The Second Black Renaissance

The Second Black Renaissance
ESSAYS IN BLACK LITERATURE

C. W. E. Bigsby

Contributions in Afro-American
and African Studies, Number 50

GREENWOOD PRESS
WESTPORT, CONNECTICUT • LONDON, ENGLAND

Library of Congress Cataloging in Publication Data

Bigsby, C W E
    The Second Black renaissance.

    (Contributions in Afro-American and African
studies; no. 50   ISSN 0069-9624)
    Includes index.
    1.   American literature—Afro-American authors—
History and criticism.   2.   American literature—
20th century—History and criticism.   I.   Title.
II.   Series.
PS153.N5B52   810′.9′896073   79-7723
ISBN 0-313-21304-6

Library of Congress Catalog Card Number: 79-7723
ISBN: 0-313-21304-6
ISSN: 0069-9624

First published in 1980

Greenwood Press
A division of Congressional Information Service, Inc.
88 Post Road West, Westport, Connecticut 06881

Printed in the United States of America

10 9 8 7 6 5 4 3 2 1

COPYRIGHT ACKNOWLEDGMENTS

Portions of this book were originally published in *Forum, Theatre Quarterly, LILE, Journal of American Studies,* and *Poetry Nation Forum,* where they appeared in a slightly different form.

For permission to reproduce materials, we are indebted to the following:

From "I Have Seen Black Hands" by Richard Wright, from *New Masses: An Anthology of the Rebel Thirties,* edited by Joseph North, International Publishers, New York, 1969. Reprinted by permission of the publisher.

From *catechism of d neoamerican hoodoo church* by Ishmael Reed. Reprinted by permission of Ishmael Reed.

From *The World of Gwendolyn Brooks:* lines from "The Sundays of Satin-Legs Smith"; lines from "Negro Hero." Copyright 1945 by Gwendolyn Brooks Blakely. Lines from "The Children of the Poor." Copyright 1949 by Gwendolyn Brooks Blakely. Reprinted by permission of Harper & Row, Publishers, Inc.

From *On These I Stand* by Countee Cullen: lines from "To Certain Critics"; lines from "Scottsboro, Too, Is Worth Its Song." Copyright 1929 by Harper & Row, Publishers, Inc.; renewed 1957 by Ida M. Cullen. Reprinted by permission of the publisher.

The verse from *The Big Sea:* Copyright 1940 by Langston Hughes. "Union": Copyright 1938 by Langston Hughes. Copyright renewed 1965 by Langston Hughes. "Don't You Want to Be Free": Copyright 1938 by Langston Hughes. Copyright renewed 1965 by Langston Hughes. Reprinted by permission of Harold Ober Associates Incorporated.

From "Understanding But Not Forgetting" by Don Lee, from *Think Black*, copyright 1970. From "Two Poems" by Don Lee from *Black Pride,* copyright 1968. From "History of the Poet as a Whore" by Don Lee, from *Black Words that Say: Don't Cry, Scream,* copyright 1969. From "Move Unnoticed to be Noticed, a Nationhood Poem" by Don Lee, from *We Walk the Way of the New World.* Reprinted by permission of Third World Press, 7524 South Cottage Grove, Chicago, Illinois 60619.

Dedication

This book is dedicated to the memory of Maynard Gough, Julius Hamilton, Charles Martin, George McKinney, Sr., George McKinney, Jr., and Albert Miller, who died at the hands of the local police in Kansas City, Missouri, following the disturbances sparked by the assassination of Martin Luther King, Jr., in 1968. They can, most charitably, be described as victims of the decade.

Contents

Preface

This book is not offered as a comprehensive study of black creativity in the last forty years, but as a series of essays which attempt to examine aspects of a broad cultural renaissance. It follows that a number of distinguished writers do not appear at all or are mentioned only in passing. This is a consequence of my critical strategy and not an indication of their status as writers.

Black writing has yet to attract the serious critical concern which is its due, and, too often, such studies as have appeared have been engaged in political debates, which have made them more valuable as evidence of the pressures exerted on black writers than as guides to the now considerable and impressive corpus of black writing. I am not so foolish or presumptuous as to imagine that I am immune to this critical virus. But, perhaps, as many black writers discovered, the European vantage point offers the possibility of a perspective which is sufficiently different to command interest if not agreement.

The Second Black Renaissance

Introduction

The First Black Renaissance (formerly called the Harlem Renaissance or the Negro Renaissance) can, with some confidence, be confined to the decade beginning in the mid-1920s. It was a brief but powerful explosion of black culture which placed the Negro, for a time, at the heart of a national myth and dramatized a self-image at odds with that offered by American society as an adequate account of black life. The Second Black Renaissance, as I have chosen to call it, is less easily contained. Admittedly, a case could be made for the special significance of the period from 1964 to the end of the decade, as evidencing the energy of the Black Arts movement. But, for all its distinctiveness, this was part of a development in black writing which had begun with Richard Wright and which had continued throughout the 1950s, 1960s, and 1970s.

The Second Renaissance did, indeed, have its roots in the work of Richard Wright, who, in a sense, contained within himself the conflicting passions which, for the next four decades, defined the nature of the black American's debate with himself and with his culture. In a lifetime spent in the pursuit of an adequate definition of the selfhood which, instinctively, and despite occasional statements to the contrary, he felt to be the clue to group identity, he sought personal and public meaning firstly in the confident determinisms of the Communist Party, and subsequently in the philosophical assurance of existentialism and the liberating power of a newly independent Africa. As he himself remarked, ''Men create the world in which they live by the methods they use to interpret it.''[1] And Wright's private search for meaning was reenacted by a new generation in the 1960s, some of whom once again looked to versions of Marxism (Angela Davis, Huey Newton, Bobby Seale) and some of whom looked to Africa as a clue to identity (Stokely Carmichael, Ted Joans, Amiri Baraka).

Though he explained, in *Black Power* (1954), that his kind of thinking was impotent when it came to explaining life in ''racial terms, '' suggesting instead that he was concerned with ''the reaction of human beings to a concrete social environment,''[2] it was as a black American that he perceived the problem, and that double heritage was as apparent in his decision to join the Party as it was later in his decision to leave it. Wright did not join simply because of its racial policies. He had glimpsed its deeper human appeal, as Bigger Thomas, the protagonist of *Native Son* (1940), dreamed of a similar underlying community of human feeling. If history constantly appeared to obtrude a dissonant note, then Wright set himself to disrupt that historical determinism by bringing the warring elements into some kind of dialectical relationship which was not material. It is perhaps not surprising that such an effort should have taken him beyond communism and existentialism to what amounted to a visionary tran-scendentalism, in which feeling conquers will and tensions are dissipated in the great chain of being.

The extent to which this process was a fully conscious one may be in doubt. Wright was frequently naive and confused and, though he was fascinated by philosophical ideas, he lacked the rigor of a philosopher. But his desire to relate the individual consciousness to its social determinants and, subse-quently, to its metaphysical and cultural context is clear enough in works like *Native Son* (1940), *The Outsider* (1953), and *The Long Dream* (1958).

In his early collection of stories, *Uncle Tom's Children* (1938), Wright's determination to dramatize a resistant black identity coexisted uneasily with an equally powerful desire to stress the Negro's role as a symbol of deprivation. Caste does battle with class as an explanation of suffering. But the pre-dominant tone of the book is one of black assertiveness. Much the same could be said of most of *Native Son*. This is the Wright enthusiastically acclaimed by cultural nationalist critics like Donald Gibson and Addison Gayle, Jr. But, there is another Wright, one who emerges in the short story "The Man Who Lived Underground," in the concluding pages of *Native Son*, in his autobiog-raphies, and in his later novels. This is the Wright who chooses to see the Negro as an appropriate image not only for the American, but also for man. Marginality and irrational persecution were, after all, realities which seemed to many to be a key to the modern experience, more particularly in a Europe which had just survived a reign of irrationality which had brought to the individual a feeling of vulnerability and contingency with which the Negro was all too familiar. Wright, indeed, took considerable pride in the fact that *Native Son* and *Black Boy* (1945) had apparently been widely read by members of the Resistance in France and Italy: "Negro literature, coming of age during the last days of the Depression and the beginning of the war, impressed the millions of European whites who then lived under the cruel domination of Hitler. Here, for the first time, the voice of the U.S. Negroes sounded a truly human and universal note which struck deep into the hearts of men living an existence full of pain and terror."[3]

This was a note which resonated particularly strongly in the America of the 1950s, and Ellison and Baldwin were at first welcomed for their assertion that in many respects the black experience of dispossession and alienation was akin to the American experience and that the question of personal and national identity was central to blacks and whites alike. They had, in other words, transformed social fact into metaphor. Indeed, as the racial stiuation became, for more than a decade, the principal moral problem confronting the American state, so the Negro writer, and especially James Baldwin in *The Fire Next Time* (1963), became a kind of mediator between America and its principles, between a troubled present and a past which refused to stay buried. The Negro stood as evidence of the failure of American liberal principles and thus he became the chief advocate of those principles.

Indeed, together with a concern for the black writer's ambiguous struggle with a language scarred with historical guilt, the suggestion that a central tradition of black writing over the last thirty years has been essentially a liberal one, provides the subtext of this book. This does not mean that black writing shares nothing with other powerful traditions. It is, for example, not merely in the influence of Faulkner on writers like William Melvin Kelley and Toni Morrison that the impact of the South can be detected; there is, in other words, a conservative impulse at work, too. The South, after all, differs from other regions of the United States, not merely in its history, but also in the value which it chooses to grant to that history; not merely in the persistence of a determining myth, but also in the ways in which that myth presses on the individual sensibility and the public structures of society. The difference between North and South, as far as the writer is concerned, derives not simply from the power of history but from what one is prepared willingly to offer by way of expiation. And for the twentieth-century northern writer the answer has tended to be, nothing. He has chosen, on the whole, to retreat into admittedly fragile and self-annihilating fictive structures and has accepted the resulting ironies. The southern writer, on the other hand, has been more inclined to pay his dues and engage the tragic consequences, for his is a society which still claims access to moral values deriving from tradition rather than from the contingent structures created and sanctioned by the self. He could still envisage a tragic sensibility, as the northern writer, for the most part, could not.

And this is where the southern experience touches that of the black American. The past is undeniable; it is the key to present reality. It is imprinted on the features of the self and the community alike. And, in many ways, the central task of the black writer is to discover the basis on which that past may be confronted. But where for the southern writer history is often simply the face of determinism, a force whose demands can never be satisfied, for the black writer it stands as a symbol of myths and realities which are to be acknowledged only as a necessary prelude to transcendence. And it is the possibility of transcendence which deflects what could have been a wholly conservative impulse into liberalism, into the powerful myths and realities of black cultural nationalism, and, less significantly, into radicalism. The central theme of black writing is the recreation of the self and the community, the rebirth of the black Lazarus.

What, then, is liberalism? In his book, *American Liberal Disillusionment in the Wake of World War I* (1977), Stuart Rochester laments the difficulty of defining the word "liberal" in America. He recalls Max Lerner's comment that it was the most disputed word of his generation. It is, indeed, notoriously difficult to pin down, more particularly in a country where it frequently masquerades as conservatism. The Swedish sociologist, Gunnar Myrdal, has rightly said that "America is conservative. But the principles conserved are liberal."[4] In *The Liberal Imagination* (1950), Lionel Trilling reminds us that Goethe says that there is no such thing as a liberal idea, only liberal sentiments, and this is the sense in which Trilling himself chooses to use the term. It is "a large tendency rather than a concise body of doctrine." It is a set of sentiments and ideas whose political meaning is defined by "the quality of life it envisages, by the sentiments it desires to affirm."[5] Perhaps, therefore, it can best be defined descriptively, by identifying the admittedly changing ideas and sentiments which have become associated with liberalism.

In terms of the nineteenth century, liberalism implied a faith in the inevitability and reality of human progress; it asserted the centrality of man and the importance of the individual; it believed in the need for personal fulfillment, but saw this as being allied to an acceptance of a personal responsibility for one's society. It assumed the desirability of, and the need for, change. It recognized the need for free thinking, for the individual to hold conflicting ideas in the mind without ceasing to function. By the end of the century, however, belief in laissez-faire economics, a noninterventionist model of government, and the political significance of individualism had effectively been appropriated by conservative forces. The response was for liberalism to reconstitute itself as a corporate liberalism, an interventionist philosophy, reformist in intent, which tried to come to terms with the new determinisms of urban life by abandoning a stress on the individual, moving closer to a pluralist position, and assuming that happiness can best be maximized by legislating away some of the worst excesses of monopoly capitalism. Clearly this approach gained its greatest success in the New Deal period, though some World War I legislation suggested the availability of an enabling mechanism. In this guise it shared something with socialism, but never embraced radicalism's desire to change the whole economic basis of society, to effect a fundamental shift in national values.

But a more classic model coexists with this, a model more amenable to the individual perspective of the writer. And it is this liberal spirit which primarily interests me, what Trilling calls "its first essential imagination of variousness and possibility."[6] It is this spirit, I suspect, which makes Ralph Ellison such a conscious descendant of the nineteenth-century tradition, which lies behind the pieties of James Baldwin, which was the force equally animating Lorraine Hansberry's dramas and the protest novels of the 1950s and 1960s. Thus, it is possible for the Negro writer to use the word "progress" unironically at a time when few postwar American white writers could. Violence might be threatened in modern black writing, but it is seldom offered as a sacrament (except during the 1930s—see Countee Cullen's ''The Black Christ''—or in the brutal ''revolutionary'' rituals of LeRoi Jones in the 1960s). The apocalypse is threatened, but not, for the most part, enacted. The absurd holds little attraction. Neither does the neoromanticism which seized the imagination of so many whites in the 1950s and 1960s and which was invoked as a justification for refusing to acknowledge the social world or its demands. For the most part, the model of identity embraced is liberal; the self is something which must be created out of the collision with a public world which is part threat and part the source of legitimate demands.

In terms of literature, the liberal tradition, as I suggest in Chapter 5, implies a continued tension between self and society which is often expressed through an openness of literary form, a suspicion of resolution. The attraction of what Saul Bellow has called ''a good five-cent synthesis'' is acknowledged but resisted. For the cultural nationalist, of course, such a synthesis is presumed to exist. Personal identity and social cohesion are rooted in a racial consciousness which is unquestioned and untroubled. It is both the point of departure and the objective. For the radical, too, present division implies inevitable synthesis. If it is objected that this model of liberalism, endlessly projected, would imply cultural and personal madness, I would reply that if guilt, angst, and tension are defining characteristics of the liberal imagination in the twentieth century, then so, too, are optimism, a cautious faith in the social contract, and a confidence in the human spirit. The fact that this model implies a constant dialogue between a private and a public self, and that there is acknowledged to be a tension between the needs of the individual and those of the society to which he is joined, partly by agreement and partly by the exigencies of his situation, is the source of the cultural dynamism of liberalism; and, of course, where the two pulls are of equal force, there exists the possibility of a dangerous immobility and a capacity for equivocation. This, indeed, is the special vulnerability of the liberal imagination. And if it is possible to detect an underlying liberal spirit in major back writers, it is equally clear that this has coexisted with other approaches, antithetical to the presumptions of liberalism. The liberal tradition is plainly not the only one, as I hope this book acknowledges.

Indeed, in the 1960s, as political and cultural forces polarized, those who had attempted to reanimate American idealism, those wishing to see the black experience as an image of the modern experience, became obvious targets. For the cultural nationalist and the black radical alike, the route to definition lay through exclusion. There was to be no compromise with fact or language. History, like literature, was a weapon, and liberalism was dangerous, not only for its past failures, but also for its anti-apocalyptic presumptions. For a time literary criticism became a simple tool of political and cultural ideologies which required that art should constitute a conscious process of myth-making and a primary instrument of social change. And, to a degree, some black writing became precisely that—but rarely simply that. Beneath the absolutist language was a recognition of moral necessity; behind the public images, a private concern for the values which had to be presumed to survive the apocalypse. And, in the end, the apocalypse was deferred. The fierce documents of protest could now be located against a longer tradition than that invoked by the rebel for whom everything had to be remade anew.

The Second Renaissance has not finished, but it has changed. The black writer is no longer, as for a few brief years he appeared to be, the cutting edge of history. But he, or she, is the embodiment of a hard-won right to see literary and personal identity outside the axial lines of passivity and revolt. The American identity can now be claimed because it is claimed on something approaching equal terms. The black identity need no longer be stridently asserted; it is now an undeniable fact of cultural life. The last few decades have witnessed a remarkable rebirth. The black Lazarus has not simply reemerged; he has, as Ralph Ellison implied, become the chief inheritor of American liberal values.*

---

*See Ralph Ellison, *Shadow and Act* (New York, 1972), pp. 182-83.

The Second Black Renaissance 1

When Sartre remarked in *Anti-Semite and Jew* that "if it is true, as Hegel says, that a community is historical to the degree that it remembers its history, then the Jewish community is the least historical of all, for it keeps a memory of nothing but a long martyrdom, that is, of a long passivity,"[1] he touched on a dilemma which essentially applies equally to the black American, though both Negro and Jew would vehemently deny the absoluteness with which Sartre proposes such an historical innocence. Indeed, in recent years, black Americans and Jews alike have sifted the past assiduously and enshrined moments of rebellion as containing the real essence of a history driven out of memory by culturally myopic historians or a self-protective denial.

For the black American, that past lies distantly and ambiguously in Africa, and for both the First Renaissance of the 1920s and the Second Renaissance, inspired by Richard Wright's seminal *Native Son*, but coming into its own in the 1950s, 1960s, and 1970s, it was a vital world of myth and fact, a crucial key to private and public meaning.

The image of Africa repeatedly appeared in the black poetry of the 1920s, where it stood as the source of an innocent lyricism in black life, largely driven out by the realities of America. It was a clue to a lost dimension of black identity or to a grace which could be glimpsed still in an occasional word or gesture. But, for Alain Locke, whose collection of essays, poetry, and prose by black and white authors, *The New Negro* (1925), was the central text of the First Renaissance, it was the present which mattered. Speaking particularly of Marcus Garvey's back-to-Africa movement, but in the context of a discussion of black American cultural influence, Locke asserted that "the possible role of the American Negro in the future development of Africa is one of the most constructive and universally helpful missions that any modern people can lay claim to."[2]

There is, indeed, some evidence that renaissance writers, and in particular Claude McKay, inspired a number of African leaders, while Amritjit Singh quotes Peter Abrahams's observation that "I became a nationalist, a color nationalist, through the writings of men and women who lived a world away from me."[3] Etienne Lero, who was the inspiration for what was later called *negri-*

tude, said, "The wind that arises from Black America will speedily sweep away from our West Indian Islands the abortive fruit of a decadent culture." And he suggested that it was in writers like Langston Hughes, Claude McKay, and Countee Cullen that he found "marinated in red wine, the African love of life, the African joy of love, the African dream of death."[4]

Marcus Garvey's Universal Negro Improvement Association, originally founded in Jamaica in 1914 but coming into its own in America in the early 1920s, was in some respects the political embodiment of this concern with Africa as image and fact. Garvey advocated a back-to-Africa policy which assumed that that continent was the spiritual, if not the actual, home of the American Negro. It was the first genuinely mass movement of American blacks and, despite its ignominious end—Garvey's projects foundered one by one and he himself was imprisoned for fraud and was deported—its significance was considerable. The black writer Amiri Baraka was later to recognize in Garvey a crucial figure in an emerging black nationalism. But, ironically, Garvey's hubris with regard to Africa—he declared himself provisional president of a continent he never visited—was a product of the very cultural presumptions against which he was ostensibly revolting.

By the time of the Second Renaissance, the boot was securely on the other foot. Beginning with the Sudan and Tunisia in 1956, gathering pace with Ghana and Guinea in 1957 and 1958, and then exploding in 1960 with the Central African Republic, Chad, the Congo, Dahomey, Ivory Coast, Gabon, Madagascar, Mali, Mauritania, Niger, Nigeria, Senegal, Somalia, Togo, and Upper Volta, African nations seized their independence, offering a persuasive paradigm for the black American. And, though Richard Wright was aware of the cultural gulf which remained between emergent Africa and American blacks who, even if discriminated against, were still part of a technologically advanced nation, he did recognize the essential symbolic value of decolonization as an image of the birth of individual and cultural identity. His 1957 book about his visit to Africa was entitled *Black Power*, a phrase which, when echoed by Stokely Carmichael nearly a decade later, had acquired a new significance.

In 1965, Elijah Muhammad could say, "Many of my people, the so-called Negroes, say we should help the nations of Africa which are awakening. This has been said as if we owned America. We are so foolish! What part of America do you have that you can offer toward helping Africa? Who is independent, the nations of Africa or we? The best act would be to request the independent governments of Africa and Asia to help us. We are the ones who need help. We have little or nothing to offer as help to others. We should begin to help at home first."[5] Indeed, in 1964, the Organization of Afro-American Unity was founded on the model of the Organization of African Unity, which was established the previous year in Addis Ababa. It was an organization which included "all people of African descent in the Western Hemisphere, as well as our brothers and sisters on the African continent.'' It was created because ''it is important for us to know that our history did not begin with slavery's scars. We come from Africa, a great continent and a proud and varied people, a land which is the new world and was the cradle of our civilization. Our culture and our history are as old as man himself and yet we know almost nothing of it. We must recapture our heritage and our identity if we are ever to liberate ourselves from the bonds of white supremacy. We must launch a cultural revolution to unbrainwash an entire people . . . This cultural revolution will be the journey to our rediscovery of ourselves. History is a people's memory . . . Armed with the knowledge of the past we can with confidence chart a course for our future. Culture is an indispensable weapon in the freedom struggle. We must take hold of it and forge the future with the past.''[6] The story of the Second Renaissance is the story of that cultural revolution.

For all the differences of emphasis, however, there was a sense in which the Second Renaissance could be said to reflect the First. Africa remained a potent source of imagery abroad, while at home the Black Muslim demand for a separate black state, spelled out in 1962, was itself an echo of the demand made in 1928 by the Communist International at its sixth World Congress held in Moscow.

More significantly, Alain Locke identified the process whereby black writers ''stopped speaking for the Negro'' because now ''they speak as Negroes. Where formerly they spoke to others and tried to interpret, they now speak to their own and try to express.''[7]

The First Renaissance was born out of a distrust of rationalism, a celebration of sensuality, an atavistic drive which was seen, paradoxically, as the source of moral progress, a faith in a self sundered from social imperatives, and a belief in the virtues of improvisation in personal affairs. Authenticity was a matter of the sensibility rather than of logical process. Jazz was the symbol of the age because of its spontaneity, its creation of a cooperative method, and its assumption of a empathetic community. And, although one does not find that sense of disillusionment and despair that one does in white writing, Heming-way's private code of sensual integrity, his assertion that morality is a personal affair to be measured by some unexamined and undefined process of private verification, derives from the same reaction against liberal values that is apparent in the romanticism of much black poetry of the period or in the incipient naturalism of some of the novels.

Curiously, the Second Renaissance emerged at a similar moment of roman-tic assertiveness. The beats of the 1950s gave way to Norman O. Brown's calls for a Dionysian body mysticism and to Herbert Marcuse's announcement of the need ''to activate repressed and arrested organic biological needs,'' and thence to the improvisational thrust of performance theatre and the atavistic establish-ment of communes, the search for personal transcendence, and the brief blooming of flower power, transcendental meditation, and other mystical cults. While, in some ways, black art once again offered a paradigm of the neoromantic life-style (urged on by Kerouac and Mailer), there was by this time a stronger resistance—a liberal reluctance to concede the collapse of social responsibility and a radical refusal to endorse a counterrevolutionary elevation of the self and the authenticity of sensual truths. There was, in other words, a fiercer debate about the nature and function of black art, a self-conscious drive for definition which accompanied a similar debate about the methods and objectives of the civil rights movement.

Where Alain Locke had seen the First Renaissance as evidence of the claim which blacks were making to be seen as an essential part of American society, those involved in the Second Renaissance had much less confidence in that objective. To be sure, the 1950s opened on a similar note. In 1950, *Phylon* produced a special issue on Negro writing which, for the most part, welcomed what many of the authors took to be the new-found desire on the part of Negro writers to escape "the trap of cultural segregation." Just as the logic of the newly stirring civil rights movement was to seek integration in American society, so the goal of the black writer was to lie in the transcendence of racial identity. The ambiguity of such a stance was never far beneath the surface, however. Just as Herskovits had suggested, in an unfortunate phrase in *The New Negro*, that "the proudest boast of the modern young Negro writer is that he writes of humans, not of Negroes . . . he seeks to be a writer, not a Negro writer,"[8] so Nick Aaron Ford found himself praising the "raceless" novels of Frank Yerby and Willard Motley thirty years later, precisely because of their refusal to write of their ethnic background.

Of course the First Renaissance did not in fact simply exemplify the desire for cultural universalism expressed in some of the essays in *The New Negro*. Indeed, the volume itself contained, and was evidence of, an ambiguity which has always been a crucial factor in black writing.

Locke objected to protest literature precisely because "it perpetuates the position of group inferiority" and "speaks under the shadow of a dominant majority."[9] Thirty years later Baldwin made essentially the same point in "Everybody's Protest Novel." Protest literature confirms the impotence of the writer, it concedes a hegemony of power to the dominant group, and implies a passive model of the self.

In his study of the Negro novel, Robert Bone, writing in the late 1950s, suggested that there had been a decline in the protest novel as a result of the lack of activity on the civil rights front. It is not an observation that is easy to substantiate. The phenomenon is more complex than this. There was certainly a flight from America and an engagement with issues which seem at first tangential to the racial situation, but it would be hard to see the work of Motley, Smith, Himes, Mayfield, and Killens as "raceless" in the way that Bone suggests, and certainly the spirit of protest dominated the black novel from Richard Wright onward. But the phrase "protest novel" would be as inadequate a description of *Native Son* as it would be of later works.

Locke had suggested of the new black writers of the 1920s that "race for them is but an idiom of experience."[10] In other words, it was not the prime cause of their art, nor even their main concern. Yet there is, of course, more than a linguistic irony in the proposition that black writing should be seen as virtually a local color school. And there is a curious contrast between the desire to emphasize a cultural pluralism and the social realities of the day. After all, if "the culture of the Negro" was really to be seen as "of a pattern integral with the times and with its setting,"[11] one might have expected a direct engagement with the painful realities of segregation, electoral impotence, and brutal victimization.

In a sense, Locke becomes a kind of black Matthew Arnold, recognizing the danger of incipient anarchy and erecting a protective construct of art. This is surely in part what he meant by saying that "for the present the Negro is radical on race matters, conservative on others, in other words a 'forced radical,' a social protestant rather than a genuine radical."[12] It was also, of course, half apology and half finely calculated threat. Even the emergence of Marcus Garvey, surely the most important phenomenon of the 1920s, hardly makes an appearance in the black novel of the period (he is attacked by Countee Cullen in *One Way to Heaven*). Garvey, whose support was largely working class, though often seen as a natural counterpart of the First Renaissance, was much more sensitive to political realities.

The First Renaissance did however explore the fact which gave it birth—the city. But, despite a common awareness of the inhospitable nature of the physical surroundings, there is marked divergence between black and white writers and their perception of the cityscape and its human consequences. For the white writer, urbanism is synonymous with the loss of innocence, the collapse of those rural values which were the source of puritan righteousness and frontier individualism. For Brockden Brown, in the nineteenth century, the city was associated with plague; for Melville, it implied squalor; for Howells, a dubious arena in which morals were placed under pressure; for Norris, Crane, and Dreiser, it was a corrupting force in which appearance assumed greater significance than reality and personal volition deferred to social, economic, and biological determinism. Curiously, and suggestively, the America of the post-World War I period shunned the city (Hemingway, Fitzgerald, Faulkner, Steinbeck), concentrating on the small town (Anderson, Lewis) or opting for rural, preindustrial values (Tate, Warren, Eliot). Many of these writers were not themselves products of the city, coming from the South, the Midwest and the West. But for the immigrant, the city was inherently ambiguous, part promise and part bitter reality (as, indeed, it was for Fitzgerald). And in this period, a high proportion of blacks were immigrants—immigrants from the South.

The black experience in the twentieth century, but particularly in the 1960s, is an urban experience. And the city, in the American context, had assumed a central position as an image of betrayed ideals, tawdry illusions, and the loss of liberty. Its size seemed to guarantee anonymity and thus the collapse of moral identity. If the classic American model had been the battle to sustain selfhood against an enormous sweep of physical geography, now selfhood had to be sought in the arabesques of the metropolitan landscape.

The myth of space, embodied in the idea of an expanding frontier, had never contained as much substance for the black American as it did for the white American. Though he did play a part in frontier settlement, the black American never did take imaginative possession of that myth in the single generation which came between Emancipation and the closing of the frontier. If the frontier myth offered a world unstained by history, it is hard to see how it could accommodate the Negro. In *Invisible Man*, Ellison's hero goes to a Western and, though he responds to its images of freedom, he notes that "there was no one like me taking part in the adventures."[13] For the Negro, the question of whether society, as such, was a good or a bad thing remained for long an academic one. But the individuality which the myth pitched against that social world was equally fragile. The black equivalent for what Irving Howe has called the "Edenic nostalgia"[14] of American literature is, of course, the Negro's response to Africa. But that never constituted a present reality nor even really an available symbol of moral independence, and it was only invoked when the prevailing reality was urban.

In many city novels by black writers (Claude McKay's *Home to Harlem*, 1928; Chester Himes's *The Third Generation*, 1954; Julian Mayfield's *The Hit*, 1957; Willard Motley's *Let No Man Write My Epitaph*, 1958; Warren Miller's *The Cool World*, 1959), the urban landscape becomes the same antinomian world that nature had been in the white novels of the nineteenth century. There is no effective law; there are no universally acknowledged values; there is no social system with the self-evident right to demand obedience. Social values have disappeared to be replaced by the code of the streets, the authenticity of action, and, on occasion, an assertive masculinity. Identity depends upon role. Lacking physical space, the individual seeks to create psychic space, like Rinehart in *Invisible Man*, by deploying a range of roles which can identify without defining. Cross Damon, in *The Outsider*, seeks in the metaphysical space of an undefined self what so many American heroes had sought in the physical space of the American environment. And for him, as for them, it was a tryst between good and evil, dramatized within the self rather than contained by the clash of that self with its environment.

But the city also has a more positive role as far as the black writer is concerned. After all, the northern urban center constituted an escape from the South. In the city, for the first time, the black American felt the potential political, economic, and cultural power which was a by-product of ghetto life. In this sense, the city became, as for most white writers it did not, something to celebrate. Its streets constituted possibility. It was southern agrarian life which constituted determinism for the Negro and not, at first, the urban realities which for white writers had constituted the social correlatives of fate. For the black writer, that disillusionment with the city came rather later.

After the Progressive era, in which liberals had felt in tune with history, they found themselves, after World War I, curiously impotent. (See Stuart Rochester's *Liberal Disillusionment in the Wake of World War I*, New York, 1977.) Liberal ideals seemed to many to have been destroyed not only by the war but also by the loss of the free moral and physical world of the nineteenth century and, more immediately, by the collapse of Wilsonian policy after the war. (However, as several historians have reminded us, there is an underlying continuity to liberal thought, so that the corporate liberalism of the Progressives eventually triumphed in the New Deal policies of Roosevelt.)* And if the idea of the war as a watershed no longer carries quite the conviction which it once did, it is clear that in the 1920s liberals could no longer feel that they provided the governing ethos; while those who sought more radical solutions to America's problems did not hesitate to charge them with political impotence. Lewis Mumford felt obliged to make a public declaration in 1930 that he had never been a liberal.

But, whatever liberal theorists may have felt, American creative writers, a surprising number of whom had been to Europe and had seen the realities of war (as many of those theorists had not), were certain that civilization had indeed reached a clear watershed. Indeed, this conviction was shared equally by a writer like Scott Fitzgerald who never ceased regretting his failure to experience the European war. To these writers, at least, liberal pieties had been exposed as just that—pieties. Progress was a sham; rationality, nonfunctional; the supposed symbiosis between society and the individual, inoperative. The prevailing tone was one of cynical stoicism, the dominant mood was ironic, and the only recourse was a retreat from engagement, a refusal to acknowledge any feeling which might lead to vulnerability. And since this was conceded to be impossible, narrative became an account of the failure of fact to approximate to ideal. The prewar literary rebellion had been iconoclastic, but it had also been exuberant. Writers had been in rebellion against presumptions and styles of writing and living which meant nothing to them. After the war, they lamented the eclipse of values to which they were themselves partly attracted and which had to some degree been the emotional and spiritual baggage they had taken with them on their real or imaginative trips to Europe.

*Christopher Lasch, in *American Liberals and the Russian Revolution* (New York, 1962), concludes that there was no real loss of illusions, or questioning of basic assumptions, only a despair that those principles would ever be enacted. Henry May stresses that the war was not the crucial event it was taken to be, that fundamental changes were already in hand. For an account of Progressive views on the war, see J. A. Thompson's "American Progressive Publicists and the First World War 1914-1917," *Journal of American History* LVIII (June 1971 to March 1972), pp. 364-83. *See also* Burl Noggle's *Into the Twenties: The United States from Armistice to Normalcy* (Urbana, 1974), which offers an interesting account of the careers of Progressives after World War I.

But such a public confession of the collapse of an old vision was not, for the most part, reflected by black writers. Indeed, the idea that America had lost its innocence in the nineteenth century, as Henry May suggests in his book *The End of American Innocence*, or with World War I must have struck the Negro as somewhat bizarre, since he had not encountered that innocence except in the sense of a brutally simplistic vision. *The New Republic* may have charted the rise and fall of liberal confidence, but this was not a graph which commanded the attention of Negroes who had their own practical realities to deal with. Lacking such illusions, they lacked also the consequent despair, which so suffused the work of white writers. There is thus no real equivalent in black writing to that lament over the decline of liberal individualism which one finds in Fitzgerald or Nathanael West, and none of that desperate creation of discrete linguistic and physical enterprises in which alone the solitary figure can snatch meaning from chaos. There is, in other words, no black Hemingway. And, because a direct connection between the plight of the individual Negro and the state of the nation was made implausible by the unapologetic exploitation of his labor and his vote, there was no black Dos Passos either. The black writing of the 1920s tended to be neoromantic, emphasizing a free self without responsibility to society; that of the 1930s described a deterministic world in which the Negro was a simple product of American social forces.

When Randolph Bourne, himself a radical critic of American social values, wrote of the dangerously illusioned liberals of the time that they were "like brave passengers who have set out for the Isles of the Blest only to find that the first mate has gone insane and jumped overboard, the rudder has come loose and dropped to the bottom of the sea, and the captain and pilot are lying dead drunk under the wheel,"[15]* he was talking about a domestic sense of betrayal, of lost values and self-deception which could simply not be felt with such shattering force by those who had long since understood the surrender of moral control by those who still wished to think their enterprise moral in origin and liberal in conduct.

The Negro was seen as, and to a degree collaborated in becoming, the id to be contrasted with the superego of white society. White literature of the 1920s was full of references to sterility, from Eliot's fisher king, to Hemingway's Jake Barnes, to the homosexuals of *Tender Is the Night*, or to Babbitt's anemic wife. Such characters were the deracinated result of the simultaneous destruction of past and future. The immediate past was defined by war, the collapse of both rationality and mysticism; the future could be little more than the projection of an empty present. In the circumstances, hedonism seemed justified, moral sanctions having melted with the snows of Hemingway's Swiss mountains, or later with Fitzgerald's snows of 1929, which went away if you paid sufficient money. The only reality seemed to be the ineluctable process of the

*See also Randolph S. Bourne, *War and the Intellectuals* (New York, 1964).

natural world or the hard-edged substantiality of money. This was the age of the Caesars, pictured by Spengler in *The Decline of the West* (1918), a book which seemed to many to be an accurate account of the collapse of social, cultural, and metaphysical values.

The Negro seemed to stand to the side of this. In an age which considered the city as the image of social alienation, Harlem seemed to offer the virtues of a community unified by a shared experience and by a public imagery which sought to close that gap between appearance and reality which is the clue to cultural heterogeneity and ultimate personal meaning. If there was a bitterness, as there was, it had a specific, identifiable, and potentially rectifiable object. Music and religion emerged out of a deeply felt black experience, as for the whites, on the whole, they did not. And while the cultural enthusiasms of the 1920s concealed social realities which art could only sentimentalize, the self-consciousness which marked the black sensibility was not a sign of modernist conviction but a genuinely liberating sense of racial and personal identity.

The white American writer felt compelled by the pressure of his own punctured naivety to present an image of man as maimed, incomplete, exhausted, and defeated—crushed by warped ideals or the sheer weight of money and the machine. Self-pity and a pervasive sense of betrayal were the principal emotions, and the only legitimate response was a cool irony, a detachment from everything but the natural world, the desperate retreat offered by the mind, or that grace under pressure which could so easily slip into sentimentality or mannered despair. Curiously, the black, who had more reason than most to withdraw from the social world, responded in a completely different way. He revealed what was wholly lacking from the white literature of the age—an energy which could genuinely pass for passion. No wonder he was subsequently required to become the avatar of sexuality for a society which perceived itself as an old bitch gone in the teeth.

The 1930s saw a shift in emphasis for the Negro. At the Amenia conference of 1933, some of the younger black intellectuals (Ralph Bunche, E. Franklyn Frazier, and Abram Harris) launched an attack on what they saw as the ill-conceived ideas and strategies of those leaders, like W. E. B. DuBois and James Weldon Johnson, for whom race was the dominant issue. Indeed, as James Young has suggested in *Black Writers of the Thirties*, "Besides repudiating the provinciality of the older generation, they went on to attack their old-style liberalism."[16] Criticism of the principal Negro organizations had been particularly strong following the Scottsboro case of 1931, in which nine young blacks were accused of rape. It seemed clear that justice could not be secured by slow tactical reformist measures. Hence, these younger black intellectuals proposed a class, rather than a racial, interpretation of the Negro's plight (though, in fact, behind their public stance, there remained an understandable ambivalence). Like Edmund Wilson, who in 1931 had charged liberals with sustaining a decadent capitalism which was otherwise in a state of crisis, they felt that liberal reform could not tackle the basic issues of inequality.

For Richard Wright, later in the decade, liberalism lacked the practical drive and disciplined strategy of communism. He had written a poem denouncing the inefficacy of liberalism—"Child of the Dead and Forgotten Gods"—and, as organizer of the weekly meetings of the John Reed Club, had arranged for Lawrence Martin to speak on "The Collapse of Liberalism." Indeed, as late as 1945, he announced that he was convinced the problem would only be solved "when those liberal and kind whites are out of the way, when their fear reaches that point where no Negro can meet a white in his drawing room,"[17] a thought close in spirit to that frequently voiced two decades later.

In 1934, the Communist Party announced that the capitalist world was passing from the end of capitalist stabilization to a revolutionary crisis. The new corporate liberalism of the New Deal seemed to offer little to the black American. It certainly lacked any coherent strategy. As Raymond Wolper points out in *Negroes and the Great Depression*, some economic recovery agencies did establish policies which ensured fair treatment for black Americans, but the blacks were too poorly organized to put pressure on the administration or on any of its principal agencies. As A. Philip Randolph, president of the Brotherhood of Sleeping Car Porters, pointed out, "True liberation can be acquired and maintained only when the Negro people possess power; and power is the product and flower of organization—organization of the masses, the masses in the mills and mines, on the farms, in the factories."[18] And this is what the Communist Party had to offer. It seemed to incorporate DuBois's notion of consolidating what was, in effect, already a separate black nation with a simultaneous, if contradictory, effort to ally the poor black with the poor white. In other words, it claimed to reconcile what had always been an ambiguity in black thought. Established black liberal groups, like the NAACP and the National Urban League, continued to press government for reform, but the black writer and younger intellectual increasingly responded to the public imagery of the Party, which seemed to acknowledge black autonomy while subsuming it in a great alliance with the world's oppressed peoples.

For Richard Wright, the chief failure of black writing had been its unconcern with bridging the gulf between the writer and the black masses. The First Renaissance had been essentially a middle-class movement, exemplifying Lenin's observation that oppressed minorities tend to reflect the techniques and concerns of the bourgeoisie. Despite ther sense of racial identity, this had, he felt, been expressed in terms and in forms which stressed the emergence of an individual rather than a group identity. And, in "Blueprint for Negro Writing" (1937), he regretted the fact that "two separate cultures sprang up: one for the Negro masses, crude, instinctive, unwritten, and unrecognized; and the other for the sons and daughters of a rising Negro bourgeoisie, bloodless, petulant, mannered and neurotic."[19]

The failure of the 1930s to remedy this was underlined by the late date of the essay's publication. Though obliged as a Party member to forswear a strictly nationalist stance, it was clear that that was precisely the vital link between those two cultures. So, while declaring that "it should be known that no attempt is made to propagate a specious and blatant nationalism," he immediately confessed that "the nationalist character of the Negro people is unmistakable."[20] Since the American Communist Party was at that time itself transfixed by just this same ambiguity, simultaneously committing itself to a view of the Negro as a colonial subject and as a member of a raceless proletariat, it was an ambivalence which he could carry off with less fear of attack than might otherwise have been the case. And it was plain that he *was* claiming the existence of a discrete culture which derived from the special nature of black experience and whose existence was not recognized only because black writers had failed to establish a form commensurate with that experience or to tap the living source of its unique qualities.

It was not a wholly accurate account of the recent history of black writing, but his emphasis on folklore, on the homogenizing power of suffering, and on the shaping force of black institutions indicates his concern with identifying elements of what would later be seen as a black aesthetic. But it was a nationalism which had to be accepted in order to be transcended—a nationalism "that knows its limitations, that is aware of the dangers of its position, that knows its aims are unrealizable within the framework of capitalist America."[21] And it was, of course, just such a conviction which led LeRoi Jones from a nationalist to a Marxist stance more than thirty years later, and which informed the polemical essays and autobiographical works of so many key figures of the 1960s. For Wright, as for Baraka, nationalism was to be a key to self-possession, but, as such, only a stage in the realization of a political interdependence.

The burden which Wright wished to lay upon the black writer was extreme, even absurdly so. Thus, every work by a black writer, every "short story, novel, poem, and play should carry within its lines, implied or explicit, a sense of the oppression of the Negro people, the danger of war, of fascism, of the threatened destruction of culture and civilization, and, too, the faith and necessity to build a new world."[22] It was a tall order, but the point at least was clear and not as easily reconcilable with his Marxist faith as he suggested. The values to which he appealed were not primarily those of the brotherhood of man nor yet the established culture of an urban proletariat. For all the reality of folk tradition, this had left the Negro singularly ill-prepared for the realities of urban life. Thus, he sees black writers as performing a central task. "They are being called upon," he said, "to do no less than create values by which their race is to struggle, live, and die. They are being called upon to furnish moral sanctions for action, to give a meaning to blighted lives, and to supply motives for mass movements of millions of people."[23] And yet, from his position as Marxist, such motivations should have been self-evident. It was a contradiction which was not resolved in the writing of the 1930s, and rather than creating the myths and symbols through which the black individual could relate to his own past, perceive the reality of his present, and project the possibilities of a future not defined solely in terms of material objectives, it provided a revolutionary iconography disturbingly unrelated to the task which Wright had identified and too often simplified to the point at which it denied the complexity which was the essence of the Negro's bid to escape from stereotype.

And in his poetry, Wright was as guilty as anyone of this reductiveness. The problem in reaching for a new audience was to render complexity in a simple way—what Wright, borrowing from the Russians, called "complex simplicity." The phrase was a concession to the difficulty of creating a valid revolutionary art. It was a skill which Langston Hughes had demonstrated in the 1920s, precisely by tapping the distinctive myths and rhythms of black experience; but in the 1930s, the compulsion to serve a different cause confused the issue. Marxism may, as Wright suggested, have been "but the starting point," a phrase which must have struck his Marxist colleagues as, at the very least, disturbingly ambiguous. But the questions remained, What precisely was the nature of the animating principle to be found behind the seductive humanism of Marxism and how was the distinctively black dimension of that principle to be presented? In terms of poetry, he had, in fact, very little to offer, and neither did those other black poets who wished simultaneously to protest racism and to accept the view that it was an aberration of capitalism. An identity of aims and a presumed identity of experience, the latter never convincingly rendered because it was never fully felt, inevitably worked against attempts to locate and define a cultural distinctiveness. The contradiction is clear in a short story like "Bright and Morning Star," as it is, indeed, in *Native Son.*

Wright's pains to insist that the heritage of the Negro writer included Eliot, Stein, Joyce, Hemingway, Gorky, and Barbusse merely intensified the problem and was, anyway, not a fact reflected in most black poetry in a decade which was distrustful of the lack of commitment to be found in modernism. His suggestion that Jack London was also a part of the black writer's heritage must have struck a number of such writers as especially ironic, given the social-Darwinist views of a man who, unaccountably, was one of Lenin's favorite authors.

The truth was that Wright was acutely aware of the problem facing the black writer—the need to acknowledge and absorb the cultural forms of American life while reclaiming a past which included a distant African experience and accepting a history of abuse at the hands of those who had forged that American culture. Black culture was clearly formed not merely of heterogeneous elements, but also of inherently contradictory ones. Indeed, the need to absorb the black past in America was largely at odds with another responsibility—that of giving artistic form to ''all those forces which help to shape the consciousness of his race toward a more heroic cast.''[24]

Thirty years later, the contradictions remained as much in evidence. The mind which renders experience so neatly into opposing heroic and destructive forces, while serving the immediate need for definition, does not necessarily delineate the subtle and ambiguous nature of a culture which coalesces around fictions and realities whose potency lies in their evasion of simple presentation. Wright was certainly not unaware of this. Indeed, he defended the ''functional autonomy'' of the artist. But this autonomy could too easily be seen as a concomitant of the Negro's social isolation, so that the pressure in art, as in the sociopolitical sphere, was to choose freely a social role which called for the surrender of that autonomy in the interests of, first, racial and, then, class solidarity. The freedom to deny that responsibility existed but was not historically real. The unity of Negro writers and the Negro masses led logically to the proposal of a unity with the proletariat as a whole. The history of social and cultural isolation existed to be transcended.

Wright's is a crucial document. Its contradictions were, and have in large part remained, those of the black writer dedicated to resolving in his or her own sensibility the conflicting demands of history and the future, of a black cultural autonomy and the powerful patterns of American national identity; of the desire to capture the subtleties, the myths, and the symbols of black life in a form which does not sunder them from those who, in their daily lives, embody those myths and symbols. Wright recognized that black nationalism could take a reactionary as well as a progressive form, but he also believed that Marxism had to subordinate itself to a sense of life which could not adequately be accommodated within the absolutes of ideology. His own fictional career exemplified these tensions; his poetry less so. And, for the most part, black poetry of the 1930s offered little advance in the history of developing black literature.

Faced, on the one hand, with a literary model which, in the form of Fitzgerald, West, and the early Hemingway, seemed to document the collapse of idealism and the failure of community and, on the other, with one which proposed a positive art involving social commitment and an active role for the imagination beyond a desperate and losing game with fate, there was perhaps little doubt as to which direction black art would take. Besides which, the images deployed by the Communist Party seemed to be endorsed by the political actions of those who took such elaborate pains to establish their concern for the black community (witness the bitter struggle for control of the Scottsboro case). The Party also proposed a central role for the artist—a role which, for the black American, potentially placed him at the center of events for the first time. It offered the possibility of inclusion and a theory of history which explained past suffering and charted a new sense of community apparently without demanding the surrender of identity, except insofar as it should prove necessary to the immediate and, as regrettably it turned out, the continuing needs of class conflict.

Black writers were all too aware that the First Renaissance had in part been a product of fashion—a fashion which, if it could raise a Langston Hughes from elevator boy to the status of poet, was quite capable of reversing the process. And, although it was to be several more decades before Zora Neal Hurston completed the cycle by ending her life as a domestic servant, the fragility of the achievement marked by the 1920s suggested the need for a more solid foundation. What better basis than the logic of history and the scientific analysis of economic forces; what better purpose than the freeing of the world's poor; what better images than those precipitated by the conflict between the forces of reaction and those of progress. From the disregarded parochial art of an oppressed minority to the standard-bearers of the literary and social avant-garde in a single generation—it was a temptation which could scarcely be resisted, and few saw the point of such resistance. After all, in the name of what tradition, which values, which heroic imagery, and which eternal cultural verities was the new cosmos of political and artistic truths to be resisted? By reference to what aesthetic principles and social ideals were the new symbols of committed art to be denied? It was a period of high hopes during which many black writers came to share political convictions with the white writers whom they met in the WPA. By the same token, it was a period which led to a disillusionment which provided some of the energy from which the literature of the 1940s and 1950s and, in particular, the fiction of the period derived. For, despite an imagery which pictured black and white hands joined together in the common struggle, black writers also looked to the Party to serve another function. Its policy of pressing for a separate black state in the South was a public image of the cultural pretensions of the Negro, the longing for a recognition of the special status and experience of the black American. And when the Party switched its policy in 1935, the vision began to collapse. Earl Browder, head of the Communist Party of America, announced that while the old determination to establish an independent Black Belt in the South remained an ultimate objective, the Negro masses were ''not yet ready to carry through the revolution which would make possible the right to self-determination.''[25] The change of policy was more symbolic than actual, but it confirmed Wright's sense of disillusionment and marked the end of the Negro's flirtation with the Party until the 1960s, when a new generation of young black activists and intellectuals once again responded to the Marxist vision, though few became formal members.

Yet, despite its brief success with intellectuals who responded to what they took to be its humanism, the Communist Party did not, of course, dominate the politics of the 1930s, though it was a powerful force for a number of writers. Nor was the plight of the black American ignored by the American government. Some New Deal agencies (primarily the Farm Security Administration, the Public Works Administration, and the Works Progress Administration) did attempt to secure equal treatment for blacks. The NAACP continued its legal campaign against discrimination. And when the war came, the exigencies of the situation created the momentum for subsequent improvement. At the same time, the American pacifist movement was instrumental in establishing the Congress of Racial Equality in 1942, an organization which operated on Gandhian principles of the kind which Martin Luther King, Jr., was to embrace in the 1950s.

After the war, indeed, the immediate political objective was desegregation; the prevailing tone of black literary life, a liberal one. The special circumstances of black life were presented as in some way an image of modern life (William Demby, *Beetlecreek*, 1950; Ralph Ellison, *Invisible Man*, 1952; Richard Wright, *The Outsider*, 1953; William Melvin Kelley, *A Different Drummer*, 1959). The confidence inspired by the 1954 desegregation decision was reflected in novels like John Oliver Killens's *Youngblood* (1954), and John A. Williams's *Journey Out of Anger* (1963); plays like Lorraine Hansberry's *A Raisin in the Sun* (1959), Ossie Davis's *Purlie Victorious* (1961), and Loften Mitchell's *A Land Beyond the River* (1963); and in the poetry of Margaret Walker, Robert Hayden, and the early work of Gwendolyn Brooks.

But as "all deliberate speed" turned out to be remarkably slow, so a number of young writers and activists began to resist what they saw as the prevailing tone of black moralism and white pragmatism.

Subversion of the political machine seemed increasingly necessary, as did public, sometimes violent, gestures of dissent; what was lacking was an ideological base which could prove attractive to the liberal. And it was that typical refusal of ideological commitment which attracted the opprobrium of Carmichael, Cleaver, and others. For the liberal's inherent distrust of ideology, strengthened by the guilt with which many looked back on the naivety of the 1930s, conflicted with the newly discovered need for ideology on the part of many blacks. To some, the whole civil rights strategy of nonviolence and passivity seemed increasingly demeaning, not only because it took as its premise the desirability of integration and the implicit passivity of the black, but because, as a movement, it lacked any coherent vision of social and political realities, any analysis which went beyond a simple wish to inherit the American dream. Both cultural nationalists and black radicals rejected such strategies in favor of an assertion of coherent racial and political objectives. The ideologies which surfaced were either racially based, proposing a discrete black culture, or were radical, proposing political revolt.

Much the same might have been said of the 1930s, but the strategy in the 1960s was not to win over the liberals, or to destroy the always dangerously uncommitted middle ground, but to detach the black from a debilitating faith in political action *as defined by whites*, in a freedom conferred on them as a result of white action. For the assault was not aimed at liberalism so much as at *white* liberalism. The rationale was simple and familiar enough from colonial situations. Freedom conferred by others is not freedom. Attacks on white liberalism were designed for black consumption. They were part of a necessary process of racial aggrandizement; they were concerned with an essential restoration of pride.

In some ways, liberal involvement in civil rights was an extension of resistance to the conservative assault on civil liberties which was a mark of the late 1940s and early 1950s. It was also a broadening of the alliance, a recognition of new political realities, which perhaps explains, and in part justifies, some of the attacks which came from blacks who recognized a pragmatic impulse where they had looked for a moral commitment.

The civil rights movement created the logic from which black power was born. Although its objective was integration into an America whose values and objectives went largely unchallenged, its very success not only raised expectations but also demonstrated the inherent power of an organized minority and the potential for action in a group previously forced to accept its own subservience. There was also an admitted failure of liberal will, as seen by many blacks, revealed for example in the refusal to seat the black delegates of the Mississippi Freedom Democratic Party at the Democratic Convention of 1964.

Meanwhile, the antipoverty program of 1964 had the effect of bypassing the regular civil rights channels and funneling money directly to local communities. And though the program failed, it did serve to strengthen the separatist impulse, creating a conflict between the established civil rights leadership and the local black communities, suggesting that the best solution might not lie in a black middle-class flight to the suburbs (as dramatized by Lorraine Hansberry in *A Raisin in the Sun*), but in a consolidation and enrichment of the ghetto. Some OEO (Office of Economic Opportunity) money was used, for example, by LeRoi Jones's Black Arts Repertory Theatre in Harlem, which, for its brief life, became the focus of black cultural separatism. This, in turn, was reminiscent of the way in which the Federal Theatre used New Deal money to indict the very government which funded it. The result was the same in both cases; funding was withdrawn. Liberalism has its limits. A minor irony was that, for a while, both the Federal Theatre and the Black Arts Repertory Theatre offered some of the most inventive theatre then available.

The civil rights movement undoubtedly had its greatest achievement in the 1964 Civil Rights Act, but the power and influence of direct action began to wane. When James Meredith was shot while on a voter registration drive in Memphis, Tennessee, Martin Luther King and Stokely Carmichael joined together to continue his march. But it was Carmichael's advocacy of black power which caught the imagination of blacks and whites alike. And though it was by no means clear what the term meant, in the years that followed it acquired a definition. The immediate and clear issues of legal segregation having largely been settled on paper, the problem was translated into symbolic form. In 1965, the Watts riot marked the end of a stage in the civil rights movement.

The Marxist-oriented Black Panthers were founded in 1966. Their policy, like that of other such groups, was black control of the ghetto, the restoration of pride and dignity for the Negro. A new concern for the Negro past sprang up. Courses in black history and literature were instituted at universities. The magazine *Negro Digest* changed its name to *Black World*. An increasing number of books on black culture were published. White interpreters of black culture were warned off.

The civil rights movement was an appeal for justice. Its literary counterpart, therefore, was the protest novel, which was directed in large part at those in a position to offer that justice. It was a Catonian warning about resentment, about the fire next time. It was an enumeration of sufferings, offered in the conviction that the failure of white society was at least partly a product of ignorance. Its tactic, therefore, tended to be an assertion that racial differences were basically insignificant, that American pluralism should expand to incorporate the Negro as it had historically so many other diverse groups. The principles to which it addressed itself were the liberal ones of justice and human dignity; the image which it deployed was the Negro as metaphor for the dispossessed.

But it was Du Bois, writing in 1920, who urged his fellow Negroes to "train ourselves to see beauty in black."[26] He warned, indeed, against precisely that "universalism" which critics of the 1950s so much admired. "Just as soon as true Art emerges, just as soon as the black artist appears, someone touches the race on the shoulder and says, 'He did that because he was an American not because he was a Negro—what is a Negro anyhow? He is just a human; it is the kind of thing you ought to expect.' "[27] Already he was challenging the desirability of cultural and social integration. Where, in 1959, Lorraine Hansberry was to question the wisdom of being integrated into a burning house, Du Bois, in 1926, was asking, "What do we want? What is the thing we are after?...We want to be Americans, full-fledged Americans, with all the rights of other American citizens. But is that all? Do we want simply to be Americans? Once in a while through all of us there flashes some clairvoyance, some clear idea, of what America really is. We who are dark can see America in a way that white Americans cannot."[28]

For some black writers, the problem of cultural identity was best solved by exile. Of course, in a sense, all writers are exiles by definition, but for the black writer the situation is especially acute, and many black writers felt they had to leave America in order to reclaim it; they had to create sufficient space for new images to form and for the urgent chaos to resolve itself into an order which was not simply that of victim and oppressor. But like many American writers before them, they found that the process of removal changes more than perspective. It is not simply a gesture of refusal—a denial of public structures and coercive forms. The mind is, after all, not a camera, and the organism changes with an alteration to its environment. Richard Wright was changed by his life in France, as was James Baldwin or William Gardner Smith or Carlene Polite. Chester Himes was altered by Spain, as was Willard Motley by Mexico—which is not to imply that they were cut off from their roots. Roots, after all, are not determined by physical space. But the complex fate of being a black American is perhaps never more complex than when that self is located in the center of another culture, with its own tensions, limitations, and possibilities. Wright's and Baldwin's sense of available freedoms came, at least in part, from lived realities in France—realities which were admittedly simultaneously denied to those black Africans whom they were invited by their American counterparts to identify with as fellow oppressed. The ironies developed fast and far. Black Americans' European and African experiences have always generated ironies—whether it is the most obvious contradiction between democratic freedoms defended abroad and abrogated at home, or the subtle guilt which resulted from the attainment of that freedom which seems to come with distance from moral commitments.

Nor were the exiles fleeing blindly. The countries they chose, primarily France and Spain, were the countries which other writers had chosen. The France of Camus and Sartre drew the black writer for many of the same reasons which had attracted Hemingway, Fitzgerald, and Stein. And, not surprisingly, the literary influences which formed their sensibilities, despite the urgent exhortations of the 1960s, were white American and European. Asked which writers had most shaped their own work, Cyrus Colter named Melville, Dostoevski, and Joyce; William Demby suggested Virginia Woolf, Camus, and Ellison. For Ernest Gaines, it was Tolstoy, Chekhov, and Turgenev; for Julian Mayfield, it was Du Bois, Hemingway, Dreiser, and Thomas Wolfe; for Ishmael Reed, Nathanael West; for Alice Walker, Kate Chopin, Simone de Beauvoir, and Doris Lessing; for John Wideman, T. S. Eliot; for Charles Wright, James Joyce; for Ralph Ellison, Dostoevski. Given the nature of cultural history, it could scarcely be otherwise; but it is in the light of this pattern of influence that the painful and bitter attempt to precipitate out a quintessential blackness becomes simultaneously an understandable but forbidding necessity for those who wish to isolate a racially specific organism.

It was Emerson who said that we go to Europe to be Americanized. And this tended to be equally true for the black American, more especially for Baldwin, who saw himself as uniquely placed to mediate between black and white Americans whose incomprehensions were frequently a measure of their joint experience. "From the vantage point of Europe," he suggested, an exile "discovers his own country. And this is a discovery which not only brings to an end the alienation of the American from himself, but which also makes clear to him, for the first time, the extent of his involvement in the life of Europe."[29]

Certainly, if Wright's and Baldwin's American experience had stressed the differences between the races, their European experience stressed the similarities. For Wright, the Negro became a metaphor; for Baldwin, he became a desperate soul in search of completion, an individual seeking to cauterize social and personal pain with love. As the latter remarked, "White men in this country and American Negroes in this country are really the same people. I only discovered this in Europe; perhaps it was always very obvious, but it never occurred to me before."[30]

But in truth, the process was more complicated for the black American. The journey across the sea becomes a metaphoric retracing of steps. For if the black writers did not, for the most part, return to Africa, they did return to a Europe which held at least a clue to their present. It was a Europe which should have inspired the deepest scepticism. As blacks and, in some cases, as southerners, they had a sense of the past which was more acute and more necessary to them than for the average American. But what they looked for in Europe was less the mark of Cain than a racial innocence to contrast to that of America. It was not as the heart of imperial darkness that they perceived it, but as a liberated and liberating force; a response having as much to do with their American identity as it did with their sense of black selfhood. In a 1952 essay called "I Choose Exile," Wright declared, "Yet, exile though I am, I remain unalterably and simply American and, as such, I've often asked myself, if, armed with these gloomy thoughts garnered from an exiled life, I could somehow aid my country in its clumsy grappling with alien realities; shivering world; if I could in some way ingest into the American consciousness a consciousness of their consciousness."[31] He offers himself, in other words, as mediator between a Third World, which he imperfectly understood, and a white America, whose implacable myths and realities had sent him into exile. He finds himself in precisely that cultural no-man's-land whose existence had been a recurrent theme of *Native Son*, but which is now transformed from existential void into a kind of cultural neutrality as he seeks the meaning of his blackness in Africa and the meaning of his Americanness in Europe. "I am an American," he asserted, "but I realize and sense that the meaning of my revolt that made me an American can be sensed only in relation to that rich and fecund Europe against which America once rebelled."[32] This is, indeed, a very American conviction, and it must be said that as his life progressed, he sought to resolve the perpetual dilemma of the American Negro by asserting a very nineteenth-century vision of the American —that of a self-dramatizing within itself the conflicts of the culture which it inhabited. What he describes, in other words, is a liberal tension between conflicting racial identities, the compulsions of affirmation and revolt. As he said, "I am an American, but perhaps of the kind you have forgotten, self-reliant, irritated with authority, full of praise for those who can stand alone, respecting the socialness that I feel resides in the higher personality . . . I am that sort of American . . . an amalgam of many races and many continents and cultures; that I feel that the real end and aim of being an American is to be able to live as a man anywhere.''[33] It was a declaration in tune with the period, if we mean by that the drive to escape a cultural identity defined either by the compulsions of revolt or by a national chauvinism which severed the self from its universal ambitions. It was, after all, another decade or more before the word ''universal'' was seen as a term of abuse, a hopelessly diffuse objective, and a denial of cultural identity. In the 1950s, the black American sought to claim rather than deny his American identity. Negro critics tended to celebrate the maturity of black writing to the degree that it avoided what they increasingly saw as racial chauvinism.

The distance between America and Europe was a distance also between experience and perception, between inchoate events and the structure which the individual seeks to impose on them. Released from playing the American game in its full complexity, the black writer was able to determine the direction and moral stress patterns of his culture more easily. And if that very facility carried its own dangers, it also granted, at least potentially, a privileged viewpoint of racial identity and of the America which was an inevitable component of that identity. Wright, Baldwin, Himes, Motley, and Polite escaped from the grave of America and were reborn as Lazarus in an Old World from which they could survey both their old selves and the America which had first buried them and then given them, as Prospero had Caliban, the language with which to curse them and measure the extent of their own independence. It was a rebirth which had the effect, not only of redefining the reborn self, but also of transforming the world which that self observed.

To inhabit two cultures—three if one counts Europe, America, and the black world—is to create a kind of existential triangulation which may locate the self with greater precision, or at least generate overlapping selves which defeat the more simplistic models provided by racial stereotype and national myth. American mythology was not easily claimed. Africa and Europe offered alternative versions. Yet Africa had little perception of America. Europe did at least engage the kaleidoscope of American fact and fancy. It granted full weight to the problem of America, seeing it alternately, or even simultaneously, as promise and threat—precisely the kind of ambiguous response felt by the black American whose history was both an ironic comment upon, and a paradoxical vindication of, the American dream. The journey from African hut to U.S. Senate was, after all, a muted and belated version of log cabin to White House.

There is little doubt that it was the European setting which made Baldwin speak as an American rather than as a black, just as it had been as an American that Wright had confronted Africa. It was, indeed, as Americans that they were received. And the very absence, or relative absence, of racial antagonism which they found when removed from America, actually diminished the sharpness of a racial identity which had always been, at least in part, the product of white intransigence.

They were engaging in a debate not only with America but with their own selves, now newly liberated from the forces which had shaped their identities as writers and individuals. Freed from the pressure of what Hawthorne called "the Present, the Immediate, the Actual," they felt able to break through the social and racial surface to the metaphysical beyond. But the act of transcendence can, of course, also be seen as an act of betrayal, and there was a subtle web of guilt which was spun by so obvious a retreat from the daily indignities of black life. It was a guilt which pulled Baldwin back to America from time to time, and which created in Wright a sensitivity which could flare up into bitterness.

What is striking, however, is the almost complete absence of interest in Europe as such. American expatriate writers of the nineteenth century were concerned with engaging the Europe of fact and myth; those of the early twentieth century tended to see it as a backdrop against which their frequently neurotic heroes and heroines enacted their entropic lives. For Wright, Baldwin, and Smith, it virtually disappears altogether. It is present, of course, in *Giovanni's Room*. But this is not so much a real Europe as an image of implacable determinism, which is the closest analogy to racial imperatives which Baldwin can find outside of a homosexuality which is itself part metaphor. Europe simply does not feature. The eye remains securely focused on America.

The black writer clearly feels an obligation laid upon him which offers a role as ineluctable as his skin color. As Richard Wright had insisted, the Negro writer is "called upon to do no less than create values by which his race is to struggle, live and die."[34] The desire to evade that role is entirely understandable, for though it may indeed prove the path of personal and racial catharsis, it is also a direct consequence of that social determinism which his art is designed to deny. This is the black "Catch 22." Stephen Dedelus, in Joyce's *The Portrait of the Artist as a Young Man*, expressed the fear clearly enough: "When the soul of a man is born in this country there are nets flung at it to hold it back from flight. You talk to me of rationality, language, religion. I shall try to fly by these nets . . . I will try to express myself in some mode of life or art as freely as I can and as wholly as I can, using for my defense the only arms I allow myself to use—silence, exile, cunning."[35] And these are precisely the defenses deployed by the black writer anxious to avoid the commitments which are the price to be paid for being born black in America: the silence of Ellison, the exile of Wright and Baldwin, the cunning of Reed.

Black writers are, in a sense, unavoidably spiritual exiles. It goes with the territory. The process of physical expatriation is merely an expression of a spiritual banishment. As Richard Wright said in *Twelve Million Black Voices*, "The word 'Negro,' the term by which orally or in print, we black folk in the United States are usually designated, is not really a name at all nor a description, but a psychological island whose objective form is the most unanimous fiat in all American history; a fiat buttressed by popular and national tradition, and written down in many state and city statutes; a fiat which artificially and arbitrarily defines, regulates, and limits in scope of meaning the vital contours of our lives, and the lives of our children and our children's children."[36] Expatriation in this sense is not a willed choice; it is a fate. No wonder that social and metaphysical theories of alienation should have proved so compelling to black writers.

No wonder, either, that black writers in the 1940s and 1950s should have been so drawn to the work of Camus and Sartre. The idea of the alienated outsider was familiar enough to someone pressed to the very margins of society, made external to all available social and political models. Invisibility was an entirely appropriate consequence of the casual indifference of those who defined the contours of his existence in such a way as to deny the black man any substance. In the introduction to Horace Cayton and St. Clair Drake's *Black Metropolis*, Richard Wright quoted William James's observation about the terror of inhabiting a world in which everyone ignored his presence. "No more fiendish punishment could be devised, were such a thing physically possible, than that one should be turned loose in society and remain absolutely unnoticed by all the members thereof. If no one turned round when we entered, answered when we spoke, or minded what we did, but if every person we met 'cut us dead,' and acted as if we were non-existent things, a kind of rage and impotent despair would ere long dwell upon us, from which the cruelest bodily tortures would be a relief; for these would make us feel that, however bad might be our plight, we had not sunk to such a depth as to be unworthy of attention at all."[37]

For the black in America, shut up for so long in a cultural cell, with no ability to influence the social system or to deflect the thrust of political development, it was as though reality were indeed located elsewhere. As Irving Goffman has remarked in a different context in *The Presentation of the Self in Everyday Life*, "To stay in one's room away from the place where the party is given . . .is to stay away from where reality is being performed. The world is, in truth, a wedding."[38] The room to which Goffman refers is that of the "unperformed" self, apart from the interesting roles projected by those whose games constitute an agreed reality. For several hundred years, the Negro was simply not invited to the wedding.

Of course, being shut up in that room may result in the construction of a self uncorrupted by external influences, as Thoreau implied in his retreat to Walden, or as Ellison's protagonist belatedly discovers in *Invisible Man*. But, as Wright suggests in *Native Son*, it may also create a personality and a cultural group which can only gain access to the dominant fictions through an act of violence. Melville implies as much in *Typee*, where the cost of entering history is the striking of a blow and the acceptance of a consequent guilt and responsibility.

Bigger Thomas is as responsible for his own self-creation as is Jay Gatsby, but where the latter is destroyed by his own potent self-imagining, a failure to perceive the other side of an insistence on the platonic ideal, Bigger owes his fate to his sudden presence in time, to his reentry into a world of cause and effect, in which his life cuts a vector across public mythologies and social determinisms alike. Many American heroes are, in effect, parentless, constructing their identities out of the dialectical relationship between self and environment. In

Bigger's case, however, that environment is no more than an image of a determinism too willingly accepted as economic fiat and moral evasion. His identity coheres only when he can accept that such determinisms exist to be transcended, and that to have meaning that transcendence must be spiritual rather than material. He transforms his life by taking possession of his experience. The act of seizing that selfhood, of wrenching it free, is perhaps necessarily a violent one.

Creative writing itself, of course, is a sign that transformations are possible. The act of writing is in itself an assertion of freedom, an insistence on the individual's ability imaginatively to shape his world. And this process of taking possession of reality is available as a social model. Sartre reminds us that when the French used to drink their wine, they would say, "One more that the Prussians won't have."[39] Much the same could be said of the black writer's assertion of his hegemony over experience from the slave narratives onwards. In doing battle with a reality which had formerly demonstrated its substantiality through social dictat, the black writer is simultaneously denying territory to white paternalists and enemies alike and describing a moralized landscape in which it becomes possible to reassert control and hence responsibility and, if you will, guilt. As a pure social construct, as an individual denied access to history and to time, he was condemned to an irrelevance which was the moral equivalence of innocence. Thus, he has to smash this image in order to emerge into history and a sense of the self. This is why the necessary gesture becomes a violent one, as it did for Melville's Tommo. Psychic territory is surrendered no more readily than physical territory. The act of violent rebellion, which one finds in Chesnutt's *The Marrow of Tradition* and in Wright's *Native Son*, is thus an image of that challenge, as the books themselves stand as testaments to the desire on the part of the black writer to regain psychological and artistic control of his experience.

The appeal of an existentially liberating violence, which Carmichael found in Fanon and which Fanon, perhaps, found in Sorel, is a familiar one to readers raised on *Native Son*. The act of violence kills more than the oppressor; it destroys also that image of passivity which was taken to stand between the individual and his authenticity. In the American context, however, the revolution took symbolic and rhetorical, rather than literal and physical, form. Even though the language of black revolutionaries frequently invoked the image of colonialism, the possibility of armed revolt clearly never existed. It was violence as myth rather than violence as reality which appealed. It was to the possibility of breaking out of a role which had become coterminous with an identity that the black American now looked. And it was this fact that Baldwin ignored in his response to Wright's Bigger Thomas. It was a misunderstanding of this fact that set American police to their shameful destruction of the Black Panthers.

Wright's work, like Fanon's studies, tends to examine the points of intersection of the social and psychological, the Freudian and the Marxist, with all the consequent confusions and contradictions. *Native Son* and *Soul on Ice* both turn on the understanding that the individual psyche offers the real point of impact for social distortions. As Fanon remarks in *The Wretched of the Earth*, ''At the level of individuals, violence is a cleansing force. It frees the native from his inferiority complex and from his despair and inaction.''[40] For Fanon, this was a first step towards perceiving the complex nature of social and economic realities; it was an act of release which made perception possible. For Wright, and to a lesser extent for Cleaver, it was the basis of perception, and Wright was not ready to deliver his protagonist up to another form of restraint. He could not follow Fanon down the path of militant socialism, though for a number of years he embraced a harsh discipline which itself seemed to offer the possibility of action and an identity with the forces of history.

Yet it is precisely that historicity which offers some kind of benediction for violence by placing it in a dialectical position. The synthesis is to be the revolutionary society, at peace with itself and the world. Wright offers no such vision of past or future, except for Bigger Thomas's momentary dream of transcendental unity, which remains precisely that—a dream. Since his act is unconnected with any systematic perception of the world, and since, despite Max's efforts to the contrary, it remains outside any ideological conviction, it leaves no residue of political energy. It expresses a liberal conviction about the potential of the self and a romantic view of social connectiveness. But it does so through the ironic inversion of moral values to which such convictions would normally lay claim. The irony is that this social gesture should have been seen as an implicit threat, a confirmation of the stereotype and even a despairing confession of determinism.

There is something irremediably antimodern about black writing, not merely in the sense in which, until comparatively recently, it had eschewed aesthetic experimentation, but in the convictions which the black writer embraces. The contemporary American writer has come increasingly to feel that fiction itself contains the incubus of social control, that the manipulations of the writer are coterminous with those of the political and even cosmic realm. This has prompted a mode resting on parody, irony, and linguistic self-doubt. Language is seen as an arch-betrayer; truth loses its essence in the process of utterance. As Roland Barthes has said, the writer had the choice of being true to the present, or to the literary and linguistic forms which he has inherited, but scarcely to both. The black writer faces that problem in a more acute and specific form, in that the language which he employs contains the essence of those defining forces which he needs so desperately to defeat. The cultural traitor is within the gates. And, although this is true for all writers, it is so much the *subject* of the black writer's dilemma that the paradox is the more disabling. But for the black writer, communication is a moral necessity. The result is a curiously ambiguous response to language—an assertion of its deceptive qualities, paradoxically expressed in words which try to locate and define the nature of black anguish. So, too, with the symbol. Having been forced as individuals to enact symbolic roles, they frequently wish to smash the metaphoric trap; and yet they know simultaneously that for an oppressed minority the individual is necessarily a public symbol, containing the history and potential of the group.

The black creation of myths, of political exemplars, of cultural signs, derives out of a recognizable impulse. In his book on contemporary American fiction (which is surprisingly reticent on the subject of black writing), Tony Tanner quotes Blake's observation in "Jerusalem," "I must Create a System or be enslav'd by another Man's."[41] And this, of course, is the essential problem of the black writer. The social and literary models which he is offered are conditioned and defined by the white world; the language which he inherits is the instrument of his oppression, carrying as it does the tracery of history.

The problem of the black writer, more than the white writer, is to create a space between the self and the conditioning forces which surround that self, a space in which the autonomy of the individual and the cultural group itself can cohere.

The basic dilemma of the writer—the fact that he must always express the present in terms of the past, that his work contains the very history it is designed to deny—must be felt more acutely by the black writer for whom the past is anyway a dubious heritage and literary form an image of the constraints against which he rebels. Roland Barthes has spoken of the "tragic element in writing" which derives from the fact that "the conscious writer must . . . fight against ancestral and all-powerful signs which, from the depths of a past foreign to him, impose Literature on him like some ritual, not like a reconciliation." And for the black writer, language and form potentially create a barrier between himself and the experience which he would engage, between his perception and the communication of that perception, for, as Barthes suggests, "Either the object of the work is naively attuned to the convictions of its form, Literature remaining deaf to our present History, and not going beyond the literary myth; or else the writer acknowledges the vast novelty of the present world, but finds that in order to express it he has at his disposal only a language which is splendid but lifeless." Thus, "in front of the virgin sheet of paper, at the moment of choosing the words which must frankly signify his place in History, and testify that he assumes its data, he observes a tragic disparity between what he does and what he sees. Before his eyes, the world of society now exists as a veritable Nature, and this Nature speaks, elaborating living languages from which the writer is excluded: on the contrary, History puts in his hands a decorative and compromising instrument, a writing inherited from a previous and different History, for which he is not responsible and yet which is the only one he can use."[42]

For writers like Wright, Baldwin, and others who wish to articulate black suffering, who feel a direct social obligation, the dilemma has a moral dimension. One response is to desert fictional strategies entirely for the apparently neutral language of reportage or, more usually, the self-confessing conventionalities of polemical rhetoric, where language and form are closer to the familiar registers and metaphoric impulses of religious practice. The form and language are conventionalized to the point of ritual, ideal for casting out devils and describing a Manichean world. Perhaps significantly, it is almost impossible to find a major black novelist in recent years who has not also been an essayist. The middle ground, however, is the realistic novel. Though its language and form are heavily conventionalized, the familiarity of its structure and its narrative strategy convey at least an illusion of engaging reality directly. It is an evasion, but literature is an art of evasion no less when it is confessing to its deceptions, as in the work of Ishmael Reed.

There is certainly a distrust of fiction in black writing, but it is not, for the most part, the same as is felt by white writers. It derives from the feeling that countering a potent reality with fictions betokens a massive failure of nerve, a shifting of the essential conflict to the safe battleground of words. The essay and the autobiography promise truth, fact, authenticity, a courageous confession of painful realities. Fiction offers Pyrrhic victories, fanciful structures of words bereft of social content and tangential to crucial economic and political realities. The naturalistic novel offers a compromise, an apparently direct engagement with the real. As Wright explained, "I read Dreiser's *Jennie Gerhardt* and *Sister Carrie*. . . .It would have been impossible for me to have told anyone what I derived from these novels, for it was nothing less than a sense of life itself. All my life had shaped me for the realism, the naturalism of the modern novel."[43] But, balancing this, was always a perception of the need to reach through the simple claims of a tangible existence to a world of possibility. The pressure of a transcendent vision coexists with his compulsion to delineate the contours of black suffering. In a letter written at about the time he concluded *Black Boy*, he wrote, "We must beware of those who seek in words no matter how urgent or crisis-charged, to interpose an alien and dubious curtain of reality between our eyes and the crying claims of a world which it is our lot to see only poignantly and too briefly."[44]

Alain Locke, writing in the 1920s, observed that "all classes of people under social pressure are permeated with a common experience; they are emotionally welded together as others cannot be. With them even ordinary living has epic depth and lyric intensity."[45] But, in turn, the need to break out of such determinism created a counterpressure which always threatened to subvert the realistic drive.

Realism appears to be democratic both in its accessibility to a larger public and in the equal weight which it agrees to give to physical and mental realities alike. Its positivist assumptions are reassuring; its paradigm of truths concealed beneath the penetrable masks of private and public deceptions, an agreeably simple and plausible reduction of complex forms and fears. Plot has a central and necessary role because it is from the impact of events that meaning is presumed to emerge. There is an agreed world and a unified vision.

The content may be anguished and self-doubting, but the form is confident and secure. The amassing of detail is presumed to imply the accretion of truth. And the pressure of fact is more likely to obsess and overwhelm the black writer for whom the solid realities carry a determining force not felt by whites. Such books are a means of grasping meaning through things. Like Dickens' Gradgrind, their authors feel that to locate an irreducible factuality is to pin down meaning. It is a conviction mocked by Melville in *Moby Dick*, but celebrated by the naturalist. A sense of place and time and social norms provides the coordinates for an identity which can be adequately defined by this kind of triangulation.

But it is a strategy which is not without its elements of nostalgia, its failure of nerve. For if these parameters do indeed have a constraining power, they do not constitute a final and defining influence. That, after all, was the point of *Native Son*, in which the communists remain encysted in a deterministic world which releases the individual from guilt even as it liberates him from responsibility, but does so at the cost of his personal identity and at the price of social change which is anything but structural. The moral universe cannot contain a model which relies on simple inversion. If change was to be of any significance, Wright implied, it had to take root in the individual sensibility. History was anything but the succession of inevitabilities outlined by Marxist theorists. For Wright, it thus became necessary to snap the bonds of naturalism, as it did to relinquish a comfortable illusion of impotence. And the drive of his major novel was through the naturalistic surface to the symbolic core. Not that this was a wholly conscious impulse, for just as Bigger Thomas learns to strike through the pasteboard masks, so, I fancy, does Wright himself, who, while increasingly alienated from the Party, was still persuaded of the rightness of its economic analysis. But the familiarly naturalistic biological metaphor with which the novel opens—a black rat in a white-constructed cage—is slowly broken down as Bigger perceives the degree to which such a metaphor can itself become a trap. For color, he suggests, derives its potency precisely from its metaphoric, rather than factual, thrust. It stands for qualities, attitudes, abilities. The black man, in other words, has moved around in an image created by whites, an image whose power ultimately lies not so much in the gun or the club as in the ability to define the public fictions within which the individual must operate. The black man's mistake is thus presented by Wright as lying in the decision to treat image as fact. Hence, Bigger's decision to strike through the mask of social determinism is the essence of his freedom. Liberation is transcendence; stylistically it inclines to realism, morally to a new cosmology of symbols which frequently subvert that realism.

The stylistic revolt of *Invisible Man*, which for many black critics allied Ellison uncomfortably with the literary avant-garde, could more profitably be seen as an analogue of that resistance to defining contours, which is the subject of the book and the necessary task of the black writer. Much the same could be said of Wright's denial of the naturalistic logic of *Native Son*. There is a centripetal force driving the public world back to the self, a force which places naturalistic assumptions under pressure.

This process is, perhaps, at its most obvious in the work of an author like Ishmael Reed, who deliberately subverts the language which he uses, turning words and myths back on themselves, mocking and celebrating the craft of the writer and the culture in which he operates.

Clearly a writer like Amiri Baraka foregrounds language, deliberately deconstructing lexical structures, collapsing words, investing them with special meanings. In one linguistic act he seeks to subvert the language which he has inherited and assert a different pattern. He forces language back against the joint, dislocating cultural presumptions, not so much because he is trying to capture the tone and nature of black English, but because he wishes to disassemble the component parts of an assumed system. Revolution operates on a linguistic as well as a political level.

The irony, of course, is that, as Richard Poirier has suggested, the American writer has taken as his subject and stylistic principle the necessity to resist models of reality which subordinate the self to the environment. While the pull of moral commitment is never far away, the escape into imagination is a constant temptation, working to resist the pull of time and place and simple facticity. So that, seen in this way, the black writer's desire to break out of linguistic and cultural constraints is familiar enough in American writing actually to constitute the tradition.

Nevertheless, the main thrust of black writing has been social. Why should this be so? It is, perhaps, for the reason that Sartre suggests in discussing the plight of the Jew; because he has been trapped in the social. He is "the social man *par excellence*, because his torment is social."[46] "His life is nothing but a long flight from others and from himself. He has been alienated even from his own body; his emotional life has been cut in two; he has been reduced to pursuing the impossible dream of universal brotherhood in a world that rejects him."[47] And the cause of this is not merely racism but equally a condescending liberalism.

Sartre has said that "the Jews have one friend . . .the democrat," but argues that "he is a feeble protector" because "he recognizes neither Jew nor Arab, nor Negro, nor bourgeois, nor worker, but only man . . .It follows that his defense of the Jew saves the latter as man and annihilates him as Jew. . . .This means that he wants to separate the Jew from his religion, from his family, from his ethnic community, in order to plunge him into the democractic crucible whence he will emerge naked and alone. . . .This is what, in the United States, is called the policy of assimilation."[48]

It is precisely this fear which had led to the difficult relationship between the black writer and the white liberal—a relationship which is not always rational and which was, for a time, the source of genuine anguish to many whites who had devoted their energies, and on occasion their lives, to what seemed, for a crucial decade, to be the central issue facing the nation. Partly, of course, the difficulty arose from a deep and historically determined scepticism, a recognition that moral causes come and go. But increasingly it derived from the conviction that identity was finally as menaced by friend as by enemy. Confronted, on the one hand, by the defining opposition of racists, and, on the other, by the well-meaning homogenizing instincts of the liberal, the black American had to assume the difficult task of delineating an identity not wholly separable from that forced on him by the racist. As Sartre said of the Jew, "The inauthentic Jew flees Jewish reality, and the anti-Semite makes him a Jew in spite of himself; but the authentic Jew *makes himself a Jew*, in the face of all and against all."[49]

I am not unaware of the danger in presenting Negro and Jew as brothers in alienation, nor am I unaware that their experience of America has been radically dissimilar, and that the black and Jewish diaspora are different in kind and meaning—though Eldridge Cleaver proposes a parallel between the plight of Negro and Jew in "The Land Question and Black Liberation."[50] The parallel which I propose is limited to a concern with the degree to which the question of authenticity is socially derived, the nature of acquiescence or resistance being equally provoked and determined by social pressure, by forces emanating, in part at least, from outside the self. For Sartre, of course, the leap from the social to the metaphysical is attained only by an existential decision to embrace one's fate. And in this respect, Wright's Bigger Thomas, like Ellison's nameless protagonist after him, is an appropriate example. And though Sartre observes that "the authentic Jew abandons the myth of the universal man,"[51] just as during the 1960s those black writers and those critics identifying a concern with using the individual as springboard to the universal were roundly denounced (indeed the very word "universal" became a code word for lack of commitment), it is clear that for writers like Wright, Baldwin, and Ellison the drive toward a general view of human nature was strong. Indeed, Wright confided to his journal the conviction that "when the feeling of the fact of being a Negro is accepted fully into the consciousness of a Negro there's something universal about it and something that lifts it above being a Negro in America."[52] For they saw racial identity as a necessary key to human indentity. *Invisible Man* and *Another Country* are both concerned with the need to break through social determinants, even in the knowledge that that revolt is itself an image of those determinants. The paradox, however, was potentially disabling, and neither Wright, nor Ellison, nor Baldwin has ever succeeded in dramatizing a self liberated from its social determinants and operating freely in the social world.

But, paradoxically, there is a greater confidence in the nature of reality and in the ability of language to reflect and, indeed, construct that world than one finds with contemporary white writers, though Wright's "The Man Who Lived Underground" is an articulate confession of self-doubt. Wright's and

Baldwin's works, primarily, are offered as versions of the real. Their claim is to specialized knowledge, to a perspective denied to those who contrive to describe the social world from within. The basic claim is that marginality confers a special vision, and that experience stripped of casual urbanities and the protective myths of order, progress, and an effortless technology is more real and closer to the marrow of existence. Life in the ghetto is life without a veneer, even if it is a life of masks and roles.

But to resist America is, of course, an act of definition which is American in origin. LeRoi Jones's revulsion against American trivia, against false social and moral values, is scarcely different in kind from that of Thoreau. Disengagement is seen as the only legitimate path to the self. Paradoxically, Ellison's protagonist discovers as much in his cellar.

The experience of the modern is the experience of inhabiting a world which has lost agreed values and shared experiences and substituted only a common situation—the uncommunal city and a common series of fictions. And the black writer takes as his setting a physical world characterized by disintegration and decay, a moral world distinguished by the collapse of human values, and a social world in which the individual is the victim of institutional violence. Paradoxically, this does not, for the most part, generate the entropic, attenuated, intransitive, and reflexive literature of Pynchon, Kosinski, Coover, Purdy, and Hawkes—a literature drained of ethical tension. Instead, it produces works which presume the substantiality of the self, the availability of a language largely uncorrupted by irony and the persistence of a reality which can be defined in terms adequate to the individual who confronts it, that is primarily in social and psychological terms. The self may be under stress, but it exists; society may be menacing, but it is not, for the most part, seen as a tantalizing fiction, its deceptions being pragmatic devices.

The very rigor of black suffering creates a resistance which *requires* an unambiguous world and a self which, if it can adopt disguises, nonetheless remains intransigent in its assertions of identity. The risk is that the disguises will become the origin of corruption, a danger which Ellison recognizes in *Invisible Man*. But even this worry implies the existence of a real self—not a romantic self adrift in the void, feeding on it own substance, but a self reaching out to other selves in an attempt to heal a wound which is part contingent and social and part primal and metaphysical.

"A writer is committed to what is real and not to the sanctity of his Feelings," [53] LeRoi Jones insisted in 1963. Outside of Ellison and Reed, there seems little doubt among black writers as to what constitutes the real. The pressure is to see literature as a social act, a moral gesture which, in a sense, requires the minimum mediation by the author. The aesthetic is distrusted as deceptive, distorting. As James Walker says in the *The Slave*, "The aesthete came along after all the things that really formed me. It was the easiest weight to shed." [54] Addison Gayle, Jr., has said that for the black writer "substance is more important than form . . .the social takes precedence over the aesthetic. . . . each act, gesture, and movement is political.''[55] Clearly, much black writing is presented as testament.

As Tony Tanner has pointed out, the narrative lines of contemporary American literature ''are full of hidden dimensions, plots, secret organizations, evil systems, all kinds of conspiracies against spontaneity of consciousness, even cosmic take-over. The possible nightmares of being totally controlled by unseen agencies and powers is never far away in contemporary American fiction. The unease revealed in such novels is related to a worried apprehension on the part of the author that his own consciousness may be determined and channelled by the language he has been born into.''[56] How much more literally the black writer feels the victim of conspiracies, the focus of manipulating powers, can be imagined. Pynchon's conspiracies are cosmic. His characters are comic-strip heroes desperately searching for meaning in invented worlds. The conspiracies identified by black writers are all too substantial. If theirs seemed a paranoid fiction, it did not seem so for long. The apprehension about the determining power of a temporally and culturally alien language is acute and literal. Tanner suggests that, for the American writer, the twin fears are that the self will dissolve into an amorphous lump, a gelatinous creation of featureless cells, on the one hand, or become a fixed, immutable form, whose contours are determined not by internal pressures creating a moral shape from within, but by the molding power of externalities. The self is threatened in one direction by pure fluidity and on the other by fixity resulting from social or metaphysical stasis. The same apprehension can be found in black writers, but here the menace to identity stems from a definable act of racial hostility. Richard Wright describes an occasion on which he was maneuvered out of a job by the irrational hatred of two white men. The result, he explains, was that ''for weeks after that I could not believe in my feelings. My personality was numb, reduced to a lumpish, loose, dissolved state. I was a non-man, something that knew vaguely that it was human but felt that it was not. As time separated me from the experience, I could feel no hate for the men who had driven me from the job. They did not seem to be individual men, but part of a huge, implacable, elemental design towards which hatred was futile. I felt doubly cast out.''[57]

To speak is to use the language which has historically been used to justify their oppression. The act of cultural assertion becomes an ambiguous act, undercut by its very expression. It is a familiar paradox, but one whose social and political implications, in the case of the black writer, produce an angry and brittle rhetoric. The black writer has not for the most part moved towards silence as a resolution to the paradox of language. The compulsion is to speak, to define, to recapture a past, delineate a present, and project a future.

There is an irony to *Native Son* in that as Bigger Thomas feels his way towards articulateness, a sense of an identity distinct from the defining pressures of environment and cultural presumptions, that very articulateness becomes a new determinism. It is an irony not fully engaged by Wright. It is, after all, language that becomes the real cause of his isolation, in that it connects him only with those who seek to destroy him either through simple hatred or through political reductivism. Ellison rightly objects to Bigger's ability to express thoughts beyond the reach of his character. More tellingly, he gains control of words which deny him access to his self at the very moment he is laying claim to its discovery. What Bigger actually claims is that he is the product of his actions and not of his environment, that he makes himself and is not created out of racial or economic stereotypes. Since the actions which define him are themselves partly involuntary and partly the result of circumstance, his freedom lies only in the decision to regard those acts as willed. It is, in other words, an act of appropriation, a fiction which offers more scope for selfhood than the events themselves can render up. When he asserts that ''what I killed for I am,'' it is an inherently ambiguous claim. After all, just what did he kill for?

The pity is that Wright's concern for the self in its struggle with externalities gave way to a fascination with Sartre and Camus. His own language, as reflected in *The Outsider*, begins to pull him away from the tensions and crude authenticity of his earlier work, in which the struggle for identity was reflected in the search for an identifiable voice. The failure of Wright's later work lies in his mistaking submission to language for mastery of language. Arguably, his failure lay in his increasing articulateness.

The fact is that historically, for the black, language was an essential part of the process of manipulation and control. The systematic denial of his own language and the superimposition of another was not a consequence of enslavement, it was the essence of it. The impress of language not only stands as a symbol of cultural subordination, it is the prime agent of it. Reality was defined anew. Whole clusters of images and myths were offered, as was a highly selective sequence of observations about the individual's relationship to himself, to his environment, and to others, which was presented as a descriptive definition of the real. Reality was what white American language asserted it to be. And it was that special panoply of fictions which the black has struggled to escape from that moment since. But, since the act of communication must always be an act of self-betrayal, the black American becomes a kind of Sisyphus, who must exult in an act of rebellion which usually remains wholly contained in the self. Communal action, insofar as it rests on a suspect linguistic act, is subverted at the moment of its birth. The process of defining is a process of exclusion. Hence the movement towards a black language, a cultural autonomy which was at first a substitute for a missing ideology.

In *The End of Ideology*, Daniel Bell argues that ''one finds, at the end of the fifties, a disconcerting caesura. The new generation, with no meaningful memory of those old debates, and no secure tradition to build upon, finds itself seeking new purposes within a framework of political society that has rejected, intellectually speaking, the old apocalyptic and chiliastic visions. In the search for a 'cause,' there is a deep, desperate, almost pathetic anger . . .a restless search for a new intellectual radicalism. . . .The irony . . .for those who seek 'causes' is that the workers, whose grievances were once the driving energy for social change, are more satisfied with the society than the intellectuals. . . ..The young intellectual is unhappy because the 'middle way' is for the middle-aged, not for him; it is without passion and it is deadening. . . .The emotional energies—and needs—exist and the question of how one mobilizes these energies is a difficult one.''[58] While this obviously does not apply directly to the young Negro, who had no need to search for a cause and who, in the beginning, for the most part, treasured no romantic notions of class solidarity, he also found himself in an ideological vacuum.

The ideologues of the 1930s were still around to play out the radical rituals of the past—denouncing the drift from social realism in the black novel and expressing a familiar distrust of cultural nationalism. But they did so with less conviction, though scarcely less stridency. The emerging civil rights movement was at first nonideological. Its vision of society was liberal, deriving from Thoreau via Gandhi; its strategy was pragmatic; its appeal was to abstract principles of justice and morality; its demands, though sometimes formulated in terms of immediate objectives, in essence call for dignity and for inclusion in the ideologically barren world accurately described by Bell. There was, in other words, an ideological vacuum which many young blacks felt acutely. Where the civil rights movement dealt in epiphanies, they were drawn to apocalypse, which they shaped at first in racial and then increasingly in political terms.

But the irony of a disengaged majority existed for them, too, for though all blacks had a vested interest in change, the vision of society which they shared was essentially that of modern consumer America, redefined only to include them in its capitalist enterprise. The result was the invented ideology of race, sometimes attached to imperfectly perceived religious myths, sometimes an inadequately understood version of African liberation, sometimes growing out of a real but still undefined sense of cultural identity which irritatingly contained a past which could not always bear inspection until it could be offered the grace of retrospective invention. Alternatively, it was an international radicalism, learned at third hand from African and European models and recast into models of third-world solidarity or an imperfectly argued class unity.

Much of the energy of such people was predictably discharged, not at the social system which dominated them or through opposition to which they gained their identity, but through internecine battles and clashes of myths, symbols, and systems oddly tangential to the immediate issues of transforming American society to the point at which it would acknowledge their existence. The dissonance, which frequently existed between an imprecise and frequently confused language, and the perceived reality of daily existence, became itself a source of frustration. Frustrated hopes were displaced into a rhetoric which became daily more shrill until, in the late 1960s, with a sudden jolt, like two geological systems brushing against one another to produce a convulsive shock, reality tried to approximate itself to the rhetoric. The blow at capitalism became literal; the apocalyptic spirit was acted out in dozens of cities across America. The trauma, followed by the benign indifference of the political system, shocked many blacks into a conservatism from which they have yet to recover.

The symbolic victories, the victories apparently desired by the majority, were slowly being won by the nonideologues. Though the economic structures remained unchanged, the social fabric had been transformed, largely through legal means backed up by direct action. But, arguably, the new intellectual radicalism of those who felt excluded, not only by American society, but also by the language and tactics of the civil rights movement, created the distant prospect of apocalypse necessary to give iron to the diffuse aims of the majority. And revolutionary times inevitably increase the pressure on language. As Roland Barthes, speaking of the French Revolution, has said, this was "in the highest degree one of those great occasions when truth, through the bloodshed that it costs, becomes so weighty that its expression demands the very forms of theatrical amplification."[59] Revolutionary writing was the "one and only gesture commensurate with the presence of the guillotine."[60] And while the changes in American society in the 1960s did not always get beyond the verbal act itself, it was still true that the sense of society undergoing fundamental change (the supposed crisis of capitalism, the "green revolution," the youth movement, and, most of all, the collapse of black acquiescence) generated precisely that theatrical amplification of which Barthes speaks. It was this rhetoric that was at the heart of the attempt to raise fact to the status of myth.

It was against this background that the Second Renaissance took place. It was this reality which the writer had to engage and against which he projected his fictions. It was into this fierce debate that he interjected his symbolic structures, and it is no wonder that he should have been so closely inspected for his orthodoxy or that each defection from the pure line of a longed-for social and aesthetic norm should have been denounced with the fervor of a Puritan divine haranguing the sinful celebrant of a beauty detached from its divine root. Literature could not be permitted to slip into mere frivolity. For the one, its sole justification lay in its service to God; for the other, in its service to man. There was, said LeRoi Jones, to be no closet poetry unless the closet was as wide as God's eye. And Puritan divine and black radical each arrogated to himself the definition of God and man and, hence, the role of critic, deliberately subduing in the process any aesthetic pleasure for fear that it might detract from the higher purpose, for fear that it might prove the first step towards a formalism which each would equally agree to be the highest sin. So, Ellison is indicted for his use of symbols because they create a distance between his work and reality. Craft becomes a crust between the artist and his human source.

At least the Puritan divine, believing the whole world to be an emblem of God, had the means at hand to reconcile himself at last with art; the Marxist is denied such absolution—as, I suppose, is only right. One might have thought that the black nationalist could have applied something of this Puritan logic, since the author's race should be absolution enough, but dealing in images so much himself, he was, and is, apt to challenge anyone who usurps his hegemony over versions of black consciousess not commensurate with a black revolutionary upwards mobility. Hence Trueblood, in Ellison's novel, is seen not as an avatar of white consciousness, a projection of the white id, but as a potential slander on a race in the process of ransacking history for evidence of black rebels and saints. And where in his wandering through time the black writer came across a white writer sifting through the same boneyard, they fought desperately for possession of the prize. William Styron chose entirely the wrong moment to attempt his leap into black historical consciousness, for that was precisely the moment chosen by blacks for the exorcism of white spirits who were unwise enough to stray outside the legitimate confines of their patrimony. But to balance things up, of course, they were equally prepared to apply the same stringent restrictions to those black writers who presumed to animate an alien white consciousness, for they were by definition deserters, putative whites, who exposed their own predilections and sought access to a cultural heritage outside the remarkably thin tradition of black writing that they were prepared to validate.

Simply to be a black writer in the 1960s was to offer yourself up as a sacrificial victim, public spokesman, potential Quissling, hero, villain, a virtual Manichean image of black society itself. To be a black writer was not a career; it was a fate. And, in turn, each was seared by the heat of a burning conviction about the appropriate range, direction, and motivation of black art. James Baldwin, who had for his own psychic reasons once attacked Richard Wright, was himself reduced to tears by Eldridge Cleaver's excoriation of his own work and personality. The need to cast out devils knows no limit. Denunciation becomes itself proof of orthodoxy, and withdrawal from the arena proof of one's detachment from social engagement. But there is a case for saying that the themes of Richard Wright, Ralph Ellison, and even James Baldwin, are closer to the modern impulse than those critics who are still applying theoretical models derived from nineteenth-century economics or vague theories of class solidarity would grant. The prospect of Amiri Baraka searching for an "advanced working class" in contemporary America, for example, is ironic in a number of ways. As a cultural nationalist in the 1960s, he wrote for a race which did indeed share some of the characteristics once justifiably applied to class. In particular, it possesses precisely that cultural homogeneity which he now has to reinvent for a group which must be made to correspond to largely defunct social and economic models. The radical critique of black culture, in other words, runs the risk of destroying the very thing which it would wish to describe. The cultural nationalist, on the other hand, recognizes and stresses a cultural homogeneity but too often seeks to distill out a racial essence by denying the economic, political, and cultural context in which it unavoidably locates itself and which, inevitably, forms part of a personal and social identity.

One thing was clear, however: black Americans felt no need of the ersatz sense of community pursued by people like Julian Beck, the theatre director, and others in the 1960s. Theirs was a community which had no need to break out of the constraints of rational society and the overburdening materialism of American life. On the contrary, they had for decades been trying to break into it. And if now there was a strong feeling that there was little to be gained by free access to the white social structure, the model advanced was not, for the most part, a romantic one, simply celebrating experience outside of a moral world, parallel to but detached from the downward plunge of American society. That was too close to the cliché use to which whites had put them over the years, the image in which they had been ensnared by Kerouac (*On the Road*, 1957) and Mailer ("The White Negro"), as much as by white racists. No. The model which they embraced was a liberal one, derived from America's past. The self was not located in some spiritual void in which other selves brushed briefly and ecstatically against them, only to pass on further into a sensual universe. It derived its meaning and its location from a social world which had to be reaffirmed in order for the self to invent itself in relation to others. The blacks required a moral world in order to accuse. They required an ethic of connectiveness in order to confirm their own rights. In the First Renaissance, sensuality was seen as a virtue, a clear contrast to a white world which chose to dramatize its sense of social and moral impotence in sexual terms. Despite some consciously abrasive art, black writers, on the whole, chose to test the lyric potential of a newly asserted racial identity. For the writers of the Second Renaissance, lyricism, where it existed, had to be sought in the interstices of a public struggle. Community was something which cohered around public images of personal and group identity.

If bourgeois capitalist society lacked a transcendent dimension, that dimension had to be sought in the moral responsibility which was the basis of the claim now being laid before that society by the civil rights movement; and, despite the ill-considered attacks on Ellison for his supposed detachment from the struggle, his work bore the impress of this need to reinvent America in its own former image as much as that of any other writer, except, perhaps, Saul Bellow (see Chapter 5). Art is not seen by Ellison as a refuge from chaos, but as a moral instrument. "A man's character is his fate," Ralph Waldo Emerson had remarked. In *Invisible Man*, Mr. Norton and the ironically named Mr. Emerson had derived from Emerson only a justification for capitalist enterprise; self-sufficiency for them implied rigorous individualism and laissez-faire economics, the deflection of classic liberalism into conservative virtues. For Ellison, Emerson is the poet of connectiveness, who finds transcendence not to be external to man but to emerge from a confident selfhood and from that self's moral and social relationships. This is the America which he seeks to invoke and which Wright's Bigger Thomas had glimpsed in his jail cell. It is also the America that Baldwin tries to re-create through the sexual pairings in his novels. The irony is that the values endorsed by the black writer should be those abandoned by many white writers in favor of a seductive romanticism or an existential and ironic despair.

The black's situation on arriving in America was existential in a literal sense. Thrown into a world of hostile forces, unable to decipher the symbols of that world, his whole history in America has consisted of his attempt to gain possession of himself through gaining possession of his environment. The central irony of his existence, more especially in the twentieth-century, has been that as those alien symbols have resolved themselves, as he has penetrated the mysteries, so he has discovered that the code which he has broken contains no meaning of itself. Behind the immediate mystery lies another which is more profound. As he begins, perforce, to feel more at home in the social world, so he has come to realize that this in itself is only a desperate attempt to conceal an awareness of contingency and menace. At precisely the moment that he began, in the 1940s and 1950s, to take imaginative possession of what he had now come to conceive as being his country, he found a people themselves perplexed as to the meaning of identity and the substance of reality, projecting a literature which generated images themselves expressive of absurdity.

It is scarcely surprising that black writers should have been drawn to apocalyptic imagery, or should, like Wright, have expressed a supreme consciousness of social and metaphysical absurdity. But the really striking thing is the extent to which they have retreated from the brink, have subsumed the absurd in a rebellious or, more usually, liberal image of individual freedom and responsibility. The idea of human existence as a kind of brutal game played out by conscious or unconscious role players in a world spun out of the imagination is seen by the serious black writer as a temptation to be resisted. Rinehart offers a possible tactic for dealing with absurdity; by merging with it you become invulnerable, by surrendering your identity and suppressing a moral self you become immune to the ironies which are the product of maintaining an ethical stance in an antinomian world. For a time in the 1960s, such Rinehart figures appeared in novels of black city life: the confidence man as hero. But to Ellison, it was a temptation to be resisted. Irony was perhaps the price to be paid for maintaining one's independence from the absurdity which it was necessary to confront.

As argued above, the black writer, more than most, has every justification for sharing the contemporary conviction about the strangeness of language, its ironic claim to approximate the reality which it purports to describe. For, not only had that language once been wholly alien, but the gap between language and reality had for most of the time in America been the source of his suffering and the root of his social absurdity. The gap between American liberal rhetoric and the reality of deprivation, prejudice, and judicial injustice was a fissure in which the black had been invited to live out his existence. Language provides the possible, rather than the actual, borders of action. It is, thus, itself, the well-spring of irony, as, indeed, it is in another sense. As Roland Barthes has pointed out, "Language is never innocent: words have a second order memory which mysteriously persists in the midst of new meanings,"[61] that is, it is historically derived, indeed in a sense it contains history, as style, he suggests, contains a personal past. But more important, in his mind, is the mode of writing, which is perforce "an act of historical solidarity."[62] It is in this area that some freedom persists; for there is some choice, however limited. Hence, "writing is precisely this compromise between freedom and remembrance." For Ellison, however, this is also a model of human existence which is lived out precisely within the tension created by freedom and control, the pull of history and the pull of the future. The border is the natural place for the individual, and the very act of writing becomes a paradigm of the individual's task of recognizing the conflicting claims of self and society, of past and future, of order and release. The process of writing, like the act of composing a life, is a compromise between the given and the possible, and it is in this tension that the hero of Ellison's novel discovers the meaning of his quest.

And yet writing is inevitably coercive. As Barthes insists, it is "closed" in the sense that it is not a channel for communication but a self-contained system. Ellison is clearly aware of this. His book is full of unreliable documents which deny the freedom they purport to guarantee. His strategy for dealing with this paradox of literature, therefore, is to foreground its process, as Tanner points out that Melville does at the beginning of *Moby Dick*, to undermine even the coercive quality of the book which warns against coercion. Similarly, the openness of the ending, the unexplored future of his protagonist, is a deliberate gesture of incompletion.

The changed circumstances of the 1960s made Saunders Redding's comment (in Herbert Hill's 1966 collection *Anger, and After*) that the gulf between black and white audiences had closed and that it was now possible for a "Negro author" to "create that which rises above race" and reach out, in the words of James Weldon Johnson, " 'to the universal in truth and beauty,' "[63] seem singularly inappropriate. Indeed, the situation in the middle-late 1960s was such that it bred a mutual paranoia, with J. Edgar Hoover and numerous police forces around the country launching a campaign of vicious and illegal assaults on black individuals and organizations, and blacks, generalizing out of this experience, talking about genocide. LeRoi Jones was not alone in quoting the

Jewish experience in World War II. The "riots" of 1967 and 1968 seemed to validate this dramatic image, and, in an essay called "Survival Motion: A Study of the Black Writer and the Black Revolution in America, " Stephen Henderson went so far as to say that "the question is not . . .whether America is capable of genocide; not *whether* the white man would exterminate the black (if he could), but *how*."[64]

Indeed, in a sense, LeRoi Jones's book of essays, *Home*, marks not only his personal transformation, but the shift which took place between the 1950s and the 1960s—a change in attitudes, strategies, and values in the civil rights movement and in black writing which made Jones's career seem exemplary. *Home* measures those changes in the form of essays written over a period of five years. A visit to Cuba in 1960 introduced him to the idea of revolution as a practical reality. He began to feel uneasy about his own relative uninvolvement, his view of literature as personal liberation, as a search for a form to express and contain a comfortable alienation. As he said in the essay which reflected on his Cuban visit, "The rebels among us have become merely people like myself who grow beards and will not participate in politics. Drugs . . .complete isolation from the vapid mores of the country, a few current ways out."[65] But at this stage he could see no possibilities, recognize no program, which could deal with the problem. The challenge which he offers—"name an alternative"—betrays a loss of imaginative energy which may itself partly account for the dramatic change which came over his life and that of others shortly afterwards.

"Cuba Libre" was written for *Evergreen Review*; it shows no sense of black consciousness as an animating force. But in the essays which follow, that sense of an available cultural solidarity strengthens. Beginning with an assault on what he sees as a liberal equivocation, defining liberals as "people with extremely heavy consciences and almost non-existent courage,"[66] he moved quickly to outlining the basis for a black nationalism whose model he found in the black African struggle against colonialism—"The Negro's struggle in America is only a microcosm of the struggle of the new countries all over the world."[67] The aim remains personal freedom, but the route to that liberation of the self is now seen as lying through the release of the group. And, where earlier he had defended the use of the term "Afro-American," he now chooses the name "which the rest of America has pounded into our heads for four hundred years, *Black*."[68]

Yet Jones continued to locate this cultural experience as essentially an American one, quoting approvingly William Carlos Williams's observation that the American Negro was a pure product of America, in essays which were for the most part designed primarily for a white reading public (being published in *Cavalier*, *Evergreen Review*, *Saturday Review*, *The Nation*). Where his tradition of literary excellence had derived from Melville and Joyce rather than from Chesnutt and Wright, he now began to propose a model for black writing which anticipated his own later work and the black culture movement which developed in the mid-1960s. He called for a black writer who would do what he had manifestly not done before, namely, "propose his own symbols, erect his personal myths,"[69] speaking from "a black country, " a "no-man's-land" (Wright's favorite image).[70] He implied, however, that such black writing did not as yet exist, while he continued to betray his own ambivalence both in his own work and in the essay "The Myth of a Negro Literature," which saw the black culture which he proposed as "an invisible strength . . .of a more profound America."[71]

Yet, by 1963, the tone of his essays began to change. In a brutal article in *Kulchur*, he attacked James Baldwin and the South African writer Peter Abrahams, denouncing them for their "spavined whine,"[72] for creating a literature which celebrated their own individual sensibilities, and for wishing to evade a commitment which was an unavoidable obligation of the black writer. In the same year, he began a review of three anthologies of black poetry with the prophetic words "This review or chronicle might be my last liberal . . . act."[73] He was all too aware, however, that the equivocal nature of his position as a writer whose very fluency could be taken as a token of his assimilation, and whose admiration for the powerful and sophisticated literature of a cultural tradition which was in some profound sense alien to him, was an ironic commentary on his own efforts at definition. He knew and acknowledged that "semantic philosophers are certainly correct in their emphasis on the final dictation of words over their users," but clung to the necessary belief that "words have users, but as well, users have words. And it is the users that establish the world's realities."[74] As suggested above, his response was to parody his own articulateness, as in "The Last Days of the American Empire (including some instructions for black people)," an essay addressed to black people, in which grammar and syntax shifted away from a familiar fluency, or in "The Revolutionary Theatre," in which he outlined the objectives of black theatre in a way which made clear his concern with generating precisely those symbols and myths whose absence he had earlier regretted. Liberal language and rational argument give way to a use of language as an instrument of assault. So, he calls for a political theatre which will be "a weapon to help in the slaughter of those dim-witted fatbellied white guys."[75] It must "accuse and attack because it is a theatre of victims. It looks at the sky with the victims' eyes, and moves the victims to look at the strength of their minds and their bodies."[76] Rational art is replaced with consciousness-raising rituals whose function is to parade a new panoply of heroes and villains. Hence, the white man is represented as effete, even homosexual, and the black as either an accommodating self-destroying pseudo white man or a black revolutionary hero. Images largely replace language, and the vibrant energy of revolt replaces that enervation which he had identified in 1960 as typifying America and which at that time he could see no way of transcending.

In a speech which he delivered as director of the Black Arts Repertory Theatre in front of the Hotel Theresa in 1964, he called for black unity in the face of the "white devil," as, in an essay on the legacy of Malcolm X, he saw cultural separation as a primary route to black identity, offering by way of definition the observation that "race is feeling" while "culture is the preservation of those feelings in superrational to rational form."[77] Stokely Carmichael had somewhat surprisingly said in *Black Power*, "The extent to which black Americans can and do 'trace their roots' to Africa, to that extent will he be able to be more effective on the political scene."[78] For Carmichael, it was a matter of practical politics, of learning from foreign models, while for Jones, it was a resource of available myths. But, together with Ron Karenga, who in some respects had been Jones's teacher, they were agreed on a cultural nationalist stance which was in contrast to the Marxist-Leninist position of writers such as Angela Davis, Huey Newton, and Bobby Seale.

This, of course, implied a black audience. Indeed, Conrad Kent Rivers announced that "if we fail to write for black people, we—in effect—fail to write at all."[79] The division between LeRoi Jones's early plays and his black revolutionary plays was in effect a consequence of his changing audience as he began to create potent images of black pride and revolt, as he asserted a racial absolutism.

Indeed, a degree of absolutism seemed a natural product of this period as it had done in the 1930s. While older writers like Arna Bontemps could say, as late as 1968, that "all a sincere Negro artist needs to do is to be himself"[80] and Loften Mitchell that "the role of the artist is to protest the human condition,"[81] Julius Lester said, "If the black artist does not commit his art to the liberation movement . . .he is not fulfilling his responsibility . . . . At this point in history the black artist has no other responsibility."[82] At the same time, Hoyt Fuller, managing editor of *Negro Digest*, announced that "the Negro community will not accept direction and evaluation from the white community," though, somewhat paradoxically, this did not prevent his calling on the Ford and Rockefeller foundations for support. The publication of these views in the University of Wisconsin's *Arts in Society* in 1968 coincided with the death of Martin Luther King and the arrest, among others, of LeRoi Jones. And despite his political differences with Jones, Killens was by now calling for essentially the same response from black writers, urging them to "write our own black history, create our own myths and legends."[83]

The argument over the publication of William Styron's novel, *The Confessions of Nat Turner*, essentially a battle for simultaneous possession of the past and present, became part of a systematic assault on what was taken to be a white manipulation of black experience. In March 1968, the Association to End Defamation of Black People, based in Los Angeles and supported by Ossie Davis and Louise Meriwether, sent letters to David Wolper, of Wolper Productions, and to Norman Jewison, of United Artists, warning them against making a film version of Styron's novel. When a paperback edition of LeRoi Jones's and Larry Neal's *Black Fire* was published in 1969, it carried a note that William Morrow, the publisher, had refused to include additional material by black writers because "these devils claim it costs too much to reprint," adding that this served to indicate "the frustration of working with these bullshit white people."[84] And, in February 1971, Ed Bullins published an open letter in *Black Theatre*, attacking Richard Watts, the drama critic of the New York *Post*, characterizing him as "a conservative senile fool" who produced only "idiotic, demented ramblings" and whose "classic know-nothing American" intelligence could not "stretch to encompass Black Visions."[85] In the renamed *Black World*, Hoyt Fuller sustained a continuous assault on white critics and those black writers who failed to accept their historic role in the revolution.

Accompanying this was an attempt to create black publishing houses. These particularly lent themselves to the business of publishing poetry, but the costs involved meant that these concerns could never offer a genuine alternative to white publishers. As Dudley Randall, founder-publisher of Detroit's Broadside Press (founded in 1965), pointed out in an article in *Black World*, the largest of these, the Johnson Publishing Company, published five books in 1972, as compared to Harper and Row's one thousand four hundred twenty-six. Broadside Press, itself, aimed to publish four books a year. Individual writers did establish their own imprint, but for anything other than poetry, they were dependent on white publishers.[86] Nonetheless, *Black World* still managed to identify twenty-one black publishing concerns in 1975, most of them founded in the late 1960s and early 1970s (including Jihad Productions—later renamed Vita Ya Watu—founded in 1967 by Amiri Baraka; Third World Press, 1967; Third Press, 1970).

If the dominant form in the 1950s had been the novel, in the 1960s, it was the public arts, drama, and poetry in performance. The political and cultural emphasis on the idea of black community, on art as both a stimulus to identity and action and as an expression of it, led to a form which could literally dramatize these images and leave space for community involvement, in the manner of the black church. The establishment of black theatres was both evidence of a cultural autonomy, which could serve as a concomitant of the political shift in the civil rights movement, and of a means to forge images and myths of a utilitarian kind.

It was a theatre which broke with a dramatic tradition which had examined the nature of the Negro's victimization. The plays which were produced were no longer pathological studies. The dialogue was essentially internal to the black community. The unavoidable ironies of protest literature—whereby appeals against injustice must inevitably be made to those who are themselves the source of that injustice, and the impotence of the victim becomes the source of the moral claim—are evaded by making the black sensibility, the black ability to define the past and present, the subject of the work. The appeal of Lorraine Hansberry's *A Raisin in the Sun*, as of James Baldwin's *Blues for Mr. Charlie*, had essentially been that of Langston Hughes's *Mulatto*, written twenty years earlier. A wrong was being done which could be corrected only by those whose human failings had turned suffering into tragedy. Indeed, in a curious way, the very inflexibility of the white world was transformed into a metaphysical determinism which was a necessary element in a tragic vision. By contrast, black art is nontragic. It is a celebration of blackness. It exudes the unfettered optimism of revolutionary art. It has no place for nihilism, rejects the absurd as an expression of capitalism in extremis, and sees art as a transforming mechanism. So, the black poet declaims on black beauty, the dignity of the black male, the serene and supportive heroism of the black woman. It is presented as an antidote to the destructive realities of ghetto life. Indeed, the junkie and the pimp, the religious fanatic and the putative white, become the enemy. The black family, under so much strain, becomes the model for the new community which may be won with the gun but which is an existent reality for those with eyes to see.

The Black Arts movement was an attempt to destroy what, in another context, Du Bois referred to as the double-consciousness, by simply denying one element of a dialectical process. It was perhaps not a credible method in a cultural sense since the dilemma of the black American, after all, resides precisely in the fact that he is both black and American. The Black Muslim call for a separate nation within America, like Jones's emphasis on a collective inner city which already constituted such a nation, was an attempt to deny the paradox by evading it. The image had a compelling force to it, but its impracticality was also potentially the source of a dangerous disillusionment. But even a revolution of the psyche needs a program, an ideology, an enabling process to sustain itself. Black art, insofar as this implied the elaboration of black heroes and myths, was a gesture which could not be endlessly repeated and, indeed, was not designed to be so repeated. Its value was as a cultural shock therapy, a reminder that social myths and rituals were just that—elaborations of deeply held, but often unexamined, beliefs in social processes rarely engaged by the conscious mind. No wonder that prosecutors and judges found the metaphors of black liberation so perplexing—in the trials of LeRoi Jones and Angela Davis attempting a literal reading of deliberately cabalistic signs.

There was, indeed, an unreality about the bitter debates over the existence or meaning of the black aesthetic, whether it was Hoyt Fuller's solemn attempts to set up a committee to define it, or Martin Kilson's severe proscription of Addison Gayle's desperate attempts to parade pieces of the true black cross. The ritual attacks on white critics such as Theodore Gross, Robert Bone, Herbert Hill, and Irving Howe were public acts of exorcism having little to do with the failures of scholarship of which they were accused (Gayle's endearing definition of scholarship as the accumulation of "the proper number of foot-notes, quotes, addendums, and a bibliography which no 10 men, let alone the author, could possibly read in a lifetime,"[87] making it clear how irrelevant such charges were—charges, moreover, in the best tradition of American anti-intellectualism). The point was that black art was to be addressed to blacks, and the presence of white intermediaries was too familiar an act of cultural appropriation to be tolerated.

The problem was that the black aesthetic, according to Gayle, was to be judged not according to any innate quality in the work, but by its effect on the audience, and this potentially displaced not only the white critic but any critic. As he said, "The question for the black critic today is not how beautiful is a melody, a play, a poem, or a novel, but how much more beautiful has the poem, melody, play, or novel made the life of single black man?"[88] The critic who is able to assess the degree of beauty in an individual life and the degree to which it was culturally derived has yet to be born. When he adds that the black aesthetic is designed to "offer logical, reasoned arguments" as to why the black man should not join the "polluted mainstream of Americanism,"[89] his description is strangely at odds with most of the work which lays claim to exemplify that aesthetic; for the most part it relied on the irrational and the illogical, the stunning image, the ironic caricature, the striking metaphor, the ennobling paradigm, the dramatization of a black self which had no need to define or justify, and certainly not to engage in, any kind of dialogue with an America which was assumed to be implacable and invulnerable to appeals based either on the mind or general invocations to humanity.

Hoyt Fuller's premise for rejecting the white critic lay in that critic's supposed failure to recognize "a fundamental and obvious truth of American life—that the two races are residents of two separate and naturally antagonistic worlds."[90] This was, after all, essentially the conclusion reached by the Kerner Commission in 1968. But, as part of an attempt to locate and define the black aesthetic, it was essentially tautologous; that is culturally separate which is manifestly culturally separate. The real question—what the nature of that identity was and in what sense the two worlds were "naturally" antagonistic, beyond a willful historical record of abuse—remains unexplored. But in a sense, that mattered less than the public assault on white criteria. The black aesthetic was a declaration of independence, and the nature of its constitution mattered less than the fact of revolt.

Black art was an enabling mechanism which stood at the other extreme from the blues. The latter implied resignation, the transmutation of suffering into an acceptable form; the former is concerned with resistance, with a rejection of suffering and the projection of art as a model for life. John O'Neal's incantation, "We are an African People. We are simply not an American People,"[91] is a mantra designed to clear the mind. Its literal meaning is undefined. Aesthetic theory is thus subordinated to social imperatives which themselves are exemplified by an art which offers itself as a model for social action—a closed circle of imaginative symbols, private and public, an endless series of reflecting mirrors.

As Larry Neal said in *Black Fire*, "The artist and the political activist are one. They are both shapers of the future reality. Both understand and manipulate the collective myths of the race. Both are warriors, priests, lovers, and destroyers. For the first violence will be internal—the destruction of a weak spiritual self for a more perfect self. But it will be a necessary violence. It is the only thing that will destroy the double consciousness—the tension that is in the souls of the black folk."[92] The creation of a new self required the destruction of an identity which was merely the dark shadow of American economic and social imperatives. And art was required to be the agent of this transformation, its value lying solely in its ability to provoke this change. Thus, for Ron Karenga, "all art must reflect and support the Black Revolution, and any art that does not discuss and contribute to the revolution is invalid."[93]

It is a logic which naturally leads to a wholly utilitarian view of literature and a deliberately provocative rejection of cultural values which are alien to the immediate business of revolt. Hence Karenga's attack on the teaching of Shakespeare: "Why should somebody be teaching Shakespeare today, with his 'thee' and 'thou'. People don't talk that way any more. I don't want to hear it. White people can . . .they like that sort of stuff. But it's not the real world to us, tight pants and funny hats."[94] The curious blend of know-nothing anti-intellectualism and assault on an icon of white culture is finely calculated. It is a piece of necessary destruction to clear the site for the erection of the golden cities of black art. But it is two-edged. An attempt to define by elimination is a dubious enterprise.

The Second Renaissance was not only an explosion of new literary talent, but a rediscovery of the past. It relied, therefore, on the reprinting of books long-since out of print, the publication of anthologies of black writers, past and present, and ultimately the introduction of black studies courses in universities, whose job was both to teach this material and to provide the context for the new sense of black identity. And this process went ahead with remarkable speed. Despite the isolated success of figures like Ellison and Baldwin in the 1950s, the main outburst of activity was a factor of the mid-1960s and early 1970s, sparked by the achievement of LeRoi Jones's Black Arts Repertory Theatre and the growing autonomy of black political forces signaled by Stokely Carmichael's call for black power in 1965 and given moral authority by the death of Malcolm X in the same year.

And though there was finally no clear agreement about the precise nature of that revolution, in retrospect it is clear that the Second Renaissance was indeed one of those remarkable moments in the development of a culture when the writer sounds a note which reverberates in the community he addresses. More than in the First Renaissance, he addressed all levels of the black community across America and, perhaps unavoidably but paradoxically, thereby enriched that very American society in opposition to which he sought a personal and cultural identity.

The Self and Society: Richard Wright's Dilemma

In the first volume of his autobiography, *Black Boy*, Richard Wright confesses that his "inner resistance had been blasted" that he "felt emotionally cast out of the world," and "made to live outside the normal processes of life"; that he "had been conditioned in feeling *against* something daily, had been accustomed to living on the side of those who worked and waited."[1] In due course, the act of writing became, for him, the agent of his release from this alienation. It became an assertion both of private and cultural identity. The primary urge now was to speak for the mass of blacks. As he explained in the second volume, *American Hunger*, he wanted to reveal the vast physical and spiritual ravages of Negro life. "I wanted to voice the words in them that they could not say, to be a witness to their living."[2]

Like so many other black writers, he was acutely aware of the significance of language. Speaking of conversations with communists, he says that "words lost their usual meanings," as he had earlier lamented in relation to the white world in general that "the very meaning of words I spoke could not be fully understood."[3] And yet, of course, what else does the black writer have but language. "All I possessed were words,"[4] says Wright. And the gap between language and the experience which it attempts to express was precisely the essence of the writer's dilemma. But rather than derive from that gap an absurdist conviction about social and metaphysical reification, Wright expresses a liberal conviction that he should "try to build a bridge of words" between himself "and that world outside, that world which was so distant and elusive that it seemed unreal. I would hurl words at this darkness," he insists, "and wait for an echo, and if an echo sounded, no matter how faintly, I would send other words to tell, to march, to fight, to create a sense of hunger for life that grows in us all, to keep alive in our hearts a sense of the inexpressibly human."[5] What had first enthralled him in reading books by Mencken, borrowed on a white reader's ticket from the Memphis Public Library, was that here was a man who could use words as weapons. And this was how he came to use them in the crude and powerful stories and poems which he published in the 1930s.

The act of writing is an act of transformation, an assertion of control. It offers an imaginative possession of experience. For the black writer, confronting a reality which resists the imprint of his social self, such a fictive assurance offers a potent attraction. Writing is both a form of escape and a positive gesture of inclusion, a means of access into American reality. But for Wright, it increasingly offered an opposing set of images no longer simply defining the self's relation to a given American reality, but projecting a system of values and signs forming part of a dialectic of which only one element was constituted by the daily environment which he inhabited.

Black Boy ends with a vision of social hope, with the possibility of change in his economic and social circumstances. As Michel Fabre has shown, this is something of an accident of publication, in that this first part of the autobiography was severed from the second half. But the second half ends with another glimpse of a possible world—a world, this time, which is a world of art. No longer was he submitting himself to circumstance. The world he set about constructing now was a world of words, designed not simply to describe a deracinated self, but "to keep alive in our hearts a sense of the inexpressibly human."[6]

In *Black Boy*, Wright describes the process whereby dogs are rendered voiceless by an operation which cuts their vocal chords. It is not only a potent image of silent suffering, which has clear political implications for the Negro, but it also has implications for the writer who seeks to sound (in the sense of plumbing the depths as well as vocalizing) that suffering. And this double sense can be felt in what is, in many ways, the best piece of writing he ever produced, "The Man Who Lived Underground."

Freddie Daniels, falsely accused of a murder and beaten until he signs a confession, escapes from the police station and hides in the sewers. Once there, he loses all sense of time and place and all sense of identity. Wandering in and out of the city's basements, he is offered glimpses of the real nature of the world which presents its public face on the surface. At the same time, he is forced to recognize the fears and compulsions which have accounted for his own passivity. The result of this anguished process is a self-destructive drive back to the surface where he can expiate a new-found sense of guilt and pass on his new and potentially dangerous perceptions.

It is, indeed, an inverted world, a platonic paradox, as he tries to distinguish the reality of his own being and the animating power of the culture from the limited vantage point of what amounts to a cave. Alongside him sweeps the sewer, the effluent of material society, including the dead body of a baby, which stands as the most obvious evidence of that society's callow brutality and inhuman reductivism. Above him, the "real" world is oddly transformed; the sun is described as "dead," "obscene," "dark," and "cruel." Below, in the brief glow of a match or the dim light of a single lightbulb, he sees more clearly than ever before. All his experience underground begins to cohere into a symbol more eloquent and revealing than the public fictions which he has lived on the surface—a world in which he had been forced to sign a confession to a crime he had not committed, to endorse, in other words, a reality he knows to be false. Now he comes to realize the symbolic wisdom which his situation betokens—that truth lies beneath the surface, that real meaning derives not from a language apparently sculpted for deception, but from a felt truth, a mute but ambiguous symbolism.

Hence, the dead baby, like the dogs in *Black Boy*, is described as having its mouth wide open in a soundless cry. The dead body which he encounters in a basement mortuary is similarly silenced. The singing in a local church, which he hears through the crumbling brick wall of the cellar, contains its meaning in its tone and timbre rather than in its words. "Glad, glad, glad, oh, so glad. I got Jesus in my soul!" sings a young black girl, "but what her words did not say, her emotions said as she repeated the lines, varying the mood and tempo, making her tone express meanings which her conscious mind did not know."[7] What he detects is a feeling of guilt which emerges from the gulf between the singers' aspirations to happiness and their doomed reality. Similarly, when he sees a movie audience laughing at the platonic images on the screen, the reality lies not in their laughter but in the gap between that laughter and the reductive nature of their lives. But he himself has perceptions which he cannot articulate in language. Like Bigger Thomas in *Native Son*, "he thought with his feelings and no words came."

In many ways, the story is about the process of writing. For the writer is the man who lives underground, who seeks a form adequate to the expression of truths unavailable on the surface. The subject of this story is, in a sense, language; not the language of words, but of symbolic perception. Meaning, as the protagonist of the story comes to realize, lies in the totality of his experiences: in the trappings of material society which he collects from store basements he breaks into, in the inarticulate sufferings he observes, transmuted sometimes into religious ecstacy and sometimes into mindless entertainment. "He remembered the singing in the church, the people yelling in the movie, the dead baby, the nude man stretched out upon the white table. . . .He saw these items hovering before his eyes and felt that some dim meaning linked them together, that some magical relationship made them kin. He stared with vacant eyes, convinced that all of these images, with their languageless reality, were striving to tell him something."[8]

This languageless reality is at the heart of Wright's social and aesthetic concerns. The paradox which faces the writer lies precisely in articulating this reality when language itself is temporally and culturally inadequate to that task, a material means to express the immaterial, a strategy for concealment rather than an agent for truth.

Wright is also aware that while the impulse to write may itself be an attempt at self-definition, it may also constitute a flight from that self. When the protagonist finds a typewriter, he tries to type his name only to find that he has forgotten it—his experience in the underground world having destroyed those referents which had given his life its apparent meaning. For a moment, he feels a genuine terror and, then, deliberately, he begins instead to type out the beginning of a story, "itwasalonghotday." Michel Fabre has pointed out that this was originally to have been the first sentence of the story, so that the whole piece would have been a reflexive fiction, reflecting on its own processes—a post-modern contemplation on the vulnerability of the fictive mode to the anarchic spirit of the public world.

Like Baldwin after him, Wright was fully aware of the ambiguous pressures which lead the black American to turn to fiction. This short story is in essence a debate with himself over the morality and, ultimately, the utility of doing so. After all, in the end, nobody will listen to the protagonist who wishes to reveal the truths he has discovered. But the writer, like the protagonist of the story, and, later, the protagonist of Ralph Ellison's *Invisible Man*, has to emerge into the flow of time and risk his perceptions in a world in which the material replaces the spiritual and destructive fictions are preferred to painful truths. By a kind of homeopathic logic, the writer offers his own fictions as alternative visions. Yet his own detachment, his own manipulations as author, his own status as observer, imply a moral culpability which is displaced onto his protagonist, whose stuttering attempts at composition make him a putative writer.

Seeing all, Daniels is tempted by a chilling amorality. He watches unmoved as a boy is beaten for stealing a radio purloined by the protagonist himself, feeling that "perhaps the beating would bring to the boy's attention, for the first time in his life, the secret of his existence, the guilt that he could never get rid of."[9] When a nightwatchmen shoots himself in the head after the police have beaten him for the protagonist's theft of jewels, again he can only say that doubtless he "was guilty, had always been guilty,"[10] just as he had earlier contemplated shooting a man whom he finds sleeping. He is stranded, in other words, between the brutal pragmatism of the surface and the primal venalities exposed by his trip underground, surely a Freudian model of an anarchic subconscious and a deliberately deceptive rationalism.

The temptation is to an absurdist license, an antinomian perspective whereby everything becomes possible, for "if the world as men had made it was right, then everything else was right, any act a man took to satisfy himself, murder, theft, torture."[11] But in fact, the protagonist is struggling towards a new set of perceptions. He comes to feel that guilt derives from a failure to see clearly that the sun is indeed a false sun. And if he stops short of Ahab's conviction that the true man is the man of woe, he does come to feel that man is the inventor of his own tortures. Just as he had been shocked into a new state of mind by the police beating and his subsequent plunge downwards into self, so he feels, with Bellow's Henderson, that "truth comes in blows."

This is Wright's *Heart of Darkness* (the last words of the story are "the heart of the earth"), in which the terror of the loss of identity, the fear consequent upon a sudden viscosity of time, the pain derived from a realization of human cruelty, are not transposed to a symbolic Africa, but are literally beneath the feet of those who move about so confidently. And if Conrad also knew that the real heart of darkness existed at the very center of the imperial machine and the human soul, he sought a moralized landscape in which to dramatize it, a world in which intellect and pagan emotionalism could expose a revealing savagery implicit in human nature. For Wright, a similar perception is transposed into a Freudian dualism. But his text is self-doubting, the truths which it offers prove inoperative. They cannot be passed on. Like Plato's philosopher, his protagonist, and perhaps behind him the writer himself, faces a world which would rather live with fictions which can be bent to serve the interests of the moment than confront the truth of human nature. Driven back to the surface, he finds that he is exchanging his world of ''dark light'' for the ''cruel sunshine'' above and that nobody will listen to him.

The two levels are as much two parts of his own experience—intellectual and emotional—as they are physical locations. ''His mind said no; his body said yes; and his mind could not understand his feelings.'' He succumbs to the need to ''go somewhere and say something to somebody.''[12] He stumbles first into the church, determined to give them the benefit of his new understanding, but he can only stutter a few incoherent words, for the truth is that the statement which he wishes to make cannot be reduced to language, that ''he was the statement.'' But, insofar as the meaning of his life is decipherable by others, it is too dangerous to acknowledge. As the policeman who shoots him explains, ''You've got to shoot his kind. They'd wreck things.''[13]

Fred Daniels is a Lazarus figure made suddenly aware of his spiritual narcosis. The paradox is that his intuitions crumble in the open air and the world cannot afford to acknowledge his subversive discovery that guilt is self-created, the material world irrelevant to human needs, and public reality only a series of agreed fictions. He is unable to influence those people who are ''sleeping in being, awake in their dying.''[14]

For the writer, early in his career, it is perhaps also a confession of self-doubt, an expression of his fear that invisibility can infect both writer and story, that urgent truths of a personal and cultural kind are finally incommunicable. In this story are the germs of his central themes and his private fears: a concern over the destructive power of public fictions and myths, but a parallel suspicion of the moral anarchy of the self sundered from his society; a compulsion to articulate experience, but a suspicion that fundamental truths are not communicable or, worse, that the process of communication is itself a form of manipulation.

But as a black writer, particularly in the early part of his career, such subtle self-doubts deferred to a more immediate need, the necessity to bear witness to the power of the public world and of history to crush the individual, and the consequent necessity for the individual to resist this pressure through a renewed sense of self and a recognition that a shared plight offered the possibility of shared strength. The credo of the writer, and that of the protagonist of his first novel *Native Son*, are summed up in a sentence from *American Hunger*: "If you possess enough courage to speak out what you are, you will find you are not alone."[15]

In 1929, history caught up with America; or, as it seemed to many committed left-wing writers, America caught up with history. And yet it is a minor curiosity of the period that the tangible realities which assumed such significance for the neonaturalists should have spawned a literature so unreal in its perception of the individual and so detached from the actual nature of political and social truth. There was a curious and informative dissonance between style and content. A rigorous commitment to description, an obligation to present surface reality in authentic detail, was wedded to utopian politics, a stereotypical view of character, and a Manichean dramatization of social dynamics. Just as liberalism was out of vogue in political terms until the massive assault of the New Deal, so the presumptions of liberal literature were brushed aside in favor of a literature of action, an art which could act as a weapon.

The fact that *Native Son* was published at the end of this decade made it appear something of a culmination of this movement, a brutal document which neatly concluded the literary militancy of a decade of protest. Alternatively, it was seen as a throwback to turn-of-the-century naturalism, a dispassionate attempt to build a picture of reality from the tangible injustices of social and metaphysical determinisms. Neither interpretation was adequate. Though Wright invited such treatment with his use of such stabbing deterministic abstracts as "Fear. Flight. Fate," as section titles in *Native Son*, the novel itself creates a crucial irony as the action and the contemplative energy of the book transcends such Pavlovian reflexes.

The social situation in the 1930s was itself crude; individuals and groups had been reduced to a simple level of existence. Survival was at a premium. And the literature which sought to dramatize this reality was itself simplified. The aesthetic was to be bare, reduced, hard, as was the ideology which, for the most part, it embraced. The power of such novels derived from the kinetic energy of social collapse—the widening space between rich and poor, between the races, between American aspirations and reality. And that power often coalesced in crude violence, as it did in the society which it wished both to reflect and influence. There is a relish in the brutal smashing of a man's face in Steinbeck's *In Dubious Battle*, for example, which makes it plain that this is an individual act which is seen as embodying the essential conflict within the culture. It is presented as literal truth, but its real force is as metaphor and exemplar. The oppressor must be confronted, and, because the actual enemy is too diffuse and intangible (capitalism, exploitation, prejudice), it has to be rendered visible and vulnerable. It has to be attacked through its agents and, by striking through them, evil itself will be destroyed. But in the process, the writer becomes as guilty of reductivism as the society which he wishes to indict. The deputy whose head is smashed with a shovel in *The Grapes of*

Wrath is presented only as an anonymous extension of the industrial machine which he serves; but the worker who strikes out, does so to save his family and his vision of America.

Wright offers none of these simplicities. In raising moral issues to metaphysical status, he is vulnerable to ethical attack, but his casuistry is of different order than that of the party-liners who so unconsciously undermined the human principles which they claimed as their inspiration and objective. But then Wright had had no 1929, no sudden and blinding revelation about American society. It scarcely took the collapse of the stock market and the spreading of Hoovervilles to convince him of the injustices of American capitalism. After all, he himself had nearly been forced into a criminal career in his youth and he knew better than white Americans the hypocrisies of his society and the violence which can so easily fill the gap between social promise and actuality.

To characterize *Native Son* as a naturalistic novel, as Alfred Kazin has done, or as a protest novel, as James Baldwin was to do, is not only to simplify the book, it is to simplify the experience from which it emerges. Obviously, the killing of Mary Dalton and, in particular, the grizzly business of her decapitation and incineration, described in such detail that naturalistic fact becomes seductively tactile, is in part a form of fantasy revenge. The interest of the novel, however, does not lie in the racial and political symbolism of the event, but in its philosophical significance. The process is no less cold-blooded than the proletarian writer's transmutation of human blood into communist sacrament, but it is a clear indication of Wright's commitment to press beyond the material, to create a model of individual existence which is not predicated on the transcendence of one set of determinisms as a simple prelude to the submission to others.

It is true that race is the fact which provokes the events which lead Bigger Thomas to his death cell; it is not clear that racial justice would have solved the problem to which Wright addresses himself. For none of the characters in the book possess a clearer sense of their own identity outside of the racial, political, and social myths which they embrace. Jan, the naive communist, is no more in touch with his being than is Bigger. Wright's ''protest'' is not even directed primarily at racial injustice, though this is clearly a central concern of the novel. His real target is the failure of the individual—any individual—to recognize the extent of his freedom to act and the responsibility which consequently accrues to that individual. Identity is under assault, and, for the black man in America, the assault is harrowing and radical. But it is not the black alone who has slipped into a sleep of the spirit. And in its emphasis on transcendental unity or a community of selves, the conclusion of the novel is not even addressed primarily to the racial situation.

Wright, like Camus (in an article on ''The Human Crisis''), rejects the Hegelian principle that man is made for History, not History for man. Though he was attracted by its symbolic overtones of human unity, he was ultimately as appalled as was Camus by the chilling rationalism and implicit antinomianism of the Hegelian progress from anarchy to feudalism, to nation state, to empire, to world society. If history was a force independent of man, it was a steam roller which could and did crush the individual. Wright's temptation, and Bigger's, is precisely that identified by Camus when he suggests that the double temptation offered to the men of his generation is "that of thinking nothing is true" and "thinking that abandonment to historical fate is the only truth."[16] The only possible response is that adopted by Bigger Thomas—to live in the present, or to generate a conviction that, as Camus puts it, "Men live and only live by retaining the idea that they have something in common." The problem is that while "one always imagines that if one speaks to a man humanly his reaction will be human in character...we have discovered...there are men and women one cannot persuade."[17] It is that knowledge which makes it impossible for Wright to dramatize the rage with which Bigger faces his death. But *Native Son* is clearly not a protest novel aimed at shocking the consciousness of the white world; it is a plea to sustain a human vision. And that cannot be sustained by the Party, for, as Camus lamented, "What counts now is not whether one respects a mother or spares her from suffering, what counts now is whether or not one has helped a doctrine to triumph." It is precisely this perception which drew Wright away from the Party and which leads Bigger eventually to reject the articulate defense offered by his lawyer.

In summing up his view of the human crisis, Camus suggests that it can all be traced to what he calls "the cult...of abstraction." This, he says, is why "man in Europe today experiences only solitude and silence. For he cannot communicate with his fellows in terms of values common to them all. And since he is no longer protected by a respect for man based on the values of man, the only alternative henceforth open to him is to be the victim or the executioner."[18] So, too, in *Native Son*, the question at stake is not whether the whites hate the blacks, but the fact that they embrace no values by which their actions may be judged. And the book is a warning directed equally to whites. It is not a plea for justice, but a recognition that, as Camus himself observed, even the executioner is a victim since he is trapped inside the same destructive determinism.

In such a crisis, where will meaning come from? For Camus, the act of revolt was itself a value—a revolt not consciously chosen or deriving from any acknowledged principles. His generation simply found itself fighting a war, a campaign of resistance against those who sought to determine their lives. In the circumstances, they looked for the meaning of those lives in the only place they could—in the act of resistance itself. This was the affirmation they had been unable to find elsewhere. And it was a common revolt. Their shared experience made them feel that they shared something more than simply that experience. But Camus offers more than revolt. He asserts, with Wright, that fatalistic thought is a kind of murder and that, insofar as we allow such fictional determinisms to dictate the shape of reality, "we are all murderers to one degree or another."[19] It is in this sense that Bigger Thomas is a native son. Wright is not identifying a necessary organic determinism which destroys Bigger Thomas. The forces which drag him towards the death cell are man-made.

The freedom which Bigger claims and which Wright endorses is ultimately that which Camus offers as his own description of the liberated self. Conceding that "our life belongs to others" and that "it is proper that we give it to others when that is necessary," he asserts that "our death belongs to ourselves alone." Such, he suggests, "is my definition of freedom." But neither for Camus nor for Bigger is this to be an act of solipsism; it is, instead, a rejection of public ideologies. Bigger's vision is of a world of imprisoned individuals, each denied access to others. But in his mind, at least, he can imagine a connection between himself and those others, an act of imagination which would have been impossible for the man who, at the beginning of the novel, was trapped inside his own alienated personality. As Camus suggests, the way out of that trap lies through "a universalism . . .through which all men of good will may find themselves in touch with one another," but this must be a sense of community rediscovered by each individual since "no mortal man, today or tomorrow, can conclude that his truth is good enough to justify imposing it on others."[20] What better description could there be of the unfolding moral conviction which lies at the heart of *Native Son* and *The Outsider*?

As Camus has said, for communication to exist, men must be free: "Since master and slave have nothing in common, since one cannot speak or communicate with a slave . . .bondage is silence . . .the most terrible of all."[21] This is precisely the subject of "The Man Who Lived Underground" and of *Native Son*. There is simply no available language to bridge the gap between black and white, between experience and its social meaning. That silence may express itself in an apparent inarticulateness or in lies designed to confirm the reality projected by the dominant group. It may also express itself in a life in which action and style are substituted for communication. When Billy Budd is denied access to language, he strikes out. Bigger Thomas does likewise. There are no words he can use, when he finds himself in Mary Dalton's bedroom at night, which can obviate the meaning implied by the myths which circumscribe black and white alike. As Camus observes, "Injustice . . .slavery and terror" are the "three scourges which impose silence on men, fence them from one another, make them indistinct to one another, preventing them from discovering the one value which can save them in this despairing world: the long fraternity of men struggling against fate."[22]

The image of the fence or wall recurs in Wright's fiction, while his black characters frequently perceive the whites indistinctly, as vague blurs, as looming white mountains or threatening wraiths. For Wright, moreover, the essential battle is indeed the struggle against fate—racial identity being merely one form of that determinism—and the need to perceive other people in clear outline as individuals rather than as integers in a public mythology. Bigger's perception is ultimately Camus's, though he lacks the facility to express it: "It is because the world . . . is finally absurd we must give reason to it."[23] And Wright, like Camus, attempts to "unite a pessimistic view of the world with a profound optimism about man."[24] That Camus failed then to perceive the irony of an article in which he contrasted the "violence and repressed hatreds" of Europe with the "humanity . . . taste for freedom and for happiness . . . visible in the face of the great Americans"[25] is perhaps understandable, but in claiming as his objective the need to "escape from the humiliating dumbness of those who have been beaten and conquered as a result of having entertained scorn for man for too long a time,"[26] he was echoing a central theme of *Native Son*. It is no wonder, then, that he and Wright should have become friends and mutual admirers when Wright began his long exile in Europe the following year, though Wright was, admittedly, not the intellectual equal of Camus, whose own moral equivocations and shifting perspective make him such a useful touchstone of mid-century moral philosophy. Wright was admittedly no philosopher, but his concern with the alienated individual, with the meaning of violence, the question of identity, and the nature and extent of personal responsibility for social forms and actions, placed him momentarily in a context in which the invocation of Camus becomes more appropriate than it might otherwise have been.

Alfred Kazin is clearly wrong in suggesting that Wright was simply a child of his generation and that his resources were "no different in kind from the resources of naturalism and the left-wing conception of life and literature to which, like many Negro writers, he surrendered his thinking."[27] If his sole intention had been, as Kazin implies, to destroy the reader's apathy with respect to the racial situation, then there might indeed have been "nothing left but to go round and round in the same vindictive circle."[28] That, after all, was exactly what Baldwin was to claim more than a decade later. But Wright is no more "captured" by the assumptions of naturalism than he was by the assumptions of Marxism. Like the Steinbeck of *The Grapes of Wrath*, whose characters finally break through the membrane of their material concerns and glimpse a wider community which is not conceived primarily in political or economic terms, Wright is trying to trace the problem to its root, beyond the limits of Marxist analysis and outside the potent, but not irreducible, realities of industrialism and urbanism.

Wright and Steinbeck share a kind of sentimentality. They bring their characters to the brink of a vital perception about themselves and the world in which they move, but, seeing no way in which that perception can operate, except at the level of symbol, they leave them stranded at the end of the book.

We are offered what is clearly designed as a crucial insight, but its visionary quality makes it nearly impossible to see how such a vision can be realized in the inflexible reality of the present, which both writers have been so careful to document. The result is a failure of nerve whereby the book's moral resolution, in both cases, is displaced into style, a lyrical symbolism which abstracts character from time and space. Their protagonists move in what Wright repeatedly calls a no-man's-land, a territory in which the full rigor of conflicting forces is suspended and the idea of fraternity can flourish. But there is no territory to light out for. As Ellison knew, hibernation is a temporary state. The logic of the earlier naturalistic detail is that the space in which such vision can operate is threatened. Yet it is precisely that vision, akin to but transcending that offered in the proletarian literature of the day, which constitutes the power of both Steinbeck and Wright. Both of them had an instinctive distrust of party dogma, preferring to emphasize the importance of the individual in restoring a sense of community. That neither of them could dramatize with any conviction the terms on which that individuality could function in a world so irredeemably hostile to individuality was the essence of their dilemma and the source of the sentimentality which is apparent in the closing pages of both novels. For Wright in particular, it was the source, too, of the pressure of the symbolist sensibility which constantly threatens to fracture the naturalistic surface, generating lurid images which are a kind of symbolic equivalent of the social anomie and spiritual frenzy which he cannot entirely accommodate to the naturalistic style.

There is clearly, in fact, a gothic element in Wright's work. Poe is never far away, whether it is in the form of the white cat in *Native Son* who seems intent on revealing the protagonist's guilt, or in Cross Damon's own urge to betray himself in *The Outsider*. And just as the Marquis de Sade suggested that the gothic novel itself had been the realistic art of a revolutionary age, so, here, the lurid gothicism of some passages of Wright's novel is offered as a correlative of the dissolution which threatened American society and the myths with which it had protected itself. Wright's path to the real lies as much through the nightmare, which he invokes as image and fact, as it does through his elaboration of the details of the environment from which that nightmare emerges.

And Wright is not unaware that, having proposed the individual's need and power to invent himself, he has begged a central question of morality. When Bigger Thomas acts spontaneously, he kills. When Cross Damon, in *The Outsider*, is freed from social constraints, he kills. The protagonist of "The Man Who Lived Underground," cut off from society, levels a gun at the head of a sleeping man with the same chilling detachment as the neanderthal subjects of William Golding's *The Inheritors*, who use their new-found intelligence simultaneously to shape a life and plan a murder. The central character of *Savage Holiday* moves inexorably towards an act of pure violence.

Just what, then, is this self detached from its social moorings? In *The Outsider*, it becomes clear: it is a natural killer, not for environmental reasons, but from nature. So the acknowledgment of a contract between individuals, the elaboration of a social code, becomes a necessary protection not only against prejudice but also against the anarchy within, of which the outward sign is brutality, injustice, and irrational prejudice. It is clearly no romantic self. Indeed, in *Native Son*, since we never see that irreducible self in intercourse with the external world, it has no contours at all. It simply threatens to dissolve into the universe, and that is one of the reasons for an uneasiness about the end of the novel.

Wright begins his career by describing solitariness as a social condition, but presses towards a conviction that it is ultimately a human condition. That is, within his work, particularly in *Native Son*, one finds a transition from realism as defined by Lukacs, to modernism; that is, from man as a social animal whose individual existence "cannot be distinguished from" his "social and historical environment,"[29] to man as a social being, solitary, detached from the defining power of the environment. The quintessence of the latter Lukacs finds in Heidegger, whose description of human existence as a "throwness-into-being" is, of course, a persuasive description of Bigger Thomas in the latter half of *Native Son*, as it is of Cross Damon in *The Outsider*, a man whose reading includes the works of Heidegger. Both are, in effect, without prior histories, having been reborn. Yet the fact of race ties them into society in a way that is not true of the conventional modernist hero. Bigger Thomas's Chicago is not simply a backdrop, though in his more clearly existential works, "The Man Who Lived Underground," and *The Outsider*, it is. For the protagonist of "The Man Who Lived Underground," the outside world literally disappears, the only reality being that of the inner world. But even for Bigger Thomas, it is constantly threatening to dissolve until, at the end of his life, he cannot accept a social definition of a life which now creates its own reality. At the beginning of the novel, he is trapped by his environment; his world is defined by the walls of his slum apartment. At the end, the bars of his cell no longer contain his questing mind or his expanding identity. As Wright says in *American Hunger*, "My life as a Negro in America had led me to feel—though my helplessness had made me try to hide it from myself—that the problem of human unity was more important than bread, more important than the physical living itself; for I felt that without a common bond uniting men, without a continuous current of shared thought and feeling circulating through the social system, like blood coursing through the body, there could be no living worthy of being called human."[30]

It is as though his environment were described in such detail precisely so that its substantiality could be parodied and transcended. What gives *Native Son* its special quality is not its sense of the defining power of history, but the dramatized conviction that ultimately the battle lies beyond the net of history. At the beginning of the novel, with the insistent ringing of the alarm clock, Bigger is the victim of an objective time which ties him into the process of history; at the end, the only time he acknowledges is subjective. The moral commitment which he feels never crystallizes into social action. Here, as in *The Outsider*, it remains an unrealized potential, a moral completion which the reader must imply from the failure of social connectiveness by those whose limitations have been exposed under pressure. Wright's failure to dramatize this, however, is a token of his ambiguity. Drawn to an absurdist stance but feeling a commitment to transcendence, he compromises.

Of course the *isolato* is a common enough figure in American writing. In a sense, it is difficult to find an American hero, from Deerslayer, Hester Prynne, Ahab, and Huckleberry Finn through to Frederic Henry, Jay Gatsby, and Henderson, who is a full part of the society through which he or she moves. The isolation is a moral one. It involves an act of judgment or a passion so strong as to abstract the individual from his cultural setting. Yet there usually remains social commitment, sometimes acknowledged through action, sometimes through the vigor with which it is rejected.

At first glance, the black protagonist is in a similar position—outside the social world, at war with its values, entrenched within a self which must sustain itself in isolation. What is largely lacking, however, is the cultural commitment. Black isolation is, in origin, the consequence of expulsion and exclusion rather than willed isolation. The solitary self has to be forged initially out of negativity. Slavery and its consequences resulted only in a deeply menaced identity which left the individual lacking the ethical resources of a Huck Finn or Hester Prynne. And if the early twentieth-century American hero is much less assured, assaulted by debilitating realities and ironic myths, and cut off from spiritual conviction, he nonetheless can still lay claim to some shared presumptions about the value of action and a personal morality. But it is precisely the new sense of exclusion without real moral assurance, in more recent fiction, which makes the black protagonist seem so central to contemporary concerns. His invention of a self wholly outside the axial lines of the society through which he moves has increasingly come to be seen as the prototypical task of the individual in the modern world. When Ellison's protagonist states in *Invisible Man*, "Who knows but that on the lower frequencies, I speak for you,"[31] he is claiming an affinity which derives from precisely this conviction.

But to be outside society is not to be immune to its claims. Far from it. The special plight of the *isolato* is to be fully accountable to the world which excludes him. For the nineteenth-century hero, that injustice is the dignity of his position; for the twentieth-century writer, the absurdity. When Bigger Thomas is put on trial by the society which having excluded him now wishes to hold him accountable, the fundamental injustice is theirs and not his. And this absurdity is examined further and more self-consciously in *The Outsider*, in which Richard Wright lays claim to the paradigmatic nature of the Negro's plight. Increasingly, he sees the black man's experience of social alienation as an appropriate image of metaphysical alienation. Nor is he unaware of the ambiguities which derive from an existential decision to create the self. And it would be as much a mistake to believe that Wright identifies himself uncritically with Bigger's exultant sense of purposive action following his murder of two girls as it would be to regard Cross Damon as a model for an existential freedom which Wright admired.

The image which recurs in *Native Son* is that of a no-man's-land (a phrase used both by the narrator and by the prosecuting attorney). Bigger feels that he exists in the psychic territory between white hatred and black passivity. It was an unacknowledged territory, "a shadowy region,"[32] which, lacking solid reference points, denies the individual any means of confirming his existence: "He felt he had no physical existence."[33]

Yet there is an important irony here. The freedom which he believes himself to have created is highly limited and self-defeating. He consoles himself with the thought that he need no longer feel afraid now that he has his own destiny in his hands. But the formulation of that freedom is such that its negative quality is underlined. For he felt free only "as long as he could decide just *when and where he could run to*."[34]* Similarly, when he feels that "for the first time in his life . . .he was moving away from the threatening penalty of death,"[35] the sense of "fullness" which he moves towards was one that he had "inadequately felt *in magazines and movies*."* In escaping one myth, he presses towards another, the existential drive being at this stage simply a partially understood version of American values. The irony is further underlined by Wright's use of the passive voice in a way that denies his faith in Bigger's self-invention. "In all of his life these two murders were the most meaningful things that had ever *happened to him*."[36]* The problem is that this denial of lexical meaning extends beyond Bigger's consciousness to that of the narrator. The paradox of the observation that "never had his will been so free as in this day of *fear and murder and flight*"[37]* is that this self-denying statement implicates the narrator in the reductive ironies which derive from the yoking of a claimed freedom with manifest determinisms. Nevertheless, the fact is that at the very moment that Bigger lays claim to a new sense of freedom, Wright insists on a passive construction: "Hunger came to his stomach."[38] Moreover, the symbolic quality of that hunger and its passive nature are emphasized some pages later when we are told that "passively, he hungered for another orbit between two poles that would let him live again."[39] These linguistic contradictions become the basis of his narrative strategy. Cognitive meaning is contradicted by stylistic form. The passive voice implies the lack of agent, and this, of course, is a linguistic correlative of Bigger Thomas's social plight. The dropping of that voice in the final scene signifies, if not the collapse of that irony, then at least the achievement of an equanimity deriving from a knowledge of the limits to freedom as well as its potential.

*Italics are mine.

Wright had used a similar device at the end of his short story "Bright and Morning Star," in which a woman whose whole life has been an expression of passive acceptance, at the moment of her death and having just killed a white man, discovers an identity which gives meaning to her life. "Yuh didnt kill me," she insists, "Ah come here by mahsef."[40] Bigger's crimes were not active. The first murder was accidental; the second is, once again, described in a passive voice. He does not so much kill Bessie with a brick as find himself the simple agent of an uncontrollable determinism. "This was the way it *had* to be . . . his hand gripped the brick and shot upward and paused a second and then plunged downward through the darkness . . . . He lifted the brick again and again, until in falling it struck a sodden mass."[41] The positive element lies not in the murders but in their subsequent acceptance, in the molding of meaning out of the contingent. The true self-possession comes in the concluding pages of the novel and not earlier when Bigger claims to have found the meaning of his life in acts of blind violence. Hence, Wright evades the moral problems which might otherwise confuse the novel's thematic integrity.

Robert Bone is clearly wrong in suggesting that at the end of the novel Bigger is "repossessed by hate,"[42] as is Baldwin in asserting that it is "his hatred and his self-hatred . . . which causes him to die."[43] In embracing his crime, he is not accepting the validity of hatred. Indeed, he recognizes that though his violence is an expression of his failure to sublimate that emotion, the meaning with which he chooses to invest the murders is not hatred. He sees them as assertions of his existence. To deny these murders, to claim, as does Max, that they were the result of simple determinism, or to confess, as well he might, that they were the accidental consequence of circumstance, would be once more to accept a passive view of himself, to sink back into invisibility again. Hatred has no place at the end. Far from it. His last words to Max, a white man, are a request to him to convey his regards to Jan. It is not the murders which enable him to relate to other people, as Bone suggests, but the fact that he has sufficient belief in the substance of his own identity to make the notion of social responsibility viable. The sense of control over his own destiny which he feels after committing the murders is illusory. The act of violence which apparently releases him also imprisons him; the act which is to free him from determinism is itself a product of determinism. It is a paradox which he is unable to deal with and which he is certainly unable to express until the end of his life. But, then, the whole question of articulateness is crucial to the novel.

The difficulty Wright has in investing Bigger with an articulate consciousness which is able to offer an adequate account of his changing perceptions is not simply a problem of craft, though it is certainly that (his desperate strategies for dealing with the problem lack all credibility—"he never thought of this in precise mental images; he felt it,"[44] "in a sullen way Bigger was conscious of this;"[45] "though he could not have put it into words."[46]) The fact is that Bigger is crossing the boundary from feeling into thought, and though he would clearly not possess the resources to articulate his new self-perceptions in quite the language which Wright affords him, he has to find some way of expressing his new state to himself. He is engaged in what D. H. Lawrence has called "the struggle for verbal consciousness."[47] All his life he has lived within the defining power of white language. Early in the book he watches as an aircraft spells out words against the sky in white smoke, and it is under that panoply of white language that he has lived out his life. As Max asks in his closing speech, "Out of what can they [the Negroes] mold a new existence ...but what we *are* and own?"[48] And language is in many ways the most important such possession, which is why Bigger values the act. Just as Billy Budd, deprived of language, substitutes an appropriate violence, so, too, does Bigger; but the blow no more frees him than it did Billy Budd. Now he is no longer just a "nigger"; he is a "murderer." The real struggle is to locate a means of transcending such a definition, and this is what Bigger struggles towards in his prison cell as he counterposes his feelings and his new spiritual perceptions to the public myths which threaten to destroy his individuality.

It was Lévi-Strauss who observed that myths turn facts into signs. And this, of course, is the source of the potency of American racial mythologies. The black man is required to read his environment and his relations with others symbolically. Every action, every word, every feeling has to be inspected for its cultural meaning and adjusted accordingly. The death of Mary Dalton is a consequence of such a reading for Bigger knows that to be found in a white girl's room can only have one meaning in the myth which governs his life. His sense of freedom at the end of the novel thus results from his creation of other myths and other symbols. That he has no power to enforce these no longer matters; what is important is that they can sustain him, they confer a retrospective meaning on his life and, more importantly, on his death. What matters is that they establish the possibility of human contact and deny the significance of what he had imagined to be a dominating materialism.

What Bigger discovers is a world of possibility, flaws in the apparently seamless garment of determinism. Imprisoned in his cell, he discovers space for the first time, space in which identity can cohere and a new vision of life can be generated. In *Black Boy*, Wright actually asked himelf, "What was it that made me conscious of possibilities? From where in this southern darkness had I caught a sense of freedom? ...What was it that made me feel things deeply enough to try and order my life by my feelings?"[49] The answer he offers is that in part he had been sustained by literature, by the truth-telling potential, or simply the distinctive force of art. But the real power lay in the negative compulsions of revolt. "In a peculiar sense, life had trapped me in a realm of emotional rejection; I had not embraced insurgency through open choice. Existing emotionally on the sheer, thin margin of southern culture, I had felt that nothing short of life itself hung upon each of my injunctions and decisions."[50] To live on the edge is to see each action as potentially destructive, to construct a self out of the pressure of contingency. Yet life in the city seemed to undermine the expansiveness which prompted the move north. As he confessed in *American Hunger*, "What could I dream of that had the barest possibility of coming true? I could think of nothing. And, slowly, it was upon that sense of nothingness that my mind began to dwell."[51] This became the new starting point for a consciousness which would no longer be defined by the simple pressures of American life. Indeed, like Bigger in his cell, he rebelled against the "material way of American living that computed everything in terms of the concrete"[52] and searched for an identity and a sense of purpose which, unlike party dogma, could be expressed in human terms. And this of course is the problem with Max's defense of Bigger Thomas. In trying to secure Bigger's release, Max ensnares him more thoroughly in a determinism which he now feels able to escape.

The trouble with Max's speech is also that it expresses too thorough a knowledge of Bigger's inner life and that it borrows both the language and the analysis of the narrator. The complex of emotions, conflicting motives, and social and psychological explanations offered by Wright are now vocalized in a powerful speech which is persuasive in its logic but unconvincing in its context and in the depth of perception which it ascribes to Max. That Wright should have the lawyer, in the explosive context of the trial, suggest that the murder of Mary and Bessie was "an act of *creation*"[53] or that murder was "his way of *living*,"[54] says more for his determination to underline an existential moral than it does for the credibility of the narrative moment. It is, of course, his solution to a problem of craft—how to articulate the plight of the inarticulate.

The unexamined irony, however, lies in the fact that it is a white man who, in articulating Bigger's unexpressed feelings, necessarily commandeers that experience, translating it into his own terms. In offering him his identity, he deprives him of it. But Wright's narrative strategy, rather than his political commitment (which was by now too ambiguous to dictate character or action as he admitted it had done in his early stories—"I remembered the stories I had written, the stories in which I assigned a role of honor and glory to the Communist Party and I was glad that they were down in black and white, were finished. For I knew in my heart that I would never be able to write that way again, would never be able to feel with that simple sharpness about life, would never again endorse such passionate hope, would never again make so total a commitment of faith,"[55]) will not permit this paradox to be pressed. Bigger senses a remaining barrier between himself and Max, but he can no more acknowledge the paradox than can Wright himself. The fact is that Max literally speaks for Bigger, completing the circle of language which has closed around him and which had begun to trap him from his first contact with whites. Hence, when he meets the blind Mrs. Dalton and her family, it is he who feels blind as he is unable to penetrate the language which is the mark of their race and class. "The long strange words they used made no sense to him . . .it was another language. . . .It made him uneasy, tense, as though there were influences and presences about him which he could feel but not see. He felt strangely blind."[56] He inhabits a cultural void, receiving back no confirmation of his worth or indeed his existence. He becomes, like Ellison's protagonist, invisible. "He felt he had no physical presence at all. . . .It was a shadowy region, a No Man's Land, the ground that separated the white world from the black that he stood upon. He felt naked, transparent."[57]

The naturalistic method lies in accumulation; the salvation for his protagonist lies through reduction. He has to abstract himself from the layers of fact and fiction which crush his identity (what Wright persistently and confusingly calls "personality"). Ironically, at the time he was writing the novel, Wright was actually engaged in assisting in the preparation of WPA guides to the states, the assembling of details which taken together claim to offer an accurate account of truth. But *Native Son*, which in a sense claims to constitute a guide to the underworld, works on the assumption that truth is not available through such a strategy. It is a document which starts out to show that if individuals are the product of history, history is also the product of individuals. But the crucial development of the novel, the fact which raised it above a hundred other attestations of human inconsequence, was the struggle to articulate the basis on which the individual can escape from the grave of myth and fact.

Such interpretations do not, however, appeal to those who wish to identify an unfolding logic of history and who see the individual as no more than an agent of that history. One such is Addison Gayle, Jr., the principle advocate in the 1960s and 1970s of the black aesthetic. For Gayle, in his study of the black novel, *The Way of the New World* (1975), the moral of *Native Son* is that "only by accepting violence as an ethic might black men chart the path to salvation."[58] It is in this sense that it becomes "the model for the novelist of the nineteen seventies."[59]

Obviously an act of violence is indeed the catalyst which shocks Bigger Thomas into a new sense of identity, but there is nothing in the novel to suggest that Wright is advocating such violence as an "ethic." Indeed, the perception towards which Bigger works is of a world in which divisions between individuals dissolve, a world in which such tensions as provoked his own actions will disappear. He does not, to be sure, wash his hands of responsibility, but he does see beyond the act to a symbolism which is decidedly not that of the simple rebel.

Wright, Gayle asserts, came to realize that "peace between black and white man is an impossibility."[60] I know of nothing in Wright's work to justify such an assertion, and none is offered by Gayle. What he does present is an account of the novel which reverses the logic of its development. He suggests that Bigger's murder of Mary Dalton is "an attempt to validate manhood,"[61] apparently forgetful of the actual circumstances of the killing and of the vital distinction to be made between Bigger's motivations at the time and his subsequent attempt to gain imaginative and moral possession of the act. Gayle asserts that the murder, Bigger's subsequent attempts at extortion, and his desperate flight from the Chicago police are signs that he is "a man of strength,"[62] where Wright sees this as evidence of the determinism, the hapless imitation of white inhumanity, and that conditioned response which must be transcended. To Wright, strength lay in the acceptance of moral responsibility, in the projection of a vision of human unity which found no justification in the casual inhumanities of white society, in Bigger's creation of an identity out of the harsh reality of his life, not in the brutal dominance of violence itself. Indeed, in "How Bigger Was Born," he goes to some pains to stress that Bigger contains a potential for fascism. But, for Wright, that potential is not realized within the novel, except in the brutal killing of Bessie. Indeed, the ethic of violence advocated by Gayle is specifically rejected by Wright. It is for this reason that Gayle finds the novel's conclusion anticlimactic and sees the murder of Bessie as "disconcerting."[63] It is disconcerting, of course, because it shows that Wright is indeed not advocating violence, an assault on the white world, that he is fully alive to the dangers of a totalitarianism of the self of the kind which he subsequently examines in detail in *The Outsider*. To Gayle, the murder serves primarily "to substantiate the integrationist rhetoric of Communists and liberals" or, alternatively, to turn Bigger into a psychotic for whom race ceases to exist because reality ceases to exist. Since such an interpretation will not serve his purpose, he attempts a logical U turn based on an illogical premise. "The rationale [by which I take him to mean "argument"] against black vengeance and retribution does not hold, however, because the murder of Bessie Mears is the weakest incident in the novel," and because "for a black to murder another is to commit the most heinous of crimes."[64] This statement seems to have the distinction of combining bad logic with bad literary criticism with bad morality.

Thus, Gayle offers us two Bigger Thomases: the first is presented as a black rebel, conscious and heroic; the second, who appears after Bessie's death, is "as much the brainchild of Communists and liberals as he is of Richard Wright."[65] It is this latter whom we are told "the modern black sensibility will not accept."[66] The former alone is "acceptable to black readers" who know that "only when black men move collectively to accept violence as a new ethic, as a force for change, as the only instrument capable of bringing about a just society," can the violent "universe in which he lives be confronted."[67] To be told that "two years after the publication of *Native Son*, Europe's war became worldwide and validated the practicality of the ethic of violence" is the ultimate irony, as Gayle turns Wright's desperate and prophetic warning into simple advocacy. The practicality of an ethic of violence has never been in doubt since Cain and Abel, as Wright well knew: The question was how could the logic of dispossession be denied? How could the individual break out of the cycle of deprivation and violence and thereby obviate an apparent historical inevitability?

It was always a visionary aspect of communism which seized Wright's imagination, a vision which often left him blind to, or willfully ignorant of, moral issues. Hence, in an unpublished article written in 1939, he had said,

"The rightness or wrongness of a given set of tactical actions by the Communist Party does not strike me as being of any great importance." What mattered, and what his imagination responded to, was that is adherents were "rebels against the limits of life, the limits of experience as they know it. They are (and not in a mystical or religious sense) striving against the world."[68] One suspects that Ellison, himself drawn to the Party, would have responded equally to this vision while rejecting the shameless pragmatism which Wright never entirely got out of his system (namely his cynical advice to the black political leader in *Black Power* and the equal cynicism with which he advocates American interference in Indonesian affairs in *The Colour Curtain*, on the grounds that "civilization itself is built upon the right to interfere"[69]).

And when the Party's strategy switched away from overt support of the Negro cause, Wright was left with a vision but no program for realizing it, an ideological dispossession which drove him back on the authenticity of individual action—a shift clearly visible in *Native Son*. But, given his own earlier attacks on what he called "personalism," it was a strategy which could hardly engage his imagination entirely. It was not that he had been a wholly uncritical adherent of the Party—one only has to read his short story "Bright and Morning Star," unaccountably reissued by International Publishers in support of the Earl Browder Defense Fund, to realize that. Indeed, his inclusion of Boris Vian's translation of the story in the first issue of *Présence Africaine* suggests that Wright was committed to its wider, more existential implications. But the fact was that the Party had constituted a powerful image of social action in terms of which the individual could define his own sense of cultural identity. It provided a necessary tension for Wright, and once it went, the constant danger was that he would relapse into a sentimentality of the self a focus on an individuality independent of historical realities. His virtue was that he recognized this and, in *The Outsider*, explored something of the danger which had perhaps been implied even in Bigger Thomas's final sense of personal absolutism. For the irony was that he could finally only re-create himself by re-creating the world in which that new self could operate. Hence, the past had to be reinvented, and accidental or unwilled actions claimed as deliberate and crucial; the future had to be plotted in an image of human solidarity which existed only in an imagination pressed to the extreme. Wright was clearly correct in suggesting that Bigger contained the germ of totalitarianism. In *The Outsider*, he pursues that thought and, giving a new Bigger Thomas the freedom and the articulateness which he had formerly lacked, sends him forth to realize his imagined world, to bend reality to fit his dreams. The consequence is indeed a totalitarian mind, willing to impose the principles which he invokes by a force which he sees as simply the agent of justice.

But Wright did miss the Party. Its loss closed the only avenue to transcendence which he could see. It had provided the only concrete route to that sense of human unity which Bigger had yearned for, even if the Party had too often itself been too taken up with political divisiveness ever to dramatize such a vision with any conviction. The struggle by the individual to free his identity from the encroachments of American life had to be accomplished alone and, as he showed in a succession of books, it was an uneven battle. For to move beyond the social world is to risk a dangerous antinomianism; it is to break the thread which ties that individual to a moral world. It was a dilemma which he never really solved. The hero of "The Man Who Lived Underground" becomes the root of human suffering and is killed; the protagonist of *The Outsider* realizes on his death bed that in order to sustain his own innocence he has become the source of evil. The central character in *The Long Dream* takes a tentative step towards resisting injustice, but leaves America, unable to function any longer in a world which he can see no way of transforming. It was, after all, Wright himself who said, "I want to leave the hatreds of race and the pressures of the United States behind and go and live in a foreign land."[70]

Wright eventually tried to replace the Party with a vision of Africa. This was to become the instrument of transcendence. As he wrote in his journal in 1945, "I had once thought that communism was an instrument for that, but now I don't know. They beat you down too much with dictatorial methods of work and feeling and thought. . . .I've not had of course a sense of oneness from the past of Africa; but I feel the need for one now in the future and I'm looking forward to it."[71] But for the moment, he chose to press another concern, one implicit in *Native Son* but fully articulated in *The Outsider*. He took a crash course in existentialism, which included personal discussions with Paul Tillich.

The Outsider's central character, Cross Damon, is a man who has permitted himself to become trapped in a self-created prison. Allowing his life to be determined by passion, he falls first into marriage and then into an affair with an underaged girl. Threatened with jail for statutory rape, on the one hand, and simple blackmail, on the other, he tries to blot out his awareness of the situation with drink. Then his problems are suddenly solved by a freak accident. The subway train on which he is traveling is involved in a crash, and another passenger, whose face he has had to batter in order to free himself from the wreckage, is subsequently mistaken for him. But before he can leave Chicago for New York, he is recognized by an old acquaintance and has to kill to protect his new identity.

Now a literal outsider, inhabiting a world which he himself has to invent, he is reborn as an observer of life, detached morally as well as socially. The transformation is complete and not wholly realistic. Thus, he changes from a mindless sexual being into an articulate intellectual who can cross swords with the district attorney, Houghton, whom he meets on the train to New York and who soon stumbles on the secret of his dangerously amoral stance, his freedom from all external moral sanctions. For the gift of his detachment is an objectivity which enables him to see more clearly the needs and tensions of the human heart. The cost, however, is an ethical neutrality which is chilling in its disregard for individual life. Determined to pull the world into some kind of ethical shape, and opposing himself to those whose cruelty is destructive of human values, such as the members of the Communist Party whom he meets, he kills three more people who threaten his image of human interdependence. It is a self-denying strategy which he recognizes as such only on his death, as the absurdity which he validates even while opposing it finally reaches out and destroys him.

In many ways, it is an unskillful novel. The abrupt change, which transforms Cross Damon from a pathetic caricature into a self-possessed articulate philosopher, lacks credibility, while the constant references to "dread," "anguish," and "the outsider" bear witness to Wright's personalized course in existentialism rather than to the reality of the characters who are forced to voice them. So, too, Cross's observation that "a man creates himself" is appropriate to the Lazarus who dominates most of the book, but not to the man who actually voices that sentiment in the early chapters. Nevertheless, the novel clearly goes to the heart of Wright's concern with the terms on which the individual can lay claim to his identity and establish a relationship both with his fellow man and with his metaphysical situation.

All the main characters are presented as outsiders: Cross, as a Negro; Houghton, the district attorney, because of the physical deformity of a hump-back; Gil and Hilton, the Communist leaders, by virtue of their positions; and Eva, Gil's wife and Cross's lover, as an orphan. Yet, fundamentally, their status as outsiders derives less from their special circumstances than it does from a condition which is shared by everyone in the novel. Indeed, although Cross is a Negro, Wright stresses the fact that "there was no racial tone to his reactions," that "he was just a man, *any* man who had had an opportunity to flee and had seized upon it."[72] Nonetheless, the relevance to the plight of the Negro is clear. "His past," we are told of Damon, "had come to him without his asking." But now that he is reborn, now that he has assumed a new assertive identity, untrameled by the constrictions of a personal history, "his past would have to be a deliberately constructed thing";[73] "only the future must loom before him so magnetically that it could condition his present" and enable him to "build a new past."[74]

His freedom does indeed derive from his marginality. Outside the axial lines of society, he is unbounded in thought and action by the disabling presumptions of that society. Bigger Thomas had been protected for a while by white resistance to the notion that he was capable of decisive action or thought. Captain Delano had made a similar mistake in Melville's "Benito Cereno." But it is not primarily racial myopia which concerns Wright in *The Outsider*; it is a blindness which derives from a denial of human freedom, from a failure to recognize the real potential of the individual, a potential to be realized only by those who transcend the boundaries of social definition. Wright's blackness, like the district attorney's humpback, lifts him beyond habitual patterns.

Just as Camus proposed that moment in which the individual becomes alert to the nature and force of absurdity precisely through his sudden awareness of the routine nature of his existence, so, Wright's protagonist comes "gradually to a comprehension of the force of habit in his and others' lives."[75] His own break with routine "disturbed the tone and pitch of reality."[76] Unhappily, Wright feels obliged to spell out his convictions in detail, dividing these observations between his protagonist and the white district attorney whose language and perceptions are indistinguishable from those of his black alter ego. Indeed, it is the district attorney and not Damon who offers an observation which is clearly a direct expression of Wright's conviction, as it is a paraphrase of Du Bois's remarks in *The Souls of Black Folk*: "Negroes . . .are going to be gifted with a double vision, for, being Negroes, they are going to be both *inside* and *outside* of our culture at the same time. . . .They will not only be Americans or Negroes; they will be the centre of *knowing*."[77]

Damon's comparative insulation from racial matters, however, in a sense belies this. In his case and, one suggests, in Wright's, the conceit is an intellectual one, and there is, perhaps, more than a little relevance to Wright's own situation as an expatriate who was actually writing this novel in England and France. For, although in his earlier life he had assuredly encountered racial antagonisms brutally and directly, he was now protected from them, and his concern with identity, perhaps inevitably, was thus broader than that posed by the specific racial dilemma. "Practically he was with them," Damon confesses, "but emotionally he was not of them. He felt keenly their sufferings and would have battled desperately for any Negro trapped in a racial conflict, but his character had been so shaped that his decisive life struggle was a personal fight for the realization of himself."[78]

Having sloughed off his old identity, and with it his responsibilities, Damon is faced with an opposite dilemma. For now he found himself formless and adrift in a world of possibility, desperately projecting on his surroundings his own renewed desire for order, and looking for an experience sharp and total enough to engage. Reborn as Lazarus, he not only creates his own life, but becomes a manipulator of others. Like the protagonists of Kosinski's novels, Damon feels that his new self-conscious awareness gives him a freedom of action which is godlike. Seeing, suddenly, beyond the surface of life, he feels that civilization is nothing more than a pattern invoked to conceal disorder, a disorder which derives from, rather than determines, human nature. His new conviction that "man is nothing in particular"[79] is the horror which such complex illusions are designed to conceal. For if it is true, then everything is indeed possible. Accordingly, he lives out this absurdist logic, allowing his feelings to constitute a moral code, enforcing his will on those around him. As he says to himself, if "the Party was justified in coercing obedience from others purely on the basis of its strength, what was there, then, to keep an individual from adopting the same policy?"[80]

Murder is not an act of release or even self-creation, as it had in part been in *Native Son*; it is an expression of the protagonist's own status as outsider, as one released from the determining definitions of the social world. And yet, while he feels free to kill, he does so in the name of a principle of human solidarity and right action which is potentially undermined by the act itself. Like the central figure in Kosinski's *Blind Date*, he kills to sustain a moral vision which he derives from his own sense of natural justice, but, in doing so, naturally allies himself with the forces which he wishes to destroy. Indeed, the justice which he invokes is a strategic device, a desperate attempt to identify a unifying and absolute principle beneath the anarchy of life. As a communist leader points out to him, he is trying to create a space between appearance and reality in order to sustain an image of the self and its setting which can create transcendent purpose: "You're seeking for something that doesn't exist. You want to redeem life or this life with so-called meaning—But what you see before your eyes is all there is."[81] Outside society, and subject therefore to none of its constraints, he constructs his values out of his feelings. The impulse is a totalitarian one. But where Kosinski and Coover are aware that such totalitarianism extends to the writer himself, who is, of course, a supreme manipulator, Wright stops short of such a reflexiveness. The pathos of the protagonist's attempts to project order does not extend to the work in which that attempt is documented. Wright's creation of a physical and moral world is not, apparently, susceptible to the ironies which infect that of his protagonist's, despite the ironies which he had identified in "The Man Who Lived Underground."

Hilton, the Party member, justifies the suffering which the Party inflicts by insisting that life is, anyway, "bare, naked, unjustifiable . . .existing there for no reason and no end."[82] When Damon kills, it is an attempt to destroy such a view; it is a gesture of moral outrage, where morality is presumed to begin and end in the sensibility of the free individual, unconditioned by the culture in which he moves. Insofar as he is offered as a prototype of modern man, severed from the values of the past and with no transcendent vision of the future, he stands as a warning. But the battle which he fights for a resistant individualism is lost from the start precisely because individualism relies for its definition on a cultural commitment which menaces the self but which is finally the only source of identity. Damon kills with clear deliberation, in an exercise of will and passion, and yet, as he realizes, he is hopelessly caught in the coils of his own actions; "subverted by the contagion of the lawless, he had been defeated by that which he had sought to destroy."[83] Repelled by the drive for power which he sees in others, he exerts his own moral absolutism, invented to condemn others' guilt; invented, in other words, to assert his own innocence. By enacting the dilemma, he exposes it. Wright is presenting a theory of history, in essence making the same point which Lowell was to make in *The Old Glory* and Miller in *After the Fall*: "Perhaps he was staring right now at the focal point of history: if you fought men who tried to conquer you in terms of total power you too had to use total power and in the end you became what you tried to defeat . . . Was all action doomed to this kind of degredation?''[84]

And this was to prove a potent question for the black American in the 1960s. Amiri Baraka, as LeRoi Jones, acknowledged the problem in *The Slave*, but could offer only the pragmatic response that ''you had your chance, now these other folks have theirs.''[85] For Wright, beneath the certainties of ideology as beneath racial tensions, lies the individual will to power which derives, not from the existence of values which can be freely invoked and whose enforcements create the contours of history, but from the nonexistence of such values and the nullity which is presumed to be human life.

Wright's novel has clear Spenglerian overtones. The world which he describes is close in spirit and in detail to what Spengler described as the age of the Caesars. The only realities are money and power; the only determinants, industrialization and urbanization; the only active agents, those who subordinate everything to naked will. Hence, some passages in the novel sound like little more than paraphrases of Spengler's apocalypticism. ''Industrial life plus a rampant capitalism,'' says Wright, ''have blasted the lives of men in these cities; those who are lucky enough not to be hidden are ridden with exquisite psychological sufferings. The people of these cities are lost. . . . They haunt the movies for distraction; they gamble; they depress their sensibilities with alcohol; or they seek strong sensations to dull their sense of a meaningless existence.''[86] The natural consequence is a move towards the totalitarian and the absolute; it is a reduction of life to a sport.

For the modern man, for the communists, for the district attorney, life is a game; its only significance lies in the meaning with which they arbitrarily choose to invest it. The same is true in part of Cross Damon, himself, who violates the basic human contract. Like Hemingway's Frederic Henry, he can no longer believe in the liberal virtues (he cannot accept words like ''glory, culture, civilization and progress,''[87] as Frederic Henry could not accept ''glory,'' ''honor,'' and ''sacrifice'') since both have glimpsed the absurdity which lies behind them. Both respond by inventing worlds in which some provisional meaning can cohere. But where Henry declares a separate peace, refusing to take life, after himself conspiring in the general absurdity and anarchy by aiding in the killing of one of his own men, Damon assumes a messianic role, trying to kill that absurdity and restore a human order as Hemingway's bullfighters had tried to kill death by administering it.

The Outsider seems to be Wright's lament over the death of liberalism. Damon strikes at the very idea of a social contract. He ''had no party, no myths, no tradition, no race, no soil, no culture, and no ideas—except perhaps the idea that ideas themselves were, at best, dubious.''[88] Indeed, he declares liberals to be an extinct breed, well-meaning, dedicated to destroying illusion, but unable to build a new world: ''Had it not been for those liberals, the full flood of a senseless existence would have long since broken through the myths of progress which have sustained modern man so far. They did an impossible job with great skill, those liberals. Future history will regard the liberals as the last great defenders of that which really could not be defended, as the last spokesmen of historical man as we've know him for the past two thousand years.''[89] Yet the lament is put in the mouth of such a self-deceiving individual that Wright's own sympathies seem entirely with a faith which counterposes itself to the absolute.

Damon's failure lay in his inability to see through himself. Having rejected God, he reinvented him in his own image. As Houghton says, ''You peeled off layer after layer of illusion and make-believe and stripped yourself down to just simply naked desire and you thought that you had gotten hold of the core of reality. You felt that what obstructed desire could be killed.''[90] The lesson which Damon essentially learns as he lies dying is in part that learned by the dying Harry Morgan in Hemingway's *To Have and Have Not*. ''The search can't be done alone. . . .Never alone. . . .Alone a man is nothing. . . .Man is a promise he must never break.'' Like Morgan, he wishes that he could communicate his message, which is ultimately a liberal one. The need is to ''make a bridge from man to man.''[91] But his own path of a totalitarianism of the self is the wrong one. ''Tell them not to come down this road,'' he insists, ''We must find some way of being good to ourselves. . . .Man is all we've got. . . .Man is returning to the earth. . . .For a long time he has been sleeping, wrapped in a dream. . . .He is awakening now, awakening from his dream and finding himself in a waking nightmare. . . .The myth men are going. . . .The real men, the lost men are coming. . . .Somebody must prepare the way for them. . . .Tell them what they are like.''[92] And the real horror of these last men, as Damon manages to gasp out as he dies, is not that they perceive themselves as evil, but that they believe themselves to be innocent. As Arthur Miller's Quentin observes in *After the Fall*, to remain innocent, we ''kill most easily.''[93]

The questions which he has asked himself are basic to Wright's work: ''Was there really no direct bridge between the subjective worlds of people? Was the possibility of communication only a kind of pretence, an arrangement assumed to exist but which really did not? Was the core of the subjective life of each person sealed off absolutely from that of another?''[94] It is that isolation, perhaps social and racial in origin, perhaps metaphysical, which places moral responsibility on the individual. It is a responsibility in which Damon fails. Eva, who wishes in her painting to create ''images common to everybody, symbols that can link men together,''[95] eventually commits suicide, having seen her dreams destroyed by Damon's inhuman defense of the ideal.

So, if the novel condemns the bad faith of ''the far-flung conspiracy of pretending that life was tending toward a goal of redemption, the reasonless assumption that one's dreams and desires were realizable,''[96] it equally denounces the potent conspiracy of those who mobilize ''the natural hopes and anxieties of other men for their own selfish ends.'' Damon is suspended between precisely those twin dangers which have always been the special perils identified in American writing: an inflexible self which sustains itself only by virtue of removing itself from the chain of being, and a flexible self which flirts with the anarchy which at base it expresses.

Wright's last published novel, *The Long Dream* (1958), returned to the South of his first book, *Uncle Tom's Children*. The book is set in the South in the early 1950s and is concerned with the education of Fishbelly Tucker in the realities of race and power. His father is an undertaker who, literally and symbolically, is concerned with burying ''the long dream'' which is the life of the Negro. Tyree Tucker makes his money on the side from investments in brothels—buying the influence and respect which the white world otherwise denies him. When one of these brothels is destroyed by fire and forty-two people are killed, he is threatened with jail. In order to secure his freedom, he attempts to blackmail the chief of police, Cantley, with canceled checks which are evidence of the payoffs Tyree has made to him over the years to secure police protection and immunity from the fire regulations. Such a blatant challenge to white power results in Tyree's murder. A white reformist politician, to whom he had entrusted the checks, is unable to help him when they are stolen by Cantley's men. Tyree's son now inherits the business. Suppressing his bitterness, he prepares to continue his father's dangerous but profitable collaboration with whites when a second collection of checks falls into his hands. Suspicious that further evidence exists, Cantley frames the boy on a rape charge and then sends a black informer into his cell. Though the rape charge comes to nothing, Fish's fierce attack on the informer results in a two-year sentence. When he is released, he takes his money and flees to France, sending the checks to the white liberal.

The crucial realization towards which the young protagonist moves is that people like his father had indeed collaborated in their own destruction. Tyree had offered his son essentially the same advice that the grandfather offers the invisible protagonist of *Invisible Man*: ''The only way to get along with white folks is to grin in their goddamn faces and make 'em feel good and then do what the hell you want behind their goddamn backs.''[97] But the implacable realities of life in the South only permit such a strategy to the point at which the real interests of the whites are placed at risk. At that point, dissembling ceases to operate. Tyree had accepted the role thrust upon him by whites in the mistaken belief that it was a mask and that his essential self remained unaffected. But the reality is otherwise, as Fish comes to realize. ''The difference between them was that Tyree automatically accepted the situation and worked willingly within it. Fishbelly also accepted the definition, but he did so consciously and therefore could never work within it.''[98] As a result, he comes to realize that Tyree has become ''a crawling black scavanger battening upon only the black side of human life, burying only the black dead, selling only the living black female bodies to the white and black world, buying justice, protection, comfort from these sordid dealings and calling it business.''[99] He debates with himself, as Tyree does not, the cost to his selfhood and dignity and recognizes in himself, perhaps scarcely credibly for a boy of his age, the twin temptations of an almost sensual respect for white power and a willing submission to it. It is this temptation to collaborate in one's own victimization which Fish recognizes early, through his own experience with the police, and, later, in the black community's willing subservience to white definitions of the real. Yet in the terror of the white world, its fear of the image which it has itself created, in the very rigor of its brutality, Fish detects an admission of worth, the possible source of an identity. It is an ambiguous one because it is a consequence of white psychosis, and it is an identity which, he learns, cannot consist simply of a violent opposition which is neither strategically credible nor philosophically tenable since it would, paradoxically, offer further evidence of white power.

Early in the book, Fish "could not imagine any way of meeting" white people "other than of violence,''[100] but the events which bring him to such a rapid maturity teach him that the problem is more complex. For Fish admits that "his fantasies had often pictured him as battling in the racial arena . . .his imagination had always pitted him physically against a personal enemy." But now he comes to feel that the real enemy "was vague, was part white, part black, was everywhere and nowhere, was within as well as without, and had allies in the shape of tradition, habit and attitude.''[101] And this surely is Wright's point. The battle is not to be fought in the convenient arena of physical confrontation. The essential war is internal. It has to be waged with the self, with the past, and with the institutionalization of prejudice. Far from advocating violence, Wright suggests that this is simply a convenient way of displacing one's social impotence into anarchic action which leaves the world unchanged. Hence, the crucial action of the book is concerned with the need for the young protagonist to break free from his father's values, from his own tendency towards acquiescence and guilt, and from the temptations of power and wealth. To the extent that this is true, Addison Gayle's comment that "whatever Wright's intentions, characterwise, Tyree Tucker is the major protagonist of the novel''[102] is wide of the mark, a fact that is even apparent in the concession implicit in the gap which the critic admits to exist between his stance and that of the author. Fish survives the South not because "the teachings of his father can be called imminently [*sic*] successful,''[103] but because he rejects his father's values, methods, and convictions; because he has the courage to choose a free life before wealth and pledges his faith in the possibility of change.

In a sense, *The Long Dream* is Wright's justification of his own exile. In America, the whites are seen as an "ever lurking enemy who shaped your destiny . . .curbed your ends . . .determined your aims . . .stamped your every action with alien meanings. You existed in the bosom of the enemy, shared his ideals, spoke his tongue, fought with his weapons, and died a death usually of his making.''[104] The logic was clear; "there was nothing left for them but flight . . .maybe to a foreign country . . . . But such a country was beyond Fishbelly's imagination.''[105] But not, of course, beyond Wright's, and, by the end of the novel, Fish does indeed reenact Wright's journey to France. And since this implies leaving the scene of the battle (insofar as a component, at least, of that battle is external), Fish is given a weapon, in the form of the checks, to fight that battle vicariously from Paris, just as Wright saw himself doing, using his work in a similar manner. It was, perhaps, a morally ambiguous stance, but one with which Wright himself was all too familiar. And Wright was saddled with another ambiguity, one which is endemic to the black writer, for, like Tyree, his service to the black community is simultaneously the root of his own power and independence. The very act which is offered as a gesture of solidarity distinguishes him from those on whose behalf the gesture is made.

Not that Fish escapes the paradox into which he has been born. He does come to believe that there are whites who are willing to fight for his rights, but the violence which has been done to his life, the erosion of his spiritual and imaginative being, has left him trapped in a ''flat, pallid present.'' He is free now—physically and emotionally—but lacking a tradition which can give meaning to his life and any vision which can invest mere existence with purpose and direction, he flirts with the idea of voluntarily offering what the violence of the South had failed to make him render up compulsorily—his allegiance. But the world to which he offers that fealty is not quite what it had been. It has been changed by his own knowledge, his self-conscious awareness, and by the existence of a white man, not only more honest than other white men, but more honest than himself. There is at last a small crack in the monolithic structure of white hostility. It is a tenuous basis on which to found a new life, and he is far from clear about the nature of the social contract which he is now drawn falteringly to endorse, but he sees the world with other eyes than his father's and he has found a response other than apocalypse. ''That in him which had always made him self-conscious was now the bud of a new possible life that was pressing ardently but timidly against the shell of the old to shatter it and be free. This resolution of denial and acceptance that he was now making was not born of a will towards deception; he was not acting now; it was a free gesture of faith welling up out of a yearning to be at last somewhere at home; it was his abject offer of a truce. Knowing that he was relatively free from fear and pressure, he was now more willingly anxious than ever to confess that he was maybe wrong and that others might be right. He was now voluntarily longing to pledge allegiance to a world whose brutal might could never compel him to love it with threats of death.''[106]

But it is not the same world. He is traveling now, at the end of the novel, on an aircraft, surrounded by whites who show and apparently feel no animosity towards him. If he still feels the urge to cover up his black hand, it is because he has yet to exorcise the values which southern society has forced him to internalize. But the desire to break through to another world is there as strongly as it had been in Bigger Thomas; indeed, he now flies above America in a plane which had been an image of freedom for Bigger, and lays claim to an existence which is beyond Bigger's powers of imaginative possession. Thus, if this novel details the nature of southern brutality and spells out the terrible cost in human terms of injustice and deprivation, it also pledges some kind of faith in the existence of other values, in the possibility of reform, and in the ability of black Americans to avoid the double jeopardy of self-abnegation and violence, which were precisely the twin dangers implicit in the civil rights movement then in the process of challenging the apparent inflexibility of the South.

It is a novel which, like most of Wright's work, has its weaknesses. The rhetoric is at times banal (''A man's got to do what he's got to do''[107]) and at times baroque (''He prayed wordlessly that a bright, bursting tyrant of living sun would soon lay down its golden laws to loosen the locked regions of his heart and cast the shadow of his dream athwart the stretches of time.''[108]). His effects are too often overdone: it is not enough that the existence of the American flag should create obvious ironies to the youth who is being denied justice, he has to feel ''that the glittering eagle was about to swoop down upon him and peck out his eyes.''[109] His images are too frequently and unnecessarily underscored: when the young black boys taunt a homosexual, the point is clear enough without the unnecessary statement that ''mebbe it's like being black.'' He is also faced once again with the problem of articulating the subtleties of his perceptions through an adolescent who cannot credibly be presented as so perceptive and expressive. His solution is the same as that in *Native Son*; he falls back on transparent devices (''he felt rather than thought this; it came to him in flashes of intuition''[110]). But it is a better novel than is usually suggested and, while capturing the spirit of aggressive reformism and bitter complaint then manifesting itself in America, it raised more fundamental questions than those of black access to the political system.

Although Wright believed that ''the word Negro in America means something not racial, or biological, but purely something social, something made in the United States,''[111] in something of a contradiction, he increasingly came to see Negro culture as an international phenomenon which incorporated African art. In this, he differs fundamentally from Ralph Ellison who, in 1958, remarked that ''what I understand by the term 'Negro culture' is so vague as to be meaningless.''[112] Since the word ''Negro'' was a deliberately reductive word which ignored the many and profound differences between African tribes, Ellison rejected any idea of culture being genetically transmitted. The black American was most sensibly seen as a subgroup of American culture. But for Wright, though he was tempted to concede that the American Negro writer was dominated by American modes, the idea of a transnational racial culture provided the only real alternative after the apostasy of the Party. However, his own confused encounters with Africa and Asia, described in *Black Power*, *The Colour Curtain*, and *White Man, Listen!*, did little to demonstrate his understanding of these cultures, and his suggestion that the proofs of *The Colour Curtain* should not be sent to Ellison, Baldwin, or Horace Cayton because they would not be independent enough to give their honest reactions to it, betrayed a certain defensiveness on his part. He had little time, however, for the sentimentalities of negritude, being increasingly attracted to the ethnopolitics of anticolonialism. But his analysis was surprisingly naive.

His relationship to America remained highly ambiguous and ironic. As he remarked in 1950, "I may complain about America but I'm still a citizen of the United States. The only thing that Paris has that the United States does not seem to have is humanity."[113]

In Europe, Wright began to see Negro life as an image, first, of American alienation and, then, of that felt by Western man. It was, he asserted in a lecture on "The Literature of the Negro in the United States," simply white life "lifted to the heights of pain and pathos, drama and tragedy. The history of the Negro in America is the history of America written in vivid and bloody terms; . . .it is the history of men who tried to adjust themselves to a world whose laws, customs, and instruments of force were levelled against them. The Negro," he declared, "is America's metaphor."[114] But he is an image, too, of something wider, for *White Man, Listen!* was dedicated to "the lonely outsiders who exist precariously on the clifflike margins of many cultures—men who are distrusted, misunderstood, maligned, criticised by Left and Right. Christian and pagan—men who carry on their frail but indefatigable shoulders the best of two worlds—and who, amidst confusion and stagnation, seek desperately for a home for their hearts: a home which, if found, could be a home for the hearts of all men." And these men were no longer the dispossessed masses but "the westernised and tragic elite of Asia, Africa, and the West Indies." Accordingly, he looked for a merging of "Negro expression with American expression."[115]

For Wright, ideology was "a means towards social intimacy,"[116] just as nationalism was to be seen as a starting point and not an end. In "Blueprint for Negro Writing," he had asserted that "Negro writers must accept the nationalist implications of their lives, not in order to encourage them, but in order to change and transcend them."[117] And yet, the need for an animating principle was clear throughout his life. In *White Man, Listen!*, he makes the plainly unconvincing statement that "I do not hanker after, and seem not to need, as many emotional attachments, sustaining roots, or idealistic allegiances as most people. I declare unabashedly that I like, even cherish, the state of abandonment, of aloneness; it does not bother me; indeed, to me it seems the natural, inevitable condition of man, and I welcome it."[118] While he was certainly drawn to the intellectual fascinations of abandonment, equally clearly he spent a lifetime trying to discover ways of nullifying it through precisely that attempt to discover sustaining roots and forge idealistic allegiances which he here so strongly and significantly disavows.

The Flight of Words: The Paradox of Ralph Ellison   3

Writing in *Commentary* in 1964, Ralph Ellison explained that "the act of writing requires a constant plunging back into the shadow of the past where time hovers ghostlike."[1] But that past is presented as being inherently ambiguous. For Ellison, the "temptation to interpret the world and all its devices in terms of race" was "deadly and hypnotic"[2] and to be resisted. And yet, what did that past consist of if not history shaped by the fact of race? Time, after all, contains precisely that racial component which he ideally wished to evade, and he himself acknowledged the paradox which led him simultaneously to celebrate and attempt to transcend that fact.

The plunge back into the past seemed to require an equal and opposite pull—a flight into the future, a soaring, unaffected by the gravitational pull of history. And, indeed, such an image suffused his early work. In a short story called "That I Had Wings," the protagonist watches a young robin's first attempt at flight, seeing in it a striking parallel to his own situation as a young boy testing the limits of his freedom. In "Mr. Toussan," the same boy contemplates a butterfly and a pigeon and speculates, with his friend, on what he would do, given wings:

> "Where'd you go, man?"
> "Up north, maybe to Chicago."
> "Man, if I had wings I wouldn't never settle down." . . .
> . . ."I'd go to New York" . . .
> . . ."Or anywhere else colored is free."[3]

In the background. a woman sings the spiritual "All God's Chillun Got Wings," with its theme of freedom.

But flight is an inherently ambiguous term, connecting freedom and desertion alike. And the image collapses. In "That I Had Wings," young chickens thrown from the roof of a hen house simply break their necks in the dust; while in "Mr. Toussan," the fantasies of flight from racial identity give way to racial pride in the achievement of Toussaint L'Ouverture, who was excluded from their history books but newly discovered by the young boys.

So, freedom is discovered in time, in a psychic space won within the given, rather than projected beyond the axial lines of personal and group identity. So it is that in his essay "On Becoming a Writer" Ellison turned to jazz as his paradigm for writing, for the musicians were "artists who had stumbled upon the freedom lying within the restriction of their musical tradition as within the limitations of their social background."[4] Their flights of sound were rooted in an experience which their art transcended but did not deny.

And for Ellison, as for other black writers, the nature of this balance between the prosaic and centrifugal nature of experience and a transcending centripetal language becomes crucial. For the flight of language, the liberating power of the word, is potentially a denial of the reality which it begins by expressing—language having its own seductions, its own momentum, its own cultural imperatives. For those critics who suspect Ellison of a fundamental betrayal, it is this balance between experience and language which he does not sustain because his art is an evasion. Hence, Clifford Mason suggests that he is "unable to deal in a world of tangible reality, he must make artifice of it,"[5] while for Ernest Kaiser, his writing is "unemotional, uncommitted and uninvolved in his people's problems."[6] But, in truth, Ellison has, from his earliest work, been sensitive to this dilemma, so much so that it becomes the subject of a brilliant early short story, "Flying Home" (1944).

Ellison has said that every serious novel is, beyond its immediate thematic preoccupations, a discussion of the craft, a conquest of the form, and a conflict with its difficulties. And this is no less true of "Flying Home" than it is of *Invisible Man* itself. In a way, it is a warning to himself against literary hubris, as it is a recognition of cultural identity and moral responsibility. It picks up the image of the aircraft as a symbol of escape, which one finds in *Native Son* and *The Long Dream*, and creates a dense but lyrical metaphor of racial relationships. Todd, a Negro pilot, crash-lands into a field in Alabama and breaks his ankle. One black farm worker, Jefferson, stays with him while his son goes to a nearby white man for help. As they talk, Todd's fears and ambitions are gradually revealed. Eventually, the white man and his friends appear and, partly as a joke, put the pilot into the straight jacket of a madman who has escaped from a nearby institution. It is one of the minor ironies of the story that the black serviceman and not the mad white man ends up in constraint. Eventually, his fellow blacks are allowed to take him back to the airfield.

Lying in the field, Todd is embarrassed to be face to face with old Jefferson, precisely that self-image which he had fought to escape. The mistake which had led to his crash is bad enough, not simply because it will be taken as proof of his own incompetence, but because, inevitably, it will be adduced as evidence of racial inferiority. In success and in failure he is reduced to public symbol, and his identity is denied. Now his situation is exacerbated; having plunged, literally and symbolically, back to his origins, he resists the notion of being seen with the man who now offers to help him. Todd feels that Jefferson has knocked him "back a hundred years,"[7] like the black buzzard which in striking the windscreen, had thrown him into the panic which had caused his crash. He feels that "the closer I spin toward earth the blacker I become."[8] He has moved from a high technology world back to a "peasant's sense of time and space."[9]

The irony is, of course, that for him humiliation exists in both spheres. The progress of society (itself ambiguous since these events take place in the middle of a war) is precisely technological and not moral. The trained black pilots are kept on their southern bases for fear that their achievement in combat might undermine the myths which sustain southern culture and which even the desire on the part of blacks for flight seems already to threaten.

For Todd, the plane is his dignity, as Bigger had felt it was for him in *Native Son*, and as, in a sense, it proves to be for Fish in *The Long Dream*. Told, as a boy, that such things were in the sole possession of whites, he made the mistake of believing that the symbol was coterminous with the reality—that it was the source and not the proof of power. As a child, he had seen a plane, "a gleam in the sun like a fiery sword,"[10] dropping white cards with the symbol of the Ku Klux Klan and the printed advice: "Niggers Stay Away from the Polls." His horror and fascination at the sight is a model of his response to white society. To wipe out the humiliation, he has to gain possession of the sword. But to fly the plane, as he discovers, is not to own or dispose of it. He is inside it, as he is inside American society, as Jonah was inside the whale. As a consequence, his is a fragile dignity because it is essentially external to his drive for identity. The whites have only to change the rules for the gesture to become absurd.

Flight thus becomes an image of his own desperate attempt to exist on the border between white condescension and what he takes to be black ignorance; but it is a no-man's land which necessarily takes him outside of any human relationship: "His course of flight seemed mapped by the nature of things away from all needed and natural landmarks...his path curved swiftly away from both the shame the old man symbolised and the cloudy terrain of white man's regard."[11] "Flying blind," he believes that the meaning of his life can only finally cohere through action, through the violent clash of warfare in which his identity will consist entirely and exclusively, in the eyes of the enemy, in his success or failure as a killer. The truth, in other words, is that he has locked himself into a logic whereby only his death will confer meaning on his life. He will become hangman or victim. It is a truth which his mind slides away from; its absurdity is too familiar in the setting in which he now finds himself, in which the local white farmer has a reputation as a killer of Negroes, the oxen cast "queer, prehistoric shadows against the dry brown earth," and the fingers of the black peasant are like "gnarled dry wood"[12] in contrast to the bright metal of the plane. His "advance" consists of a simple return to paganism. That is the nature of the anarchy which is a constant threat. The distance between the natural world of dry brown earth and the plane flying its free arabesques is precisely that vital space which Todd wishes to maintain between past and present—his own and that of his race. But a single mistake, a single accident, can close that gap in a second. Space, then, becomes a void, rather than a tension.

To pass the time until help comes, Jefferson tells a folk tale of his trip to heaven in which he had discovered that black angels were required to wear harnesses which prevented them from flying properly. When he insists on flying nonetheless, he is sent down to earth again. Todd, recognizing the relevance to his own situation, feels a sense of guilt and humiliation "that only great violence would wash away." And this, of course, is an emotional image of the situation in which Todd finds himself as he waits to go to war. In trying to be an eagle, he is simply turning into a black buzzard feeding on death. He is "fighting pain with counter pain."[13] When the aptly named Dabney Graves appears and has Todd put in a straight jacket, because " 'you cain't let the niggah git up that high without his going crazy,' "[14] it is Jefferson who comes to his assistance "as though somehow he had become his sole salvation in an insane world of outrage and humiliation," as though only he "could release him from his overpowering sense of isolation."[15] It is an assumption which is reflected in the linguistic strategy of the story. For the old man's speech and Todd's thoughts are run into one another so that it is not always apparent who is speaking—a stylistic confirmation of the kinship of the two men, a kinship which Todd wishes at first he were able to deny. So, too, the narrative moves from third person to first person, once again uniting Todd's private world with that of his fellow blacks.

As Jefferson and his son carry Todd back to the airfield on a stretcher, and he realizes finally his literal and symbolic reliance upon them, he accepts that cutting himself off from his past, from his own community, and from a common sense of humanity had not been a solution to his injured pride and threatened identity. Flying free, removed from time and place, was actually only a prescription for solitariness. Now "it was as though he had been lifted out of his isolation, back in the world of men. A new current of communication flowed between the man and boy and himself." The touch of genuine humanity even transforms the black buzzard, whose nickname is Jim Crow, into a bird of beauty; "like a song within his head he heard the boy's soft humming and saw the dark bird glide into the sun and glow like a bird of flaming gold."[15] This is the "home" of the story's title—it is a renewed sense of solidarity with the black community and that sense of humanity which is only accessible through an acknowledgement that the self derives its identity from its relationship to others. The story is a parable of black identity and human interrelationship and, as such, stands as a statement of Ellison's sense of his own responsibility as a black writer who threatens his moral and artistic credibility if he presumes that his reputation depends upon creating a gulf between himself and his origins, in tracing arabesques of language against the sky as a way of affirming his freedom and achievement.

The story underlines Ellison's convictions that essential human truths exist to the side of history, that they manifest themselves in the interstices of time—a conviction which he repeats in *Invisible Man*, a novel which also challenges the presumption that movement is progress, that symbol transcends reality, and that the self can sustain its moral form in isolation. The paradox which the protagonist of his story has to negotiate is that, flying high in his plane, his selfhood is constantly threatened by the void, while on the ground, it is menaced by history. But, dislodged momentarily from time (he tries to reach the clock in the cockpit but is unable to do so), he no longer perceives his life and that of his race as a kind of narrative progression. Time collapses so that he sees the nodal points of his personal history and, in the person of Jefferson, the history of his race. As a consequence, we are offered the suggestion that progress does not lie in winning a place in American society, but in discovering an identity built on something more substantial than flight and in acknowledging a community other than that proposed by a society which is at war with itself and others. The wish to be part of the onrush of history stems from the belief that meaning derives from events, from unfolding social structures, but, as he speculates in *Invisible Man*, "what if history was a gambler. . . .What if history was not a reasonable citizen, but a madman full of paranoid guile."[16] The model he is tempted to choose, in other words, is the wrong one. History is not something one opts to join, not something with the power to confer meaning. It is a product of individual choices, and this realization is one that his protagonist in *Invisible Man* eventually chooses to embrace.

The question of identity is central to the novel, and, significantly, the protagonist is described as living in "a border area," for it is at the border that questions of the boundary of identity and action are most likely to occur. This border is not only that between Harlem and the white area of New York City, where the central character ends his odyssey living in a cellar, tapping into the city's electrical supply; it is the no-man's-land in which the black American writer has constantly insisted that the Negro American has to live out the dialectical nature of his existence, hoping that meaning will distill out of ambivalence. Various syntheses are offered in the form of black nationalism and the Brotherhood, a clear version of the Communist Party, but the novel's logic leaves the central figure continuing to negotiate with opposing demands. As Tony Tanner suggests in *City of Words*, it is this lack of a clear boundary to the self which lies at the heart of the protagonist's dilemma. This is the area which he wishes to throw light upon ("Light confirms my reality"[17]). Thus his act in tapping into the power lines of the Monopolated Light and Power Company (an echo of Wright's "The Man Who Lived Underground") is an act of sabotage which goes beyond commercial deceit; he is intent on undermining white power to define the real: "The truth is the light and the light is the truth."[18]

Safe in his underground hideout, the protagonist determines his own time. Indeed, his invisibility gives him "a slightly different sense of time." Instead of "the swift and imperceptible flowing of time, you are aware of its nodes, those points where time stands still or from which it leaps ahead. And you slip into the breaks and look around."[19] And, as in "Flying Home," this collapsed sense of time offers a special insight into history. It is the sudden perception which halts the flow of time, just as a professional boxer's "violent flow of rapid rhythmic action" is halted by one sudden unscientific blow from his yokel opponent because "the yokel had simply stepped inside his opponent's sense of time."[20]

For a black protagonist who finds himself in a cellar "shut off and forgotten during the nineteenth century," it is precisely this discovery which enables him to see through the apparently flawless web of white reality, no longer to be distracted by the seemingly invulnerable positivism of white society. Now, he feels the force of a past which explains the ambivalence which afflicts him in the present. For him, history is a boomerang; it will turn back on itself, as it has for the Negro, repeatedly offering him the same lesson. Not appreciating the meaning of his past, he is doomed to repeat it until it proves possible to break out of the cycle.

But history is not to be seen as an implacable public structure paraded by whites, for, if formlessness is a threat to identity, so, too, is a rigid structure. Indeed, it is in the anarchy of the Golden Day that a bedrock of truth is glimpsed.

The problem is to negotiate one's way between a shapeless flux which destroys the self and a threatening rigidity which reduces the individual to role and event to simply causality. Order does indeed assume a menacing quality. It lies behind the harmonies of the songs sung at the bequest of white visitors to the black southern college attended by the protagonist, an obedient performance which constitutes "an ultimatum accepted and ritualized, an allegiance recited for the peace it imparted, and for that perhaps loved. Loved as the defeated come to love the symbols of their conquerors." It exists in the nonemotional, logical appeals of those who preach acquiescence and submission, in sermons which exhibit a "formal design requiring nothing more than the lucidity of uncluttered periods, the lulling movements of multisyllabic words."[21] Language conceals the truth that experience should convey. The appeal of being part of a vast and "formal ritual" lies in the sense of identity and belonging that it appears to offer. But even the bewildered protagonist feels the pressure of violence behind the language of those less subtle in their approach, those "who trailed their words to us through blood and violence and ridicule . . . who exhorted and threatened, intimidated with innocent words as they described to us the limitations of our lives and the vast boldness of our

aspirations, the staggering folly of our impatience to rise even higher
. . .their most innocent words were acts of violence.''[22]

And this is the chief message of the book—the need to penetrate symbols,
including the symbols which are language, for this has a seductive logic of its
own which is independent of the experience it purports to capture and explain.
It is ''more sound than sense, a play upon the resonances of buildings, an
assault upon the temples of the ear.''[23] The protagonist becomes as practiced at
such orchestration of subservience as the preachers whom he mimics. He
becomes a ''bungling bugler of words,'' building false linguistic structures for
those who are attuned to ''voices without messages . . .to the vowel sounds and
the crackling dentals, to the low harsh gutterals of empty anguish.''[24] He
becomes the source of ''a river of word sounds . . .playing Ha! as upon a
xylophone; words marching like the student band . . .blaring triumphant
sounds empty of triumph . . .the sound of words that were no words, counter-
feit notes singing achievement yet unachieved.'' He tosses ''word sounds . . .
like bright-colored balls in a water spout,'' seeking validation from those who
believe that they will ''never be fooled by the mere content of words,''[25] but
who respond, in spite of themselves, to a rhetoric legitimized by its very
familiarity, its cadenced rhythms of hope, success, and acceptance—a linguistic narcosis punctuated only by a repeated monosyllabic irony—''Ha!''—of a
kind later used by Heller and Vonnegut.

Ellison's protagonist inherits a language, as he does a habit of acquiescence.
Neither is adequate to the task of rendering him visible to himself or others;
neither can enable him to operate in a present in which reality is constantly
rupturing the thin skin of his linguistic world. It is a lesson which he is
repeatedly offered, but one which he finds difficult to learn precisely because
he has internalized the values which that language celebrates and because he
finds it impossible to understand words which expose the reality of his position. When the veteran in the Golden Day sheds light on his own plight, the
young boy can only say, ''What are you talking about? . . .What?'' As the vet
realizes ''He registers with his senses but short-circuits his brain. Nothing had
meaning.''[26] Later, as he listens to the college principal, Bledsoe, outlining
his pragmatic version of truth, he feels that he is drowning in a ''disgusting sea
of . . .words.''[27]

And yet the author, of course, by definition, is himself a manipulator of
words, a creator of order. His obsessive need, as Ellison has confessed, is ''to
play with the fires of chaos and to rearrange reality to the patterns of his
imagination,''[28] and *Invisible Man* does not absolve the writer whose own
fictions purport to release the imagination, but, in fact, entrap it in the coils of
an arrogant personal vision. The book itself thus becomes a further document
to be treated with the scepticism ironically implied in its own methodology.
Elsewhere, indeed, Ellison has alarmingly suggested that his protagonist is
''something of a liar,'' a possibility which breeds a logical metafictive distrust

of writing as simply another manipulative agency. No wonder that he should say of his novel that "for me, of course, the narrative is the meaning."[29]

Indeed, the protagonist is not only a victim of language, but he is also its chief agent. Thus, his final destruction of a briefcase of printed papers, which together constitute the totality of his false selves, becomes a vital act in his own liberation. Experience is the only reliable truth, an accumulation of events which, on a social level, adds up to history. For the book offers what is in effect a psychic history of the Negro in America since slavery, beginning with the accommodationism of Booker T. Washington, whose Atlanta address is presented in parodic form, through the flirtation with communism and the nationalist fantasies of Marcus Garvey. It is a psychic history which runs parallel to, but stands in contradiction of, the public version. In the memory of Ellison's protagonist, Tuskegee and its philosophy of pragmatic apoliticism is represented not by its reflection of the green fields and pleasant buildings of white institutions, but by a broken, corroded, and dry fountain and the yellow contents of a cistern which spreads over the lawn's dead grass.

The informed narrator, waiting to emerge from his subterranean refuge, is present throughout the book as an ironic voice commenting on his own and his race's naivety. He is Ellison's strategy for presenting appearance and reality simultaneously—the boy who has to deny the evidence of what he learns and cut himself off from his own past, and the man who sees the effect of such denials. The advice of the veteran, "Learn to look beneath the surface,"[30] and of the young white businessman, Emerson, to look for "what lies behind the face of things,"[31] is woven into the narrative method of the book. It is not that the universe is a symbol, a code to be read, but that truth has been buried so deeply beneath the level of appearance, of language, of public role and private aspiration that the cost of resurrecting it is a revolution in consciousness. Beneath the whitewash supplied by the Liberty Paint Company (whose slogan is "Keep America Pure with Liberty Paints"), lies another America.

The veteran is right in suggesting that Mr. Norton, the northern benefactor, is a "trustee of consciousness," but the real price of wresting that consciousness free is not simply an alarming challenge to the white world, but the kind of shock that sends the veteran himself to an asylum. By the nature of things, a challenge to established versions of the real is likely to incur public hostility and private guilt. As the veteran remarks, "There's always an element of crime in freedom"[32] and, he might have added, sin. For if, in insisting that the boy should play a double game, he is exposing him to the risk of the "straight jacket or a padded cell," in proposing that he seizes a freedom that he himself has not attained, he is aware that he is advocating an independence from all authorities, secular and spiritual, from "the white folks, authority," but also from "the gods, fate, circumstances . . .The big man who's never there, where you think he is."[33] The world of possibility towards which he urges the young boy is a solitary world. Once the veils of blindness, which afflict so many of the book's characters, are lifted, it is by no means certain that the individual can survive. The veteran and the young Mr. Emerson are both driven to psychiatric care, as Melville's Pip was shocked into insanity. None of them can face the logic of their own perceptions.

When the protagonist goes north, he warns himself to acquire a watch, wishing to adjust his own time sense to that of the white world, but the pace and direction of his life is as directed by others here as it had been in the South. Things speed up until, in the explosion at the paint factory, he is blasted into a new phase of existence. Like the central character of Wright's "The Man Who Lived Underground," he can no longer remember his name. As the style of the book slides into a kind of nightmare surrealism, the doctors, who entrap him in a machine, discuss the possibility of shock therapy which will destroy the spaces in his life which are the source of his frustrations and of those ambiguities which seem to reside in every experience. The discussion is part medical and part historical for, as one doctor explains, the case "has been developing for some three hundred years."[34] But though effectively born again, when he escapes from those whose plans to lobotomize or castrate him have clear historical referents, he is still trapped in a white world which continues to define meaning and deny him access to a language which can adequately explain his life.

The hospital section is in fact a parodic version of slavery and Emancipation, in which selfhood and past are destroyed, in which words directed at him are meaningless, and identity seems to consist of nothing beyond the mere facts of "blackness and bewilderment and pain."[35] He plots rebellion, but concludes that "he wanted freedom not destruction," that "he could no more escape than [he] could think of his identity." Then he comes to a crucial perception: "When I discover who I am, I'll be free."[36] Immediately he is released.

Again, in a parody of Emancipation, he is tempted to stay rather than face the unknown, and then he is told that, though free, there is no work for him because he is not "prepared for work under our industrial conditions." For the hero, like the Negro after slavery, is reborn still the victim of the "vast stretch of . . .whiteness"[37] and having to spell out his personal meaning in terms of the "jumble of alphabets" which define the provisional freedom granted him by society. The hero, like the ex-slave, is released clutching his freedom papers (in this case, insurance claim forms to compensate him for his suffering) and torn by the conflicting emotions of hatred towards his manipulators and gratitude towards his emancipators. Yet, after a plunge down into the subway, he begins to see things in a new light—gaining insight below the surface. He sees through the illusions which had attracted him and which still attract others: black capitalism, the consolation of a religion based on nothing more than a fear of the real, freedom through education. He has broken through the gestalt imposed by the whites, but he still lacks any positive direction of his own. Angry words spill from his lips, but they offer no definition because he is still looking for that identity in the external world; they are words over which he admits having little control. It is this gap between the words he uses and the self which they should express which he desperately wishes to close.

As the novel develops, the "emotion-freezing ice" which had conditioned his life begins to melt. He recognizes now that even his flight to New York had been "an unconscious attempt to keep the old freezer unit going."[38] But a few drops of hot water had obtruded themselves, just as in the factory he had dropped black dope into white paint and turned it translucent. Now he begins to see through the surface of society, as his free-flowing experience brings him, through the heat of political rebellion, eventually to a clearer understanding of himself.

The first and necessary step is to come to terms with his own past, which he does symbolically by eating a hot yam, a link with his black origins which would have appalled Bledsoe, who wished to detach the young black student from his past. The protagonist's ironic observation that "I yam what I am" is a serious enough perception, though one that does not as yet become a determining principle of his life.

His first encounter, thereafter, and one which leads to his involvement with the Brotherhood (a transparent version of the Communist Party), is with a dispossessed old couple whose belongings are tumbled onto the streets by the white authorities. Together, these objects constitute a record of the black man's experience of "freedom" in America; an emblematic history consisting of a faded tintype of Abraham Lincoln, their freedom papers, "knocking bones" used in minstrel shows, a newspaper report of Marcus Garvey, an Ethiopian flag, a "dream book," and a cutting from a Hollywood magazine: eighty-seven years of frustrated hopes. These are those nodal points of time brought together, which contain a meaning which transcends that of the individual moments they record. Together, their ironies are manifest, especially spilled out across the snow-covered streets by two white "trustees" operating under the orders of a white marshal.

The protagonist is stung into action, trying at first to stop the violence which is imminent as a black crowd gathers and closes in on the white men, and then letting the irony spelled out by the old people's possessions enter his speech. Yet he does not intend to provoke the violence which ensues, so that the Brotherhood's approach to him is, from the first, based upon a misreading of the black reality which its members see only in ideological terms. Like everyone else in the story, they see only imperfectly, reshaping the world to suit their preconceptions, and seeking meaning only within the boundaries of their own invented determinisms. History becomes an implacable force, a Darwinian principle, favoring some groups, some ideas, and selecting against others. He is offered the choice of running with history or being discarded by it. But history is rigged, like the fight in which a black man had been blinded and which had taken place in the same arena where the protagonist now makes his debut as a Brotherhood spokesman.

Scientifically sculpted, history becomes detached from experience, a pattern wholly imposed from without. But the Brotherhood does offer an apparent means of possessing the past and a coherent vision of the future; it implies a rational world. Nevertheless, while submitting to party discipline, Ellison's protagonist also glimpses a central truth, not only of his own being but of history itself, a liberal conviction which was to make Ellison himself a prime target for attack by both Marxists and cultural nationalists. For he recalls a college lecture on James Joyce which placed the individual at the heart of history and cultural identity (Richard Wright recalls the same passage in "Blueprint for Negro Writing," where he uses it as a symbol of the need for black writers to "show the Negro to himself")[39]: "Stephen's problem, like ours, was not actually one of creating the uncreated conscience of his race, but of creating the *uncreated features of his face*. Our task is that of making ourselves individuals. The conscience of a race is the gift of its individuals who see, evaluate, record. . . .We create the race by creating ourselves and then to our great astonishment we will have created something far more important: We will have created a culture."[40] Yet, for the protagonist, this is a perception which stands between him and the success and identity which the Brotherhood seems to offer. Accordingly, he accepts the new identity which they present to him, bends his will to theirs, and subordinates himself to the mechanism of history as they choose to define it.

Once again he finds himself inside a machine, this time a political one, and though tempted, like Tod Clifton, to "plunge outside history,"[41] he continues to surrender to it until his literal plunge into the ahistorical world of his subterranean refuge. He continues to adjust himself to a sense of time external to his needs and his experience, the Brotherhood insisting on punctuality as rigidly as did his southern college and the northern paint factory. He wryly observes, "I am what I think I am,"[42] and struggles to reach the top by "climbing a mountain of words,"[43] by learning the language of the new power as his ancestors had learned the language of the old. Indeed, as he waits to make his first appearance for the Brotherhood, his mind traces and retraces over his past. Time is no longer reassuringly sequential. The various clocks in the narrative run at different rates. Time, and hence history, and hence identity, are thus, in his mind, not rational constructs; and the meaning of his own life is concentrated in these nodal experiences, as the history of his race had been in the scattered objects of the dispossessed couple.

The book thus stands as a warning against the appropriation of meaning through the surrender of freedom. Control of the past is secured only by a sacrifice of the present. It is a warning against "reading" experience only through the distorting lens of materialist ideology, a reductive symbolism stemming from a need to contain disorder and exert discipline in an unruly natural world. As he says: "I lived with the intensity displayed by those chronic numbers players who see clues to their future in the most minute and insignificant phenomena: in clouds, in passing trucks and subway cars, in dreams, comic-strips, the shape of dog-luck fouled on the pavements. I was dominated by the all-embracing idea of the Brotherhood. The organization had given the world a new shape, and me a vital role. We recognized no loose ends, everything could be controlled by our science. Life was all pattern and discipline."[44]

But the death of Tod Clifton at the hands of a white policeman brings him to a realization that history itself is a fiction, an expression of the need for order rather than an expression of order itself: "History records the patterns of men's lives, they say. . . . All things . . . are duly recorded. . . . But not quite, for actually it is only the known, the seen, the heard and only those events that the recorder regards as important . . . are put down, those lies his keepers keep their power by. But the cop would be Clifton's historian, his judge, his witness and his executioner."[45] This is the history which he had tried to inhabit—a fiction, a conspiracy, offering a seductive sense of order at the cost of truth and meaning, at the price of identity.

The demands of the real, of a self-justifying pragmatism and a self-serving power elite, are revealed as simply a fiction which assumes the appearance of the real by virtue of social sanctions. It is a myth which has captured and subordinated the black man more effectively than the reality of power, because it has the authority of an imagination yearning to make some sense of social and metaphysical indignities. Those who control history have the power to define it. And now, with the death of Clifton, the protagonist begins to think that his very historical invisibility, the fact that he and other blacks live life at a tangent to the supposedly closed world of historical time, might prove their own and society's salvation: "By all historical logic we, I, should have disappeared around the first part of the nineteenth century, rationalized out of existence."[46] They are the last representatives of a world whose rhythms are determined by human and not industrial cycles; they are individuals resisting that surrender of the self which seems a prerequisite for survival in a material world bereft of transcendent values (when Tod dies, the cause of death is given by the narrator as "resisting reality"). Yet, if history is indeed fiction, Ellison does not push this perception to the logical limits explored by Pynchon, Coover, or Kosinski. For where they see a relativism which breeds only irony, an irony which reaches out to include the fiction which contains it, Ellison is drawn to a liberal model in which the individual invents himself through his dialogue with society. Yet he is not unaware of the danger of countering one fiction with another. If language is by turns disturbingly plastic and alarmingly coercive, the writer himself is alternately the source of deceit and a prime example of the authoritarian spirit. His only recourse is either a metafictive confession of complicity with the forces which he indicts, or an assertion that, whatever its complexities and willful deceptions, the alliance between writer and reader constitutes a valid model for the kind of social contract which relies on the reality and moral necessity of the drive for communication and meaning, but not on its facility or completeness. As he has said, "The main task of the Negro people is to work unceasingly toward creating those democratic conditions in which he can live and recreate himself." And such an attitude implied that "moral responsibility for democracy" which Ellison saw as "the chief significance of *Invisible Man*" and as the painful but inescapable inheritance of the individual.[47]

Clearly, the risk of stepping outside of time is embodied in the figure of Rinehart, for whom there is no reality, only a series of possibilities. His world is without boundaries—fluid, anarchic, invisible by virtue of his infinite number of masks; antinomian, plastic, absurd. But, nonetheless, he offers a clue to the protagonist who comes to feel that the meaning of his life lies, not in adjusting himself to the models offered to him by other people, but in the authenticity and defining power of his own actions, in the experiences of his life, drawn together, like the belongings of the dispossessed couple, and seen as the real history of his selfhood. It is, in other words, an existential conclusion: "I saw that they were more than separate experiences. They were me; they defined me. I was my experiences and my experiences were me."[48] Tod Clifton, selling black Sambo puppets on the streets of Harlem, had simply been confessing to his own manipulation. He became an emblem of his own surrender of self, and his death thus stood as a correlative, a logical extension, of self-abnegation. So, too, the protagonist realizes the fallacy of what he takes to have been the meaning of his grandfather's advice, as he appreciates that "by pretending to agree I *had* indeed agreed."[49] The result of following this advice is the chaos of the race riot, an apocalypse in which black and white fight to retain their hold on an ordered world by destroying one another. But the real absurdity lies deeper than social manipulation.

All are fatally illusioned. The only affirmation he can contemplate is of the principle on which the country had been built and which had thereafter been systematically compromised. This is the point of the references to the protagonist's connection with the nineteenth century, for Ellison, who formerly taught a course on "Democracy and Literature" at New York University, is convinced that "the moral imperatives of American life that are implicit in the Declaration of Independence, the Constitution, and the Bill of Rights were a part of both the individual consciousness and the conscience,"[50] of the nineteenth-century American writer and the nineteenth-century mind. The only form of transcendence for the protagonist thus lies in the values which he has seen abrogated by whites and those blacks who had felt that their own destiny lay in affirming power rather than principle. As he waits in his cellar, he realizes the necessity to endorse these values, for without them, there is no moral universe to invoke, nothing but an absurdist world. The irony is that such an affirmation necessarily makes the individual responsibile even for those who have abused him. Thus, the Negro becomes, not merely the test of American liberal principles, but their repository.

Those principles involve possibility, freedom. The problem, as ever, is to avoid the straight jacket of ideology, restrictive myths, and scientific positivism on the one hand, and the anarchic, formless absurdity of pure relativism on the other. Thus, the border territory is precisely the area where meaning coheres. Tension is meaning; tension between the self and society, between rigidity and fluidity, between an external and an internal world. The diversity which he had feared, he now embraces. Where once he had wished to be white, feeling that this was the only reality, he now comes to feel that "America is woven of many strands," as is reality itself. The American motto becomes a central strategy for survival: "Our fate is to become one, and yet many,"[51] while the real struggle, he comes to feel, is not against other people but against determinism and especially against the final determinism of death.

And the act of writing, for all its admitted ironies, becomes a part of that resistance and an expression of the commitment to others, to society, which the protagonist now professes. The book is itself a public gesture, and its publication stands as evidence of the hero's reemergence into the world and his belief in the efficacy of communication.

If it is the job of fiction to convert experience into symbolic action, then identity itself is rendered by a similar process, as, on a broader scale, is a culture. So the process of creating literature, creating a self, and creating a culture involve the same act of imaginative appropriation. And this perception lies at the heart of *Invisible Man*, which, itself, constitutes an act of definition in private and public terms. Ellison has said that "consciousness and conscience are the burdens imposed upon us by the American experiment,"[52] and the process of his novel lies precisely in the growing acceptance of that burden by its protagonist. But in that acceptance, he simultaneously lays claim to a culture which he had thought external to himself and which had, anyway, largely abandoned its own moral task.

When Ellison says that, for him, learning to write was "a struggle to stare down the deadly and hypnotic temptation to interpret the world and all its devices in terms of race,"[53] he does not mean that he wants to transcend race, but that he wishes to break out of the symbols generated by others. *Invisible Man*, like *Moby Dick*, is a warning against capitulation to other people's symbolic reading of the world. For Ellison, throughout history the Negro has been America's metaphor only to the extent that he has been forced to play a required role, to accept a reduced version of his identity and his potential for action. Specifically, he has been made to function as an image of sensuality, deprivation, violence, spontaneity, revolution, submissiveness, cunning—

whatever serves the interests of those who recast him in the form most useful to their own psychic, social, or sexual needs. "I am invisible," announces the narrator-protagonist, because "when people approach me they see only my surroundings, themselves, or figments of their imagination."[54]

To be an American Negro is a complex destiny, and it is that complexity which Ellison wishes to confront. Ellison believes reality to exist (as opposed to history, which is simply a version of that reality), but he also believes it to be various. The problem of the writer is to render complexity in a form which is inescapably reductive. For writing necessarily renders down spontaneity, simultaneity, the contingent, the complex, into immutable order, sequential narrative, purposeful action, and the analagous image. Yet, if its ineluctable distillation of order out of chaos constitutes a potential distortion, it also mimics what Ellison has described as "the triumph of the human spirit over chaos."[55] Indeed, for Ellison, the writer's role is fundamentally a moral one. His duty "is that of preserving in art those human values which can endure by confronting change,"[56] and though he is not unaware that to transform pain into aesthetic form is at best an ambiguous gesture, he does render that pain into a form in which it may be perceived as a moral reality as well as a social fact. The writer's struggle with form is a displaced version of the individual's struggle with experience, and, in the case of *Invisible Man*, the book itself (presumed to be written by the protagonist) is generated by the shifting perception of the hero and by the disintegration of the social world which he had thought to be so solid and assured.

But if, on a pre-thematic level, the very fact of the novel implies that mediation between the individual and the society which gave birth to it, which Ellison still sees as the prime function as well as the subject of art, the self-doubt of the writer is also available within the text. Ellison has said that "the novel constitutes a portrait of the artist as a rabble-rouser,"[57] and certainly the protagonist is at his most unreliable when he makes speeches, just as everything written down in the novel is either false or ironic. And the author is, of course, the speechmaker par excellence, while Ellison takes pains to indicate that even the advocacy of freedom may imply coersion. But that dilemma is a familiar enough liberal paradox. The writer cannot help but create the experience which he describes, and Ellison accepts that responsibility, which he sees as putting him in that tradition of American writing which was, with some exceptions, interrupted by the amoral scientism of naturalism and those formal concerns of modernism which had led the writer to declare a separate peace from society and from the moral issues which had animated works like *Moby Dick* and *Huckleberry Finn*.

Thus, he offers himself as an American writer whose subject matter happens to be the Negro. Indeed, *Invisible Man* is a projection of a process which is at the heart of both the black experience and American culture; the need to create a self outside the defining structures of ideology and social imperatives and in the face of an attractive antinomianism. Tempted equally, like Huckleberry Finn and Leatherstocking, by the comforting certainties of the public world and by the moral anarchy of a self wholly free of social responsibility, Ellison's protagonist, like them, has to forge an identity out of an acceptance of the past and a projection of those moral values which will permit the individual to conceive of a socially responsible self.

Ellison has, indeed, always been at pains to locate his novel in the context of American moral writing, a literature which has engaged the diversity of American life, the fluidity of its social forms, and the openness of its issues debated through the encounter of the individual with that variegated reality. With the exception of Faulkner, he sees this as essentially a product of preindustrial America. In the twentieth century, the writer had either become obsessed with factuality as a defining force or with opposing the patterns of art to those of the social world. Nineteenth-century writers, by contrast, ''took a much greater responsibility for the condition of democracy and, indeed, their works were imaginative projections of the conflict within the human heart which arose when the sacred principles of the Constitution and the Bill of Rights clashed with the practical exigencies of human greed and fear, hate and love.'' His view was essentially that of Langston Hughes's poem: ''Let America be America again, / Let it be the dream it used to be, / Let it be the pioneer in the plain, / Seeking a home where he himself is free.''[58] As he explained when he was presented with the National Book Award in 1953, it was no wonder that he should be attracted to such writing because his fate as a Negro and as an individual was intimately connected with the application of those principles. Moreover, as he recognized in using a quotation from Melville's ''Benito Cereno'' as the epigraph of his novel, the Negro had, anyway, cast a long shadow over American history, providing an ironic reminder of the animating principles of that society and representing, he suggested, in a phrase with obvious relevance to his own novel, ''the mysterious underground aspect of human personality.''[59] It is that inner world which Melville and Twain dramatized. The Negro became the image of submerged truths which held the key to individual and national identity. The image is a compound of the black slave described by Crevecoeur, left to die in a cage, his eyes picked out and his flesh lacerated, and the black rebel of ''Benito Cereno,'' who had reduced the white man to a similarly sightless skull. It is this moral potential which Ellison examines in a book in which the plunge down into the cellar at the end of the book is in fact a descent into the psyche in order to face the demons of the self and of history.

And since, for Ellison, the function of moral literature is to celebrate life, he found himself at odds with what he took to be the dangerous reductivism of *Native Son*, a response no doubt sharpened by Irving Howe's unfavorable comparison of *Invisible Man* with the naturalistic drive of Wright's novel. For Ellison, the imaginative enterprise involves more than an engagement with the texture and substance of social reality; it implies a familiarity with, and a conscious learning from, writers who have confronted the task of dramatizing the individual's collison with history, myth, and social fact in other contexts than that of racial relations. Ellison's argument with Howe is only partly a discussion of the function of writing. Mostly, it is Ellison's attempt to resist co-option into an image of the black writer that is too restrictive.

If Richard Wright and Langston Hughes were, by virtue of their color, literary relatives, then Hemingway and Eliot were ancestors. Racial kinship was not a matter of choice; literary influence was. His value, he feels, is as an artist and not as a spokesman, though his own convictions may make such a distinction difficult to sustain. The act of transcendence is the essence of artistic creation; to see it in social terms, as an evasion of the conditions which give rise to it, is to misunderstand the nature of art. It is not that the writer has no responsibility towards the realities which provoke his work, but that that responsibility may be most appropriately expressed in their imaginative transcendence. As he said, he was released from the "segregated" idea of human possibility, not by the propagandist or by the example of Richard Wright, but by the example of writers and composers whose works, which "by fulfilling themselves as works of art, by being satisfied to deal with life in terms of their own sources of power, were able to give me a broader sense of life and possibility. Indeed," he added, "I understood a bit more about myself as Negro because literature has taught me something of my identity as Western man, as political being."[60] When Western man came to be seen as the enemy of emergent African nationalism and of black cultural myths, it was no wonder that Ellison should also have been made into an enemy of the new black aesthetic.

In the immediate mood of the early 1950s, Ellison seemed squarely in the spirit of the Negro's aspirations to break out of restrictive racial stereotypes. But within a decade, the mood changed abruptly. In the late 1960s, a phrase like "the sacred principles of the Constitution" seemed to ring with an irony too obvious for the kind of oblique critique offered by Ellison. And, despite the calmer mood of the 1970s, Addison Gayle, Jr., writing in 1975, could still object that his "art was simply a celebration of the racial acquiescence of its author." The flaw, for Gayle, lies in the fact that "when he might leave his underground sanctuary and emerge as a black man. . .Ellison's protagonist chooses death over life, opts for non-creativity in favour of creativity, chooses the path of individualism instead of racial unity."[61] This is not simply a failure to perceive the actual reemergence of the protagonist at the end of the novel, his decision to accept the implications of his simultaneous existence as individual and social animal, it is a positive assertion that personal and public identity are racially based; that race is not a particular circumstance, one mark of social exclusion. It is the source of meaning. For Ellison, such a view is inimical to his beliefs and to the thrust of the novel. To claim that the ending is a flaw in a work which otherwise celebrates the resources of black heroism is a simple failure to understand the moral purpose of the book. If the protagonist had left his cellar only as a black man, how would he have been distinguishable from those at whose hands he had suffered and who likewise see the word only in racial terms? The moral world, Ellison implies, operates subcutaneously. Ellison's hero does not deny his blackness; indeed, a crucial stage is reached when he can embrace all aspects of his black past—its humiliations as well as its triumphs. He leaves the cellar, therefore, with a new understanding of himself, but determined not to be trapped in any system. When Gayle says that he should have emerged as a black man, he implies a clearly defined version of blackness which is itself simply another prescriptive version of cultural identity. To be black is to demonstrate certain definable characteristics. It is to be a rebel, to eschew white cultural and political forms; it is to assert a whole panoply of agreed opinions, to act according to a new model of revolutionary orthodoxy. But, if Ellison's protagonist has learned anything, it is to avoid becoming ensnared in such determinisms.

Ellison is all too aware that the question of naming lies at the heart of American writing. From Cooper's Deerslayer, defining and redefining himself as his identity is slowly built up by choices made and deeds done, through to Arthur Miller's heroes, calling out their names against urban anonymity or the aggressions of society, the question of clinging to a clear notion of self has lain at the heart of the American endeavor. And from the beginning, the act of individual definition was unavoidably linked to the question of national identity. Ellison has said that "it is through our names that we first place ourselves in the world. Our names, being the gift of others, must be made our own."[62] Much the same could be said of America, which had to be repossessed not only from its original inhabitants, but also from the myths from which it emerged. The parallel between this process and that whereby Father Divine's and Elijah Muhammad's followers rejected their "slave names" is clear. They, too, were defining a self and a nation simultaneously. In *Invisible Man*, therefore, the process whereby the individual moves towards possession of himself is precisely that act of cultural definition for which Addison Gayle, Jr., had called, but which he was unable to recognize for what it was. He is anonymous throughout, not because he has no identity, but because he fails to perceive in the experiences through which he passes the material out of which that self is forged. But for Ellison, the self, like America, is essentially pluralistic. Nor can it function outside of the cultural context which is a part of its meaning.

And Ellison finds his model as surely in the world of black music as he does in white literature. Indeed, he sees in black music precisely that act of pure social balance which his namesake, Ralph Waldo Emerson, had advocated. "The delicate balance struck between strong individual personality and the group during these early jam sessions was a marvel of social organization, I had learned too that the end of all this discipline and technical mastery was the desire to express an affirmative way of life through its musical tradition and that this tradition insisted that each artist achieve his creativity within its frame . . .and when they expressed their attitude toward the world it was with a fluid style that reduced the chaos of living to form.''[63] What better description could there be both of the narrative strategy and the cultural philosophy which lies at the heart of his novel? It is precisely through an acceptance of the past, through the generation of a fluid personal style, and through the acceptance of the fact that individual identity operates in a social context that the anonymous protagonist is able to survive and prevail.

But, musically, Ellison regards himself as being heir both to a classical and a black musical tradition. And, as he resists attempts to separate those traditions in music, attacking a writer like LeRoi Jones for doing so in *Blues People*, so he does in literature. Technique, he insists, is the key to creative freedom for the musician, the writer, and the individual faced with imposing his own patterns on experience. For the true synthesis of cultural tensions lies in the sensibility of the individual.

Ellison, in other words, is asserting with Sartre that ''we . . .in the very depths of historical relativity and our own insignificance are abso-lutes . . .and our choice of ourselves is an absolute,'' and that the inter-relationship between these selves is the real stuff of history and the real nature of time. ''All the vital and passionate choices that we are and that we are constantly making with or against other people . . .all the bonds of love and hate that unite us with each other and that exist only in so far as we feel them . . .this whole discordant and harmonious life combines to create a new absolute which I like to call *time*. This time is intersubjectivity, the living absolute, the dialectical wrong side of history.''[64] For Sartre, as for Ellison, art ''is a meditation on life, not on death,'' so that the judgments of history matter less than those of his own time for, as he says, using a conceit which anticipates Ellison's own, ''I have not yet entered history, and I do not know how I will enter it.''[65] For Sartre, history is the future which he will not live to see; for Ellison, it is the present that he must learn to forge out of intersubjec-tivity. But for both, the work of art is itself a gesture of intersubjectivity since, in Sartre's words, ''to read a book is to re-write it,'' and time thus becomes, not the process defined by history or scientific rationalism, but the imaginative moment of communication. The novel crushes time and meaning into its own arabesques of thought.

Historically, it has been the Negro's experience in America to be treated as an object, available for sale or lease, directed to specific physical locations, employed, largely, in mechanical roles, required to conform to specification. The story of the individual has been one of resistance to that state—it is an existential resistance to objectivization. Like the hero of Camus's *The Stranger*, Ellison's protagonist has no real subjectivity. He, like the briefcase which he carries with him, contains versions of reality having no real connection with his own needs. In a material world, he is himself an object bearing the impress of social and ideological forces. He looks for meaning in style, in modes of response spun out of history as simple process—what Ellison in speaking of Hemingway called "a morality of technique."[66] What is lacking is any distance between himself and process; he lacks perspective, vision, an awareness of the fragility and contingency of the world to which he surrenders his authority. And this understanding comes to him only when he drops through the surface into his cellar, when he realizes that what he had taken to be solid was, in fact, hollow. This plunge into subjectivity leads him to recognize the provisional nature of those realities which he had taken to be so substantial, and leads him to the resolution with which the book ends—the resolution to reemerge and accept the resultant responsibility and guilt which stem from an acceptance of responsibility for one's own actions.

Paul Tillich, in *The Courage To Be*, interprets Heidegger's concept *Entschlossenheit* (resolve) as a "symbol of unlocking what anxiety, subjection to conformity, and self-seclusion have locked," and asserts that "once it is unlocked, one can act but not according to norms given by anyone or anything" for "nobody can give directions for the actions of the 'resolute' individual. . . .*We* must be ourselves, we must decide where to go. Our conscience is the call to ourselves. . . .It calls us to ourselves out of . . .the adjustment which is the main principle of the conformist." But, "having the courage to be as ourselves we become guilty, and we are asked to take this existential guilt upon ourselves."[67] And it is in this sense that Ellison suggests that the protagonist of the novel is responsible for his own near-destruction. His final realization that the essense of man is his existence places him back in control of his own destiny, but also makes him responsible for the world into which he must reemerge. And his first act, we are to presume, is the publication of the book which recounts his progress towards that sense of responsibility to self and others, of which the book itself is primary evidence. Ellison leaves his protagonist with the familiar two-term dialectic of American writing, the simultaneous assertion of individualism and an unavoidable social duty, and with the problematics of language which are the source of the protagonist's dilemma and, in many ways, the subject of the book.

The Divided Mind of
James Baldwin

4

Baldwin is a man who spent the first part of his career compensating for his deprivation and the second part compensating for his success. He sought invisibility in racial terms by going to Paris and ended up by becoming the most visible black writer of his generation. His career was, in part, generated by the rise of the civil rights movement, as white America looked for an explanation for the crisis which had apparently arrived so suddenly; and it was eventually threatened by that movement, which, in time, produced demands for racial and aesthetic orthodoxy which left him stranded in his equivocal role as mediator and prophet, when the dominant model for black art became fierce commitment and cultural separatism. Having fled a role as writer and individual which was determined by the color of his skin, he discovered that that color was, in fact, to be the key to his art. Wishing to dispense early with the obligation to act as spokesman, he came to recognize a responsibility to articulate, if not the demands, then the feelings of those whose own frustrations and courage were otherwise expressed in mute suffering or simple action. What Baldwin has become, he once traveled four thousand miles not to be.

And both the act of refusal and the ultimate acceptance are characteristic gestures of a writer who has always been drawn in two apparently mutually incompatible directions. It was not simply that his early faith in the moral responsibility of the individual and the possibility of social change was destroyed, though he has said as much: "There was a time in my life not so very long ago that I believed, hoped . . .that this country could become what it has always presented as what it wanted to become. But I'm sorry, no matter how this may sound: when Martin was murdered for me that hope ended."[1] It is that from the very beginning the optative mood had been in battle with a historical determinism. Catonian warnings in his work have alternated with expressions of sensual salvation. His has, indeed, always been a schizophrenic style, as he has in turn presented himself as suffering black and alienated American, social outcast and native son. It is a rhetorical style which, at its best, captured the cadences of hope and rebellion which characterized the early days of the civil rights movement, and which, at its worst, degenerated into unashamed posturing of a kind which failed to inspect with genuine moral honesty the realities he had once exposed with such authority. He was a crucial figure in the Second Renaissance. His polemical essays dramatized the moralism of the civil rights movement; his novels, with the notable exception of *Giovanni's Room*, attempted to inspect the relationship between racial identity and social role. He was, for many, the most visible symbol of black resurgence. But in time, he also became a paradigm, for some black writers (most notably LeRoi Jones), of the black writer who looked primarily to a white audience, who regarded with suspicion the more forthright examples of black assertiveness, and who, hence, should no longer be regarded in any meaningful sense as being black. He was, however, never as simple as such an accusation would imply. Indeed, he sought to make a virtue of the conflicting pressures operative in his life and work, regarding them as exemplary. In part, he was justified in such a suggestion, but in part he was rationalizing a lack of intellectual rigor which became progressively more disabling.

For Baldwin, the self is sometimes a series of improvisational gestures and sometimes a moral constant which has only to be exposed to become operative. And there is at the heart of his work, beneath the level of contingent event and social determinant, an unexamined confidence in the possibility of action and the recovery of ethical purpose. Constraints are arbitrary and irrational; hatred and rage the products of a history which is real but capable of transcendence. Though assailed from within and without by a corrosive mythology, he suggests that the individual consciousness contains resources entirely adequate to the task of distilling meaning from social chaos, while the alliance of consciousnesses provides the principal means of resisting an isolation which is part social and part metaphysical.

At the heart of his own work is a Christian belief that grace is a gift of suffering and that love has the power to annihilate the primal space between the self and its perception of itself, between the individual and the group. Racial and national categories, though real and though reflecting a symbolic heritage, exist to be transcended, for he is convinced that society clings so desperately to rigid definitions—sexual and social—more from a need to project a sense of order than from a belief that such distinctions contain any real clue to the nature of human possibilities. The Negro, in fact, is in large part a fiction, a convenient hierarchical invention. As an emblem of unrepresssed needs and of uninhibited sexuality, he becomes a convenient image of the dark, spontaneous, and anarchic dimension of human life.* His social subordination thus stands as a symbol of society's control over its own anarchic impulses. As a consequence, he is offered a role whose significance is not limited to its social utility. Thus, when he resists that caricature, the consequent appeals by the dominant society to "law and order" have metaphysical as well as pragmatic implications.

---

*For an historical account of white views of Negro sexuality, see Winthrop D. Jordan, *White Over Black: American Attitudes Toward the Negro, 1550-1812* (New York, 1968).

In Baldwin's work, the self resists the peripheral role which seems its social fate, and the primary agent in this resistance is the imagination. It is an imagination with the necessary power to project alternative worlds, to conceive of a society which can escape its own myths and consciously break its own taboos. The communicative act involved in art (virtually all of his protagonists are artists of one kind or another, including musicians, actors, and novelists) becomes in itself a paradigm of a desired social interaction, while the individual's imposition of order, implied by the creative act, becomes a model for a coherence which is generated by the sensibility and not imposed by social fiat. And this presumption of an imaginative control of the world necessarily implies a rejection of that religion which historically has proved a secondary means of social control. Rejection of God is a natural extension of rebellion against the power of the state.

There is a demonstrable logic of revolt. The creation of an autonomous self relies, first, on a rejection of the authority of the father (his personal revolt against his father recurs in his work) and, then, the authority of white society and of God. The self emerges, in a familiar liberal way, by a slow rejection of elements extraneous to that self. Such a process frequently involves pain, and Baldwin remains enough of a puritan to believe that this is a key to truth. But salvation, paradoxically, lies in a leap from belief into scepticism. Baldwin replaces the authority of social and metaphysical dictat with an authority of the sensibility. Faith gives way to a secular belief in the authenticating power of the self.

Baldwin's characters are highly self-conscious, reflecting not only upon their social situation, but on the nature of their consciousness itself. The question of identity is constantly presented to them; indeed, it is often a clue to literal survival. So it becomes in itself a literary event. And the particular problem which confronts them is that the usual strategems of definition now fail. History, memory, and belief are at odds with the drive for self-creation and the need for personal alliances which can deny the reality of boundaries. Thus, his characters tend to adopt an ambiguous stance with regard to time, appropriating to themselves the right to define process and resist versions of historical progress which threaten to subordinate them to an alien logic.

His use of the internal monologue itself implies the existence of a resistant self which is apart from and not contained by the externalities which otherwise seem to define the limits of action and character. This is the functioning imagination, the artist within, which creates even as it analyzes. His are not novels primarily concerned with social change in the sense of a reallocation of power; what matters to him is the altered consciousness of the individual. He is interested in process, in the interplay between the experiential and the given. The stream of consciousness becomes an image for the flow of experience and responses which provide the basis for a definition of the self. And, in a sense, one can find in William James's discussion of the stream of consciousness a justification for Baldwin's attempt to have his cake and eat it: his feeling that the self is both its own creation and an existent fact which has merely to be exposed to another level of consciousness. In *The Principles of Psychology*, William James says that ''if the stream as a whole is identified with the self far more than any outward thing, *a certain portion of the stream abstracted from the rest* is so identified in an altogether peculiar degree, and is felt by all men as a sort of innermost centre within the circle, of sanctuary within the citadel constituted by the subjective life as a whole.''[2] For Baldwin, this is less a spiritual essence than a sense of moral certainty, an intimate reality available to the individual who learns the necessity to engage experience with a sensibility undistorted by social presumptions.

The problem Baldwin fails to engage is precisely how that integrity of the self can be projected onto a social scale; why the withdrawal into love should be seen as an adequate model for social action since it is frequently born out of a denial of that social action. This is something which he largely leaves to his essays. Baldwin can dramatize the moment and even the process which results in that moment; but he is, for the most part, unable to sustain that moment to the point at which it becomes an enabling strategy. The impersonal power which limits individuality seems too immune to such epiphanies to grant anything but momentary release from its definitional authority.

For Norman Mailer, the world can be made over by the personality, which can counterpose its own energies to that of society and which can release a neutralizing flood of language which, in effect, reduces the physical world to the status of backdrop: the subject of the drama is the self, the social world exists only insofar as the individual is prepared to grant it a role. Personal history becomes as authentic as public history. But for Baldwin, history cannot be shrugged off with such a casual gesture. His lack of social freedom as a Negro contrasts markedly with that of a man who can seriously run for the office of Mayor of New York City and who apparently has a kind of romantic faith in the fact that social forms are plastic enough to be molded by the sheer power of the will. As Baldwin has never tired of telling people, the black American knows otherwise. He is all too aware of the injunctions, written and unwritten, which spell out the limits of his freedom; to cross those boundaries is to risk a reaction which is real in the sense of Dr. Johnson's definition of the term. Yet, in fact, he himself was tempted by solutions every bit as romantic as those advanced by Mailer, and his commitment to invoke the sinister lessons of history is always balanced by a contrary faith in a grace which can dissolve such determinism.

In his attack on Baldwin in *Advertisements for Myself*, Mailer accused him of not being able to say ''fuck you'' to the reader. It was an even more naive remark than it seemed in that it failed to recognize that sense of oppression from which Mailer was immune but which had led Baldwin to be a writer; it also failed to recognize that all of Baldwin's work was in effect an attempt to discover a basis on which such a contemptuous dismissal of society could be effectuated, while longing, as LeRoi Jones and Eldridge Cleaver cruelly pointed out, for precisely that gesture of inclusion which would obviate such a response.

For Baldwin, will, crucially allied with imagination and a sensitivity to the pressure of other selves, becomes a force with the power, if not to overcome social realities, then to forge alliances other than those sanctioned by history and power. But this is not quite the confident self of the transcendentalists. In each of his books, self-analysis is not only provoked by pain; it is the source of pain. Society's power is scarcely diminished. The most that the individual can hope for is to win a small psychic territory within which the harsh pragmatics of the public world no longer operate. Nor is love quite the panacea which it appears, for it, too, is infected by materialism, by the urge to power, and by the demands of history and myth. And though, as suggested above, Baldwin is never clear as to whether identity is laboriously constructed out of the interplay of sensibility and event or whether it is a resilient moral principle concealed beneath social habiliments, in neither sense is he confident of its ability to command public acquiescence. (And this, of course is the source of the pressure which led him to social protest outside of his novels. As a public spokesman, he sought to provoke changes which would allow greater space for the self which, as a novelist, he felt was the real agent of transformation.)

Like Emerson and Thoreau, he felt the need to resist those conventions and beliefs which passed for an adequate description of the real, in favor of a spiritual self-reliance limited only by its obligations to remake the public world, whose deceptions and inadequacies were rejected not in the name of privatism but of truth. But Baldwin inhabits a more skeptical world, and his racial identity is forced to concede more power to social fictions than did the New England moralist.

In a sense, of course, America has always prided itself on its improvisational qualities; and, in his essays, Baldwin has repeatedly insisted on the parallel between the Negro in search of selfhood and the American intent on distilling a national identity. And he was clearly right in insisting on his Americanness. It is stamped on his imaginative enterprise. But the fluidities of the American system have historically not extended to the Negro. Where everything else has changed, to Baldwin, this, at least, has remained a constant. And in this respect, the experience of black and white is dissimilar. Certainly the irony of Baldwin claiming an America heritage at the moment when facilities in southern towns, which he himself was not to visit until his early thirties, were still segregated, was not lost on his critics. Yet Baldwin's view was that though American identity and history had indeed been built on a denial of human complexity and freedom, this was a denial of an essential American idealism to which he wished to lay claim. His resistance to protest fiction and, implicitly, to the naturalistic novel lay precisely in the fact that it denied access to this idealism, that it made the self into a simple product of biological and environmental determinism. It denied the possibility of escape. And that, arguably, is at the heart of Baldwin's work; the need to forge a truce with determinism and with punishing social constraints, a truce which can sustain the individual even, perhaps, in the face of the knowledge of its inevitable collapse. The escape to Europe is simply an attempt to create geographically that space for maneuver which, in America, has to be won through an exertion of imagination or will.

But the ironies emanating from his American identity were not simply those contained in the obvious dissonance between American idealism and reality. As he, himself, fully realized, his very articulateness is itself fraught with ambiguities which seem to nail him permanently to a paradoxical view of self and cultural identity. Indeed, Baldwin has always been aware of the special problem of language for the black writer. "It is quite possible to say that the price the Negro pays for becoming articulate is to find himself, at length, with nothing to be articulate about."[3] The word becomes a barrier, indeed a protection, between the self and experience. The reduction of social event to language becomes in itself a form of escape. Initially, experience intervenes between the self and the articulation of that experience, but, in turn, language intervenes between the self and the experience. He is crushed from two directions. It was not for nothing that Stokely Carmichael used to introduce his speeches with a quotation from Lewis Caroll: " 'When I use a word,' Humpty Dumpty said in a rather scornful tone, 'it means just what I choose it to mean—neither more nor less.' 'The question is,' said Alice, 'whether you can make words mean so may different things.' 'The question is, 'said Humpty Dumpty, 'which is to be master—that's all.' "[4] The right to define logically implies mastery.

"The root function of language," Baldwin suggests, "is to control the universe by describing it."[5] But the black finds that access to language is not access to power, to control over his environment, or to himself. Language becomes dysfunctional. Historically, of course, it betrayed him more fully into the power of those who sought to control him by offering means to effectuate that control. And once in possession of that language, he becomes, perforce, heir to those very cultural presumptions to which he is formally denied free access. In turn, he is then blessed or fated with a fluency which draws him steadily away from his own past. He is thus left with a cultural inheritance characterized by ambiguity, self-doubt, and linguistic paradox. And Baldwin's work carries this mark. The personal pronoun, as he applies it, means sometimes Negro and sometimes American, a pronominal uncertainty which goes to the heart of that concern with identity which characterizes so many of his essays and so much of his work. And when he assumes an identification with his American self against his racial identity, the effect is more than ambivalent. For the cultural nationalists of the 1960s, his assertion that "our dehumanization of the Negro . . . is indivisible from our dehumanization of ourselves: the loss of our identity is the price we pay for our annulment of his,"[6] is an expression of a desire for cultural assimilation which goes beyond a rhetorical device.

His rhetorical style, particularly in the latter part of his career, is, in fact, a product of the battle to enforce his authority over language, to make it accommodate itself to an experience which it had been designed to justify and impose. As he put it, "You've simply got to force the language to pay attention to you in order to exist in it."[7] The central problem, as he explained to Margaret Mead in 1970, was "how are we ever going to achieve some kind of language which will make my experience articulate to you and yours to me? Because you and I have been involved for all our lives . . .in some effort of translation."[8]

Protest was implied in Baldwin's stance as an essayist. He was indeed a mediator, explaining the Negro to America by translating his experience into American terms, by establishing his own struggle for identity as of a kind with that of the American, anxious to distill meaning from history and experience. Like Ellison, he is essentially calling for the restoration of American idealism, and he sees the route to that as lying through the individual: "And honest examination of the national life proves how far we are from the standard of human freedom with which we began. The recovery of this standard demands of everyone who loves this country a hard look at himself, for the greatest achievements must begin somewhere, and they always begin with the person."[9]

His trip to Paris was an American search for personal and national identity in an Old World which could render up an image of the New, partly from its own desire to translate promise and threat into concrete form and partly from its own ability to conceive of an America luminous with a meaning derived from those very contradictions which the American writer frequently found so disabling. In part, of course, it was the old game of discovering the limits of the self by abstracting it from the viscous world of its daily setting; it was an attempt to see what could survive such spiritual surgery—an act of definition by elimination, an attempt to find which conflicts were internal and definitional and which were part of a dialectic between the unexamined self and the social projections of that self. For a black American, it afforded the only opportunity to venture outside of the myth which defined him and, in a curious way, protected him, insofar as it offered a self-image requiring only acceptance. Here, as Baldwin knew, he would be judged for himself, or at least in the context of compulsions other than the familiar ones. Yet it was as an American that he found himself responding; it was as an American that Europeans perceived him. And what he learned was the impossibility of distinguishing a clear line between the self and the culture in which that self develops. Once in Europe, he felt as "American as any Texas G.I.," freed from the necessary reflexes which had once concealed his own identity from others and hence, eventually, from himself.

It was a move which sprang from the conviction that neither an unquestioned community of suffering nor an assumed American homogeneity offered a real clue to personal meaning. Baldwin "wanted to find out in what way the *specialness''* of his ''experience could be made to connect'' him ''with other people instead of dividing''[10] him from them. And that specialness could only be abstracted by removing himself from a culture whose definitions of him sprang from compulsions shaped partly by history and partly by the pressure of a perverted puritanism and a hermeneutic of suffering and guilt.

''Everybody's Protest Novel'' was less concerned with a necessary assault on a major icon of black literature than it was an expression of his desire to resist the role which he could feel being pressed upon him. To be a Negro writer was to be reduced to a socio-literary category. His subject was not just himself, in the sense that it always is for a writer, it was himself *as Negro*. And his assault on the protest novel was an attempt to create sufficient space for himself to operate outside of the terms which it seemed his fate to embrace. As he said in the introduction to his first book of essays, ''I have not written about being a Negro at such length because I expect that to be my only subject, but only because it was the gate I had to unlock before I could hope to write about anything else.''[11] At the beginning of his career, already writing his first novel, he felt the need to establish his own right to be seen outside the terms which seemed to mark the limits prescribed for the black novelist by white society, on the one hand, and by the moral demands of black suffering, on the other.

He reacted against Bigger Thomas, he admitted, partly because he seemed to represent a possibility which had to be rejected if he was to escape a self-destructive rage. In an early story, called ''Previous Condition'' published in 1948, he displaces this violence into the imagination of his protagonist, ''I wanted to kill her, I watched her stupid, wrinkled frightened white face and I wanted to take a club, a hatchet, and bring it down with all my weight, splitting her skull down the middle where she parted her iron-grey hair.''[12] But Baldwin is less interested in the literal discharge of hatred than in its power to distort the psyche, to warp personal and private history. It was precisely to escape such a distortion that he fled to Europe, a process which he describes in ''This Morning, This Evening, So Soon,'' which remains one of his best stories and one which is crucial to an understanding of his position. It concerns a black American actor-singer who lives in France with a Swedish woman, Harriet, and their son and it is in part an explanation of the sense of release which expatriation granted to him. For though he concedes a determining power to race, religion, and nationality, the story is offered as evidence of the fact that such determinants are deadly if they are not transcended: ''Everyone's life begins on a level where races, armies, and churches stop.''[13] And the gift of expatriation is precisely such a transcendence, for it enables individuals to confront themselves and others outside of the constraining power of myth.

Black men and white women free themselves of a public rage and coercive power which, in America, would have become private compulsions. They are also free of a language which might otherwise throw its own reductive net around them. As the protagonist's sister observes, "Language is experience and language is power."[14] The failure of black Americans, as she sees it, is that they employ a language of power which must be ironic since it is detached from their experience. And yet this is Baldwin's language too, and the story can be seen as a confessional work of some honesty. For the protagonist recognizes that his success has in part been generated by a refusal to be identified too closely with the misery of his people, by associating himself, on the contrary, with those responsible for their suffering. It has also been dependent on his refusal to grant any ambiguity to French racial attitudes. France had removed the cataract from his eyes with respect to America at the cost of a moral myopia with regard to French attitudes.

A brief return to America reminds him that there his life is a concession offered to him by whites. But a conversation with his French director also reminds him that suffering is not a black prerogative. For he had lost a wife and a son in the war and knows the weight of history as well as the black American. The real American sin is presented as an innocence of history, a failure to perceive that the past demands a price from the present. And this is a message which Baldwin himself felt increasingly obliged to underline as his career developed.

For Baldwin, Europe's function was precisely to release him from an identity which was no more than a projection of his racial inheritance. It was not, as LeRoi Jones was later to imply, that he wished to deny his color, but rather that he recognized the danger implicit in allowing public symbols of oppression or resistance to stand as adequate expressions of the self. As he said in his introduction to *Nobody Knows My Name*, "In America, the colour of my skin had stood between myself and me; in Europe, that barrier was down. Nothing is more desirable than to be released from an affliction, but nothing is more frightening than to be divested of a crutch. It turned out that the question of who I was was not solved because I had removed myself from the social forces which menaced me—anyway those forces had become interior, and I had dragged them across the ocean with me. The question of who I was had at last become a personal question, and the answer was to be found in me."[15] For it was Baldwin's assumption that the question of color, crucially important on a moral level, concealed a more fundamental problem—the problem of self. And it is in that sense that he felt most American.

But he negotiates a privileged position for himself by claiming an American identity (while naturally disavowing the guilt for a prejudice which he did not originate and for a history which he played no part in determining), and simultaneously embracing a Negro identity (while declining the cultural temporizing and disabling pathology which he otherwise identifies as the natural inheritance of the black American). Both American and Negro search endlessly for identity. Only Baldwin, in the eye of the storm, realizes that it resides in stillness, in an acceptance, not of injustice nor of public roles, but of the authenticity of the self. His failure lies in his inability to reveal the authenticating process at work. Sexuality is clearly a part of it; in some way, supposedly, it tells the truth that the intellect denies. It offers a vital clue, he feels, both to the American need to dramatize innocence and to the real roots of prejudice. In his essay "Nobody Knows My Name," he coyly hints that desegregation battles have to do with "political power and . . . with sex."[16] Now, on an obvious level, he is clearly right. It was certainly never an argument about educational theories. But the link between that observation and the obsessive question of identity is not so clear. Meanwhile, his own sexual ambiguity was itself a confusing factor; acceptance for him meant the difficult task of accepting the real nature of his sexuality and abandoning illusion for reality.

On the face of it, the American problem with regard to sex was somewhat different. It was that sexuality had so often been presented as an absolute, as a metaphor for evil or anarchy, or alternatively, as utopian bliss, that it could not be so easily integrated into a realistic model of society. Its metaphoric weight was simply too great. But for Baldwin, acceptance implied precisely that elevation of sex into metaphor, so that in virtually all of his work it stands either as an image of exploitation and abuse, or of an innocence with the power to transform social reality: sex as weapon; sex as redemption. In other words, he is never more American than in his symbolic perception of sexuality, and what he presents as a kind of emotional realism is, in fact, a familiar form of sentimentality. It can be found just as easily in Hemingway, in Tennessee Williams, and in Norman Mailer, and it is no more sophisticated there, except that Mailer, whom Baldwin actually attacked for his sentimentality, purports to see sex as a dialectical term. Baldwin, in struggling to escape the sexual myths which surround the Negro in America, has simply succumbed to others.

He suggests that Wright placed violence where sex should have been because he was unable to analyze the real nature of the rage which he perceived; but Baldwin himself endows sex with a brutal physicality which is, in effect, a simple transposition of social violence. Having claimed in his essays that it is principal, in his novels he presents it as agent; while the ambiguities of sexual contact—in part an expression of self, in part a surrender of self, in part aggression, in part submission—becomes an enactment of the ambivalence implied in the self's confrontation with society and the tensions of racial relationships. For, if in suppressing the Negro white Americans were in fact "burying . . . the unspeakably dark, guilty, erotic past which the Protestant fathers made him bury,"[17] then the release of that erotic self should serve to heal the wound opened up by that denial of the whole man. And Baldwin was by no means alone in this assumption. What he adds is the presumption that the existence of the Negro has facilitated this disruption of identity, that he has collaborated in a myth of black sexual potency. The risk is that in releasing this sexuality in his own work he is in danger of endorsing the metaphoric presumptions of those Protestant fathers or, as bad, of generating a false image of reconciliation.

In a graceless essay following Richard Wright's death, he asserted that "the war in the breast between blackness and whiteness which caused Richard such pain, need not be a war. It is a war which just as it denies both the heights and the depths of our natures, takes, and has taken visibly and invisibly, as many white lives as black ones." For him, Wright was "among the most illustrious victims of this war."[18] Borrowing one of Wright's favorite phrases, he had, he suggested, wandered in a no-man's-land between black and white. The act of reconciliation simply lay beyond Wright's imagination. But what, then, does Baldwin offer? Only, it appears, the fact that whiteness has lost its power and that blackness will soon do so. Thus, the crucial act of reconciliation will take place in the moral sensibility of the Negro. But to be made flesh, however, it must assume a reality beyond that privileged environment. And the only way in which he can dramatize it is in the literal embrace of black and white, a coition which, like that implied but mercifully not enacted at the end of Hawthorne's *The House of the Seven Gables*, will produce a moral synthesis. The trouble is that, for Baldwin, history cannot be so easily propitiated by simple images of sexual union.

For Baldwin, society is bound together by fear of our unknown selves. In other words, he offers us a neat reversal of the Lockean model. Men form society, not to protect their freedom, but to evade it. The notion is a Freudian one, so it is perhaps not surprising that the force he invokes to neutralize this process in his work is sexuality. This becomes the key to a real sense of community. The sentimentality of such a conviction is clear and may account for the real evasions which are to be found at the heart of so much of his own work. For social evil is thus seen as deriving from a desire for order and a fear of "our unknown selves...which can save us—'from the evil that is in the world.' "[19] Indeed, by this logic, the victim creates himself by accepting the need for social structure and granting it his acquiescence, when all the time "our humanity is our burden, our life; we need not battle for it; we need only to do what is infinitely more difficult—that is, accept it."[20]

In the case of his attack on *Native Son* he is offering a severe misreading, for far from being trapped within sociological generalizations, far from reducing complexities to simplicity and failing to engage the dangerous but liberating freedom of the individual, the genuinely subversive quality of that novel lies, not in its attack on American society, but in its conviction that individual action and the individual mind are not socially determined or socially bound. It is true that Wright's novel was a curiously schizophrenic work, with the individualistic drive of the narrative operating against an adjectival insistence on constriction and the deterministic weight implied by its sectional headings. It is equally true that, if events constitute successive stages in the liberation of the sensibility, they are also, by inverse law, stages in the diminishing world of social possibilities. But Baldwin was saddled with the same paradox. He wished to presume both that the self is real and presocial and that it cannot exist apart from its determinants. The result is a curious and distinctive tension between what he sees as an American sensibility and a free-ranging existential self; yet another example of his Manichean imagination which sees himself as the product of the Old World and the New, black and white, vengeance and love, male and female, probing intellect and liberating imagination. It is a dialectical process of which the self is the putative synthesis. And, to Baldwin, this is an American process.

To Baldwin, the objective of the novelist is to serve truth, which he defines as ''a devotion to the human being, his freedom and fulfilment.'' To see the individual as only an image of a race is to exchange reality for symbol, a life for a cause. And this was the real target of ''Everybody's Protest Novel''—the retreat into metaphor. And just as Moby Dick was not to be understood either as type or as emblem, so the individual's reality lies outside his availability as public symbol. Baldwin could already feel the pressure of the public role he was inevitably offered and which he felt the need to resist. ''What is today offered as his [the black writer's] Responsibility,'' he said, ''is, when he believes it, his corruption and our loss.''[21] Curiously, *Native Son's* vulnerability to Baldwin's criticism lay less in the element of protest, which is the source of its central ambiguity, than in the vague mythologizing of the social impulse which Bigger feels. The edge of his newly discovered identity blurs at the very moment of its coalescence. Baldwin suggests that American uncertainty about identity and American disregard for the identity of others derives from a contempt for history and historical process. Doubtful of historical logic, the American has tended to distrust time and to value experience—to assume that identity therefore is the product of events outside of time. A name is no more than the emblem of a man until it is claimed in action. The result is a social formlessness which masquerades as freedom but which actually smacks of anarchy. And this breeds a Hemingwayesque pragmatic morality which is as likely to validate racism as anything else. It is, he suggests, an American confusion to think that it is possible to consider the person apart from all the forces which have produced him, since American history turns on the abstraction of the individual from his social and cultural setting. And yet, this is precisely Baldwin's assumption since, as we have seen above, when it serves his purpose, he, too, posits the existence of a primary self outside of and unaffected by history. This, indeed, is a clue to a basic contradiction in his position which enables him to use both the moral self to indict the social world and the social world to explain the collapse of self.

The recurring pain to which Baldwin avers is the alienation from self and from the cultural experience of the Negro, an alienation which is not neutralized by expatriation, as this intensifies the guilt and adds a further level of ambiguity since now he must battle for possession of an American identity which, if the source of his pain, is also the key to its transcendence. As he wrote in a 1950 essay, ''Encounter on the Seine,'' ''To accept the reality of his being an American becomes a matter involving his integrity and his greatest hopes, for only by accepting this reality can he hope to make articulate to himself or to others the uniqueness of his experience, and to set free the spirit so long anonymous and caged.''[22] More than this, like Wright, he felt that the black experience did not merely offer a clue to American moral ambiguity, but that it functioned as metaphor, that ''in white Americans he finds reflected— repeated, as it were, in a higher key—his tensions, his terrors, his tenderness'' and that ''in this need to establish himself in relation to his past he is most American, that this depthless alienation from oneself and one's people is, in sum, the American experience.''[23]

Having previously argued, in his essay on the protest novel, against metaphoric reductivism, he now strains, as expatriate, to transform his own experience into an emblem of dispossession in precisely the same way that Wright had done in a series of works starting with *Native Son* and running through ''The Man Who Lived Underground'' and *The Outsider*. Where he does try to establish a distinction is between the social and the metaphysical image, yet this is a distinction which he finds difficult to sustain. It now turns out that his real rejection of Wright's novel lies in what he takes to be the inaccuracy of its portrait, in its faulty sociology, in a conviction that the problem is being engaged too soon and at a level which denies not so much the complexity of the Negro as that of an essential human nature. For he feels that ''the battle is elsewhere. It proceeds far from us in the heat and horror and pain of life itself where all men are betrayed by greed and guilt and blood lust and where no man's hands are clean.''[24] It remains unexamined since, as Camus realized, the logic of this position is that if all men are guilty, then all men are innocent. If the sociological approach implies the possibility of facile solutions, then assertions of an immutable human nature generating social action leave one with the sentimentalities of evil and innocence, with desperate images such as that which concludes but scarcely resolves Steinbeck's *The Grapes of Wrath*, in which social realities are invited to defer before the reassertion of human goodness. For this was a paradox he was not ready to engage, indeed has never engaged, since he has continued to dramatize human action as a battle between good and evil, a battle which he believes characterizes American political and cultural presumptions. Out of the sociological frying pan and into the metaphysical fire. Knowing that ''anyone who insists on remaining in a state of innocence long after that innocence is dead, turns himself into a monster,''[25] his puritan mentality continues to play with Manichean ideas.

Baldwin's first novel, *Go Tell It On The Mountain*, is concerned with a young boy's move towards maturity. His religious conversion coincides with the first tentative stirrings of sexualtiy, which, the book suggests, can be redemptive and fulfilling or destructive and constrictive. His own hesitant perceptions are set aginst the reality of black life as implied in the memories of his family as, for their various reasons, they humble themselve before God.

His mother, Elizabeth, had fallen in love with a young black man, but the white world had intervened, falsely accusing him of a crime and driving him to suicide. She bore an illegitimate son, John, the protagonist of the novel, but was rescued from her solitariness by Gabriel—once a dissolute youth, but now the stern pastor of the Temple of the Fire Baptized. As a young man, the latter had married a black woman who had been raped by white men. The marriage was a form of penance in which there was no love, and he had an affair with another woman whom he abandons. She dies in childbirth and the boy is later killed. When his wife dies, he remarries. Elizabeth produces another child of this marriage, whose hatred for his father is a punishment for his sins. *Go Tell It On The Mountain* is an act of exorcism. It is an account of a battle with authority, expressed primarily in terms of a young boy's struggle against his father and against the religion which is deployed as a means of controlling and limiting his emerging manhood. His father's favorite text is the Old Testament invocation: "set thine house in order." But, as Baldwin implies in his essays, the desire for order can simply be an evasion of self and of reality. Thus, behind the Word is another lexicon; behind the injunctions of the Church, the implacable determinisms of white society. The iconography of the Church, which dresses its saints in white and condemns the disobedient to a black hell, mirrors a social symbolism which divides with the same confident zeal.

The Church is portrayed as both an escape from reality (in which the declaration that the first shall be last and the last first seems to promise the possibility of ultimate justice), and a covert image of social manipulation. The abject surrender of self, the abnegation of sexuality, the necessary recognition of authority, and the obedient internalization of values are a reflection of those concessions which society likewise demands. When Gabriel preaches a sermon on passivity, it is clearly intended to apply to both the spiritual and the secular world. He denounces those with "the desire to overturn the appointed times of God, and to wrest from Him who held all power in His hands power not meet for men. . . . Yes, and there were those who cried . . . that they should wait no longer, despised and rejected and spat on as they were, but should rise today and bring down the mighty, establishing the vengeance that God had claimed." But "not for nothing was it written, 'He that believeth will not make haste.' "[26] Clearly, Baldwin implies, personal and cultural identity depend upon the ability to resist such passivity. The battle is one between the Old Testament and the New, between a God-centered rite of retribution and anger and a man-centered gospel of love and forgiveness. The contradictions are manifest. Everything clearly does not work together for good for them that love the Lord, while social acquiescence is no protection in the face of white hostility.

Go Tell It On The Mountain is not a book which engages the racial situation directly, but the battle which its young protagonist wages with the constricting power of religion represents a transposed version of a social conflict. John's sexuality rebels against the boundaries defined by the Church, as his aspirations transcend the harsh limits ascribed to race.

Yet John also has to conquer and resist his father's absolutism. For him, all whites are wicked, and the anger of God is simply a sublimation of his own bitterness. As pastor, his control over others is designed to blot out his own sense of social impotence. Spiritual food becomes a substitute for the literal food which his family lacks. The rebirth, which offers a mystical religious experience for so many characters in the book, is a process whereby suffering is rationalized and the painful realities of life raised to the level of myth. It offers relief, a context for frustration, and grounds for a hope which is located outside the terms of personal degradation.

Their very names, however, trap them inside an allegory which constricts them as clearly as does their social position. Gabriel, the announcer of good news, caught between symbolic and human needs, feels the pressure of the white world upon him and those around him. Indeed, it is that pressure which creates his faith and provides him with his role. For his dignity and his sanity, like that of the black writer, lies in his power as a dispenser of the word—a word which is a substitute for action and a sublimation of hatred. For, outside of that, he is only a domestic servant, subject to the indignities and bitternesses which accompany that role, and his personal drama is enacted in the interstices of white life. All the main characters are, from the white point of view, marginal people—elevator operators, maids, cleaners. Occasionally, however, the white world obtrudes, in the form of a lynched black soldier or a raped black woman, events which are treated as though they were as implacable as those of the natural world.

The religion which lies at the heart of the book is painfully ambiguous. For it is a religion which condemned black men, as the sons of Ham, to be the servants of servants. It is a religion which makes vengeance a prerogative of God. And as John finds himself on the "threshing floor," in a space, "a sheer void . . .a mockery of order, and balance, and time" in which "all was swallowed up in chaos,"[27] he debates within himself between the ironic consolation of a religion which rationalizes his own debasement and a cold reality in which suffering operates in time and is generated anew by each generation. The question he asks himself is whether the curse lives "in time, or in the moment," and the conclusion he reaches is that it "was renewed from moment to moment, from father to son."[28] Behind the language of religion, as behind that of daily life, he now detects the rage and the pain which is the reality of black experience: the "boundless melancholy, of the bitterest patience, and the longest night; of the deepest water, the strongest chains, the most cruel lash; of humility most wretched."[29] And so the salvation which he claims is an ironic one. For the community he now enters is a community of the dispossessed and the frustrated. Indeed, the completeness of this dispossession, shared by all the characters whose inner world we are permitted to penetrate, becomes something of a personal cliché for they have no existence outside of their suffering. The expectation of betrayal becomes a defining characteristic. And, if such an emotional hyperbole has a racial sanction, given the history of America, Baldwin risks the application of his own warning against seeing Negro life as mere pathology. For their lives seem every bit as defined by white presumptions as Wright's characters had seemed to him to be. But where Wright chooses to locate the source of that manipulation in the external world, in a sociological fact turned into psychological wound, Baldwin locates it in the private sphere, in an unquestioned inheritance of personal dispossession. He leaves the white world as an assumed fact, unexamined, palpable, simply present and affecting. It is no more sophisticated in its operation than a disease. It is itself merely an image of fate or absurdity, of the threatened chaos, to be propitiated with a ritual and myth itself derived from that absurdity. The saving grace lies in the irony which is contained, not in the narrator's voice, but in the contrasts between a language of salvation and an expectation of doom.

Baldwin has, at times, felt that this amounts to a tragic sense of life, and certainly it has that double apprehension which grows from an unequal struggle with fate that one associates with such a view. But in his first novel, the ironies, which surround and penetrate a resistance which is in fact only another kind of capitulation, work against this. The moments of human contact which seem to annihilate the tensions are doomed. They have Hardy's touch of death about them; but Hardy expected no more of a malicious or, at best, indifferent universe, a dark star on which such mismatings are an inevitable expression of contingency. Baldwin wants to locate his determinism in a more specific force. And though he dramatizes the white world as an impersonal environment of malignity, the social world undermines the validity of this as an image of blank fate. For the wall of indifference is not blank and uniform. It is itself the product of specific tensions and inadequacies, and the relation between the two worlds, as he himself showed in later works, is more subtle and confused than he was ready to concede here.

And he is also prepared to grant a confusing hereditary drive towards damnation in individual lives which is not explicable, or at least not shown to be explicable, in terms of social pressures. The issues are implied but not confronted. Character is too often seen in terms of competing opposites—spontaneity struggling with constriction, anarchy with order, body with spirit —as though the natural world simply mimicked the religious divisions between good and evil and the social divisions between black and white, which at first only provided the environment for his action but which end up by providing its dialectic. Baldwin's imagination, in fact, has a tendency to dramatize the moral world on a model which he derives from the spiritual world, so that just as Old and New Testaments seem locked, in his work, in perpetual struggle, so those human qualities which he distills out of action do battle for the individual soul.

The struggle of John Grimes for spiritual manhood is portrayed as an innocent failure to perceive the moral realities of the world. The narrative offers the reader a privileged glimpse into the private despair and menacing anarchism which leads to the absolutism of religious faith. And since the main characters are as old as the century and enact that move from South to North which was the primary experience of the black in that century, the book is offered as a kind of spiritual history of the black American, as it is of its author. Baldwin, himself at one time a young preacher, knew all too well the private and public humiliations which religion was designed to dispel, the paradoxical but nonetheless reassuring rationality which it seemed to impose on a life threatened by violence and poverty. But he also knew the price which it demanded; the surrender of authority over one's life, which becomes a kind of grotesque parody of his social subordination, and the expulsion from time, which inhibits social action. Yet the novel ends with the barest suggestion of a sensuality and a personal commitment to individual relationship, which offers another possible response—a suggestion taken up immediately afterward in *Giovanni's Room*, where it is pressed to the point of sentimentality.

In *Go Tell It On The Mountain*, the baroque prose is itself an essential part of the book's irony—an elaborate filigree of language which is a counterpart to the defensive elaborations of a spiritual universe which exists quite apart from the tawdry poverty of the social environment. But every now and then a bleak fact obtrudes; the narrow way and shining road to salvation resolves, for a moment, into the reality of a rubbish-strewn street. The hymn which the congregation sings promises the possibility of walking ''in Jerusalem just like John,''[30] but the ''shining city'' which Baldwin's John confronts is the unwelcoming city of New York. The reader sees what the protagonist does not, the desperate compulsions which transform the black woman, exhausted from her labors, into a saint of the church and the filth of the ghetto into the city of God. And the iconography is undercut by a deliberately ambiguous language in which the formal imagery of spirituality is penetrated by the reality of experience. Hence, though Florence, who is dying of cancer, sometimes heard the name of Jesus ''like the swift passing of a bird into the air,'' sometimes she perceives it ''like the slow rising of the mist from the swamp ground.''[31]

John Grimes does not lose his innocence to the pressures of experience, but to the demands of those anxious to receive confirmation of their own illusions. Baldwin, like John, illegitimate, the son of an adoptive and hostile father, and a religious convert, is all too aware that identity lies outside the Calvinist language in which blackness is synonymous with evil and the passive spirit is seen as the key to salvation. Yet, there is at the heart of this book, as of so much of Baldwin's writing, a loneliness which demands some solution, a solitariness which stems from the barriers society erects and which cuts individuals off from self-knowledge and from free access to other selves. As a black, as a step-child, as an expatriate, as a writer, and as a homosexual, Baldwin felt such barriers more acutely than most, but he also felt this state of alienation to be an American characteristic, as he tried to show in *Another Country* and as he implied in many of his essays. His solution, repeatedly adumbrated, is the need to take seriously the New Testament injunction to love one another. It is the limitation of Baldwin's imagination that he has only been able to dramatize this conviction in sexual terms, his concern always tending to be expressed by an act of sexual grace, a concrete image of the violation of boundaries which he increasingly hawked like a sentimental huckster.

For a while, it was a message whose simplicity resonated in an America which yearned for the complex problems of society to be resolved by one bold gesture of the sensibility, which was free of the rational concealments and repressed hostilities and guilts imposed by the reality principle. Baldwin, in other words, was a close kin to the Edward Albee of *The Zoo Story*, the Julian Beck of *Paradise Now*, and the more simple-minded adherents of Marcuse and Brown. But, as such boundaries proved remarkably resistent to such emotional authenticities, and as the club and the gun proved such effective means of enforcing segregation, so sexuality itself became a more desperate enterprise, and love was redefined as what he chose to regard as a hard-minded bargaining with fate. Yet, at the heart of his own experience is a series of personal betrayals which never quite permit him to grant full reality to the relationships which he forces to bear so much weight. And since betrayal is apparently a human instinct in his canon, as it is admittedly for Arthur Miller in *After the Fall*, we are offered not so much a solution as a paradox which can only be sustained and not resolved.

But, in *Go Tell It On The Mountain*, he was unclear as to the connection between private completions and public hostility. The potential love between John and Elisha, lightly sketched and providing only the barest of possibilities, bears no relationship to the white world which dispossesses both of them. It offers a transcendence which is purer only by virtue of the fact that we have not seen the evasions and the treacheries which are involved in this as we have seen those implied by surrender to the Church. Both, however, offer a sensual release and both are described in sexual terms; his failure is to distinguish clearly between them, to show how a relationship based on such a passion differs from a religion equally designed to blot out the pains of daily life. What he dramatizes is a sensibility driven back onto an emotional level. The physical world of history and time has been denied or surrendered. What is left is the sense of the moment or a projected future. The result is the confirmation of another cliché. If Bigger Thomas seemed like a social integer, the distillation of social process, these characters come perilously close to that image of the Negro as sensual and emotional being so popular with white writers and integral to the assumptions of the First Renaissance. And there is surely an implied irritation with the fact that the black American has collaborated in his historical irrelevance, an irritation which Baldwin shared with Wright. For, if the former criticizes the latter for failing to convey the reality of black cultural life, he, in turn, expressed his own sense of the narrowness of that existence.

If *Go Tell It On The Mountain* was intended to lay ghosts from his own past, *Giovanni's Room* was a more daring attempt to engage his own sexual identity and to inhabit the mind and sensibility of the white world which was responsible for his own sense of exclusion. In 1954, he published an article in *The New Leader* called "Gide as Husband and Homosexual" (republished in *Nobody Knows My Name* as "The Male Prison"). This suggested that Gide should have kept his homosexuality hidden or, if not, that he should have contrived to sound less disturbed by it. Later, he was to admit that the article was an implicit comment on himself, "I was accusing myself, perhaps not directly enough, of a certain fear and a certain hypocrisy."[32] But the essay is also interesting in the way in which it links the plight of the homosexual and that of the Negro, for he makes the point that society's power to define normality is intimately linked to the need to project the existence of a natural order in the universe; that the social and the metaphysical are locked together. To breach the sexual boundaries "would rob the normal—who are simply the many—of their very necessary sense of security and order, of their sense, perhaps, that the race is and should be devoted to outwitting oblivion—and will surely manage to do so."[33] The connection between sexual and social barriers is clear, for as he had remarked elsewhere, "if people were not so *frightened* of it . . .American homosexuality . . .would cease in effect . . .to *exist* . . .the same way the Negro problem would disappear."[34]

The Gide essay appeared at a time when Baldwin, working in Les Quatre Chemins on the outskirts of Cannes, was in the process of writing *Giovanni's Room*—a book whose central thesis is that dispossession from self and society is an American fate, but that that fate is most clearly symbolized by those who transgress social taboos, a transgression which threatens the protective nature of order and propriety, raised by its adherents to the status of metaphysical paradigm. At the same time, many of his comments about his American identity have a sharper edge if a racial identity is substituted. Take, for example, the protagonist's remark that he "resented being called an American (and resented resenting it) because it seemed to make me nothing more than that, whatever that was; and I resented being called *not* an American because it seemed to make me nothing."[35] The vulnerability is racial or sexual in origin as much as it is American.

The encounter of Europe and America may have Jamesian overtones in its probing of innocence and experience, but his concern with the need to accept the terms of one's existence applies to both sides of his identity. He did not, after all, make his characters white, "just to show that he could,"[36] as Alfred Kazin suggests, but because he is aware that at least part of his own self-doubt is national in origin, just as part of his suffering is a consequence of an insecurity on the part of white Americans who seek absolution in an insistence on necessary boundaries.

Identity is a problem for the American, he implies, because the individual wishes to deny the meaning of so much of his experience, wishes to subscribe to a version of the real which excludes ambiguity, natural compulsions, shame, fear, and moral doubt. For his protagonist, "people who believe that they are . . .the masters of their destiny can only continue to believe this by becoming specialists in self-deception."[37] For the homosexual and the Negro, this is a truth which scarcely needs articulating; for the American, Baldwin suggests, it is the key to self-acceptance. But the fact remains that this simple acceptance of one's nature and of the capricious blend of the given and the possible, is not the same for the American as it is for the homosexual or the Negro. And this is a fact that the protagonist himself learns at the end of the book. The American can run back to America, can reerect protective barriers momentarily threatened by the intrusion of anarchic truths. He, or in this case she (the protagonist's fiancée, Hella), can reinvent innocence. For David, the bisexual protagonist, this is not possible. For what the world chooses to see as corruption, as a disturbing deviance from the norm, is the essence of his life. He has to live with ambiguity, as Hella does not.

It seems strange that Baldwin should have attracted such approbrium from other black writers for a novel which, far from evading racial issues, seeks to explore the meaning of social exclusion and personal identity in a context which presents that meaning outside of immediate social determinants. But, then, the transposition of racial to sexual insecurity is indeed a potentially dangerous tactic and one which, given the curiously right-wing machismo imagery of black writing in the 1960s, would be bound to attract attack. Indeed, it is interesting to note the way in which homosexuality itself became seen as a source of spiritual decadence and political equivocation in the 1960s.

Between his first two novels, his first book of essays, and his subsequent work there is a clear caesura. Despite his own expatriation, the increasing pace of the civil rights movement brought a moral pressure to bear which was intensified by the fact that he viewed it from the safety of Paris. If the 1954 desegregation decision seemed to justify the full assumption of American identity (and even, it might be said, American paradoxes, in a way which is implicit in the method and the fact of *Giovanni's Room*), the dramatization of the Negro's exclusion from that identity, in the confrontation at Little Rock, indicated just how premature such an assumption was. Indeed, having energetically resisted the role of spokesman, he increasingly found that he could not detach himself from historical process. Where, in *Giovanni's Room*, Baldwin has Giovanni mock the American sense of time as a progressive force which can resolve social and metaphysical problems so that "everything will be settled, solved, put in its place,"[38] the exigencies of the racial situation led

Baldwin himself, in that same year, to say, ''There is never time in the future in which we will work out our salvation. The challenge is in the moment, the time is always now.''[39] There was no space for irony. He now made one of his many return visits to the United States and for the first time visited the South—a trip, in one sense, against the tide of history. It transformed his view of his own role as writer as he was forced to confront the very realities he had fled so far to escape. The fact of racial struggle could clearly no longer be avoided.

Another Country was his flawed attempt to bear witness to that fact as well as to the opposite. It is the first of his novels to engage directly the question of racial hostilities; the first, too, which permitted the rhetoric of the essays to invade his fiction and which showed evidence of that linguistic escalation which was a product of the public confrontations increasingly being enacted in America's cities. The brutality of its language and of its action is a concession to his new realization that problems of personal and social identity are unlikely to defer to bland presumptions about the power of the imagination and the moral resources of the American character. As we have noted, he had, anyway, never been entirely consistent or clear about what he meant by identity, on the one hand believing that it had to be invented from moment to moment and, on the other, that it was simply waiting to be discovered. It depended, in other words, on whether he was intent on stressing the social or the psychological origins of character. Now he seems to concede the power of a history which cannot be nullified by a simple wish for reconciliation.

As suggested above, Baldwin's changed manner dated first from his visit to the South, from which he returned with the new conviction that his role ''was to speak for people who cannot speak.''[40] This was of course precisely the role which he had refused when he left for France. But now he confessed that the trip to the South had left him with a commitment which he no longer felt he could evade. He was not immune either to the significance of an emerging Africa. He might recognize that American blacks and black Africans occupied different psychological and cultural worlds, but the changed mood of the early 1960s led him to wish that he had participated in the protest at the United Nations following the assassination of Lumumba in 1962. But, perhaps significantly, he failed to join the demonstration because he was too busy with his work—a concrete example of his continued equivocation and of the special dilemma of the black writer. Yet Baldwin did feel the pressure rising. He was all too aware that ''the times are catching up with me''[41] and saw in the Black Muslim movement a menace to his own position, which he readily admitted to be ''in the middle.''[42] That description, of course, was in danger of locating him in precisely that no-man's-land in which he had placed Wright and which his own role as mediator seemed to suggest was indeed his own. Now was clearly the time to come off the fence.

And yet, while *Another Country* did, in Baldwin's words, ''discharge venom,'' it was also an attempt to ''discharge love.'' Its central assumption was that racial bitterness was simply one example of a general failure of love in America. And, in that respect, it was a very American product, as it was in its hard exterior and its soft center.

At the heart of *Another Country*, and dominating the book, is the figure of Rufus Scott, based clearly on Baldwin's friend Eugene Worth, who committed suicide from the George Washington Bridge shortly before Baldwin's exile in France. Rufus is obsessed with rage against the white world which has circumscribed him. He lacks the ability to effect the control of that rage which Baldwin had suggested, in his attack on Richard Wright, was so necessary. It lies like a barrier between him and other people. His destruction of Leona, a young southern white woman, is an expression of this destructive anger which, though directed against a representative of the white world, is ultimately self-destructive. Rufus dies because of a failure of love on his part and on that of others. This is caused in large part by the racial situation, but Baldwin's point seems to be that it is ultimately possible to penetrate beneath the level of this kind of instinctual hostility—to bypass the racial assumptions which create barriers between people and to establish a genuine relationship, tenuous at first, but feeding on trust and relying on real experience rather expectation, able at last to establish a logic and a reality of its own. This, indeed, is a description, not only of the process of the novel itself, but also of the various relationships which are developed between individuals desperately searching for individual meaning.

Part of the time the characters use one another, mistaking physical contact for communion, or they engage in therapeutic fornication, using sex to release themselves from deadening habit or from their own confusions. But behind the desperate acts of sex, there is a simple version of love, redemptive and fulfilling; an image of transcended boundaries and of completion. Indeed, the bisexuality of Rufus and of his white friends Eric and Vivaldo is offered as a patent symbol of a world without boundaries in which the main image is one of unrestrained flow.

Rufus, like the jazz musician whose music seems to call out "Do you love me, do you love me," desperately needs some evidence of human community which can nullify his own experience of a sharply divided world. But he is unable to recognize it when it is offered to him. The same situation is recreated in the interracial relationship between Rufus's sister, Ida, and her white lover, Vivaldo. Because of her own experience of hostility, Ida distrusts Vivaldo, while he doubts his own motives and the nature of her affection for him. But both finally come to realize that they are important to each other.

The personal torments, the struggle towards a valid concept of self and the ambiguities of love, do not affect only the interracial couples, however. For, as Vivaldo points out, "suffering doesn't have a colour."[43] Vivaldo's and Rufus's lack of awareness of their own identity merely mirrors a common complaint of American society as Baldwin sees it. Richard, who has produced a mediocre book and whose marriage is incomplete, is as spiritually dead as is

Vivaldo. As his wife, Cass, admits, "Why was my husband ashamed to speak Polish all the years that he was growing up?—and look at him now, he doesn't know *who* he is. Maybe we're worse off than you."[44] Nevertheless, she and her husband are forced to come to terms with what they have failed to make of themselves, and there seems to be some element of hope in that. Cass comes to understand a simple tenet of Baldwin's faith—namely, that innocence is not a condition into which we are born, but a state which one attains through suffering. As she says to Eric at the end of the novel, "I'm beginning to think . . . that growing just means learning more and more about anguish . . . You begin to see that you, yourself, innocent, upright you, have contributed to and do contribute to the misery of the world which will never end because we are what we are."[45]

Eric, as one might expect following *Giovanni's Room*, seems to be a crucial character as far as Baldwin is concerned. A white homosexual from Alabama, he has a brief affair with Rufus before leaving for France, where he establishes a liaison with a French boy called Yves. Because of his sexual nature, he has a clearer understanding than most people of the problems which face the individual in modern society. As Baldwin explains, "There were no standards for him except those he could make for himself. There were no standards for him because he could not accept the definitions, the hideously mechanical jargon of his age. He saw no one around him worth his envy, did not believe in *the vast gray sleep which was called society*, did not believe in the cures, panaceas and slogans which afflicted the world he knew; and this meant that he had to create his standards and make up his definitions as he went along. It was up to him to find out who he was and it was his necessity to do this, so far as the witch-doctors of the time were concerned."[46] Eric is a common factor between Rufus, Cass, and Vivaldo, having affairs with all three and in some way conveying to them his own sense of certainty. To Robert Bone, the assumption which lies behind this—the vision which seems to grant the homosexual a special insight—is unacceptable and is the basis of the novel's failure. Certainly Eric does tend to be idealized, while his relationships are not submitted to the kind of scrutiny which the other relationships suffer. But to Baldwin, Eric suffers the same pains as the Negro, and the imagery which Baldwin evokes is similar. For him, too, the terrors of his life are "buried beneath the impossible language of the time"; they live "underground," while he himself "had nearly perished in the basement of his private life."[47] For him, too, love was under such pressure that it could easily sour into violence. And that is the tension which dominates the book. The reiterated cry, "Do you love me," is the counterpoint to the brutal power of the material world, which corrupts the artist and crushes the spirit. Eric's experience of life makes him stand as a prototype of the artist, the black, and, indeed, of all those who fail to conform to the definitions offered them.

But beneath the supposedly realistic surface is a callow sentimentality. The narrator asserts that "one lies about the body but the body does not lie about itself; it cannot lie about the force which drives it.''[48] Nor is he consistent in his romanticism. Ida is described in her singing as deploying ''a sense of the self so profound and so powerful that it does not so much leap barriers as reduce them to atoms.''[49] Yet, in fact, her grasp on that self is so tenuous that she surrenders it in pursuit of revenge and fails to detect the direction and strength of her own affections. Her character, simultaneously committed to love and to hate, to the future and to the past, is less a convincing portrait of human equivocation than an expression of Baldwin's own double role as spokesman for black anger and as a mediator between the races.

In a television interview some years go, Baldwin told James Mossman, ''I believe in love . . .I believe we can save each other.''[50] It was a confession of faith which does much to explain his life no less than his work and which goes to the heart of his strengths and weaknesses as a writer. At its worst, such a conviction has frequently betrayed him into a painful and disabling sentimentality, a simplification of experience as potentially dangerous as the concrete realities which are thereby evaded. At its best, it has stood as the only force which could sustain him against the insistent logic of a history which he repeatedly felt obliged to direct like a dagger at the heart of America. It was this tension which for so long made his work resonate with the hopes and fears of a generation. It was a battle between Old and New Testaments, between a philosophy of revenge and a gospel of redemption, which he dramatized equally in *Another Country* and in *The Fire Next Time*, a book which established his reputation, for a brief period, as the principal spokesman of black America.

The Fire Next Time was a crucial document. It was the work in which Baldwin seemed to reflect the mood of the black community most accurately, while its tone of menace, redeemed by hope, appealed to the moral needs of a white America newly exposed to the brutalities of southern justice and black heroism. He was, as he had been as a young preacher, carrying the word. For a generation of Americans, the civil rights movement was the moral cause which Baldwin saw it as being, and the death of Kennedy in the year of the book's publication was a confirmation of its apocalyptic warning and evidence of the need for rededication.

Paradoxically, *The Fire Next Time*, despite its assault on white liberals, is as liberal a document as one could imagine. At its heart is a call for the renewal of love, by which Baldwin means the necessity to recognize the dignity and independence of others, to engage the real, to resist historical determinism, to confront the self. Love is both a process and a state; it ''takes off the masks that we fear we cannot live without;''[51] it is a state of grace to be won through suffering. Yet, it is not untouched by a regressive romanticism. He wishes to celebrate ''the force of life itself'' and advocates that individuals should ''renew themselves at the fountain of their lives,''[52] a sensual release of a kind increasingly advocated in the 1960s; a pagan, underground, kinetic energy which will circumvent the deceptions of language and a rationalism whose betrayals are evident in the bleak statistics of recent history. It is a preacher's book, a warning of the fire next time, and, in the person of Elijah Muhammad, an identification of the agent of that apocalypse.

But it also reveals a way of evading the severe logic of eschatology. The Puritan divine's dualisms come easily to Baldwin, who confesses to finding himself held by the tension between love and power, pain and rage. He deploys the fact of African emergence as evidence both of the practicality and the urgency of black political action, while asserting the need to transcend race. The effect is, at times, one of intellectual and moral equivocation. While asserting that ''African kings and heroes have come into the world, out of the past, the past that can now be put to the uses of power,''[53] he elsewhere asserts that ''an invented past can never be used'' and that the only way the American Negro's past can be used is through ''the transcendence of the realities of colour, of nations, and of altars.''[54] It is a paradox which remains disturbingly unexamined. The Negro, we are told, is ''very well placed indeed to precipitate chaos and ring down the curtain on the American Dream,''[55] and, yet, it is through an acceptance of his identity that a genuine sense of order may cohere. The threat is unsophisticated, the promise indefinite. But Baldwin was not interested in presenting a program. He stands, he fancies, at the moral fulcrum of American history, faced with the stark simplicities of the Black Muslims, on the one hand, and an unrepentant America, on the other. He endorses the logic of the Muslims' position, but offers a beacon where they offer a fire. No wonder the book appealed so much to an America on the brink of national trauma.

Clearly, Baldwin no longer felt able to stand aside from the racial conflict. The increasing momentum of the civil rights movement itself gradually pulled him into the public world. In interviews, articles, and speeches he quickly emerged as a leading black spokesman. He offered no programs and represented no organization. His was to be a moral voice calling America back to its origins and excoriating those white liberals who were content to deflect conscience into rhetoric, though this latter strategy was an entirely familiar one to Baldwin who could so easily be accused of succumbing to a similar temptation.

In particular, 1963 marked an important stage in Baldwin's emergence as a conscious spokesman. In an essay entitled ''We Can Change the Country'' published in *Liberation*, he urged the creation of a third political party, though he did not specify its program; he called for a rent strike, but did not indicate what its objectives might be; and he proposed a boycott of Christmas on the grounds that America was no longer a Christian country. He was, in other words, dealing in symbols, gestures; he was creating the secular theology of the movement. And the denunciation of the white liberal, which created such baffled rage at the time, seemed to him a necessary step towards moral autonomy on the part of blacks. Admittedly, his definition of liberalism was absurd ("What I mean by a liberal is . . .someone . . .whose real attitudes are revealed when the chips are down—someone who thinks you're pushing too hard when you rock the boat, who thinks you are better when you are vehement, who has a set of values so deep that they're almost unconscious and which blind him to the fact that in talking to a black man, he is talking to another man like himself."[56] "White liberals," he suggested, "with some exceptions—have been unable to divest themselves of the whole concept of white supremacy"[57]). But his real objection was to the passive role offered to the black by a liberal missionary attitude. A decade later, he felt able to confess to a certain element of posturing in such statements; at the time, however, the assault on liberal equivocation seemed a necessary prelude to black independence.

But such interventions in the developing civil rights struggle were not without their cost, as he had predicted at the beginning of his career. The price of entering the public arena was a narrowing of the gap between artist and spokesman, and, over the next few years, he debated with himself about his real role. In 1965, he observed that it is impossible to be both a writer and a public spokesman, concluding that he was a writer.[58] But, at that very moment, he was in the process of finishing work on *Tell Me How Long the Train's Been Gone*, which debates precisely this issue and which was an attempt to resolve his dilemma by placing the spokesman at the center of his fiction.

In *Tell Me How Long the Train's Been Gone*, Baldwin contemplates the possible alternatives which confront the black American, the ways in which rage can be sublimated, evaded, or used. The central character, Leo Proudhammer, becomes an actor, converting passion into art and thereby escaping the definitions forced upon him by his situation. His brother, having been jailed for a crime which he had not committed and also having been savagely beaten and humiliated, turns to the Church. A third figure, Christopher, becomes a black rebel, though one whose rebellion never moves from word to act. Yet, as Leo recognizes, such strategies carry their own risk: "The day came when I wished to break my silence and found that I could not speak; the actor could no longer be distinguished from his role."[59] The real risk is that the individual will become his own jailer or simply surrender to the violence of experience rather than forge meaning out of pain: "This possibility, the possibility of creating my language out of my pain, of using my pain to create myself."[60] But they are all methods of survival, and, in Baldwin's world, there are only the doomed and the survivors; and those who survive frequently have to pay a price which makes survival simply another kind of doom.

Clearly, Baldwin's own situation as a writer is at the heart of the novel, for his protagonist operates both as artist and spokesman, aware of the paradox which springs from the fact that it is his role as estranged artist which enables him to command respect as a speaker warning against estrangement. He is aware, too, that as an artist he uses the pain which he observes; he comes to appreciate the fact that art is exploitative. As he listens to a young black girl singing, he observes that "no song could be worth what this singing little girl has already paid for it, and was paying, and would continue to pay."[61] And yet, it is his feeling of moral responsibility which enables him to justify his position.

Leo's conviction about his own social utility as an actor is surely Baldwin's defense of his role as novelist. "I *could* if I kept the faith, transform my sorrow into life and joy. I might live in pain and sorrow forever, but, if I kept the faith, I would never be useless. . . .I could do for others what I felt had not been done for me, and if I could do that, if I could give, I could live."[62] But this conviction is pitched against a feeling that the world remains resistant to his art, that life has to be lived in the interstices of time. And this is Baldwin's confession of the extent of his failure.

The book has the now-familiar weaknesses of Baldwin's work. Love is presented at its most obvious level. Indeed, even his love for his brother is expressed in a homosexual embrace. Leo's women accept the news of his affairs with men with a remarkable aplomb which has nothing to do with their characters. Baldwin lacks subtlety. His sense of doom becomes mannered and sentimental, being expressed in such an extreme form that it looses all conviction. Thus, when Leo works for a while as a waiter, he lists those who visit his restaurant, thereby creating a universe of fated souls so comprehensive as to strain credibility:

Here they came: the nice blonde girl from Minneapolis, who lived in the Village with her black musician husband. Eventually, he went mad and she turned into a lush. . . .Rhoda and Sam, the happiest young couple in the Village. She committed suicide, and he vanished into Spain . . .two girls who worked in advertising and who lived together in fear and trembling . . .one of them found a psychiatrist, married a very fat boy in advertising and moved to California and they are now very successful and vocal Fascists. I don't know what happened to the other girl . . .the black man from Kentucky . . .and his trembling Bryn Mawr girl friend. . . .Her family eventually had him arrested . . .the brilliant, aging Negro lawyer who lived on whisky and Benzedrine . . . the bright-eyed boy from the South, who was going to be a writer and turned into a wino . . .the boy who had just fled from his rich family in Florida . . .and who turned into a junkie . . .the faggot painter and his lesbian wife, who had an understanding with each other which made them brutally cruel to all their playmates and which welded them, hatefully, to each other . . .the lost lonely man who . . .loved young boys and feared them and who jumped off a roof . . .the beautiful girl who painted and who ended up in Bellevue . . .the beautiful girl who was going to be a dancer and who ended up in prison . . .[63]

And so the catalogue continues.

Rather as in Hemingway's work, people pay for what they do. The brave are broken. The only area in which meaning can cohere is that created by the individual, though even this is a tragic enterprise. So that at the end, the only value is that implicit in a tragically doomed love, a morally committed or a resistant self. But the dramatization of the self in his work can so easily veer over into self-pity and neurotic self-indulgence, and this is precisely what it threatened to do in his next book of essays, *No Name in the Street* (1972).

The notion advanced in this book, that in his own person he contains the total history and suffering of black Americans, is a conceit which, if pushed too far, becomes merely ironic, more especially since the tortured sensibility which he deploys contains more than an element of personal guilt, loneliness, and self-justification. And the style itself becomes flaccid. The tightly organized essays of his early period now give way to an account which he fails to charge with a significance beyond his own self-concern. It is not that he fails to engage public issues of importance, but that the sensibility which mediates those issues is defensive for reasons other than those generated by the events which he describes. The Baldwin who writes this book is, and knows himself to be, under pressure from other black writers and is also in the business of displaying his credentials as a public spokesman and a black artist. *Giovanni's Room* has carried an epigraph from Walt Whitman: "I am the man; I suffered, I was there." The accusations which his work was increasingly designed to meet were that if he had suffered, he no longer did so, and that at crucial moments he had, indeed, been absent from the fight. He had been in France when the civil rights movement began and people were risking their lives in the South, he had not gone to the United Nations when Lumumba was killed, he did not go to Oakland when Bobby Hutton was killed and Eldridge Cleaver wounded, though he was invited to do so. He was, he admitted, in a state of shock at the time, following the assassination of Martin Luther King two days earlier. But others were not incapacitated, and his defensive acknowledgement that "I can't describe this, or defend it, and I won't dwell on it"[64] scarcely met the objections of people like Cleaver.

In *Soul on Ice* (1968), Cleaver had accused him of "the most grueling, agonizing, total hatred of the blacks, particularly of himself, and the most shameful, fanatical fawning, sycophantic love of the whites that one can find in the writing of any black American writing in our time."[65] It was an assault which had more to do with Cleaver's own psychic necessities than with Baldwin's actual equivocations, but it did exemplify the kind of pressure applied to Baldwin and reduced him to tears when he eventually read it. And, indeed, in *No Name in the Street*, he admits that he had perhaps become, "without entirely realizing it, the Great Black Hope of the Great White Father."[66] He bears, as he admits, the guilt of the survivor and he seeks the only absolution which can be offered to such a survivor: he embraces the language and the fate of the damned. He embraces the fate which his skills as a writer-survivor had enabled him to evade. But the cost in Baldwin's case was not only a terrible nervousness about his own safety and the terms on which he could relate to those actively engaged in the real and dangerous business of the black movement; it also involved the adoption of a linguistic imperative at odds with the tensions and reservations of his usual style.

His generalizations are now offered without concession to the need for evidence, for, since his sensibility is the only authenticating device which he will acknowledge, the reader is expected to accept these without question. Thus, southern women are blighted, southern men are sexually maimed, liberals are hypocrites dominated by a "guilty eroticism," Americans are ignorant of history, and so on. In resisting the defining power of American reality, he creates a fable of his own which has everything to do with his own ambiguous plight as black American writer and, indeed, with the need to create an alternative mythology to that paraded by white society, but little to do with the reality which he lays claim to describe. His essay style now becomes hyperbolic, as though this were the only form adequate to the psychic needs of the moment. The tide has passed him by; *No Name in the Street* is his attempt to understand why this should be so and, simultaneously, his attempt to generate a persona which can repel assaults from blacks who cast doubt on the reality of his commitment. He preaches sermons designed rather less for white ears than earlier in his career and rather more to assert his own racial orthodoxy at a time when the barricade seemed more than a metaphor.

His necessary realization that "the people are one mystery and the person another"[67] nonetheless leaves him with the disabling paradox that he is forced to concede the inadequacy, on a private level, of the pronouncements that he makes on a public level. Repeatedly, in his novels and essays, he sketches portraits, even loving portraits, of individuals who succeed in transcending a history which he publicly insists to be incapable of transcendence. "Nakedness has no colour,"[68] he asserts, in describing a liberating love affair with a white person, but shows no way in which that truth, apparently vital to him, can ever hope to wrestle history to a standstill. And that, of course, is the vital issue which he repeatedly identifies but never resolves.

It is difficult to take seriously Baldwin's declaration that he is a Socialist, as it is his observation that at the age of nineteen he had been a Trotskyite, when he has never publicly shown any knowledge of Socialist principles nor demonstrated the form which they would take in America. The suspicion is that this was one more necessary credential for the black writer of the late 1960s and early 1970s to deploy. Similarly, his assertion that America was the Fourth Reich, that it was an "elaboration of the slave quarters and a rehearsal for a concentration camp,"[69] is a rhetorical gesture offered to the inflated language of the moment. When he says that "it is not necessary for a black man to hate a white man, or to have any particular feelings about him at all, in order to realise that he must kill him,"[70] the language outstrips the thought. "Must," not "may have to." The imperative is in the language; it is not in the logic of his position. Indeed, he insists that he is only discussing, and not advocating, violence. The words are a façade, and the gap between the positive assertion and its immediate modification are a denial of moral seriousness. The "must" is a bid for attention, for acceptance, for revolutionary benediction. If it has a place in the logic of history, it does not in the personal lexicon of Baldwin, whose work—even, finally, this polemical book—presses towards the point at which history exists to be transcended rather than confirmed as an implacable and timeless fate. And so, even while claiming to identify "the shape of the wrath to come," as he had nine years before with *The Fire Next Time*, he still maintains the other element of his dialectic, "the most passionate love, hoping to make the kingdom new, to make it honourable and worthy of love."[71] But then hope dies hard, even for one who takes the sentimentally dramatic view that "most human beings are wretched, and, in one way or another, become wicked,"[72] except, of course, James Baldwin, clear-eyed and honest, who alone can understand the meaning of history, perceive the liberating power of love, and in some mysterious way accommodate it to the compelling need for violence, without which change can never come. Baldwin berates those who fail to respect the individual, but he, himself, does violence to that individual by subordinating him to the inclusive nature of his moral generalizations.

Many of the books which shaped the cultural and social battle of the period were written in prison, which became an image of black containment and of the boundaries which circumscribe black possibility. And, though Baldwin himself had never been so incarcerated, he did find himself a constant visitor to jails in Europe and America when his former chauffeur was charged with murder—an experience which doubtless played a role in the creation of his next novel, *If Beale Street Could Talk*.

The story is narrated by a nineteen-year-old black girl called Tish, whose fiancée, Fonny, is falsely accused of rape by a bewildered Puerto Rican woman and is imprisoned on the evidence of a racist policeman. The girl is pregnant by her lover, and, as she and her family fight to secure his release, they and she discover the casual inhumanity of a white world for which the law is merely a convenient cover for prejudice. The gestation of the baby parallels this growing insight: the baby in the womb, the man in the prison. Both await release and the birth of true understanding. Virtually all the whites in the book, with the exception of the policeman, are kind and humane, but, institutionally, the society is shown as destroying black hopes with a cynical indifference. And it is this cynicism which a white lawyer discovers at the same time as does his black client. At the end of the novel, still awaiting news of his application for bail, Fonny, a sculptor, rejects the aesthetic in favor of a more engaged art.

If Beale Street Could Talk contains the now-familiar tension between a faith in the redemptive power of love and a conviction that social injustice will not defer to simple humanity. It is an assertion of white culpabililty which nonetheless contains portraits of individual whites which potentially nullify that conviction. If it was this kind of tension which once made his work seem so central to an understanding of a culture under pressure, by this stage in his career it has become little more than a series of contradictions which are no longer contained by an imaginative economy or by a control of narrative strategy. He poses the biblical question, *"Is there not one righteous among them?"* only to reply, *"No, Not one,"*[73] despite the fact that the protagonist's release is actively sought by one such person, his meals provided on credit by another, and his apartment kept available by yet another. On the one hand, in an interview, he describes Fonny as hardening himself "to deal with a situation which is not likely ever to change," and, on the other, he dramatizes here, as elsewhere in his work, the potentially liberating power of love. When challenged to explain the contradiction, he insisted that "a society is one thing— love is another" since "society is not constructed with individuals . . . it's constructed of units who agree on the same premise, who, to put it brutally, are in packs."[74] For the writer who accused Richard Wright of dealing in sociological generalizations, this was a potentially disabling observation in that it seems to deny that very social responsibility which his work has been designed to establish.

But the contradictions of the novel affect even the narrative style of the book itself. Baldwin originally planned to write it in the third person, but eventually changed his mind, without, it seems, making the necessary adjustments. We are, for example, expected to accept the absurdity of the narrator detailing scenes in which she plays no part (when he acknowledges this, he does so in disastrously naive ways—"Joseph and Frank, as we learn later, have also been sitting in a bar, and this is what happened between them"[75]—while the language frequently transcends the sensibility of that supposed narrator). The problem is that, wanting the freedom of a third-person narrative, with its power to offer wide-ranging social and psychological insights, but also needing the emotional directness of a personal account, he strains his style to the breaking point and beyond. And one fears that this collapse of language and structure is merely a symptom of a more fundamental failure of imagination and morale. The tension, always implicit in his work and which he had formerly managed to contain within a moral, indeed liberal, framework, now stands as simple contradiction. Aware of his own inability to dramatize his faith in individual responsibility on a social level ("I'm not really very civil minded . . . . A political perspective has got to be given by people who believe in political perspectives. It is not something I ever claimed to be able to do")[76], he is forced into proposing an unbridgeable gulf between the individual and his society—a romantic stance which negates his conviction that black people's "destinies are finally in their own hands"[77] and that a human being can "change the world in which he finds himself."[78]

In part, this is an expression of the collapse of his own confidence resulting from the assassinations of the 1960s and from the continuing prejudice in American society; in part, it betokens a loss of artistic control. Man, apparently, is good only individually; in the mass, he is evil. He repeatedly insists on the need to challenge deterministic theories, as though the challenge alone would establish the reality of human freedom. But he can find no way of establishing the reality of this. While acknowledging, in contradiction of his earlier remark, that a society is the product of its individuals, he can see no social mechanism for demonstrating this and no literary form which is adequate to its enunciation. He has said, like Wright before him, that "the situation of black people in America is not only a metaphor for America . . .it's a metaphor for the Western world,"[79] but his persistent need to portray the white as hangman and the black as victim makes it difficult to take this seriously. They may basically both be victims of history, but their fates are shown as so fundamentally different that a metaphoric role is denied by the social reality. As Margaret Mead astutely observed, "Cynicism is the other thing that goes with sentimentality."[80]

The essence of that contradiction was exposed very effectively in a conversation between Baldwin and Margaret Mead which took place in 1970—a discussion in which the anthropologist acts as a useful restraining influence on the writer's sentimentalities and on his increasingly casual use of language. Baldwin was intent on establishing an historic guilt, incurred by the act of enslavement but inherited by white Americans of the present. In this respect, he admitted himself to be something of an Old Testament prophet. But he also wished to offer the possibility of absolution, and the resultant contradiction between an ineradicable guilt and a necessary grace, which has characterized so much of his work, was carefully exposed by Margaret Mead. Speaking of the process of enslavement of blacks, he describes it as "the crime which is spoken of in the Bible, the sin against the Holy Ghost which cannot be forgiven."[81] The exchange which followed reveals his tendency to let language and imagery outstrip his convictions:

MEAD: Then we've nowhere to go.
BALDWIN: No, we have atonement.
MEAD: Not for the sin against the Holy Ghost.
BALDWIN: No?
MEAD: I mean, after all, you were once a theologian . . .And the point about the sin against the Holy Ghost is that—
BALDWIN: Is that it cannot be forgiven.
MEAD: So if you state a crime as impossible of forgiveness you've doomed everyone.
BALDWIN: No. I don't think I was as merciless as the Old Testament prophets. But I do agree with Malcolm X, that sin demands atonement.
MEAD: Whose sin? I mean, you're making racial guilt—
BALDWIN: No.
MEAD: Yes. You are.
BALDWIN: I'm not talking about race. I'm talking about the fact.
MEAD: But you are . . .. You're taking an Old Testament position, that the sins of the fathers are visited on their children.

BALDWIN: They are.

MEAD: The consequences are visited on the children.

BALDWIN: It's the same thing, isn't it?

MEAD: No, it's not the same thing at all. Because it's one thing to say, All right, I'm suffering for what my fathers did—

BALDWIN: I don't mean that, I don't mean that! I don't mean that at all! I mean something else! I mean something which I may not be able to get to . . . .

MEAD: . . . but when you talk about atonement you're talking about people who weren't *born* when this was committed.

BALDWIN: No. I mean the recognition of where one finds oneself in time or history or now. After all, I'm not guiltless, either. I sold my brothers or my sisters—

MEAD: When did you?

BALDWIN: Oh, a thousand years ago, it doesn't make any difference.

MEAD: It *does* make a difference. I think if one takes that position it's absolutely hopeless. I will *not* accept guilt for what anybody else did. I *will* accept guilt for what I did myself.[82]

Jean-Paul Sartre makes a similar point in *Anti-Semite and Jew* when he observes that "if one is going to reproach little children for the sins of their grandfathers, one must first of all have a very primitive conception of what constitutes responsibility."[83]

Though this is only a brief excerpt from a continuing dialogue, it does demonstrate Baldwin's desire to present history as present reality, to establish a social responsibility which, because he chooses to dramatize it in terms of sin and guilt, he is unable to establish as an active principle. The Old Testament prophet denies the efficacy of New Testament grace. The writer who wishes to establish a racial indictment is thus inhibited from dramatizing the transcendence of race, which is a conviction he holds with equal force. His desire to establish his belief that individuals are responsible moral creatures is undermined by his simultaneous conviction that their crime is ineradicable and human beings are ineluctably wicked. The problem does not reside in the language alone, but in his own terrible ambivalences which lead him to accuse and defend, to condemn and rescue with equal conviction. The deficiency is an intellectual one.

Baldwin's work is in large part a version of emotional truth. His observation that "I've never learned anything through my mind, I've learned whatever I've learned from my heart and my guts . . . love is the only wisdom"[84] is not merely whimsical, for it is the unexamined nature of such a proposition which undermines much of his work as essayist and novelist. His belief that history operates in the present tense, that it is a constant reality governing behavior and defining possibilities, is convincing only insofar as one does not engage his simultaneous conviction that it can be neutralized by a simple gesture of human solidarity. The color of his skin may imply his past and provoke a response which itself reveals the weight of that past, but, Margaret Mead insists, he is not responsible for it. Indeed, his failure to distinguish between present and past tense is evidence of a romantic refusal to engage the actual complexities of the moral world of the present. And, clearly, his habit of describing white individuals who are free of prejudice but locating them in a society of inflexible prejudice poses questions which are not answered by his belief that societies consist only of anonymous units. For the model of society implied by his own insistence on the animating power of love is quite otherwise. This implies that individuals encounter one another entirely free of their history—as Baldwin in Paris had no longer encountered people as a Negro—and that social meaning is a projection of private consonance. His conviction that "we can only redeem the past by what we do in the present"[85] is not only at odds with the notion that white treatment of the black constitutes an unforgivable sin, but also with his belief that redeeming relationships are forged outside of time, that they involve, not so much the acceptance of history, as a release from history. Rufus Scott dies because he cannot forget his history; Ida is saved because, finally, she can. The same is true of Leo Proudhammer. But in his public statements, history becomes inflexible, an indictment which leads Baldwin to the brink of a racism which he otherwise opposes with such tenacity.

Indeed, his incautious reference to American Jews, in his conversation with Margaret Mead, earned him a deeply felt rebuke and even betrayed Baldwin into the very cliché which he would have gleefully denounced in others when, in his own defense, he claimed that one of his best friends had been Jewish. It was not simply a debating point on Mead's part. For Baldwin, the tendency to generalize out of individual experience and to project a social determinism out of history becomes a mannerism which threatens to negate his moral stance. As Mead pointed out, it is simply not true to view the killing of four black girls in a Birmingham Sunday school as the Republic's answer to Martin Luther King's "I have a dream" speech, rather than as an event which prompted a renewed commitment by many whites as well as blacks who, on occasion, risked their lives to turn dream into reality. Yet, even now, in one mood, he sees a solution in some kind of symbolic union of black and white for which he can find no historic justification and for which he can establish no social mechanism. When asked, some twenty-five years after his first essay, how he meant to go about securing his solution to the problem, his reply was simply, "I don't know yet." And then, slipping into the opposite mood which has always been the other side to this sentimental vision, he offered the only solution which he could see: "Blow it up."[86]

The Black and White Lazarus: The Revival of the Liberal Tradition

5

If one thing seemed clear in the development of twentieth-century American writing, it was that liberalism had had its day. Democratic idealism had had a hard time surviving the multiple shocks which began, perhaps, with the Civil War or with the venality of late nineteenth-century politics, and which seemed to reach some kind of apogee in the trenches of Flanders. And the blank, bureaucratic face of evil exposed by the holocaust seemed to leave little by way of a foundation for an art built on the integrity of the individual conscience and the reality of social responsibility. "After Auschwitz," said Adorno, "poetry is no longer possible."

And so, the fine moral dilemmas of Cooper, Twain, Melville, Hawthorne, and James gave way to the ironic mode which has dominated twentieth-century art—an art which presumes the coterminous nature of appearance and reality. Truth becomes personal morality, a private code generated by the need to establish a provisional sense of order to set against an acknowledged chaos beyond the self; beauty is seen in a kind of ugliness whose attraction lies in a blend of brutality and sentimentality. Art is a resource only because it can vibrate with a faint echo of an irrevocable past or because its fragmenting planes are simple screens and are thus immune to an irony which they reflect without damage to themselves. But more recently, for the post-moderns, even that assurance collapses as art itself is penetrated by the canker of anarchy or, more likely, by a manipulative dictatorship of thought and imagination whose only virtue resides in its open confession of deviousness.

Yet this is hardly a complete picture, more especially for Jewish and black writers, for although the latter were frequently strident in their attacks on political liberalism, for its betrayals, but also, paradoxically, for its successes (emasculating in its presumed paternalism), both groups had a vested interest in subscribing to a liberal view of social structure, moral values, and individual freedom, which left them, quite clearly, the principal inheritors of a liberal idealism largely abandoned by Wasp writers. And this frequently led them to a contemplation of those nineteenth-century writers whose work had consistently addressed itself to the question of personal and public responsibility, locating this against a social and moral world which they confidently believed would yield itself to the pressure of individual conscience. The self lay at the heart of this literature, not, for the most part, as a romantic conceit, but as a key to social experience, as the evidence and agent of moral freedom.

The novel was born out of liberal presumptions about the self's capacity to define its own contours and shape the environment which it inhabited. But from the end of the nineteenth-century, it existed in a world in which those presumptions were thrown into doubt. In America, liberals, who had never formed a political party, responded politically to the evolution of their own laissez-faire economics into a rapacious capitalism by advocating a new interventionist strategy—the Populists advocating government control of the railroads; the Progressives, regulations to limit the unfettered individualism which had once been a cornerstone of classic liberal thought but which had now been invoked as a justification for corporate license. But the novelists reacted rather differently. The conclusions which they drew from industrialization and urbanization, from their reading of Darwin, Marx, and Freud, was, at least initially, that the autonomous individual, whose freedom had in many ways been the subject of the novel, was a fiction. Freedom was replaced by determinism, by a description of process.

Of course the loss of confidence in language, abstract values, and a socialized self hardly destroyed art, but it did redefine its purpose. For the early twentieth-century American novelist, defeat, in all but the most private sense, became a central theme, and when, in the 1930s, that defeat was temporarily replaced by victory, it remained hollow precisely because the individual retained no convincing leverage on the public world. He seemed, in other words, a perfect product of the system with which he struggled so earnestly. Liberalism remained out of vogue, and when it returned on the political scene it had been transformed into a diluted socialism whose very motto—the New Deal—implied a blend of commercial and social innovation.

But liberal language, perhaps drained of real meaning and substance, was still a necessary weapon of the politician, despite the fact that post-World War II totalitarianism was in fact challenged not by a reinvigorated liberalism, but by a conservative conformity. Indeed, liberals were again in retreat in universities and in the arts. Arthur Miller ceased to write for the stage precisely because he no longer believed that he had an audience to address. But the very assaults, taken together with the chilling realities of the war, themselves bred a revival of liberal convictions precisely in those whose identities and whose vision of the future were most directly threatened by a disavowal of moral principle and by the notion that the function of art lay in the celebration of the sensibility, or a willed vulnerability to the assumed entropic momentum of the private and public world. Free will, albeit constrained by sexual, social, and metaphysical coercions, was felt to be a moral necessity, for its absence threatened the self which had to believe in the possibility of action if it was to conceive of itself at all. Causality, complex and deceptive, was vital if the writer was to locate his own responsibility for his actions. For, without limited free will, without causality, without a sense of self and society, and without a sense of guilt and blame, the Jewish and the black writer could discover no mechanism for accusation, hence no basis for indictment, and hence no defense against an absurdity which could swallow up the individual in the present as it had willfully destroyed him in the past.

Thus, it became more difficult after the war for a Jewish writer to write as Nathanael West or Kafka had done, though nothing that happened in Europe had invalidated the visions they presented. Perhaps Joseph Heller comes the closest, but even in his work a value is identified, even as it is willfully surrendered. His works are supremely moral, almost in a desperate fashion.

Certainly there are many black writers whose work reveals a chilling and understandable sense of determinism, a sense of the cruel ironies of the natural and social world (Ann Petry's *The Narrows*, Alice Walker's *The Third Life of Grange Copeland*, and Toni Morrison's *Sula* being merely three examples among many, though Walker at least is not without an implied faith in human potential), but the dominant mood is one of an assertive liberalism, as the promises of the Constitution are claimed not only politically but culturally. On the political level, perhaps, this can more properly be seen as an attempt to make pluralism work for the black American as it had for other groups—pluralism being, in the eyes of Robert Woolf in *The Poverty of Liberalism* (1968), a blend of liberal idealism and conservative sociology, a recognition, in other words, that it was the group rather than the individual which constituted the only credible mechanism for apportioning power and, hence, social justice. But for the liberal writer, the individual remains the focus for moral and social concern, the only possible origin for idealism, the essence of cultural identity, and the prime mover of history. Liberalism is also a philosophy, or a series of convictions, which allows for a sense of transcendence which, though rooted in the ideal, is not idealistic, in that it can deal with the notion of evil if not depravity, and illogical action if not total irrationality.

For John Locke, in the beginning "all the world was America." But clearly, in the twentieth-century, America is no longer either a tabula rasa or a transcending idea. Especially for Negro and Jew, it is stained with historical guilt, more so for the former than for the latter. Whether as forced exile or promised land, it is no longer innocent and undefined. But liberal writing has always concerned itself with the gap between ideal and reality, finding in this not a simple irony but a sense of informing tension, and it is that tension which is an identifying characteristic of liberal writing. And though the objective of this writing is the validation of a vision of democratic individualism, more especially in the context of substantial assaults on that proposition, there is a simultaneous consciousness of cultural identity which transforms myth into practical action. And though the myth of democratic individualism inevitably intersects with that of commercial pragmatism, liberalism being constantly urged towards conservatism, a scepticism about the inevitability of moral progress accompanying material advance constantly holds the liberal novel in a continuous debate with its own presumptions. And this necessarily inhibits the resolution of action or the confident transposition of moral conviction into social event. The result, in politics, is the balance of power, and in art, a functional ambiguity, a continuing tension.

This might seem a recipe for stasis in both areas, but the fear of a homogenized identity or, indeed, a homogenized citizenry was recognized from the beginning, so that while the new state was concerned with forging one out of many, it was equally concerned with guaranteeing the independence of the individual—making a myth out of that self-reliance while insisting that the duty of the free man was not only to himself but also to his fellow men. Like the human body, it was to be a state which relied on the tensions of the muscles to sustain its shape and balance. And the central tradition of its literature recognized as much, though perhaps with that tension resolved slightly in favor of intuitive truth and felt morality which asserted a natural supremacy over a public law which could never be seen as much more than an imperfect attempt to codify natual lore.

The destruction of that natural balance was thus a crucial event, or a series of events, and coincided, ironically, with America's rise to world power. Thus, at the very moment that its political supremacy could have enforced its model of moral and social action, loss of confidence in the self and in an unremitting social responsibility left it stranded in an antinomian hedonism or in a conservative retrenchment into self-interest. President Wilson's liberal principles carried conviction in Europe; in America, they no longer seemed relevant. The 1930s, of course, restored the social world to the center of attention, but felt that the individual had been superceded, the self being a product of history or, more heroically, a necessary martyr for the class, the race, the genus. There was, again, no tension, only a solidarity of purpose whose real flaccidity was momentarily hidden beneath a language of conviction, purpose, and determined action. But, lacking any sanction in the self, the series of betrayals of language, conviction, and purpose which followed left no resources, no residue of hope. And this collapse came at a crucial moment. Nihilism was not a good philosophy with which to approach a war.

Accordingly, the old principles were taken out, dusted off, and paraded along with the war bonds. Democracy, freedom, justice, social responsibility were once again placed at the center of the national myth. But it is hard to find a sanction for democratic individualism in the enforced conformity of a war economy or in military life. And the scenes revealed in Europe and in the Pacific did little to encourage belief in the autonomy of the self and man's duty to his fellow man. The question, in a sense, was thus whether liberalism was perhaps not simply an historic phase, a myth, a political and cultural presumption adequate only to a preindustrial, pre-Einsteinian world; whether all values were not ironic or generated by compulsions rooted in the State or in a version of history implacable in its mechanisms and its objectives. The choice seemed one between anarchy and total constraint, with the only defense lying either in an ironic laughter, which achieved its objective by associating the victim with his fate, or in a renewed faith in the inner world to be entered through the senses and then transformed into an asocial spirituality. But there was another alternative—one generated precisely by the compelling need to re-invent a moral world so casually disestablished by the brutal coercions of warfare and by the disorienting revelations of human cruelty. And, not surprisingly, it was the Jewish writer who felt most directly the absolute necessity to imagine a system in which the individual could be held responsible for his actions. And before examining some aspects of the liberal impulse in black writing, it is perhaps appropriate to look for a moment at the response of another embattled group intent on constructing a house of fiction in which, in Iris Murdoch's words, "free characters could live."

In 1969, two American astronauts landed on the moon. As Neil Armstrong somewhat indistinctly remarked, "That's one small step for a man, one giant leap for mankind." The moon landing was clearly one of those moments in history which seem to demand a cool assessment of the progress or otherwise of mankind. As Saul Bellow's protagonist remarks in the novel with which he marked the lunar landing, and drawing significantly on a phrase from Mark Twain's *Huckleberry Finn*, "Before lighting out, before the hop to the moon and outward bound, we had better look into some of this" because, as he explains, "at the moment of launching from this planet to another something was ended, finalities were demanded, summaries."[1] And summaries are what we have had. Norman Mailer felt the same way in his book about the Apollo venture, *Fire on the Moon*, as did the British dramatist Tom Stoppard in his play *Jumpers*, the action of which occurs at the moment of a highly unlikely British moon landing. What links all three works together is a debate over whether the liberal vision of man remains valid. Is this a giant leap either for man or for mankind, or is it the spread of barbarism, the final victory of the machine, a breath away from the apocalypse? And in terms of contemporary American literature, apocalypse was in the air. Is the movement into space merely an attempt to escape our earth-bound mortality—an egocentric thrust into the void, like Ahab striking out at Moby Dick—or is it a genuine destiny, a sudden opening up of new possibilities which make the old liberal principles seem valid again in what had seemed to be a world choking on its own despair?

This, in fact, is the question. Whatever happened to the liberal tradition in American writing? For, as Saul Bellow reminds us, though "undeniably the human being is not what he commonly thought a century ago . . .the question still remains. He is something. What is he?"[2]

The contemporary American novelist seems to have answered in one of three main ways. Either he sees the individual as a victim of a menacing society which justifies a neoromantic retreat into the self; or, with absurdist assurance, he despairs of both self and society; or he asserts a liberal belief in the need for the individual to accept his connection with and responsibility for a society which need not be regarded as destructive or oppressive.

In the introduction to this book, I confessed to the notorious difficulty which others besides myself have experienced in attempting to define liberalism. The same confusion will inevitably emerge from my treatment of writers. For in saying that they are a part of a liberal tradition, I am not saying that they are untouched by conservative impulses—James Fenimore Cooper being a good case in point—nor am I saying that they do not succumb on occasion to an essentially antiliberal pessimism—Melville and Twain providing ample evidence of this. So what is liberalism as reflected by American writers? What is the nature of the liberal imagination?

As I suggested in the introduction, for the nineteenth-century writer it implies a belief in human progress; a faith in the importance of the individual; a conviction that ''self'' and ''society'' are unironic terms and that the individual owes each his alliance. It accepts the desirability of change, which it assumes to be the dynamic behind private and public development, and while emphasizing rationality was modified by the romantic spirit of nineteenth-century American writers to incorporate a faith in intuitive values and a belief that every man is more than the sum of his parts—that he is not totally explicable. It acknowledges the need to sustain potentially conflicting ideas. For the twentieth-century liberal writer, the world is admittedly a darker place, the self under attack, rationalism discredited, the links between individual and society attenuated, the future in doubt. Yet, as we shall see, the urge to grant full value to the terms of the social contract survives; the need to resist the destructive nihilism and romantic excesses of contemporary life remains strong.

Perhaps the most important element to note is the dual allegiance to self and society. In Emerson's words, ''A man must ride alternately on the horses of his private and public nature, as the equestrians in the circus throw themselves nimbly from horse to horse.''[3] Whitman similarly announced, ''One's self I sing, a simple separate person,/Yet utter the word Democratic, the word En-Masse,''[4] or, as he explained in *Democratic Vistas*, ''Not that half only, individualism, which isolates. There is another half, which is adhesiveness or love, that fuses, ties, and aggregates, making the races comrades, and fraternizing all.''[5] This doubleness of vision typifies the nineteenth-century American novel which can envisage the destruction of the individual with some equanimity because it takes place against a background of moral and physical progress, because the society which displaces and incorporates him is, for all its weaknesses, an expression of human advancement. Hence, the death of Deerslayer in Cooper's book is redeemed by the necessary advance of civilization which will create an order in which individualism can continue to function in a more limited but humane way. The death of Billy Budd is, perhaps, similarly redeemed by the integrity of Captain Vere, who represents the necessary demands of a society which, if capable of the inhumanity of war, is equally capable of compassion and justice. The archetypal American hero is thus not a man alone confronting nature, as we are too often taught, but a man torn between the easy moral freedom of open territory and the ethical demands of social life—demands which prevent Hester Prynne from leaving her Puritan community, which tie Cooper's hero to the representatives of a painfully obtuse and even corrupt society, and which make Huck Finn long for the company of the Negro Jim, despite the fact that he is the source of his moral dilemma. Even Ahab is drawn to the black cabin boy, Pip, as he is to the domestic world reflected in Starbuck's Quaker eyes. This ambivalence, this shuttling to and fro between a desire for order and a desire for freedom, a responsibility to the self and a responsibility to society, is a distinguishing characteristic of the nineteenth-century American writer and the liberal spirit. If one wants an image of this paradox, then consider that prototypical early American experience—the settlement in the wilderness. The settlement protects the individual but necessarily institutes restrictive laws; the wilderness represents freedom but also the danger of moral and spiritual anarchy. American writing is characterized by a suspicion of a state of order which may congeal into stasis and, by degrees, corruption and a simultaneous fear of formlessness which may decay into anarchy—hence the functional ambiguity which has distinguished American writing from Cooper, through Hawthorne and Melville, to James and Fitzgerald. So the American nineteenth-century novel is a novel of tensions, of issues which remain essentially open.

The English nineteenth-century novel is, for the most part, a novel of harmony and resolution. Order and morality are restored. In the American novel, the question is unresolved. *The Scarlet Letter* envisages a society on the brink of change. In *Huckleberry Finn*, the social verities have begun to crumble flake by flake. In *Moby Dick*, the very structure of reality has been nudged out of kilter. (The only place one can find real parallels to this in English literature is in the gothic novel or in the gothic-influenced *Wuthering Heights* and, thereafter, not until Conrad and Lawrence.) Yet, despite the existence of flux and the suggestion of horror, or at least social evil, as a determinable reality, the nineteenth-century American novel still recognizes an underlying progress—a process of change and development which can be ratified because it is sanctioned both by a sharpening intellect and a growth in compassion and moral truth.

But this confidence in human progress, this faith in the integrity of the individual and the value of social institutions, did not survive the turn of the century. Where classic liberalism insisted on rationality and saw society as an expression of individuals working in concert for common goals, Freud stressed human irrationality and posited an opposition between the individual and his society. Where liberalism stressed human freedom, Darwin seemed to outline an essential determinism. For Henry Adams, the liberal dream ended with the announcement of President Grant's cabinet, which represented a prime example in his mind of the final surrender of integrity and liberal principles to the money powers. For others, confidence in the centrality and integrity of the individual died with the determinism implied by industrialization and urbanization. For others, it was World War I which seemed, as Hemingway pointed out, to destroy the meaning of liberal language and, to Fitzgerald and others, to provide final proof of the theories of Oswald Spengler—who announced the decline of the West and the eclipse of liberal values. The gulf between the nineteenth and the twentieth centuries would seem to be precisely the gulf between freedom and determinism, between Thoreau's *Walden*, with its faith in individual integrity and social responsibility, and B. F. Skinner's *Walden II*, a rigidly determined world in which individuality has ceased to have any real meaning. The "open" world of the nineteenth century has become the "closed" world of the twentieth.

Indeed, the distinction which I implied between the "openness" of the nineteenth-century American novel and the "closed" nature of the English novel could be applied usefully to the distinction between the nineteenth- and twentieth-century American novel—at least the American novel of the 1920s and 1930s and the apocalyptic and absurdist novels of the post-war scene. Indeed, not only were nineteenth-century novels characterized by a sense of openness, of unresolved moral and social issues, but this is reflected in an imagery of openness—the open forest of Cooper and Hawthorne, the sea of Melville, the free territory of Twain. Of course, constrictions do exist; they are the inevitable and necessary counterparts of that freedom—an essential element in the definition of openness. Hence, Natty Bumppo, Hester Prynne, Huck Finn, Billy Budd, and even Thoreau all find themselves behind prison bars, but only so that their essential freedom can be underscored. Washington Irving's Rip van Winkle virtually returns from the dead as, more literally, do Poe's heroines who, in clawing their way out of the tomb, assert their identity and deny the final constriction of death with all the vigor of a Lazarus.

But if the nineteenth-century novel was characterized by images of openness, that of the twentieth century has been distinguished by containment and circumscription. Man is deracinated, solitary rather than self-contained. His environment now is the city, which regards open country simply as a containing ring which is part of its own definition. The fields and forests of the nineteenth-century novel give way to the urban wasteland pictured by Pound, Eliot, and Fitzgerald. Melville's open sea becomes Gatsby's squalid swimming pool. The free territory becomes Hemingway's bull ring, a drastically limited world in which the individual is justified in declaring a separate peace from society and in seeking meaning in a self sundered from history. When Huck Finn lighted out for the territory at the end of that novel, he chose a world of possibility in which the individual could shape the moral values of his society; when Nick Carroway leaves for the Midwest at the end of *The Great Gatsby*, he returns to an area already corrupted, having seen the potential for action and integrity exposed as unreal. The great figures of the liberal past are now remote. In *The Last Tycoon*, Andrew Jackson's house has been boarded up, and presumably, therefore, his liberal values are no longer historically relevant. President Lincoln becomes a Hollywood extra, stuffing himself with fruit pie, and when one of the novel's characters receives a telephone call from what he takes to be the President of the United States, it turns out to be from an orang-utan.

The 1930s did nothing to redeem the liberal situation. The proletarian novel turned for its hero, not to the individual, but to the mass. Even Steinbeck, apparently the decade's most liberal writer, seemed to avoid the realities of city life and to preach an antinomian doctrine (there ain't no good and there ain't no bad, there's just things folk do), a dubious moral position to outline on the eve of World War II.

And this is a crucial observation. For, what did the American writer make of the war? Essentially, I am suggesting that he reacted in one of three main ways. Either he saw the concentration camps and the bombing of Dresden and Hiroshima as final proof that society was designed for the destruction of the individual and that the individual was thus justified in retreating into the self, in forging new life-styles unconnected to those of society—a stance of romantic alienation in other words; or he despaired of both elements and stressed the equal absurdity of man and society; or he felt the need to assert liberal principles. Why? And why should the liberal banner now be taken up largely by Jewish writers? I think, fairly obviously, because if they had endorsed the other strategies, they would have been in danger of validating the concentration camp and the destruction of the Jews. After all, if you concede an antinomian world in which there are no agreed moral values then what is your basis for criticizing the concentration camp guard? If you acknowledge the individual as having no responsibility for the state of his government and society, then, once again, he stands justified. To be responsible for a literature which asserts that man is a victim, social or metaphysical, is to suggest that all action is futile or ironic. To be responsible for a literature which asserts that life is best lived within the confines of the self is to suggest that there is no social responsibility. As Arthur Miller said in his essay on "Tragedy and the Common Man," "If all our miseries, our indignities, are born and bred within our minds, then all action, let alone the heroic action, is obviously impossible. And if society alone is responsible for the cramping of our lives, then the protagonist must needs be so pure and faultless as to force us to deny his validity as a character."[6] "We ought to be struggling," he insisted elsewhere, "for a world in which it will be possible to lay blame . . .for where no order is believed in, no order can be breached."[7] No wonder that the true inheritors of the nineteenth-century liberal tradition have been Jewish writers: like Arthur

Miller, who attended the Auschwitz trials in Frankfurt and who wrote plays about the need for the individual to accept a public and private responsibility; or Saul Bellow, one of whose protagonists had been shot by the Nazis in the course of a mass murder; or Bernard Malamud, whose novel *The Fixer*, though set in Czarist Russia, is essentially a transposed reaction to the inhumanity of the Nazis. No wonder, either, that Saul Bellow rejects both the other categories, having Herzog denounce "the commonplaces of the Wasteland outlook, the cheap mental stimulants of Alienation," and has him ask and answer what clearly seems to Bellow to be the central question of the postwar world. "Has the filthy moment come when moral feeling dies, conscience disintegrates, and respect for liberty, law, public decency, all the rest collapse in cowardice, decadence, blood? . . .I cannot accept this foolish dreariness. We are talking about the whole of mankind."[8] Miller, likewise, saw the absurd as a kind of moral insanity, as "something one had to be able to afford. The abrogation of cause and effect was entertaining" only "so long as one had never felt the effects."[9]

In the postwar novel, then, the two elements which coexisted in the nineteenth century, romanticism and liberalism, have split apart; the tendency toward romantic excess, always implicit in romanticism and recognized as such, an elevation of the self at the expense of connectiveness, has been realized in a literature which seems in danger at times, at least in Bellow's eyes, of establishing what is almost a totalitarianism of the self. Society is seen, if at all, only vaguely, and seen, even then, in its most obvious and immediate form. It is the threat of an oppressive and destructive system—a menace which is invoked to validate a dive down into selfhood, or a construction of discrete linguistic worlds which are counterposed, rather as Hemingway's unique world had been, to what is seen as a menacing authoritarianism and a disturbing flux. But from Bellow's point of view, to flee from social restriction or anarchy into a self-created world, a void encircled by imagination, is to create a provisional society of the mind which offers no prescription for meaningful survival. The cost of abandoning society may prove to be the surrender of any ability to deflect its path—it may be to compound its materialism, to sustain its political priorities, and hasten its collapse. In an article written in 1963, he posed the logical question to the absurdists, "After nakedness, what?" "After absurdity, what?" and regretted the tendency of neoromantics, or what he chose to call "writers of sensibility," to believe that "only private exploration and inner development are possible, that "the opposition of public and private" are "fixed and indissoluble."[10]

The fact that Bellow attacks many of the characteristics of the modern age has given him the appearance of a conservative. I take this to be misleading, for his work contains tensions of a kind inimical to conservatism. The world he is drawn to is not one of prescriptive morality and prudent behavior. The duty which he urges on his characters is not acceptance of the status quo or even the principle of continuity; it is the need to rediscover the truths of one's own nature and imagination. He does not believe with Edmund Burke that "the individual is foolish but the species wise." Indeed, he seems to feel that wisdom lives on only in a few exemplary and psychically damaged survivors, but that that wisdom may prove an inheritance for all if we can but wake from our sleep of the spirit which has lasted for more than a generation.

The liberal alternative, presented by Jewish writers like Arthur Miller, Bernard Malamud, in some moods Norman Mailer, but perhaps most significantly by Saul Bellow, constitutes a desire to resuscitate the liberal conscience—to demonstrate the basis on which the individual can cope with what all these writers concede to be the potentially overwhelming nature of the modern world without capitulating to despair or having recourse to autonomous worlds spun out of the imagination—without recoiling from history.

Appropriately enough, the image of this new liberal literature is, once again, openness, though, as with the nineteenth-century writers, the path to that openness may lie through constriction. The hero of Ralph Ellison's *Invisible Man* discovers his liberal principles when he stumbles into a cellar which, very significantly, we are told has been closed since the nineteenth century. The boards which had been nailed around Andrew Jackson's house are coming down: the world is opening up. With the acknowledgement that a culture is the creation of its individuals, Ellison's hero prepares to leave his cellar as Thoreau had left Walden. Similarly, Edward Albee's first play, *The Zoo Story*, is based on his faith that it is possible for people to emerge from behind bars of isolation to make contact with one another. The same notion is there in Arthur Miller's *After the Fall* and in Malamud's *The Fixer*. Herzog, we are told, was a man "who knew what it was to rise from the dead". In *Mr. Sammler's Planet*, the protagonist has literally emerged from the dead—having escaped from a mass murder by clawing his way out of the grave. In *Henderson the Rain King*, Bellow had identified the image. He describes his hero as a Lazarus—the man who had been brought back from the grave, who had come out into the open again. And this is the central image of the modern liberal novel—man as Lazarus—what Bellow has called a "tenaciousness against death." In his first novel, *Dangling Man*, his protagonist admits that "goodness is achieved not in a vacuum but in the company of other men, attended by love. I, in this room, separate, alienated, distrustful, find in my purpose not an open world, but a closed, hopeless jail. My perspectives end in the walls."[11] The rest of his novels have been dedicated to opening up that world, to breaking down the walls.

For the absurdist novelist, the prison is inescapable, whether it be Pynchon's Benny Profane shooting alligators in the New York sewers (an appropriate image of the inescapable labyrinth of his life) or the character in his latest novel, *Gravity's Rainbow*, who is shut up in the small compartment of a V-2 rocket which is plunging down to earth as the book breaks off abruptly. For

Pynchon, the whole world is defined and encompassed by the constricting power of gravity and exists under the menacing arc which is now the flight path of a rocket rather than the ellipse of a rainbow.

By definition, the liberal does not deal in apocalypse or eschatology, so that Bellow rejects the vision of society projected both by the absurdist and by the neoromantic. For if society is indeed technology, urban decay, crime, violence, and change, it is also an expression of the link between individuals, an expression of interdependence. In *To Jerusalem and Back*, he quotes approvingly Hannah Arendt's observation that "with word and deed we insert ourselves into the human world . . .and this insertion is like a second birth."[12] As Bellow himself remarked, "We must carefully remind ourselves that if so many people today exist to enjoy or deplore an individual life, it is because prodigious public organizations, scientific, industrial, and political, support huge populations of new individuals. These organizations both elicit and curtail private development. I myself am not convinced that there is less selfhood in the modern world."[13] Like the nineteenth-century liberal writer, therefore, Bellow sees both the dangers and the attractions of change and stagnation, the self and society. But his world is less concerned with creating what Herzog calls a "good five-cent synthesis" than with identifying and sustaining a tension, an ambiguity, reminiscent of writers like Twain and Melville. Indeed, the influence is clear. *Henderson the Rain King* is reminiscent of *A Connecticut Yankee* and draws on one of its central incidents. *The Adventures of Augie March* similarly owes a great deal to *Huckleberry Finn*, as does *Seize the Day* to *The Confidence Man*. Augie March insists that a "man's character is his fate," as Emerson had announced that "character is reality." He asserts that he is "democractic in temperament, available to everybody and assuming about others what others have assumed about myself[14] —words borrowed almost directly from Whitman. Similarly, at the beginning of *Henderson the Rain King*, the protagonist admits that "society is what beats me. Alone I can be pretty good, but let me go among people and there's the devil to pay,"[15] as Melville's Ishmael confesses to a similar misanthropy at the beginning of his voyage, which ends in a similar acceptance of human interdependence. The echoes are everywhere in Bellow's work.

As we have seen, the nineteenth-century liberal writer was more than a little influenced by the assumptions of romanticism. Total explanations, intuitive knowledge, the integrity and ultimate value of the sensibility all assumed an important part of his work, tempering the liberal ideal. Bellow, however, sees these as symptoms of the modern disease. Illusions of human grandeur are displaced by a conception of life which accepts something of the absurdist view but which continues to assert the values of individual integrity and to endorse the terms of the social contract. This is a harrowed liberalism, refined by half a century of brutality and the growth of a technology and life-style which seem to allow less and less room for the expression of a confident humanism but which have also served to underline the urgent need for a view of human existence which transcends both despair and romantic excess. But neither is this the liberalism of the early part of the century which had come close to saying that the true inheritor of liberal values was not the individual but the group. Nor is this primarily a question of optimism or pessimism, terms which, anyway, evade real meaning, but rather of the acknowledgment that though the social structure continues to change, though technology is constantly forging a new environment which places ever newer and greater pressures on the individual, that individual still has resources on which he can draw without retreating into solipsism or preaching apocalypse—resources which humanize the mechanical, which reassert involvement with others, and which give meaning to what otherwise might seem a civilization slipping into decay and dissolution.

Of course Bellow recognizes all too clearly that liberalism seems in some ways tangential to the modern thrust. Indeed, he sees the modern laments over the death of the novel as part of the assault on liberalism, saying in a recent article that "I take it for granted that an attack on the novel is also an attack on liberal principles."[16] Liberal responsibility to self and society defers all too often to the casual presumption that problems of all kinds will dissolve in the face of physical proximity or the pursuit of spiritual nirvana. All too often, personality is substituted for individuality, life-style for life—as Bellow shows in *Mr. Sammler's Planet*. Vague imprecations to "love one another" are offered as a substitute for hard-minded moral, political and cultural realism. This is a generation which, in the 1960s, could no longer say, with Thoreau, that they craved only reality; it was a generation turning on, tuning in, dropping out, either flirting with apocalypse and the absurd or seeking for transcendence in the strange byways indicated by the Maharishi, the astrologer, the demonologist, the acid-head, the macrobiotic dietician, or any of the other "reality instructors" then hawking their wares in an America which has always sought a spiritual validation for its cloying material abundance. Despite the many historical failures of liberalism in America and despite the inescapable weakness of an approach rooted in ambivalence and constantly torn between notions of the autonomous self and a liberal democracy in which individuals are held together by a common pain and responsibility, Bellow, like Whitman, sees the real value of human life, in a world of moon landings and the patterned structures of modern existence, as resting, finally, in these contradictions, these conflicting demands of self and society which characterize the terms of the liberal debate. The openness of the endings, the commitment untested in social action, often criticized as a fault in his work, is in fact entirely appropriate, for his work is concerned precisely with indicating the possibility of new beginnings. Nowhere, perhaps, is this more apparent than in *Mr. Sammler's Planet*, which contemplates the state of mankind as he begins to thrust outward towards the stars.

The protagonist of *Mr. Sammler's Planet* is symbolically and actually a displaced person—a Polish Jew who had survived a mass shooting, crawling out of the grave and hiding in a tomb. He now finds himself living in a time in which, as he explains, "liberal beliefs did not seem capable of self-defense and you could smell decay."[17] Born, significantly, in the nineteenth century, he had survived to observe a new society—a society which no longer consists of open country, the sea, and the forests in their original purity, but which has become corrupted. The water has become "unclean, insidious," while "the bushes and the trees" are merely "cover for sexual violence, knifepoint robberies, sluggings and murders."[18] Living in New York, he confesses, "makes one think about the collapse of civilization, about Sodom and Gomorrah, the end of the world."[19] But he goes on to insist that whether this is true or not, "there is still such a thing as a man. . . .There are still human qualities. Our own species fought its fear, our crazy species fought its criminality." We are, he concludes, "an animal of genius."[20] In the face of a rational science and of a technology which threatens to destroy the mystery of existence, he asserts, with Melville, that "all is not flatly knowable";[21] in the face of irrational forces which see individual sensibility as some kind of total world, he insists that "individualism is of no interest whatsoever if it does not extend truth."[22] To Bellow, the central need is to maintain some kind of order both within and without while opening up human possibilities, and, though fearing that it represents mere escapism, he is prepared to concede that the journey to the moon may play at least a symbolic role in this direction for it makes images of openness again seem possible. Where, for Pynchon, the rocket which roars into the air is packed with high explosives and programmed to describe a destructive parabola, for Bellow it suggests at least the remote possibility of new beginnings. Where Pynchon comments on the irony of the rocket launch, "The victim, in bondage to falling, rises on a promise, a prophecy of Escape,"[23] Mr Sammler remarks, "Of course it should be possible still to follow truth on the inward track, without elaborate preparations, computers, telemetry, all the technological expertise and investment and complex organisation required for visiting Mars, Venus, the moon. Nevertheless it was perhaps for the same human activities that had shut us up like this to let us out again. The powers that had made the earth too small could free us from confinement."[24] Here, then, is the image of openness again—of Lazarus. As Sammler says, "This earth was our grave. . .No wonder the human spirit wished to leave."[25] In his most recent novel, *Humbolt's Gift*, the image changes from that of Lazarus to that of Houdini, as the protagonist, newly awoken like Rip Van Winkle from his spiritual sleep, confesses to a morbid fear of stifling in the grave and recognizes the need to end what he calls "the good liberal sleep of American boyhood" that "had lasted half a century."[26]

Surrounded, then, by self-seeking individuals and prophets of disaster, and, though able to see only imperfectly, Sammler insists on the possibility of change and on the connection between individual human beings. "There is a bond. There is a bond,"[27] he repeats. And though the scope for liberal values seems limited and even restricted to the aging Mr. Sammler and his dying friend, and is not untinged with irony, yet Bellow still seems intent on justifying his earlier remark that "novelists must value human existence or be unfaithful to their calling," and Sammler's assertion that "a compassionate utterance was a moral necessity."[28] Indeed, drawing on that favorite liberal image, the social contract, he closes his novel with as direct a statement of liberal values as we are likely to find in a world whose inhabitants are about to launch out into space but who seem rooted meanwhile in despair and self-concern. "We must," insists Sammler, "meet, through all the confusion and degraded clowning of this life through which we are speeding, the terms of the contract. The terms which, in his inmost heart, each man knows. As I know mine. As all know. For that is the truth of it—that we all know, God, that we know, that we know, we know, we know."[29]

If the Jewish writer was forced to grant full weight to both elements of the social contract—the self and society—in order to point an accusatory finger at history and in order to create space for the self to occupy, a similar logic was likely to apply to another group of writers who also had a reason for invoking a moral world which still allows room for identity to cohere and the social fabric to expand—the black writer. The question was, therefore, whether black writing did indeed embrace a liberal ideology, whether there was in fact a black Lazarus.

For a group which had literally reemerged into history in recent years, the image of Lazarus may not seem inappropriate, and it should not perhaps come as a surprise to see Eldridge Cleaver writing in 1968 that "I have returned from the dead. I speak to you from the Here and Now. I was dead for four hundred years." For the black American, history has been the tomb. Indeed, Cleaver is more specific than this. He reminds us that "the New Testament parable of Jesus raising Lazarus from the dead is interpreted by the Black Muslims as a symbolic parallel to the history of the Negro in America. By capturing black men in Africa and bringing them to slavery in America, the white devils *killed* the black man—killed him mentally, culturally, spiritually, economically, politically, and morally—transforming him into a 'Negro,' the symbolic Lazarus left in the 'graveyard' of segregation and second-class citizenship. And just as Jesus was summoned to the cave to raise Lazarus from the dead, Elijah Muhammad had been summoned by God to lift up the modern Lazarus, the Negro, from his grave."[30]

And, despite the rhetoric of the 1960s, it seems to me that this conviction that the Negro is a modern Lazarus has led to an irredeemably liberal vision. The rhetoric created a carapace beneath which the familiar liberal convictions sloshed around. For black writing takes as its central presumption the existence of an attainable identity, the reality of social and moral obligations, albeit at times defined in racial terms, the compelling necessity to strip off pretense, social posturing, pragmatic value systems in order to restore oneself to an ineluctable real essence. The creation of a history and the creation of a self are presented as parallel and complementary processes. Where nonliberal white writers tend to see cosmic conspiracies, fragmented layers of experience whose coherences are contingent, a self which is either a distorting mirror or a transparent membrane offering a pathway to ultimate nirvana, the black writer distills metaphysics into politics, seeing political conspiracies. Addressing himself to Camus, Sartre once observed that "should a child die you accused the absurdity of the world and this deaf and blind God which you had created in order to spit in his face. But the child's father, if he were a laid-off labourer, accused men."[31] So that if most black writing excludes the metaphysical dimension, it is in this sense. The black writer, particularly in the 1960s, simply encounters the problem at an earlier stage, perceives it in terms which make metaphysics seem a retreat rather than a transcendence. Alienation is a matter of practical social realities rather than a generalized sense of angst. Lorraine Hansberry's embittered denunciation of absurdist literature in her play *The Sign in Sidney Brustein's Window* was thus seen by her as a moral act (a similar point is made by Carlene Polite in her novel *The Flagellators*). Ralph Ellison, who wrote what even a quarter of a century later remains probably the best novel ever written by a black American, made a similar point when he wrote that "literature is an affirmative act. . . .Underlying it most profoundly is the sense that man dies but his values continue. . . .I think human life is a move towards the rational."[32] It is hard to imagine a more essentially liberal pronouncement. And John A. Williams, one of the more impressive black novelists of recent years, has said in a similar vein, "I believe in love which means that I live in a society. I also believe that all things, revolutions included, begin with individuals and individual choices."[33] This was a view which came under increasing pressure in the 1960s but which has, as I shall indicate, reasserted itself more recently.

However, this elevation of the black Lazarus from the grave, the emergence of the Negro into history and a sense of selfhood, was not a question of a swift step out into the light of day. It has taken some time for the new Lazarus to come to terms with his new existence. Even the Negro Renaissance of the 1920s was only a tentative step. Stylistically, only Jean Toomer and Langston Hughes seemed able to break with the structures of the past—most of the writers remaining trapped in the forms and even the assumptions of the system which they saw as entrapping them. But this, perhaps, is to be expected, and Leon Trotsky, in *Literature and Revolution*, offers a possible explanation—an explanation which rests on an image which is in essence derived from the same source as that of Lazarus. Speaking of the emergence of a new race, he says that "just as an individual passes biologically and psychologically through the history of the race and, to some extent, of the entire animal world in his development from the embryo, so, to a certain extent, must the overwhelming majority of a new class which has only recently come out of pre-historic life, pass through the entire history of artistic culture. This class cannot begin the construction of a new culture without absorbing and assimilating the elements of the old culture.''[34] But there are other, more immediate reasons for the style and direction of much black writing.

The pressure for realism in the black novel is partly, of course, a matter of audience. It derives from a desire to present fiction which attaches itself to a recognizable cultural setting and therefore strives for a kind of authenticity of setting which has ceased to be the commanding reality for other writers. Experiment implies a splintering of audiences, an intellectual schism, which sides the author with an avant-garde whose spirit, in the case of the Negro writer, is inimical to his social objectives. Indeed, the model which is offered to the black writer is that of a community homogenized by suffering, whose daily life is both a token of that suffering and the source of its heroism. And this seems to me to create a bias in favor of a particular style: Alain Locke, writing in the 1920s, observed that ''all classes of people under social pressure are permeated with a common experience . . .they are emotionally welded together as others cannot be. With them ordinary living has epic and lyric intensity.''[35] And here, perhaps, is an explanation for a continued interest in naturalistic style in books such as Ann Petry's *The Street*, William Gardner Smith's *South Street*, James Baldwin's *Go Tell It On The Mountain*, Warren Miller's *The Cool World*, and Louise Meriweather's *Daddy Was a Numbers Runner*.

It also explains the central significance of autobiographical books like Cleaver's *Soul on Ice*, Brown's *Manchild in the Promised Land*, Alex Haley and Malcolm X's *The Autobiography of Malcolm X*, and other such works which, by definition, constitute an attempt to create the self but which are conceived as potential weapons. And there is a difference between this strategy and that of other American writers which derives from their different perspectives on society.

Writers like Bellow and Mailer responded to urban complexities with a subtle enquiry into styles of response, ranging from an anguished anxiety-ridden sifting of roles to a probing of the psychopathology of the self. In recent fiction, style has been shattered, and the pieces have fallen somewhat haphazardly as doubts about public forms have created a parallel series of doubts about private structures. The novelist's encounter with the external world becomes a fraught experience, not simply because of the menacing nature of that world, but because the self which confronts it is no longer so assured, nor the forms it devises for that collision so confident or easily definable. As a dialogue between private and public worlds, it becomes at times attenuated, shrill, and scarcely audible, and at other times, neurotically verbal. But Bellow can afford to contemplate the pain which springs from divorce, from the pressures of urban life, a threatening romanticism, the collapse of social connectiveness. He can debate metaphysics in a social guise because he accepts a freely flowing continuum between the two. For the black writer, on the other hand, all these experiences tend to crystallize into or be seen through the prism of his racial being—a racial imperative which provides both the impetus for his art and the reason for its ineluctable focus. And that imperative gives the writer a different perspective—creates a contrasting set of images. Charlie Citrine, in Bellow's *Humbolt's Gift*, teetering on the edge of a partly constructed skyscraper in Chicago, or Stephen Rojack, in Mailer's *An American Dream*, balancing on a high balcony in New York City, construct a self under pressure which can begin to relate them to the material of their lives and to the urban arabesques below them. Richard Wright's protagonist in the sewers of Chicago (in "The Man Who Lived Underground"), or Ralph Ellison's invisible protagonist in a New York cellar, or LeRoi Jones's anti-hero in *Dutchman*, in his subway coach in what Jones calls "the flying underbelly of the city," or E. J. Gaines's characters in their "private basements" in *What If It Had Turned Up Heads*, approach the problem from a wholly different direction. As Langston Hughes had said in *Not Without Laughter* (1930), "Being coloured is like being born in the basement of life, with the door to the light locked and barred—and the white folks live upstairs."[36] Where, like Baldwin's Rufus Scott, they too balance on the rim of the city, it is merely as prelude to a suicidal plunge into the depths. This contrast is perhaps more apparent than real in that "the edge" also operates as an image of contingency, and the white writer, as can be seen in Saul Bellow's *Mr. Sammler's Planet*, is drawn to the image of the pit with the same compulsion as Poe. But for the black writer, the underground functions as an analogue for his own social and spiritual location. The weight of the city is on top of him. Blacks were often seen by whites as Morlocks, creatures of the underworld, threatening. Or alternatively, in the 1920s, and again with the beats in the 1950s, and with Mailer in the 1960s, they were seen, even by those who envied what they saw as their free life-style, as an image of submerged, instinctual, underground responses. In Freudian terms—and Freud was invoked very easily, if mistakenly, in the 1920s and once again in the 1960s—they were seen as the id and the whites as superego. For the revolutionary, indeed, they held a revolutionary potential which may not be wholly separable from the kinetic power implied by the suppression of energy. When Marcuse quotes Norman O. Brown in *Negations*, the Marxist and the neo-Freudian are neatly fused: "The revolution is from below, the lower classes, the underworld, the damned, the disreputable, the despised and rejected. Freud's revolutionary motto in *The Interpretation of Dreams: Flectere si nequeo Superos. Acheronta movebo.* If I cannot bend the higher power, I will stir up the lower depths. Freud's discovery: the universal underworld."[37] And all too often there was a disturbing reality to an iconography which located the Negro in the basement and placed whites above him. The blacks thus have to forge their identities in the face of definitions much more menacing than those which were offered to Augie March. And the darkness of those cellars and basements offers an image which they must learn not to confuse with blackness; darkness is the absence of light, blackness is a defining characteristic. The world into which they emerge can offer them nothing except a sense of opposition against which they may forge an identity out of refusal.

And this is the risk, and perhaps also at times the strength, of black writing. *Native Son* is built on a refusal which ultimately becomes an assertion. The process of both *Native Son* and *Invisible Man* is a slow stripping of illusion, of selves—a steady progress towards a reality which is defined in terms of an authentic being. It is a liberal literature, written at a time when liberal assumptions were under pressure. And if its liberalism creates a tendency towards a realism which is in process of doing battle with naturalism, it seems to me also eventually to place that naturalistic style under pressure. A free-ranging self actively redefining past and future implies an equally loosely structured sense of style. Thus, even in *Native Son*, the style veers over into a symbolic structuring, while in *Invisible Man*, it transmutes itself as the certainties of the South give way to the fluidities of the North. John A. Williams plays with time scales in *Captain Blackman* and forces his fictional world and the public world into the same stylistic space, as does William Demby in *The Catacombs* (also deriving from an underground image), or Ishmael Reed in *Flight to Canada*—a process which Reed himself has described as "fetish making" and which might more simply be described as the unmaking of history and the construction of new paradigms of the past to protect the individual and the race from the evils of a more conventional historical fetishism.

Indeed, many novels are precisely about the process of redefining history, of slowly reconstructing the fabric of the past in such a way as to discover the roots of cultural and personal identity. This is perhaps why so many black novels are set in that past which is part tangible and part mythic; a usable past which can be turned to the purpose of locating a self which had been cut adrift in an American environment it could not define and whose direction it could not deflect. It is a past, too, which must be set against that projected by white historians like Stanley Elkins or Fogel and Engerman or implied by a social scientist like Arthur Jensen. Elkins's Sambo thesis had taken for granted a docile response from the Negro, evidenced by the relative paucity of slave rebellions, and had seen an analogy in the passivity with which Jews had acquiesced in their fate. Fogel and Engerman had suggested that, economically speaking, the slaves had not had such a bad return on their labor, while Arthur Jensen distinguished an identifiable difference in intelligence between blacks and whites, an observation which seemed to some to offer a justification for prejudice.

It is not surprising, therefore, that William Styron's *The Confessions of Nat Turner* should have provoked such a powerful and immediate reaction or that the remaking of the past should have proved such an attraction for black writers, for the tomb which the black Lazarus wishes to escape is that created by whites. Margaret Walker's *Jubilee*, Ernest Gaines's *The Autobiography of Miss Jane Pittman*, John Oliver Killens's *Slaves*, William Melvin Kelley's *A Different Drummer*, John Williams's *Captain Blackman*, Alex Haley's *Roots* are all concerned with piecing together a present from the newly discovered or invented fragments of the past. The whole process underlying *Roots*, the most successful novel ever written by a black American, is one of asserting the reality of a tradition every bit as genuine and recoverable as that posited by whites or, failing that, of sabotaging the orthodoxies of history by infiltrating corrosive drops of fiction, as Ellison's hero had dropped black solvent into the national whitewash in *Invisible Man*.

As Ishmael Reed has said, "This is what we want: to sabotage history."[38] The intermingling of fact and fiction in the work of Williams, Killens, and in Reed's own *Flight to Canada*, is designed, much as the work of Pynchon, to subvert history from within. Reed's own strategy is normally somewhat different, however. His assault in *The Free-Lance Pall Bearers* and in *Yellow Back Radio Broke Down* is launched not so much on the supposed verities of the external world as on the mind, the process of perception. Indeed, his world is evidence of an increasing commitment to aesthetic experiment in black writing, signaled by books like Carlene Polite's *The Flagellators*, William Demby's *The Catacombs*, William Melvin Kelley's *Dunsford's Travels Everywheres*, and Reed's own work. As he has said, "Let the social realists go after the flatfoots out there on the beat and we'll go after the Pope and see which causes revolution." As such, however, he has found himself the target for those whose prescriptive versions of the function of art do not include the kind of oblique subversion which he sees as his objective. Thus, though he says of himself and those who adopt his approach that "we are mystical detectives about to make an arrest," he recognizes that the consequences are that what he calls "the historical establishment . . .hire thugs who call themselves nationalists or revolutionaries to keep us in line."[39]

The hero of *Yellow Back Radio Broke Down* (1969) finds himself assailed by just such people. The Loop Garoo Kid, a black cowboy, is a comic-book hero who tries to defend the media town of Yellow Back Radio whose juvenile population has revolted in an attempt "to create our own fiction."[40] He is temporarily captured by Bo Shmo and his neosocial realist gang, who regard him as 'the alienated individual" who survives on "a deliberate attempt to obscure." As Shmo says, "The trouble with you Loop is that you're too abstract. . . . You are given to fantasy and are far off in matters of detail. . . .Far out esoteric bullshit is where you're at. Why in those suffering books that I write about my old neighborhood and how hard it was every gumdrop machine is in place. . . . All art must be for the end of liberating the masses. A landscape is only good when it shows the oppressor hanging from a tree.'' To this, the Loop Garoo Kid replies, ''What's your beef with me Bo Shmo, what if I write circuses? No one says a novel has to be one thing. It can be anything it wants to be, a vaudeville show, the six o'clock news, the mumblings of wild men saddled by demons.''[41]

But the 1960s were indeed characterized by attempts to police black writers, to demand social and aesthetic solidarity. In part, such reactions stem from a need to simplify one's situation in order to understand it. In *The Future of an Illusion*, Freud observes that ''in general men experience the present naive-ly,''[42] and there was perhaps more naivety around in the 1960s. But it is important to remember that in America, as elsewhere, it was a decade in which political and racial tension seemed to demand, and in part even to justify, a simple model of existence. Hence, the peculiar problem of a person who was simultaneously black, a writer, and an American—and who had not only entered history but seemed for a while to be the cutting edge of history. |

And there was for a time in the 1960s a curiously dependent relationship between those blacks who saw themselves as radicals or cultural guerillas and the repressive system against which they pitched themselves. Their identity as black rebels logically required the evil oppressor in order to validate the pure line of their own new-found certainties. Far from calling on white society to change, as Hansberry and Baldwin had done, they assumed an implacable determinism in white hatred because this was a necessary part of their own self-image. It was perhaps as Jean-Paul Sartre said of Jean Genet (and note especially the parallel which he offers): ''Genet does not want to change anything at all. Do not count on him to criticise institutions. He needs them as Prometheus needs his vulture. . . . He loves French society as the Negroes love America with a love that is full of hatred and at the same time desperate. As for the social order which excludes him, he will do everything to perpetuate it. Its rigor must be perfect so that Genet can attain perfection in Evil.''[43] This is the world of white devils and black heroes invoked by LeRoi Jones, reborn as Lazarus with the name Imamu Amiri Baraka.

In a sense, it could be argued that this is a form of escapism even as it is a necessary stage in the reconstruction of an identity, for, as Baldwin has said, ''most people are afraid to become individuals because to become an individ-ual means taking responsibility for your own fate.''[44] Of course, for the cultural nationalist, as for the Marxist, such talk of individuals is premature. What must come first is a restructuring of the world in which that individual moves.

But though this Manichean rhetoric seemed to dominate black writing in the 1960s and indeed did constitute a powerful gravitational pull on writers whose work was eagerly dissected for signs of cultural orthodoxy, it competed with a counterconviction—one stemming both from the writer's necessary faith in his own sensibility and from an obligatory belief in the possibility of change. It competed, in other words, with a persistent liberalism. For, while novelists like John A. Williams, John Oliver Killens, and, to a lesser extent, William Melvin Kelley moved from manifestly liberal novels like *Journey Out of Anger, Youngblood,* and *A Different Drummer,* which were written in the full flush of the integrationist phase of the civil rights movement, to books like *Sons of Darkness, Sons of Light, And Then We Heard the Thunder,* and *Dem,* they invariably failed to sustain the rigor of their own analysis. The apocalyptic ending towards which all these books rush is invariably deflected at the last moment (see Chapter 6). A last hope for interracial cooperation is voiced. The same is true of Ronald Fair's brief novel *Many Thousands Gone* and even of the ending of the television production of *Roots,* an ending false to the novel, false to history, and false to the situation of the blacks in America. And this retreat from apocalypse did, of course, presage a more general withdrawal from the barricades which has marked the 1970s. The urgencies of black emergence were increasingly submerged in other causes: Vietnam, women, the Indians, the environment, Watergate. Increasingly, writers came to feel that they had served time for the cause and even that the foundations had now been laid— that an alternative history and mythology were now available and that the simple contours ascribed to blacks and whites in the 1960s had now hardened precisely into a carapace which could only stunt growth on a personal, aesthetic, and social level. The danger of black rage in the 1960s had been that it was too often unfocused. It destroyed Baldwin's Rufus Scott in *Another Country,* as it literally destroyed large areas of the black ghettos in 1967 and 1968. The mood now has changed. In 1976, Baraka called for an interracial alliance along Marxist lines. Eldridge Cleaver appeared in a television commercial for a Christian sect. The Black Muslims have embraced the orthodox and hence interracial Muslim faith. It is now possible to express a concern for aesthetics without incurring an automatic attack such as that which was launched on Ralph Ellison in the magazine *Black World.* It is now possible to splinter the stylistic orthodoxy, to use black experience not so much as a metaphor but as a paradigm.

Where in the 1960s Ed Bullins had produced brief consciousness-raising plays about the need for black violence, by 1972 he was saying, "I don't know anyone who's political any more . . .the initial sloganeering has been done and there's no sense repeating it."[45] Now, a black critic can say, as in the 1960s he could not, that the *New Lafayette* theatre is right in trying to escape racial parochialism, that the Negro Ensemble Company, which had frequently been attacked in the 1960s, is right in advertising in white newspapers and in seeing its real objective as being the need to be accepted as a theatrical rather than a political force. John O'Neale of the Free Southern Theatre can now say that in the late 1960s and early 1970s theatre had "too much politics." The ideas which he pursues are first and foremost theatrical ideas, for as he says, "Blacks in the South tend to be less affected by nationalistic rhetoric. . . .The people have had a lot of experience with the pointlessness of simple rhetoric." He concludes, "I haven't been interested in rhetorical or didactic theatre [for years]. It locks you into a line."[46]

And though this is perhaps overstating it, it is clear that we have entered a new phase in black writing, that there is a greater flexibility, a reduction in the social pressure, a greater confidence in the past and, hence, in the present and the future. The rituals of black theatre, the aesthetic adventureousness of Polite, Kelley, Reed, and, to a lesser degree, Williams, betokens, not a retreat from liberal convictions nor even a sense that such writers wish to submerge their ethnic identity in the mainstream, but a refusal to accept an identity or a role defined simply by the compulsions of revolt. Lazarus has emerged, very often with a new name and even a new religion. But it turns out that beneath the radical language of the 1960s was always a reformist impulse and the vision of community and the role of the artist which is projected by that Lazarus in the 1970s is as irredeemably liberal as that of many Jewish writers and for many of the same reasons.

In a way, the black writer is not a modern in the sense in which Jung uses the term in *Modern Man in Search of a Soul*. For there he suggests that he is "the man who stands upon a peak, or at the very edge of the world, the abyss of the future before him, above him the heavens, and below him the whole of mankind with a history that disappeared in primeval mists. The man whom we can with justice call 'modern' is," he insists, "solitary . . .he has become 'unhistorical' in the deepest sense and has estranged himself from the mass of men who live entirely within the bounds of tradition. Indeed, he is completely modern only when he has come to the very edge of the world, leaving behind him all that has been discarded and outgrown, and acknowledging that he stands before a void."[47]

For the black writer, as for the Jew, the past is to be claimed, the implications of an alienated self to be denied, a tradition of moral responsibility to be accepted. Bellow has confessed to the antimodern state of his imagination and moral stance. His novels have the texture as well as something of the convictions expressed in those nineteenth-century novels which he admires. Much the same could be said of Ellison. For the black American, the void lies in the past not in the future; it is the dreadful caesura in history between his African and his American consciousness. He has passed through that vacuum. Having plunged into it, as in a visit to the underworld, he has emerged into a second life in which a sense of community and an overwhelming need to lay claim to an individual identity are moral necessities.

Jung suggests that "modern man" attempts to compensate for his sense of abandonment by searching for a secular spiritualism, which he finds in psychology itself, or in astrology, theosophy, the occult, yoga, and the many other byways of the spirit, or, indeed, in a new cult of the body. This frenzied pursuit of personal "truth," which Jung, not at all pejoratively, calls "the American tempo," contrasts sharply with the experience of Negro and Jew alike, for whom the old religion is not wholly dead, for whom the past— whatever its ambiguities—is of commanding and central interest, for whom the future contains a hope of social change and even spiritual salvation. The distinction, in other words, would seem to be precisely that between the liberal writer, who continues to credit a moral world rooted in tradition and intuitive values, and the modern spirit, which manifests itself either in a sense of absurdity or in a neoromantic examination of the self in isolation from its social environment.

The black American has had a series of lives, being born again as American slave, freedman, and as fully conscious controller of his own fate. And, in terms of black writing, self-perception frequently comes to the protagonist in a visit to the underworld, in a mock death, a dive down into the underground of self and society alike—surely a liberal image in its presumption of an available truth concealed beneath illusion and falsehood. Hence, Wright's protagonist in "The Man Who Lived Underground" comes to understand his life for the first time as he wanders the labyrinth beneath Chicago, as Ellison's and LeRoi Jones's protagonists perceive their crucial truths beneath the streets of New York City. But the possibility of communicating that truth is problematic. For Wright, who was early in his career, it is too dangerous to be acknowledged by others; for Jones, it was too dangerous to be acknowledged by the self. Wright's "philosopher" is killed because his truths are too painful, and we are left with a feeling of numbing hopelessness which is perhaps akin to that which we feel at the end of Toomer's *Cane*, in which Kabnis emerges from "The Hole" into an ambiguous and even ironic world. But for Ellison, the familiar liberal tensions leave his novel in the same state of openness as one finds in Bellow or, indeed, in those nineteenth-century American novels which he took as his models.

Ellison's novel repeatedly takes his protagonist underground. The deleted scene of his escape from the hospital has him wandering through the basement corridors and down into a cellar; his experience of music is of entering "a cave." His perception of his own manipulation comes to him in the subway, while his ultimate self-perception comes in the cellar, which is his equivalent of a momentary and illuminating plunge outside of history. His determination to leave that refuge, like Mr. Sammler's struggle to pull himself out of the grave, is not to be seen simply as a struggle for survival, however, but as a commitment to the social world which waits for him in all its cruelties, ironies, and imperfections. So, too, John Williams's Odil Mothersill, in *Mothersill and the Foxes*, who was shot by a former lover, literally dies, but is resurrected by the skill of surgeons to take on the racial complexities, urban terrors, and personal pains of life in 1970s America. But he finds, in the imagery of being thus raised up, the source of hope, the possibility of new beginnings implicit in the idea of Lazarus. Thus, he defines the word ''raise'' as ''to move or cause to move upward or to a higher position. To place or set upright. To cause to arise, appear, exist. To increase in size, quantity or worth. To increase in strength, degree or pitch. To begin. To arouse or stir up: raise a revolt.''[48] Indeed, for Alice Walker in *Meridian*, this rebirth of personal and social identity is too positive to be adequately represented by the figure of Lazarus, for his was a case of passive survival. He was raised up. For Alice Walker, the voice is necessarily an active one. As a character observes of her resilient protagonist, ''His first thought was of Lazarus, but then he tried to recall someone less passive, who had raised himself without help.''[49] This, in essence, is the new Lazarus of the Second Renaissance.

Judgement Day Is Coming! Judgement Day Is Coming! 6

Inevitably political developments of the last twenty-five years are reflected in the nature of black writing. The optimism of the early 1950s gave way to an apocalypticism in the middle and late 1960s as, more recently, this, in turn, has been largely superceded by a less engaged literature, a literature which, in reflecting on the fierce commitments of that decade, has come to examine more closely its own function and its own betrayals. In the 1960s, the writer was called upon to subordinate art to life, to acknowledge the functional nature of literature, and to provide the myths of cultural identity and racial dominance required by a community simultaneously threatened and exultant in its new power. The mood was revolutionary, the tone apocalyptic, the imagery eschatological. And yet apocalypse, as Goethe asserted of death, constitutes the abolition of choice, and the revolutionary, no less than the liberal, takes the existence and reality of alternative possibilities as an axiom. Hence, there is a contradiction at the heart of many works in the 1960s, a contradiction which emerges sometimes as sheer confusion and sometimes as a powerful and informing ambiguity. So that beneath the imagery of a longed-for racial battle, which will be the culmination of history and the revelatory moment of justice and retribution, is a counterconviction that the last moment may now be deferred, that a glimpse of the fire may be enough to convert the sinner and give heart to the faithful. Judgement Day is always coming, but its arrival must be perpetually deferred. Where it does occur, as in LeRoi Jones's *The Slave*, it is recognized as being destructive, not only of injustice, but of all human qualities. That play is thus a warning and a prophecy, rather than a model. With the 1970s, when the black writer felt in some degree released from the immediate task of serving the cause, novelists like Ishmael Reed and Alice Walker contemplated the cost in human and literary terms of an apocalyptic mentality. And though Alice Walker was contemptuous of those who traded-in their revolutionary credentials for an insipid literary solipsism, she has also been dismissive of those who mistook image for reality and offered an Old Testament vengeance where the need was for a New Testament compassion. As her short stories reveal, she is not immune to a conviction that the self is under immense pressure, but what she offers, finally, is what Ellison offers— the need to rediscover principles buried by racist and revolutionary alike,

principles which recognize the significance of the individual and which assert
the responsibility of that self not merely to create itself but to acknowledge a
duty towards others. And, paradoxically, that same commitment is to be found
at the heart of the most apocalyptic novels of the 1960s, for the central tradition
of the black novel since Wright has indeed been a liberal one, even though that
liberalism has had to wrestle with a potential for mutual annihilation which, in
1967 and 1968, seemed to be enacted on the streets of America's cities.

In 1963, the novelist John A. Williams undertook a tour of the United States
for *Holiday Magazine*. The resulting articles were to constitute a personal
assessment of the state of the Union. Despite evidence of discrimination and
prejudice and despite the assassination of President Kennedy, he was able to
say, "I searched and I came away with hope."[1] But when the articles were
collected a year later and published under the title *This Is My Country, Too*,
Williams added an afterword which changed the whole mood of his observations. He had come to believe, he explained, that Dallas was the symptom of a
more widespread malaise which in its turn was evidence of a steady move
towards dissolution. "I feel that the murder of Kennedy and several other key,
though lesser-known, people and the upsurging civil-rights movement, the
plunging deterioration of both Republican and Democratic parties are but the
coincidental aspects of a future toward which we have been stumbling all the
time. The result is that grim anarchy is but one crisis away, perhaps too, from
overwhelming the land."[2] This apocalyptic time came to typify the work of
several black novelists in the 1960s after Baldwin's *The Fire Next Time* had
warned of the possibility that Negroes might feel constrained to precipitate
chaos and ring down the curtain on the American dream. Seven years later,
having had a taste of that fire, Baldwin commented that "what has happened, it
seems to me, and putting it far too simply, is that a whole new generation of
people have assessed and absorbed their history, and, in that tremendous
action have freed themselves of it and will never be victims again."[3] And it is
true that writers like John Oliver Killens, William Melvin Kelley, and John A.
Williams had become, and indeed remain, fascinated with recreating the
history of the Negro in America and with establishing a link between the plight
of the individual and the state of the nation.

This latter concern is by no means restricted to black writers. John Updike's
Couples is structured on precisely this basis; he tries desperately to establish
the historical dimension of his characters—the connection between the body
and the body politic, the pubic and the public. His failure to establish this nexus
stems in part from a failure of craft, but in part, also, from the fact that these
individuals no longer hold the front line of history. It is perhaps not convincing
now to assert that the destiny of America is enacted in the small New England
town nor even, one suspects, in the clash of a Kennedy and a Khrushchev. For
an increasing number of people in the 1960s, it seemed to lie, rather, in the moral
implications of the encounter of black and white. Despite Bellow's attempts to

breed a strain of heroes who can match the neurotic frenzy of urban existence with a neutralizing neurosis, it was increasingly the black man who was presented as sliding through the psychic sickness of American society, seeing all, speaking the mystic language of the streets, and taking the quickening pulse of a civilization moving towards cataclysm.

As Richard Wright had said in 1957, "Negro life is [all] life lifted to the heights of pain and pathos, drama and tragedy. The history of the Negro in America is the history of America written in vivid and bloody terms; it is the history of Western man writ small.''[4] Ellison's hero, testing the moral reflexes in South and North, exposed far more than racial intolerance. He revealed an ethical chaos which, Ellison's optimism notwithstanding, threatened the very possibility of order and purpose.

The eye which surveys the modern world is no longer an innocent one. Armed with the insight which had been the major gift of "invisibility," the Negro writer moved swiftly from optimistic declarations of natural justice to tracing out the eschatology of the American dream. The romantic confidence drained away: John Oliver Killens's *Youngblood* (1954), which seems to endorse the work of the NAACP and look forward to interracial cooperation, gave way to his book of racial conflict, *And Then We Heard the Thunder* (1968), and the cold threat of *Slaves* (1969); William Melvin Kelley's endorsement of liberal principles in *A Different Drummer* is followed ten years later by the surrealistic assertions of *Dem* (1969); John A. Williams's *Journey Out of Anger* (1963) is displaced by the destructive insights of *The Man Who Cried I Am* (1967) and the apocalyptic prophecy of *Sons of Darkness, Sons of Light* (1969) and *Captain Blackman* (1972). Williams has said that for many years the Negro believed more fully in the American system than did the whites and that even during the early 1960s "amelioration had set in . . .enough to push back the boiling point.''[5] But, by the time of *The Man Who Cried I Am*, we are moving in a time in which "everybody knows everything,''[6] and extinction is a real and immediate possibility.

John Oliver Killens was born in Georgia in 1916. His formative years were dominated by the economics and politics of the 1930s. He has always played a leading role in cultural and racial affairs, and this has seemingly left him with a legacy of competing commitments which have created a central ambiguity in his work. His novels have certainly moved from documents of liberal assertion to prophecies of racial cataclysm, but he is constantly haunted by the ghosts of old ideologies as well as present convictions. Killens finds himself trapped in a paradox familiar enough to the American Communist Party. On the one hand, this had dedicated itself to forging an alliance between Negroes and poor whites (in essence the old Populists' dream), while, on the other, it seriously advocated the establishment of a separate black state. The Negro was seen as both an exploited worker and a victim of colonialism. The result was a curious schizophrenia, with the Party simultaneously committed to minimizing racial differences in order to facilitate working class unity and stressing racial differences in order to justify a policy of "national" independence. Killens is touched with the same double vision.

In *Youngblood*, he outlines the historic injustices suffered by the Negro and draws what seem to be inevitable conclusions from a catalog of violence, injustice, and liberal temporizing—the need for racial solidarity and, ultimately, even racial conflict, "That's the trouble with us Negroes. . . .We always fighting each other instead of the white man."[7] But the novel appeared in 1954, the year of the Supreme Court decision on desegregation and a time of some optimism in the area of race relations. Despite the friction between the two racial communities, therefore, Killens commits himself to the possibility of interracialism. Slowly, individual poor whites are forced to respect the courage and integrity of the Negroes, who are, incidentally, heroic and dignified almost to a man. Brave efforts are made to establish local branches of a union and the NAACP. A tentative, but real, alliance cutting across color lines seems possible. Yet, while Killens seems intellectually committed to the idea, emotionally, he seems to distrust it. There is little in the book to justify the confidence which is voiced by his characters. Belief in the possibility of an alliance between "the hundreds and the thousands" of southern Negroes "and the decent thinking white people"[8] seems to owe more to left-wing optimism than to reality as depicted in the novel itself.

His 1967 book, *'Sippi*, takes the racial battle a step closer to apocalypse. It is a crudely drawn account of black-white relations in Mississippi in the period between 1954 and the voter registration drives of the late 1960s and takes as its subject the slow awakening of black consciousness and a growing militancy. The process whereby the book's black protagonist and the young daughter of a southern white landowner move towards sexual and political maturity is offered as a parallel to the new self-perception and manhood of the black southerner and an emerging, if bewildered, white moralism. But, despite references to white victims and despite acknowledgments of good will on the part of anonymous whites, the southerners whom he describes are either overt racists or hypocrites. The narrative, indeed, is punctuated with black martyrs, so that the announcement by an indignant black appalled at the killing of a civil rights worker that "it's time for us to shed some white blood now . . .an eye for an eye, a tooth for a tooth!"[9] establishes the tone for the book's finale.

A black leader is assassinated as he leaves a Mississippi church, in a manner which prefigured Martin Luther King's death the year after the book's publication. The result is a systematic killing of whites and an invocation by the protagonist, addressed initially to himself but by extension to all other blacks, to join the Elders—a militant self-defense group closely modeled on the Black Panthers. The basis for a cathartic clash between black and white is established.

But, once again, Killens, like Baldwin, seems to be drawn in two opposing directions. On the one hand, he feels obliged to identify some amelioration in the black political situation, to grant some integrity to young white civil rights workers; while, on the other, he wishes to indict white America for its historic guilt, to celebrate an impending apocalypse which will punish the guilty. The result is a pressure on character and action which constantly threatens to reduce the book to crude melodrama. The dialectic is not contained within the individual sensibility; it is crudely assigned to racial character. Hence, the whites are not merely vicious, they are unbelievably explicit in their hypocrisies and in their racist convictions, the self-deceiving bourbon landowner suddenly lapsing into an uncharacteristic forthrightness when it serves the purpose of the plot. The book's chief virtue lies, perhaps, in its engagement with the contemporary, but, by the same token, its crude analysis is equally a product of the moment. It is a potboiler and bears all the marks of one. Hence, sexuality, potentially a powerful subtext of southern life and used as such by Alice Walker in her excellent novels, degenerates into mere titillation, while the complex pressures which underpin southern racism are rendered in the simplest manner.

But the persistence of Killens' double vision, his continued wish simultaneously to invoke and deny apocalypse, is itself evidence of those subtle pressures which he is himself unable to present with any conviction but which recur in the work of so many black writers as to become almost a distinguishing feature.

Killens' next novel, *And Then We Heard the Thunder*, shows much the same ambivalence as he assembles the evidence which would seem to justify a cataclysmic interracial battle and then retreats from the logic of his own stance. The book is concerned with the slow and painful initiation of Solly Saunders, a middle-class Negro, determined, if possible, to "make it" in the white world. When he is drafted into the army, he pursues the same aim, convincing himself that the battle against fascism provides a real opportunity to win the respect of white America. The realities of life in a Jim Crow army offer him repeated chances to appreciate his real position, and, by degrees, he comes to feel that he is living in a genuinely desperate position and that his only recourse is revolt. The book has as its climax an interracial battle whose apocalyptic implications are immediately subverted by a resulting brotherhood which has no justification in terms of the book's central theme and which seems little more than a gesture toward the Killens of 1954.

Solly moves towards his new perception with a bewildering slowness. Insulted and beaten by white policemen and soldiers, he finds himself in the hospital and undergoes a rebirth which is reminiscent of the similar scene in *Invisible Man*. He comes to realize that "he hated the Great White Democratic Army of the United States of America. They had taken one of their mighty cannons and placed it against his forehead and blown away forever the brains of his grand illusion about the Army and the war."[10] Together with his fellow Negro soldiers, he now signs a letter of protest sent to the northern newspapers. The final sentence anticipates the cataclysm towards which the book inexorably moves: "God only knows why we haven't taken matters in our own hands, or when we might. . . ."[11]

Yet, for all this, he still equivocates, wavering between his new militancy and the expedient conservatism which had characterized his life hitherto. Placed in charge of propaganda for his section, he finds himself delivering lectures on "Americanism versus Racial hatred," while being excluded from the significantly named Booker T. Washington Post Exchange. Finally, confronted with an ineluctable choice, he has to commit himself: "And now he knew what he hoped he never would forget again. All his escape hatches from being Negro were more illusion than reality and did not give him dignity. All of his individual solutions and his personal assets. Looks, Personality, Education, Success, Acceptance, Security, the whole damn shooting match, was one great grand illusion, without dignity."[12] Only now does he ask the questions implicit in his initial strategy: "If he signed a separate peace treaty with Cap'n Charlie, would it guarantee him safe-conduct through the great white civilized jungle where the war was raging, always raging? Would his son also get safe-passage? Anywhere anytime any place?" Only now does he realize that he has "searched in all the wrong places."[13] Yet, as if to deny the essence of this insight, Killens cannot accept the reality of his own vision. The book ends as southern white soldiers apologize for their racist brutality. The prophecy of cataclysm is muted into a plea for an eleventh-hour tolerance, "If I get back home, my brothers, I'll tell the world about your battle here in Bainbridge. Maybe it's not too late yet, if I tell it to the whole wide world, tell them if they don't solve this question, the whole damn world will be like Bainbridge is this morning."[14] The tone is entirely familiar to anyone raised on the fervent optimism of protest literature, as, curiously, is that seemingly ineradicable schizophrenia. The final page of the novel is a supreme example of Killens' ambivalence as he looks for a possible solution, not only to racial antipathies, but also to national divisiveness, while still making compulsive obeisance in the direction of black messianism. "He wanted to believe whatever was left of the world would come to its senses and build something new and different. . . .He wanted to believe that East and West could meet somewhere sometime and sometime soon, before it was too late to meet. . . .He wanted to believe that Kiplings' lie was obsolete. He wanted to believe —that all this dying was for something, beat some sense into their heads. If they don't love you they'll respect you. . . .Perhaps the New World would come raging out of Africa or Asia, with a new and different dialogue which was people oriented. . . .This is the place, where the New World is. The world is waking up again."[15]

Killens returns yet again to the notion of apocalypse in *Slaves*. As its title suggests, this poorly written book is set in slavery times (partly inspired, one imagines by the success of Styron's *The Confessions of Nat Turner*). Plunging further into history, Killens still seems to move, ahistorically, closer to the cataclysm which seems to hound his imagination. As Jericho, a bitter and determined slave, makes his escape with the help of a frustrated white woman, he issues the warning which by now has become a commonplace of Killens's novels, ''Somebody got to pay somewhere, sometime in that great gittin' up goddamn mornin'. It might not come in my time but it's comin' one of these days, it's comin', Luke! Judgement Day is coming, Luke! Judgement Day is coming!''[16] Escape and cataclysm vie with one another; a longed-for apocalypse wrestling with a persistent liberalism. It is a paradox which he fails to examine and which, in *The Cotillion* (1971), he simply abandons in favor of a satire on the black bourgeosie.

William Melvin Kelley obviously writes out of a profoundly different context. Born in New York, he went to Harvard University and studied under John Hawkes and Archibald MacLeish. Like Williams, he has led a peripatetic and decidedly cosmopolitan life, living in Paris, Rome, New York, and, more recently and perhaps significantly, Jamaica. His first work, *A Different Drummer*, which won him the Richard and Hinda Rosenthal Foundation Award of the National Institute of Arts and Letters, was a distinguished first novel which owed a great deal to Faulkner in style and mode of approach and to the nineteenth-century liberal tradition in theme.

The plot itself is extremely simple but, as in *The Sound and the Fury*, it is recounted by a number of different characters. Tucker Caliban, after years of service to the state's most important family—the Willsons—suddenly salts his land, shoots his livestock, chops down a tree which for generations had been a landmark for the Willson family, and burns his house and possessions to the ground. When he leaves, he is followed by all the Negroes in the state. This crisis serves not only to reveal the confused position of the whites, committed to regarding the Negro as expendable but frightened at such a direct attack on the pattern of their existence, but also a potential for action which time and convention seemed to have eroded. Tucker's achievement is not that he pursues a line of militant protest but that he rediscovers principles of individual moral responsibility which seem to have died, for the Negro, with slavery, and for the whites, with the nineteenth-century—killed by the shock of urbanization, the destructive impact of ideology, and a nerveless acquiescence in historical momentum. Just as Ralph Ellison's protagonist discovers a basement ''shut off and forgotten during the nineteenth century,'' at the end of *Invisible Man*, so Kelley's hero acts to reclaim an inheritance of moral self-sufficiency and integrity which historical process and human greed seem to have rendered irrelevant.

The African slave from whom he was descended had asserted his integrity the moment he had set foot in America. His ''No! in thunder'' had shaken assertions which even then were hardening into assumptions. His descendents, however, had all operated within the terms of those assumptions, excluded from moral responsibility, and thus history, by the whites. But now, with Tucker Caliban's decision to cut all links with the past, the romantic rebellion of his ancestor gains a new vitality. At the end of *Invisible Man*, Ellison's protagonist decides to move into history, to end the centuries-long ''hibernation'' provoked by white hostility and sustained by black acquiescence. Kelley's hero likewise reclaims his right to shape his own reality and, by doing so, reveals the potential for action which arises from the courageous exercise of conscience. For Tucker Caliban, belated transcendentalist, it is an instinctual action—the virus dormant through generations becoming active; for those around him, it is a lesson to be learned by his example. As David Willson, a descendent of the man who had tried to enslave Tucker's African ancestor, comes to understand, ''He HAS freed himself; this had been very important to him. But somehow, he has freed me too. . . .Who would have thought such a humble, primitive act could teach something to a so-called educated man like myself? Anyone, anyone can break loose from his chains.''[17]

The protagonist of the book is a black Bartleby, resolutely rejecting the social and personal compromises offered to him and gaining dignity precisely through his act of renunciation. But where Melville regarded this gesture as inherently ambiguous—social isolation and willful nihilism provoking moral problems of their own—Kelley sees Tucker Caliban's action as an attempt to assert pride and identity in the face of a history which has systematically denied both to the Negro. In this novel, Kelley sets out with the determination of a John Barth to rewrite history. It is an avowedly fictive world which he creates, in the same way that Hardy's or Faulkner's characters inhabit a country contiguous with, but imaginatively separate from, the world of reality. Yoknapatawpha is recognizably Mississippi, but it is simultaneously a fictive projection of Mississippi. Kelley's state has a moral rather than a geographical reality, and the changes which are wrought in its confines are achieved within the boundaries of individual conscience rather than political structure.

The book, in other words, is firmly in the liberal tradition. The possibility of action, of moral responsibility, of self-realization is available to all, black and white. In the spirit of Kelley's introduction to a volume of his short stories, *Dancers on the Shore*, it is not finally a novel about race, but about the need to reclaim a heritage which had seemed lost but which is within the reach of anyone with the courage to grasp it.

By the time he came to write *Dem* ten years later, however, this possibility seemed to have vanished. This America is a nightmare world of unreality in which myth has been superceded by illusion. *Dem* lacks the control of his first novel, yet, in a sense, this itself is an expression of a world which is falling apart. It is a world in which fantasy has the authority of reality and reality itself seems no more than a version of absurdity. The white protagonist finds it more interesting and emotionally rewarding to follow the tribulations of a character in a television soap opera than to establish contact with those who surround him. Even when he accidentally encounters this idol, he is incapable of seeing her outside of her fictional role. In this surreal world, a man murders his wife and children and then entertains his friends in the room below. Yet, of course, this kind of fantasy is too close to today's bizarre reality to be easily dismissed. And when the protagonist's wife gives birth to twins—one white, one black—we are offered a precise scientific explanation even as the husband sets out for Harlem to track down the black man with whom he shares paternity. The gulf between the races—the hero simply cannot understand the language of the black world and tries to get rid of the unwanted child—is merely one more proof of a fragmenting society. And if this satire does not end, like Nathanael West's *The Day of the Locust*, with a cataclysmic riot, it does picture a society which is slowly destroying itself by believing its own lies and discretely disposing of realities which become too insistent.

John Williams's early novels provide a naturalistic insight into Negro life. Yet, while the hypocrisy and nerveless ineffectualness of the white community, liberal and conservative, is exposed, interracial relationships can function and black individuals can retain at least a tenuous hold on their fate. Thus, despite the bitterness of his early novel *Night Song*, his characters are not without a sullen determination. Richie Stokes, the jazz-playing protagonist, becomes the embodiment of a spirit which has little to do with legal campaigns for justice or direct action for political rights. Stokes is "fire and brain; he's stubborn and shabby; proud and without pride; kind and evil. His music is our record: blues . . .Eagle is our aggressiveness, our sickness, our self-hate, but also our will to live in spite of everything. He symbolizes the rebel in us.''[18] His death at the end of the novel does not signify the extinction of this spirit, but the vulnerability of one who responds to hatred and suspicion with friendship and love. It is an indictment of racism, but it is also an attack on a society which can find no place for humanity in its frantic desire for security and success.

In his succeeding novels, anger over individual suffering broadens into a growing awareness of historical process. In *Journey Out of Anger*, a character observes that "a whole process brings a human being to anger. Multiply that eighteen million times over and you don't have a process anymore. You have history.''[19] It is this conviction which leads, in his later work, to individuals who dedicate themselves to destroying this system; to interrupting and redirecting historical process.

Williams was suspicious that his generation would follow those who had gone before, plunging from innocence to willful ignorance, and stamped, "Cause of death: resisting reality.''[20] The expatriates of *The Man Who Cried I Am* are merely visible evidence of this retreat from truth. "The task," as one character remarks, "is to tell those people to stop lying, not only to us but to themselves.''[21] The protagonists of his more recent books have found themselves living at the moment of historical balance. Like Ellison's hero, they feel the need to emerge from their hibernation. But, unlike Ellison, they do not bring a message of love and existential awareness; nor do they pledge themselves to renewing democratic principles or realizing the potential of brotherhood. They are agents become principals. They refuse to conspire in their own extinction. The conspiracy is exposed, and the long-delayed but logical battle is joined. The cancer eating away at Max Reddick, the protagonist of *The Man Who Cried I Am*, is an entirely appropriate image of the dissolution which characterizes the whole system. Nor is this simply a racial observation. The sickness goes far beyond color, which, as Reddick reminds himself, is "no match for Hiroshima and history."[22]

The Man Who Cried I Am traces the career of a Negro writer, Max Reddick, as his brand of bitter invective attracts the attention of the white world. After an unrewarding first novel, he had slowly established his reputation and made those contacts with whites necessary to success in literature and reputation in society. As a journalist, he becomes the tolerated black conscience of a liberal news magazine and, eventually, a speechwriter to President Kennedy on civil rights; as a writer, he delves deeper into his own psyche and into the reality which threatens, not merely his own developing sense of identity, but the very structure of his political and social world.

He insists throughout on the integrity of his identity, repeating with a cabalistic intensity, "*I Am, I told you, damn it, I Am.*"[23] But the very urgency of his statement reveals its falsity. In the thirty-odd years which the book covers, he is led by the logic of events and by the ironical voice of his own conscience to realize that he is as much a construction of the whites as he is of the international society through which he had worked himself with such avidity. Finally, he discovers the existence of an international conspiracy of whites—the *Alliance Blanc*. This had been established to combat the growing power of blacks in Africa and elsewhere. It operates through agents who organize coups and inspire intertribal hostility. It had contrived Lumumba's assassination and had been responsible for much of the instability on the African continent. Observing the success of the *Alliance* abroad, the Americans prepare contingency plans to deal with their own rebellious blacks. At first, this is to involve repatriation to Africa, but when this is opposed by the Europeans, a scheme involving detention followed by genocide is adopted. Another black novelist, Harry Ames, had died because of his knowledge of the plan, and now Max has to decide what to do. But as Ames had warned him in a letter, "*Everybody knows everything, now, past and present.*"[24] The truth which his whole life should have conveyed to him now confronts him in a concrete form. He no longer has scope for inaction and passes the information on before he, in turn, is killed by Negro agents of the *Alliance*.

Each recurring and ironical affirmation of selfhood marks a stage in his initiation into the reality of history. He is led little by litte to the point where he is poised between a deceptive personal fulfillment and full commitment. If these had ever been reconcilable aims, they are no longer so. To challenge the white hegemony of history is to sacrifice, not merely identity, but life itself. And this is where Williams leaves us—on the verge of apocalypse. Reddick makes his decision. He issues the challenge, and, although he dies for his temerity, the course of history may be deflected. It was after all only by his death that he could hope to reconcile what he belatedly recognizes as the twin goals of his life.

If he had ever imagined that his caustic prose could achieve anything beyond fame, he is disabused by the white world's ability to preempt his anger. Personal and racial abuse is transmuted into literature; fury becomes craft and, as such, is neutralized. This has always been the dilemma of the committed writer, and, in many ways, *The Man Who Cried I Am* is clearly Williams's appreciation of his own ambiguous position and, indeed, the all-but-impossible plight of the black American writer. Richard Wright, James Baldwin, Richard Yates, and other novelists and essayists appear in the book precisely because Williams recognizes the failure of any of them to resolve this paradox. Wright, the existentialist, and Baldwin, obsessed with the nature of personal identity, clearly face the same problems as confront Max Reddick, and even polemic and racial exhortation are presented as a substitute for stringent analysis and a massive assault on the status quo. It is arguable, indeed, that the novelist's attempts to reshape reality or to cast it in an apocalyptic mold are simply confessions of social impotence. Fiction obviously provides a convenient and secure battlefield for psychic conflicts to those unable to influence their environment or even, in the last resort, to provoke an authentic cataclysm. Williams is fully alive to this, for the novel itself constitutes a coherent critique of his own position. He recognizes with refreshing clarity the paradox which lies in describing entropy in measured prose, in berating white injustice for white publishers at $9.95 a volume, and in criticizing the self-absorption and contemplative inaction of the creative mind at times of crisis. The book is indeed a kind of *mea culpa* disguised as militant prophecy, and this gives it a shifting perspective which seems to confer a genuine integrity on his moral postures. The inconclusive ending is perhaps the most honest aspect of the whole book. The truth has been told. Everything is known, not only about the complex contrivances of white society, but also, and perhaps more importantly, about the willful self-deceit of the black victims. Yet, the logic of the book leaves the Negro curiously impotent. The whites control events so effectively that even a revelation of their power can hardly effect their position. There is nothing here, then, of the messianic role and power of the writer. There are no black heroes here striding manfully through a country that is nine-tenths white and inspiring fear and cringing admiration. Williams knows all too clearly the limitations of art and the restrictions on action, and it is his examination of these realities which gives the novel its force and honesty.

The Man Who Cried I Am is a curious mixture of documentary and fiction—the factual and the fantastic. Many of the characters are clearly identifiable, the fictional names scarcely concealing known details of their lives. Williams seems to create pasteboard masks precisely so that he can strike through them to the intangible but real source of anger and frustration which is his inheritance and the unacknowledged birthright of his protagonist. The drama itself is enacted against a clearly delineated historical framework: the 1954 desegregation decision, Yuri Gargarin's first manned orbital flight, the political assassinations of the 1960s. Williams deliberately intertwines these events with his own fiction until the arbitrary distinction between the real and the surreal is eroded. The suggestion that Harry Ames (Richard Wright) died at the hands of a CIA assassin is, in a way, no more absurd than the black comedy of events which followed President Kennedy's assassination. Those suspicious of the existence of a vast political and even cosmic conspiracy no longer seem so paranoid as once they did. To Williams, the conspiracy which the novel proposes as being responsible not only for Lumumba's death, but also for the disproportionately high level of Negro casualities in Vietnam, is at least as plausible as the public fictions advanced as explanations of those events. The plot has a truth of its own which protects him as an author from what might otherwise have been Jamesian ethical problems.

But one is left feeling that there is something a little too casual about the book and the analysis which lies at its core. If we accept, with him, the need to confront reality, to strike through the mask, then the radical simplification of that reality, the deliberate distortion of the mask, tends to undermine the direct purity of the response. The rest of the novel goes a considerable way towards validating his conclusions, but it slides away from conviction because of Williams's determination to see history as so completely the contrivance of malicious agencies. As a metaphysical observation this might be persuasive, as it is when Thomas Pynchon implies the existence of such a conspiracy and the human need to believe in such a conspiracy; as a serious comment on social and political reality, it requires something more than the personal experience of Max Reddick or the revelations of such convenient plans as those set out in the contingency arrangements of the *Alliance Blanc*.

In many way, *Sons of Darkness, Sons of Light* takes over where *The Man Who Cried I Am* left off. Eugene Browning, a black (Brown?) middle-class liberal, incensed by the police murder of a sixteen-year-old Negro boy, suddenly attains to the clarity of vision which Max Reddick had only reached at the end of his life. "How could he not have known the truth about America and Americans, teaching political science as he had? My God, you started lying with the Pilgrims and you kept right on lying. . . .He had been a victim of both accident and design, and he helped the system to function because he, a victim of the lie, abetted it by his presence in that place."[25] He hires the Mafia to murder the policeman. The killing is a catalyst. The Mafia agent, himself a Jew experienced in applying the techniques of terrorism as an antidote to persecution, decides to take the revenge a stage further, planning to kill a white southerner who has boasted of killing Negro children. He is prevented from doing so by a Negro who has his own reasons for revenge. These swift, direct actions serve to precipitate a more general violence as long-prepared plans for racial confrontation are put into effect. The police raid the ghettos; the black rebels sabotage New York's bridges.

Sons of Darkness, Sons of Light is Williams's version of Revelations. As a black revolutionary recognizes, "Remembering all the years, the false hopes, all the waiting, all the killing . . .now it was 1973 and game-time was over."[26] Described by Williams as "a novel of some probability," the book traces out what its author clearly sees as an immediate consequence of years of betrayal and distrust. As the central character discovers, "Working from within instead of outside the system, can't be done, just can't be done."[27] Yet, when the simple act of violence with which he had hoped to redress the balance gets out of hand, he retreats into an ineffectual liberalism. The Institution for Racial Justice, the organization for which he works, significantly collapses, and it is clearly too late for his decision to return to teaching to have any validity. In Browning's mind, the year 1973 joins 1935 (Ethiopia and China) and 1936 (Spain) as a pivotal moment in history, and, while Williams refuses, finally, to commit himself on the consequences of the ensuing violence, he obviously feels that revelation and revolution are not far distant. The image of regeneration with which the book ends is a fine touch of irony.

Yet, in many ways, this book marks a step backward for Williams. Browning's tentative liberalism is sketched in too perfunctorily to carry any real conviction. The genuine dilemmas of his preceding novel, which grew in part out of the problems of committed writing, are absent from a work which presents a scenario without characters. The caricatures who act out their prescribed roles owe more to the vignettes of a Chester Himes than the kind of compassionate insight which had marked his own earlier books. The novelist cannot afford to demonstrate the kind of callousness, even towards his most ineffectual characters, which he condemns in society. The truth is that with this novel, as he himself has admitted, he capitulated to the pressures exerted on the black writer in the 1960s. It was his revolutionary novel, and it lacks equally conviction and skill, as it does the imaginative grasp of his next novel.

With *Captain Blackman*, Williams probes into the past and projects a mythical future. The novel presents a catalog of racial abuse and interracial conflict, the central thread being provided by the black experience of military life.

The protagonist, Captain Blackman, is wounded in Vietnam, and, as he lies injured, so we are taken in his mind through the black experience of America's wars, from the Revolutionary War, through the Civil War, the Spanish-American War, World Wars I and II, to Korea. The conventional ironies of fighting for democracy abroad while denied it at home, of defending an American commerce which could find no space for Negro endeavor, are deepened by the historic panorama. This is history as genocidal conspiracy. The implied conflict, represented in a muted way by the uneasy relationship between Blackman and his equally significantly named white rival, Whittman, eventually reaches its apogee in a battle between white soldiers and black deserters in Tombolo, Italy, during World War II. Yet once again, significantly, the apocalypse is postdated; it was, by definition, a false apocalypse. And Blackman is fully aware that such a direct battle can never serve the interest of the blacks. It is, indeed, only in his imagination that he can plot a future in which, operating out of Africa, blacks can take over the military capability of the United States and turn it against the white oppressor. In fact, the novel ends with Blackman lying injured in a Saigon hospital, having been awarded the Congressional Medal of Honor.

Once again the apocalypse is aborted, but now his unease at a retreat which is perhaps no more than an expression of a commitment to the real is resolved by projecting a fictive apocalypse which need not defend itself against reality or the moral questions which the book has itself invoked. It is an uneasy compromise, revealing in its attempt to transcend its own assumptions.

The crucial point about these novels is that determinism is consistently deflected into hope, that the apocalypse which is a logical extension of social injustice and the collapse of values—an image of the persistent clash of black and white—repeatedly defers to a belief in transcendence, in personal and social change, which is an equally powerful and necessary tenet of faith. The battle between Old and New Testaments which characterizes Baldwin's work is equally a factor in most black writing. The need to indict, to lock the white world and hence, in some degree, the black into an ineluctable guilt born of the past does battle with the need to project a future in which the individual is freed of such necessities. But the black man can only be freed by an act of grace towards the whites, in that victim and hangman are yoked together by time and event. For, of course, apocalypse is a moment of simultaneous victory and defeat. As LeRoi Jones suggests in *Dutchman*, vengeance and suicide are fused together. The moment of truth is potentially the moment of destruction. Hence, if the apocalypse stands as one constant pole of the black imagination, as a present possibility, the other pole is an unfashionable conviction that change is possible, that the ghosts of the past can be laid if only they are freely engaged and honestly confessed.

Wright's early stories were truly apocalyptic, but by the time of *Native Son* he was concerned with seeing the self as something other than a victim or an agent of history. The momentum carrying Bigger Thomas towards a stance in which personal meaning is to be found only in violence is deflected into an image of unity and transcendence. In *Invisible Man*, the apocalyptic alternative is relegated to a fantasy of emasculation and a reality of self-destructive riot. The imagery of Revelations is finally muted and transformed. For Baldwin, too, the fire is always coming next time, and between the self and destruction there is always a redeeming love, a sense of personal commitment to art or to other wounded beings, which prevents the apocalypse.

It may be that this resisted apocalypse is an expression of the black writer's conviction that he lives in a period of transition, that his is too much an age of change to make the concept of an end either relevant or tenable. He is still too much in the process of releasing himself culturally, politically, and personally to allow a line to be drawn with too great a finitude. For a white writer to assume stasis and, hence, to see apocalypse as an appropriate end may be an expression of a social and metaphysical sense of completion—albeit ironic. For the black writer, incompletion is a fact of private and public life and the basis for social and cultural hope. The revolutionary flirts with apocalypse, uses its imagery, invokes its energy, but rarely embraces its absoluteness. If it is true, as Jaspers suggests, that crisis is a defining quality of life, how much more so is this true for those whose lives are dramatized by society and hence who become self-dramatizing as a means to meet that presumptive arrogation? A certain personal apocalypticism is inevitable; it is based on a knowledge of unavoidable fate. Socially, such a presumption deals with possibilities, not certainties. When John Williams speaks of ''the American twilight'' and says that ''we can now calculate the end of our time,'' it turns out that the prophecy of apocalypse is ultimately connected with an urge to liberal reform, for he goes on to say that ''we are required to extend our line by doing away with the cancers which have shown us quite clearly where the end of time is.''[28] History is not to be allowed its own logic. Apocalypse is to be invoked as a reason for the urgency of faith.

The retreat from apocalypse is perhaps an expression of the moral role which the black writer feels called upon to play. The open ending, the refusal to carry apocalypticism to its logical conclusion, is less a product of character or event than it is of private conviction and public role. The novelist accepts the obligation, not necessarily to detail the nature of social possibilities, but to endorse the existence of those possibilities. That is to say, the black writer's fictions are like those of the British agent described in Frank Kermode's *The Sense of an Ending*, whose stories are to be tested by a wholly critical audience—namely, the Gestapo—and which thus become quite literally enmeshed with the business of personal, and, by natural extension, public survival. Thus, as I argued in the previous chapter, the unresolved ending becomes a social as well as moral duty. A liberal retreat from the brink, whether or not substantiated by the thrust of the narrative, becomes a necessity. As John Williams has said, ''I think there is a difference in approach to 'consciousness' between black and white writers. I don't think white writers have ever had to consciously or subconsciously concern themselves about real problems of life and survival.''[29]

In the case of John Oliver Killens, the retreat from apocalypse is the product of political confusion; in that of John Williams, it is one of ambiguity. For Alice Walker, it is a conscious rejection of apocalypse—a refusal to be contained by definitions of personal and public necessity which allow change to be only a product of violence and which endorse a mythology which identifies epiphany with apocalypse. In *The Third Life of Grange Copeland* (1970), what seems to be a deadly determinism which justifies an apocalyptic violence gives way eventually to a renewed faith in change and the power of love. Grange, overwhelmed by what seems to be his inability to control his own life, abandons his wife and child to a lonely suicide, and convinces himself, like Bigger Thomas, that his life gains meaning only with the murder of a white woman. But, in the end, that conviction gives way to the notion that violence is only redemptive when it serves a purpose beyond the self—if the individual, that is, is willing to offer himself as sacrifice.

So, too, with her second novel, *Meridian* (1976). This is a clearly post-1960s novel, not only in the date of its publication, but in its assumptions about racial relationships and in its concern with the connection between craft and conscience. It begins with its heroine's refusal to embrace murder as a personally legitimized strategy for social advance and attempts to untangle the complex interplay of sexual, racial, and psychological tensions which the 1960s had sought to short-circuit with the bullet. The immediate lesson of assassination did indeed seem to be the need to neutralize sophisticated prevarications and justifications with a purifying violence; the conclusion which her tortured characters work their way towards is the culpability of each individual who chooses to endorse the chaos which surrounds him by enacting its brutal premise. It is true that the sentimentalities of the early 1960s could not survive the simplicities of public violence, that the heroine's uncomplicated compassion is broken by the assaults of a reality which will not respond to spontaneous kindness. But there remains a tenacious will which survives its own disillusionment—a courage which is the residue of idealism and a reminder of an innocence which, if no longer fully functional, can outlive a cynicism which, by definition, will destroy itself, and a callous exercise of power which contains no transcendence. As her name implies, it is Meridian and not the racist or revolutionary, who is at the heart of human experience, who feels most directly the individual needs which prompt compassionate action. Refusing to succumb to the pressure to capitulate to either extreme, she assumes the responsibility of mediating between them. It is a responsibility which, though threatening her peace of mind, is the source of her personal identity.

The tangled motives which drive black and white together and which pull them apart—motives composed partly of guilt, partly sadism, partly desperation—are both the product of history and an explanation of it. Meridian is an expression of the need to break free of this. Conceding the fact that the future may belong to the revolutionary, she sees herself as endorsing older values. ''Perhaps,'' she suggests, ''it will be my part to walk behind the real revolutionaries—those who know they must spill blood in order to help the poor and the black and therefore go right ahead—and when they stop to wash off the blood and find their throats too choked with the smell of murdered flesh to sing, I will come forward and sing from memory songs they will need once more to hear.''[30] What she offers is neither a purifying violence nor a redemptive innocence; it is compassion. As she herself writes, in a poem:

> there is water in the world for us
> brought by our friends
> though the rock of mother and god
> vanishes into sand
> and we, cast out alone
> to heal
> and re-create
> ourselves.[31]

As a result, she raises up both herself and those she serves, becoming both an agent and a model of change.

For Toni Morrison in *Song of Solomon* (1977), apocalypse is a natural enough product of recent history. And when a group of blacks forms an assassination squad called the Seven Days (one assassin being assigned to each day of the week), it is a logical response to the violence inflicted on blacks. As one of the characters laments, ''Everybody wants the life of a black man. Everybody. White men want us dead or quiet—which is the same thing as dead. White women, same thing. They want us, you know, 'universal,' human, no 'race consciousness.' Tame, except in bed. . . .But outside the bed they want us to be individuals. You tell them, 'But they lynched my papa,' and they say, 'Yeah, but you're better than the lynchers are, so forget it.' ''[32] But when this logic leads them to propose the murder of four white children in revenge for the death of four black girls killed in a Sunday-school bombing, the response is clearly too implacable. And the murder of whites, with its own necessary injustices, inevitably leads to the murder of blacks, until it becomes clear that the real offense is against human life and individuality and the real responsibility is to a version of truth which exists to one side of a murderous nature which is drawn too easily to the brink of annihiliation.

Ishmael Reed, in *The Last Days of Louisiana Red*, denies apocalypse through parody and irony; Alice Walker and Ralph Ellison (and Ronald Fair, whose *Hog Butcher* moves from threatened apocalyptic revolt to individual transformation), through the invocation of a moral responsibility apparently out of tune with the times. For Alice Walker, the revolution is over. What it has left behind is not a conviction about the efficacy of violence, but a conviction that the private and public world can be transformed: ''I believe in change: change personal, and change in society.''[33] The agency of that transformation is a self which can first imagine the world which it then creates. Nor is it without relevance that so many of the characters in *Meridian* should be writers. For their achievement is ultimately to break free of a myth which requires the resistance of the oppressor in order to sustain an identity. The world which she pictures is, as she has admitted, almost wholly menacing. Apocalypse is indeed a logical extension of its social and biological cruelties. Yet, at its heart is the resistant individual, slowly constructing a self, a society, and a culture from the detritus of human passions and neglect. And this is the heart of the liberal enterprise which, largely, is the black American novel of the Second Renaissance.

The Public Self:
The Black Autobiography

7

Alfred Kazin has suggested that "in times of crisis people prefer to take their history straight, and on the run" rather than in the oblique form of the novel, because "the documentary journalist who writes it on the run will give them history in terms which they are prepared to understand. If we ask why so many documentary journalists [in the 1930s] did more with their material than the social novelists who seemed to be working with the same material, the fact seems inescapable that because of the very nature of the crisis and the explosive strains it imposed, too many contemporary imaginations were simply not equal to it."[1] Much the same could be said of the 1960s. The deceptions of the public world seemed to demand an art which disavowed, or at least openly examined, its own deceptions. The documentary novel or play, for example, seemed to get closer to the fact, seemed to engage the crucial details of the public world more directly and hence more honestly than did the novelist, whose need to sculpt experience and language seemed, perhaps, too close to the careful editing of the public spokesman. In the case of Peter Weiss's *The Investigation*, only the brute facts of holocaust seemed adequate to the task of recording a reality which fiction could only demean—a notion scarcely disproved by American television's attempt to deal with the same subject in *Holocaust*.

The autobiography, likewise, at least seemed to have the virtue of a self-proclaimed subjectivism and advanced the familiar claim of first-hand experience for its justification. It was a report simultaneously from the front line of the self and of society. It was an experience which had apparently only been processed once; it had been filtered through the sensibility but not yet through the imagination. It was presented as a telegram from the war zone and hence was apparently more authentic than the novel or poem. And authenticity was at a premium in a decade obsessed with discovering truths about the public and private world, a decade which produced Ralph Nader and the Maharishi.

Such books give the appearance of being at the interface of public and private worlds; they document the impact of external reality on the sensibility. They represent the struggle of the self to gain possession of that public world, to create order out of random experience. To that degree, of course, they scarcely differ from novels. But there is presumed to be a kind of self-denying ordinance which prevents the individual sensibility from subverting these externalities, which inhibits the writer from turning the social world completely into a fiction. Yet, the distinction is perhaps more apparent than real. The fictional component of public events is manifest. The mere act of communication turns the most junior reporter into an historian with the power actually to transform the events which he describes and thereby to alter its supposed reality. And so, too, the autobiography is also concerned with a series of transformations—not merely the retrospective creation of an identity out of the contingent acts of a self responding to random events, but the invention of a public world which is now invoked as an explanation for that supposed identity. The autobiography offers its author a retrospective self, a control over experience; it offers others a convenient ordering of contemporary history, a paradigm of the private acquisition of authority over events. Where the novelist invents a world elsewhere which manifests a structure and direction clearly a product of the author's mind, the autobiography claims to document a familiar environment, to present a simulacrum of the real, which proposes personal experience as a reliable guide to the material of daily life. Thus, the black autobiography becomes a handbook on life, a testament to the fact that not only can the individual function amidst the chaos of events, he can prevail over them.

Alfred Kazin's remarks about the 1930s could so easily be applied to the 1960s:"The decline of the novel all through the period, a moral and physical decline, tells its own story in this respect. In so curious and difficult a revolutionary period as our own, so peculiarly hazardous a period, no one needs to be told how difficult it is for the imaginative spirit to command a necessary poise.''[2] Philip Roth was to make much the same point in his article on contemporary American literature in the early 1960s. The extremity of the ''real'' world offered to challenge fiction on its own ground. And the subconscious did indeed seem to bubble to the surface and command a public territory; from the byzantine and almost metaphysical complexities of the Kennedy assassination and, perhaps, that of Martin Luther King, to the bizarre Negrophobia of the wild-eyed Charles Manson.

The documentary impulse seemed the only way to deal with such eruptions of the psyche (*In Cold Blood* and *Helta Skelta*). Indeed, the key books of the decade were, in many ways, public documents (*The Kerner Commission Report, The Moynihan Report, The Pentagon Papers*); reportage, factual, and speculative (*Miami and the Seige of Chicago, Fire on the Moon, Rush to Judgement, All the President's Men*); and autobiographies, more especially black autobiographies (*The Autobiography of Malcolm X, Manchild in the Promised Land, Soul on Ice, Soledad Brother*). Alternatively, there were sociological or neo-Freudian studies which offered holistic explanations, personal prescriptions for the individual in a troubled present or possible future

(*One Dimensional Man*, *Love's Body*, *The Medium is the Massage*, *The Presentation of the Self in Everyday Life*, *The Greening of America*, *Future Shock*). Even the handbook made a reappearance; Spock's *Baby Care* was followed by more adult manuals on sexual technique and the reprinting of early twentieth-century texts on the mastery of self and environment.

The desperate need to understand, to find a way through what Kazin in speaking of the 1930s had called ''a series of shattering shocks and tremors that has pounded away mercilessly at the mind,''[3] expressed itself in books which offered directly to engage the public world which was the source of those shocks. And if the novel did not collapse, as indeed in part it had in the 1930s, it did recoil from the business of responding directly to social dislocation, for the most part deflecting such concerns into oblique absurdist accounts, a fictive self-consciousness which was a confession that anarchy had penetrated the membrane of art. Certainly the novel took second place to the autobiography insofar as black writing was concerned.

Autobiography presents life as a verb, and, in a sense, to treat such works as literary artifacts is to deny them their necessary dynamic—to reduce them to noun. Their value as cultural signs lies in the process which they exemplify, a process of raising personal experience to the level of social strategy. For the slave, the autobiographical narrative was not merely in itself a claim to humanity and hence to freedom; it was a narrative image of escape into freedom. It charted the move from inanimate chattel to animate individual, from simple possession to possessor of experience. Very often a physical journey to freedom would provide a concrete image of that journey into selfhood which becomes a model for black writing. But, where once the journey from South to North had provided a correlative for that sense of a liberated self, now the black autobiography is no longer likely to be written in a free physical and psychic territory. More often than not it is an account of freedom paradoxically discovered in a prison whose value lies in its force and appropriateness as an image of American society.

In *The Wretched of the Earth*, Frantz Fanon identifies that moment in a colonial struggle when a new breed of writer emerges, a stage of development in which ''a great many men and women who up till then had never thought of producing literary work, now they find themselves in exceptional circumstances—in prison . . .on the eve of their execution—feel the need to speak . . . to compose the sentence which expresses the heart of the people and to become the mouthpiece of a new reality in action.''[4] For the black American, the 1960s was such a period.

The black autobiographies of the decade from 1964 to 1974 were largely linked by a common experience—prison. A single electrical current charges the lives of those whose thirst for personal and group freedom was expressed, not only in simple opposition to the forces which so unsubtly arraigned themselves against them, but in their sometimes confused and tentative and sometimes clear-minded and determined attempts to locate the source of their strength and plot a possible program for liberation. The literalness of their struggles for survival, which found expression in words because their actions were severely circumscribed, means that in these works one can see the process of self-invention at work. And behind the struggle for self-knowledge was a wider attempt to locate underlying principles of social action—a solidarity not only with those other blacks whose experience of deprivation they had shared, but with all those whose identities had been seared and whose freedom of spirit and being had been distorted by the inflexible power of social and economic determinisms.

None of these writers needed instruction in the realities of racial conflict nor in the amoral culture of deprivation in which the frisson derived from petty crime and addiction was substituted for a dignity derived from social position and academic or economic achievement. What had been lacking was a clear understanding of the forces which created such a cycle of humiliation. Prison was a clarifying experience. On the one hand, it rendered social divisions and racial prejudice in stark form, clarifying the institutional basis of what might otherwise be perceived as individual acts of hostility and injustice; and, on the other hand, it granted solitude and time for the prisoner to examine the nature and causes of his imprisonment. The prison cell becomes like a monk's cell—a place for contemplation and the elaboration of a faith which can both sustain the self in its isolation and establish a vital connection between that self and other selves. And if the text was not the Bible, there was remarkable unanimity as to what it was. It was *The Autobiography of Malcolm X*, as later it was *Soledad Brother*; it was the history of the black man in Africa and America; it was the work of Lenin and Mao and Frantz Fanon. Malcolm X's autobiography was read by Eldridge Cleaver, as Cleaver's works were in turn read by other prisoners. Angela Davis smuggled copies of *Soledad Brother* into a New York City prison, as her work, *If They Come in the Morning*, was designed to give inspiration to those others in prison as well as to raise funds for their support. A shared situation led to a shared literature and created what was in effect a single work—an autobiography of the black man and woman in contemporary America.

There were differences, however. Malcolm X was wholly self-taught; Bobby Seale and Huey Newton only attended college briefly; while Angela Davis, from a middle-class family, studied in France and Germany and was struggling to complete her Ph.D. thesis while campaigning for the release of George Jackson. There were ideological disagreements between Stokely Carmichael and the Black Panthers, between Angela Davis and Ron Karenga's black nationalists. But beneath these disagreements was a single objective—the necessity to challenge in a public way the system which had spiritually and literally relegated the black and the poor to the other side of the tracks; the system which excluded such people from the animating myths of their society and which validated a systematic harassment which amounted to a denial, not only of due process, but of the humanity which due process was designed to protect. And since imprisonment meant that they were quite literally at the mercy of those whose abuses they were most determined to indict (the killing of George Jackson providing the most extreme evidence of this), the fact of their resistance and of the public challenges which their autobiographical essays clearly constituted was itself an indication of the courage of which these testaments were the visible evidence.

Every step towards the establishment of identity, the construction of a survival strategy, and the elaboration of a political theory had to be won in the face of abuse and hostility. The right to acquire necessary texts, to secure the conditions in which study becomes possible, to communicate with clarity and freedom the results of their self-examinations, in each case required a minor battle.

The lives which they dramatized were not, in some fundamental sense, personal. They were presenting their experiences as exemplary. As Angela Davis remarked in the preface to her autobiography, ''I was reluctant to write this book because concentration on my personal history might detract from the movement which brought my case to the people in the first place. I was also unwilling to render my life as a personal 'adventure'—as though there were a 'real' person separate and apart from the political person . . . . When I decided to write this book, after all, it was because I had come to envision it as a *political* autobiography that emphasized the people, the events and the forces in my life that propelled me to my present commitment.''[5] Much the same could have been said of any of those writers whose work is considered here. Since their prison experience was in essence a product of their identity as black Americans, they had been made exemplary by the society which chose to impose on their private lives the penalties imposed by public myths and prejudices. It was not that these people had not committed crimes, but rather that those crimes were so much a product of an experience of America which was defined by their color and their class. The punishment was one uniquely designed for those deprived of economic and social power. Hence, George Jackson, convicted of involvement in a seventy-dollar robbery, received a life sentence and served ten years before being brutally shot down by prison authorities. It was clearly not as George Jackson, a twenty-eight-year-old man, a complex individual, that he died; it was as a black man who had suffered an injustice which had inconveniently become publicly visible. George Jackson died, in Angela Davis's words, as a ''political person,'' the only difference between himself and other black victims of the American prison system being that his anonymity had been destroyed by his own self-taught articulateness. What seems, and indeed on occasion manifestly is, a political naivity—particularly when it comes to an uncritical celebration of revolutionaries whose own imperatives were just as capable of establishing a prison system to accommodate political prisoners as were those forces which they assaulted—was a natural product of the simplified world which they were themselves forced to inhabit. In the case of H. Rap Brown, the naivety of language and of analysis proved almost totally disabling; *Die Nigger Die!* offering only an inadequate attempt at consciousness-raising which was patronizing in tone and self-aggrandizing in its objective (his account of his encounter with President Johnson and Hubert Humphrey substituting arrogant abuse for a telling assault). But for most of these writers, the particular plight of the individual, which provides the necessary starting point for autobiography, is quickly subsumed in the more general issue of the situation of the black and the poor in America and of the dispossessed in the world. The individual makes sense of his or her own condition by relating it to that of the group.

In a way, of course, an autobiography, with its retrospective establishment of pattern, its necessary selectiveness, its process of reconstructing the past out of the psychological needs of the present, is no less fictional than the work which imaginatively projects experience through manifestly fictional characters. But it is a purposive fiction. The autobiography offers a lesson; it is implicitly that which experience has taught its subject. Its didacticism is inescapable. This was as true of the Puritan autobiographies as it was of the slave narratives or of the autobiographies of Washington and Du Bois. The private life is offered as public exemplar.

Biography has the force of history, as, Emerson suggested, history has the force of biography. "We are always coming up with the emphatic facts of history in our private experience and verifying them here.... All history becomes subjective; in other words there is properly no history, only biography."[6] So, history is the key to individual life and private existence, a clue to history. As Huey Newton observed, "Life does not always begin at birth. My life was forged in the lives of my parents before I was born, and even earlier in the history of all black people. It is all of a piece."[7]

The autobiography is not only an account of a life; it is potentially a method of establishing identity. As Cotton Mather remarked, "Frequent Self-Examination, is the duty and prudence of all that would *know themselves*, or would not *lose* themselves."[8] Consciousness is a necessary element of identity; it is a means of confirming a significance to experience beyond the simple level of sequential event. The persona of the autobiography is an observing self quite apart from the self which writes it.

Contemporary black autobiographies, like early American spiritual ones, take as their central event a conversion. And it is in the light of that conversion that everything else is seen. The early years of Malcolm X's life—his willing acquiescence in white values and his life as a black criminal—are seen as a prelude to his later conversion to the Muslim faith. Indeed, they gain their meaning precisely through their negative relationship to that conversion. The criminal strategy for survival is not offered for emulation, but the Muslim faith is. The point of the book *is* the conversion (in the case of Malcolm X, a double conversion, first, to the Black Muslims and, then, to orthodox Islam). Much the same can be said of Eldridge Cleaver, who describes his criminal career only so that he may demonstrate his own transcendence of it, while in *Seize the Time*, Bobby Seale offers only the briefest of accounts of his early years since his life coheres as a conscious force only with his initiation into the truths of a militant black consciousness. His early career is seen only as a period of political and personal innocence, of experience which fails to organize itself into public or private meaning. This experience is not offered as a series of events with equal and, in a sense, neutral force. The books have a crescendo at their center, a sudden distillation of meaning, which provides the real justification for the book. Without that conviction, the book would have remained unwritten. The very gesture of offering the private self to the public world is a gesture of confidence in one's present grasp on truth. It implies a confidence that experience can now be subordinated to the self, as formerly the self had been subordinated to experience. For Benjamin Franklin, the world could be reduced to rational principle, it could be subdued by simple application. For Malcolm X and Eldridge Cleaver, likewise, it could be contained by the evident truths of the Muslim faith or, in the case of the latter, the scientific principles of international socialism or, a decade later, the unscientific truths of Christianity.

MALCOLM X'S *THE AUTOBIOGRAPHY OF MALCOLM X*

The autobiography is an extended definition of the self. As Malcolm X observes, "All of our experiences fuse into our personality. Everything that ever happened to us is an ingredient."[9] But it is also a public document. The self is clearly projected as a paradigm. The escape from innocence into knowledge is proposed as a model. The black autobiography is, as Malcolm X implied, a treatise on survival, just as he had come "to view everyday living as *survival*."[10] *The Autobiography of Malcolm X*, like all biographies, is the story of an education. Four of Malcolm X's uncles had been killed by whites, including one who had been lynched, while his own father was presumed to have been murdered by a white gang. His mother, under pressure of bringing up four children on her own and harassed by welfare workers, eventually had a breakdown which led to her confinement in a state mental hospital for twenty-six years. Malcolm himself was sent to reform school where, through dint of application and a paradoxical faith in Horatio Alger, Jr., he succeeded to the degree that he was transferred to a regular school where he was elected class president. He was close kin, in other words, to Ellison's protagonist at the beginning of *Invisible Man*. Indeed, in looking back on that period of his life, he came to feel that such success as he did have was less a result of white philanthropy than a result of his invisibility: "Even though they appeared to have opened the door, it was still closed. Thus they never did really see me."[11]

He was in fact straining to be white; his standards were those of white society, the humiliating and painful ritual of hair-straightening providing an apt image of a self-damaging denial of his own identity.

His move to Harlem, to menial work, and then to crime was a consequence of his discovery that education could not win him a way out of the racism of his society. His early ambition to be a lawyer had come up against the well-meaning but inflexible advice of a white school teacher who felt obliged to disabuse the young black boy of his illusions. In Harlem, he learned the art of survival and acquired an identity which sprang from the survival techniques he learned. The nicknames of those who came into the bar where he worked— Sammy the Pimp, Dollarbill, Fewclothes, Jumpsteady—described the terms of their encounter with reality with the same precision as did that of Deerslayer. As he said, in talking of Harlem in the early 1940s, "Everyone . . . needed some kind of hustle to survive, and needed to stay high in some way to forget what they had to *do* to survive."[12] And that high might be provided by drugs, by drink, by the numbers, or by religion. They are all ways of stepping outside of time, and Malcolm X has described the feeling of timelessness which drugs gave him.

Malcolm X served seven years for robbery, during which time he educated himself, becoming articulate in the language of power and, significantly, studying history, and in particular the history of the black man, through books like Carter Woodson's *Negro History* and W. E. B. Du Bois's *Souls of Black Folk*. For the first time he discovered Nat Turner, as he did the work of Mahatma Gandhi. He began to glimpse a wider context in which to locate the collision between black and white which he had first encountered in the Midwest and then in the streets of New York. The reality of emergent Africa became apparent to him. Though imprisoned, for the first time his mind was liberated, and the chief agent of that liberation was Elijah Muhammad.

Despite Richard Gilman's assertion (in an article in which he proposed a moratorium on white criticism of black literature, see C. W. E. Bigsby, *The Black American Writer*, vol. 1, 1969) that Malcolm X's book was simply not available for critical evaluation by whites, it is clear that it, like Cleaver's *Soul on Ice*, is in large part designed for white America. Indeed, he says that it was while he was in prison that he made up his mind "to devote the rest of [his] life to telling the white man about himself—or die,"[13] for "raw, naked truth exchanged between the black man and the white man is what a whole lot more of is needed in this country—to clear the air of the racial mirages, clichés, and lies."[14] In *Seize the Time*, Bobby Seale was also to say that "we go through a long process of trying to educate the people. All of them. The hippies, whites, blacks, everybody,"[15] for "we know about the brainwashing of black people, but this is not really separate from the brainwashing of the proletarian masses of America."[16] Huey Newton similarly acted on the conviction that "we are all—Black and white alike—ill in the same way, mortally ill."[17]

The logic of his career went in two directions. Firstly, he located the black cause in the context of Afro-Americanism, drawing a parallel between black experience and that of the American Jew. Hence, ''just as the American Jew is in political, economic, and cultural harmony with world Jewry, I was convinced that it was time for all Afro-Americans to join the world's Pan-Africanists. I said that physically we Afro-Americans badly needed to 'return' to Africa.'' Secondly, following his pilgrimage to Mecca, he came to feel that his sweeping indictment of all white people had indeed been a form of racism. In the final year of his life, his objectives began to broaden. ''I'm for truth, no matter who tells it. I'm for justice, no matter who it is for or against. I'm a human being first and foremost, and as such I'm for whoever and whatever benefits humanity *as a whole*.''[18] There were, indeed, the first signs of an ideological interpretation of American racism which placed the emphasis on political and economic structures. It was a perception, still vaguely grasped and barely articulated, which never took concrete form, for the assassins' bullets struck him before he could begin fully to articulate his changing views.

The Autobiography of Malcolm X was a crucial document. Not only did it describe the emergence of a charismatic leader, but it also charted the path to selfhood of an individual who transcended the circumstances of his birth and the humiliations of his youth. Like his father before him, who combined an avid support of Marcus Garvey with the concern for spirituality of a minister, he was drawn to powerful images of black pride and independence. His importance did not lie so much in his adherence to Muslim dogma as it did in his open challenge to white power and his restoration of black pride. The very fact that a man whose family had been murdered, literally and metaphorically, by white Americans could be taken seriously as a political figure and a moral teacher transformed his life into a model of black autonomy. But, for some, it was the move away from black separatism, documented so briefly at the end of the book, which made his work an inspirational text. And one such person was Eldridge Cleaver.

ELDRIDGE CLEAVER'S *SOUL ON ICE*

Like Malcolm X's, Cleaver's education began in prison, where he discovered books with the same avidity. He read Rousseau, Paine, Voltaire, Marx, Lenin, and Bukharin and, again like Malcolm, studied public speaking. But, when released from prison, his revolt did not take a political form. He became a rapist, justifying it as ''an insurrectionary act.'' Beneath the obvious rationalization and attempted self-justification was a genuine assault on the white totem. For writer after writer, race and sex are inextricably mixed, and the history of the black man in America is a catalog of violations of which the sexual is the most obvious.

But, back in prison, his defensive theories collapsed, and, like Baldwin, he began to write as a means to sheer survival. He came to see himself as evidence of the pathological state of the country and set about the task of re-creating himself in the unlikely setting of a prison where, as he explained, individuality is more thoroughly threatened than on the streets. For this reason, his account does not go back into the past. It is a reaction to the America of the mid-1960s. And it was Malcolm X who made the greatest impact on him. His significance lay not in the precise doctrine which he preached but in "the awakening into self-consciousness of twenty million Negroes which was so compelling;"[19] it was his conversion to a brotherhood which transcends race which struck Cleaver as potentially liberating.

In contrast to Baldwin's Calvinism, Cleaver asserted that "the sins of the fathers are visited upon the heads of the children—but only if the children continue in the evil deeds of the father."[20] Indeed, he saw hope for America in the disaffection and revolt of white youth who derived their inspiration from the black revolt and who, in many cases, had served their apprenticeship in the civil rights movement. Slowly, he began to adopt a more left-wing stance and to see the plight of black Americans in a wider context of exploitation and deprivation. But, perhaps more tellingly, if not originally, he offered a sexual account of black-white relations, identifying a model whereby the white male sees himself as Omnipotent Administrator and the black male as Supermasculine Menial.

The distinction is in essence one between mind and body, rather than between ego and id, because the latter would strike too close to the heart of the white man's sexual confidence. The white man accomplishes this, Cleaver suggests, by creating an ultrafeminine image of the white woman, while denying the black man access to her. At the same time, he exerts his own freedom to control the black woman. The gulf between mind and body is thus iconographically made synonymous with the gulf between the races, and the 1954 desegregation decision becomes an attempt to "graft the nation's Mind back onto its Body and vice versa."[21] For the implications were that the black would now have access to education, as whites, largely through music, rediscovered a black familiarity with the body. It was a romantic image of consonance which did not survive the year of the book's publication—1968—a year which, for Baldwin at his bleakest, finally sealed off the possibility of communication, though he too looked to sexuality as a crucial area for the understanding of American racial relationships and a vital image of possible harmony.

Once out of jail again, Cleaver was isolated. Malcolm X's organization had collapsed and he was thoroughly alienated from the Muslims. He was contemptuous of those cultural nationalists who believed that a simple act of disengagement was possible. But in the Black Panthers, he found a committed revolutionary group with which he could work. He became their minister of information and was already suffering police harassment when *Soul on Ice* was published in 1968.

The systematic attempt by local and federal police to destroy the Panthers is now well documented and constitutes one of the more flagrant official abuses of power in a period which witnessed a massive denial of basic American principles by a wide range of federal and local agencies. The Panthers never commanded widespread support in the black community, but the vicious police assaults on them made that organization and its leaders symbols of the public confrontation between black and white in the late 1960s. Cleaver himself became a presidential candidate for the Peace and Freedom Party and barely escaped death when the young Bobby Hutton was shot in the back by the police as he and Cleaver emerged from a building, their hands in the air. This incident led to the revoking of his parole and his subsequent self-exile.

If Richard Gilman was wrong in his suggestion that Malcolm X and Eldridge Cleaver were not writing for whites, since they both clearly addressed themselves to a double audience, he is perhaps right in implying a distinction between those books and works like *The Education of Henry Adams* or *Apologia Pro Vita Sua*, which, he suggests, rise "out of an already assured stock of consciousness of technical means, building on a civilization which had thrown up many precedents and models for the extension of the self into memorial and apologetic literature—writing which *takes for granted* the worth, dignity and substantial being of the individual, his right to talk about himself in public."[22] These black writers are individuals for whom the act of writing itself constitutes an attempt to forge values, to experiment with an articulateness recently learned. Meaning is not taken to spring out of a life which, anyway, has been lived within the parameters of a system alien to that self: it is generated by a newly perceived transcendent truth in terms of which, alone, individual identity assumes meaning. The very fact of the book's existence, in the case of *Seize the Time* and Malcolm X's autobiography, sustains the image which gives it birth. The assurance is a brittle one, and the word is rushed out as a testament, an urgent message of redemption, often propounding imperfectly perceived solutions in an unexamined language. In the case of Bobby Seale, there is no certainty about the self; it remains tentative, patterned on the confident persona paraded by Huey Newton. The certainty derives from the desperate strategies forced on them by the pressure of events, strategies which become the substance of a precipitating identity.

Yet there is an irony in Gilman's suggestion that the black autobiography was "written for Negroes" because "the Negro doesn't feel the way whites do, nor does he think like whites. . . .Negro suffering is not the same kind as ours,"[23] for Malcolm X, Eldridge Cleaver, Bobby Seale, and Huey Newton were all determinedly antiracist. As fierce proponents of Fanon, they refused to be forced into a racist stance, choosing to identify themselves not only with their fellow blacks but with the oppressed everywhere. The black experience of America was, indeed, different, and the prison cells from which these polemical documents derived were an appropriate image of the constraints, literal and figurative, which they suffered. But these books were expressions of their spiritual emancipation rather than their imprisonment. As Huey Newton remarks in *Revolutionary Suicide*, "Prison is a microcosm of the outside world."[24] The literal incarceration merely stood to emphasize the triumph of their imagination and will. George Jackson, locked in jail, still felt free. Gilman's well-meaning comments, rather like Max's in *Native Son*, were thus not only beside the point, but were paradoxically at odds with documents which were offered as evidence of a black emergence from spiritual and intellectual bondage.

For Bobby Seale, John Brown was as much an ancestor as was Nat Turner, and a white lawyer was as appropriate and reliable an ally as was a black spokesman like Stokely Carmichael. Indeed, Carmichael's black nationalist stance made him in some ways a less reliable ally. These are not books which stress the culturally unique quality of black lives, though they stress the determining power of social circumstance; they express, rather, the need to lay claim to a full humanity denied by a racist system. The heart of Malcolm X's book, as Cleaver perceived, lay, not so much in the desperate attempt to forge neutralizing black myths, as in his perception that racism was not synonymous with human nature and that other images existed with the power to liberate. The fact that, as Gilman rightly points out, "the Negro has found it almost impossible in America to experience the universal as such"[25] does not mean that these works turn about a different axis. On the contrary, they stand as assertions that "membership in the community of men" is no longer to be in the gift of those whose definitions had for so long contained and shaped black selfhood. Indeed, the Black Panthers at one time found themselves in conflict with Stokely Carmichael, whose stance they regarded as fundamentally racist, and equally in opposition to LeRoi Jones, whose emphasis on cultural nationalism seemed to them to be sterile—a view which Jones (by then Amiri Baraka) was eventually himself to share. As Bobby Seale insisted, "We know about the brainwashing of black people, but this is not really separate from the brainwashing of the proletarian masses of America."[26]

HUEY NEWTON'S *REVOLUTIONARY SUICIDE*

Like Malcolm X and James Baldwin, Huey Newton was the son of a preacher who planned a professional career for himself before the realities of the racial situation became really apparent to him. His early life did not differ materially from that of other black activists, and his autobiographical *Revolutionary Suicide* itemized the petty crimes and street fights which characterized his youth. When he left school he was illiterate, preferring the street to the patronizing tone and humiliating methods of the education system. But, inspired by his older brother, he eventually taught himself to read, discovering books with the same enthusiasm which had characterized Malcolm X's and

Cleaver's discovery of literature. His first text, laboriously spelled out word by word, was Plato's *Republic*, whose image of the cave seemed a persuasive analogue of the situation of the black in America. It was an image which Newton frequently invoked as a public speaker in later years, while in Joyce's *Portrait of the Artist as a Young Man* he found an account of the crisis of faith through which he was passing.

In 1959, he enrolled in Oakland City College, later called Merritt College, situated in the heart of the black community of North Oakland, California. He began to relate his reading directly to his experience, having no particular interest in obtaining formal qualifications. In Kierkegaard, Sartre, and Camus, he found confirmation for an instinctual existentialism; in Mao Tse-tung and Frantz Fanon, a political philosophy and strategic program which matched his growing desire to challenge the American political system. He identified a connection between racism and the economics of capitalism, while acknowledging that this nexus was not an adequate explanation for prejudice. Again, like Cleaver and Malcolm X, he was driven to a concern with history, combining this with a study of law, which he used as a protection against the police harassment which was a daily fact of ghetto life, and as a defense against charges deriving from the crimes which he continued to commit and which he justified, somewhat unconvincingly, as "liberating property from the oppressor."

In terms of literature, his taste ran to novels centering on crime and the problem of identity, books like Victor Hugo's *Les Miserables*, Dostoevski's *Crime and Punishment*, Kafka's *The Trial*, and Camus's *The Stranger*. For him, the prison cell was a literal and symbolic obsession, a key to black experience and to the mechanism of power.

The moment of "conversion" in his case, once again, came in prison. Jailed in 1964 at the age of twenty-two for assault with a deadly weapon, he felt acutely both his apparent helplessness and his potential for resistance. Though released the following year, it was his ability to survive the humiliations of that experience which gave him a sense of his own power. As he said, "Jail is an odd place to find freedom, but that was the place I first found mine."[27]

In 1965 he and Bobby Seale became members of the Afro-American Association, but became increasingly distrustful of it and began to develop their own ideas, formulating in October 1966 the principles of the Black Panther Party. Their main and immediate objective was to challenge the power of the police, who symbolized their oppression. And to that end, they publicly carried weapons and organized patrols which shadowed police cars in an attempt to inhibit harassment and instill a sense of pride and independence in the black community. As he later admitted, it was not an organization which was at first clear about its ultimate objectives and it suffered the usual internal dissension. Both Stokely Carmichael and Eldridge Cleaver split away, the former, in Newton's eyes, aligning himself with reactionary African states, and the latter, settling for careerism and a rhetoric of violence.

Predictably, Newton soon found himself in prison again, this time charged with murder, a victim, like so many other Panthers, of an institutional conspiracy. Indeed, as he astutely observed, ''During the five years since the Party has been formed, it always seemed that time was measured not in days or months or hours but by the movements of comrades and brothers in and out of prison and by the dates of hearings, releases and trials. Our lives were regulated not by the ordinary tempo of daily events but by the forced clockwork of the judicial process.''[28] For him, the prison experience was a contemporary version of the experience of slavery, but it was also an exemplary image of a political injustice which should inspire rebellion—what he described as ''revolutionary suicide,'' rather than that despairing acquiescence which he characterized as ''reactionary suicide.''

Revolutionary Suicide is a deliberately articulate book. It is liberally interspersed with telling quotations from a wide range of writers and is clearly addressed to both a black and a white audience, as the political strategy of the party was to alert both races to an injustice of which the black ghetto was the most immediate and compelling example. Newton's move towards articulateness, his struggle first for literacy and then for a command of language, itself stood as a symbol of his struggle for control over his own fate. It was also crucial to his utility as a leader. Suspicious of rhetoric and even, as a result of his religious upbringing, repelled by profanity, he recognizes ''the power of the word'' for ''words are another way of defining phenomena, and the definition of any phenomenon is the first step to controlling it or being controlled by it.''[29] Yet, the language of the book is finally less important than its spirit, its account of an individual uncowed by disillusionment and undismayed by persistent assaults. It is a record of an individual slowly abandoning the rationalizations by which he had protected himself from responsibility for his own actions. It is the brief odyssey of a man trying to find an honest way of engaging the fact of prejudice without himself being betrayed into it.

GEORGE JACKSON'S *SOLEDAD BROTHER*

When *Soledad Brother* was published, George Jackson had spent ten years in prison—seven of those years in solitary confinement—for involvement in a seventy-dollar robbery. He was a classic example of what Andrew Young, former U.S. Ambassador to the United Nations, eight years later was to describe as a political prisoner.

Genet has pointed out that ''a certain complicity links the works written in prisons or asylums.''[30] The fact of writing becomes an act of resistance—language becomes a link with a social world other than that harshly epitomized by the racism of the prison system. These are all books which are reaching out beyond the walls to a public the writer must believe in in order to sustain his sanity. In George Jackson's case, that public is primarily black, but as his revolutionary thought develops, it extends to all revolutionaries. He came to see a blanket condemnation of the white race as a fascist tactic and as indicative of a failure correctly to analyze the situation.

Jackson observes that there is a presumption of guilt for the black man in American society, a guilt which many black writers have confessed to having internalized, which makes the legal trial little more than a confirmation of an accusation implicit in every facet of race relations. Indeed, he remarks that "black men, born in the U.S. and fortunate enough to live past the age of eighteen are conditioned to accept the inevitability of prison."[31] But, as Genet observes, "the time for the blues is over." The voice of the prisoner is now strident and accusing. The humiliations of the past are rejected. The Christian religion is dispensed with early as an inadequate guide to black experience and as being irrevocably stained with historical guilt. The previous generation's painful adjustments have to be rejected as demeaning.

For George Jackson, his mother's acceptance of white values and her insistence on a Catholic education for her son is a "betrayal," placing him physically and mentally at the mercy of the "arch-foes." In his letters to them, he accuses his father and mother of failing him. The fragility of his new identity, however, is betrayed by a messianic tone in which, armed with his reading of Mao Tse-tung, he upbraids his parents for not recognizing in him a new revolutionary spirit which must prevail. "I am charged to right the wrong," he says in a letter to his father, to "lift the burden from the backs of future generations. I will not shrink from my duties."[32] It sounds like megalomania but, in fact, it is the language of a man necessarily defending his identity against hostile forces.

It is easy to imagine the dismay with which his parents must have read his letters and the despair with which he received their replies. To them, his actions were leading him inevitably to his death; to him, his parents were becoming agents of the white power structure, willing tools of those intent on destroying him. The gap of understanding was, in part, generational and, in part, a product of his need to project a persona which could resist and survive, and embrace myths and ideologies capable of challenging the established powers. He came to feel that his inability to control his fate, the complete manipulation of all aspects of his life while in prison, was only an overt instance of a basic fact of black experience in America. Indeed, he began to date his own imprisonment from the moment of his birth, and that of his race from the date of the supposed emancipation which had purportedly released them from slavery but which had, in fact, delivered them into economic servitude. In the early years of his imprisonment, the letters express a simple racial bitterness; in the later years, he discovers in Marxism an ideological explanation for his suffering and, more importantly, a program for smashing the system which imposes that bitterness upon him.

But there is a lyricism, too, which is equally a product of imprisonment, a poetic self which transcends the limitations of his circumstance: "I don't like this life, I can never reconcile myself to it, or rationalize the fact that I have been basely used, hated, and repressed as if it were the natural order of things. Life is at best a nebulous shadow, a vague contingency, the merest of possibilities to begin with. But man in general (myself most emphatically included), being at best complete and abject fools, have rendered even what small possibilities there were to love and learn null and void."[33]

The form of *Soledad Brother* was determined by the restrictions imposed by the prison authorities. California prison regulations limited the length of inmates' letters to both sides of a standard eight-and-half-by-eleven-inch ruled sheet. He was also constrained by prison censorship and by the fact that he was allowed only a limited range of correspondents, most notably the parents with whom he had such a complicated relationship.

As a prisoner, he was tied to his pain and confronted with the problem of authenticity in a way which is not true of the "free" individual. His letters offered the only way to test that authenticity beyond the confines of the prison. Thus, it is notable that he was only able to confront the crucial relationship with his father when he acquired a new correspondent, in the form of his female lawyer, Fay Stender. For the first time, he could speak frankly and without the usual restrictions of space and censorship.

At the heart of the book, indeed, is this relationship with his father, who epitomized for him an unenlightened generation, and the constant temptation of acquiescence which had to be resisted if he was to lay claim to dignity and an identity which could sustain him. It is an anguished dialogue of which we see only one side. It is a microcosm of the problem which faces all black Americans—on what terms can the past be claimed, not the distant glories of Benin and an African heritage nor yet the perhaps profitless heroics of Nat Turner, but the past locked up in the daily experience of a generation for whom survival was a prime objective and political apathy and social caution a necessary price to pay for sanity.

George Jackson came of age in an America in which the collapse of legal validations for segregation only served to expose a more fundamental injustice, unexpressed in formal statutes but manifest in the contrast between civil rights' rhetoric and the truth as encountered on the streets of the black community. He reached manhood at a time when other black voices were beginning to challenge the system in Africa and America and to discover in that challenge the meaning of their existence. The past represented by his father had to be rejected, and yet he knew that his own freedom to disavow his parents had depended on their early protection, as their continuing entreaties to submit to discipline derived from a conviction that this would be the best strategy to ensure his release. And so, in his letters, confessions of love alternate with vicious denunciations. Father and mother are accused of treachery and embraced for their love. They represent the past which must be rejected but which cannot be denied. And the resulting tension is expressed in the most powerful prose in the book—a prose which expresses as much about Jackson as it does about his bewildered and loving father. And this is no literary device, as was Baldwin's young cousin in *The Fire Next Time*. For his father was not only a link with the past, he was also one of the few links with the outside, with the world in which possibilities were still generated. And, as the book progresses, so Jackson's baffled rage gives way to a subtle appreciation of the realities which had subdued his father but which now, in altered circumstances, had transformed his son into a rebel. So that now, his letters become confessions of love and recognitions of his own ever-present potential for despair. His father becomes exemplary, a warning of the past which must be embraced as the reality of his own heritage, but rejected as the source of his humiliations:

I love this brother, my father, and when I use the word love I am not making an attempt at rhetoric. . . .But no one can come through his ordeal without suffering the penalty of psychosis. It was the price of survival. I would venture that there are no healthy brothers of his generation, none at all.

   The brother had reached the prime of his life without ever showing in my presence or anywhere, to my knowledge, an overt manifestation of *real* sensitivity, affection, or sentiment. He had lived his entire life in a state of shock. Nothing can touch him now, his calm is complete, his immunity to pain is total. . . .But he must have loved us, of this I am certain. . . .He stayed with us, worked sixteen hours a day. . . .He never owned more than two pairs of shoes in his life and in the time I was living with him never more than one suit, never took a drink, never went to a nightclub . . .and never once reminded any one of us, or so it seemed, never expected any notice of the fact that he was giving to us all of the life force and activity that the monster-machine had left to him. The part that the machine seized, that death of the spirit visited upon him by a world that he never influenced, was mourned by us, and most certainly by me, but no one ever made a real effort to give him solace. How do you console a man who is unapproachable.[34]

The implied accusation is directed at least partially at himself. They had failed to meet as people because the system had intervened, and yet the will to alter the system depended upon the solidarity in which he had failed. Anxious to assuage the guilt which he never overtly accepts, he tried to convince his father, during a prison visit, of the correctness of his political views, substituting ideology for the love in which they had both failed. The result was alarming. He had broken through the veneer of submission and practicality, but not in order to substitute his belief in self-determination through a people's government and revolutionary culture. What he released in his father was an atavistic madness, a disjointed reverie in which he rambled through the past as though George were not there, recalling long-past events, hopes, frustrations, and despair. It was a traumatic moment in which his forgiveness of his father was equally a forgiveness of himself. But still he demanded that his father and others like him should "stop their collaboration with the fascist enemy . . .and support our revolution with just one nod."[35] It is a nod which will fulfill an historical obligation. The fact is that even now and even following this encounter with his son he was unable to give that gesture of agreement because he could not believe that to do so would release his son; and it was to this end that his love led him and not to a desire to enroll in the ranks of the revolution. He never understood his son's desire to be a revolutionary and he never understood the extent to which American society had created in his son a fierce enemy for whom meaning, deprived as he was in his prison cell of any power to deflect the course of history, lay in a conviction, part practical and political, part fanciful and mythic, that he was the prototype of a generation which would destroy racism and capitalism. "This monster—the monster they've engendered in me," he prophesied, "will return to torment its maker, from the grave, the pit, the profoundest pit." He promised only "war without terms."[36] But the only weapons he possessed were his letters. He was not, he protested, a writer; he was a revolutionary. But, deprived of any practical way to fulfill that avocation, he sent out into the world a series of messages, confused cries of love and hate, of freedom and constraint, which combined to create one of the most powerful books of the Second Renaissance.

The letters document George Jackson's struggle to achieve control over himself and to elaborate a theory which will account for his experiences and sustain him through the humiliations of prison life. The very rigor of his immediate environment demands a philosophy which locates meaning first on a personal level; hence, his conviction that "only one-fourth of the sorrow in each man's life is caused by outside uncontrollable elements, the rest is self-imposed by failing to analyze and act with calmness."[37] But the self is not so assured that it can exist in a vacuum, and his letters thus become necessary lifelines. It was an irony that his first correspondents should be the parents who seemed to him to be capitulationists of the kind who threatened his identity most directly. What emerges, however, is a furious and understandable determination to imprint order on personal and social chaos, to discover an organizational principle which can "make a harmonious world out of this chaotic travesty of fact"[38] and which will constitute "a requiem" which "will be sung over the whole vast complex of disorder."[39] This necessitates a theory of social control and historical development which he eventually found in the works of Marxist theoreticians. And this, in turn, replaces the notion of a resistant self with a sense of determinism which asserts that "everything that I am, I *developed* into because of circumstantial and situational pressures. I was born knowing nothing," a "victim, born innocent, a *total* product of my surroundings."[40] Yet, paradoxically, of course, a degree of consciousness has to survive in order for the revolutionary spirit to bloom.

Such tensions were never resolved. His death denied a synthesis even as it seemed to confirm his analysis. But *Soledad Brother* is one of the more remarkable documents of a confused period. The anger, the lyricism, the hatred, the love, the solitary being, and the political animal are equally those of a whole generation of black Americans. What the book does is to offer a glimpse of the painful task involved in constructing a self out of these conflicting elements without succumbing to a psychosis which only Mailer could believe to be liberating. And this personal act of psychic reconstruction was a crucial activity of the Second Renaissance, a task which in a way underlies virtually all black writing but which has always been at the very heart of the black autobiography.

ANGELA DAVIS'S *ANGELA DAVIS: AN AUTOBIOGRAPHY*

Unlike *If They Come in the Morning* (1971), which Angela Davis helped to edit from her prison cell as a useful propaganda document in the campaign to secure her own release and that of other black prisoners, *Angela Davis: An Autobiography* (1974) was a more considered reflection on her own life and its relation to the cause of black liberation. It is an account of a middle-class intellectual's path to political commitment and a woman's rejection of a chauvinism which infected even the adherents of the cause which she shared (George Jackson's book had revealed a prejudice towards women which he eventually rejected when confronted with the evidence of Angela Davis's commitment).

Angela was born in Birmingham, Alabama, the daughter of two teachers— her father also owned a small service station. As a young woman her mother had been involved in the movement to free the Scottsboro boys. Angela herself witnessed the bombing with which whites responded to black attempts to integrate a white residential area. But her eye was fixed securely on college. Unlike those prisoners who were forced to educate themselves in a prison cell, she went north to attend a high school in New York City at the very moment that the civil rights movement turned its attention to her home town. It was an irony which deepened in later years as she found herself a student in Europe when the civil rights movement was at its height. But she did develop an interest in Marxism and in Paris she came to realize that racism was not a purely American phenomenon.

It was in Europe that she read about the bombing of a Birmingham Sunday school and the killing of four young girls, three of whom she knew personally. It was as she boarded the boat for Germany, where she was to study at the University of Frankfurt, that Watts exploded. But once there, she studied under Adorno and became involved in the fringes of the German radical movement. Nonetheless, back in the United States the civil rights campaign had taken a radical new direction, and she felt increasingly frustrated and guilty about her absence. In 1967 she returned and went to the University of California at San Diego to work with Marcuse. Here she tried to throw herself into the movement, to catch up with everything that she had been missing, only to discover the dangerously schismatic nature of black protest groups, divisions which could turn into literally deadly internecine struggles. She also encountered the sexual chauvinism which, at the time, seemed the price demanded for the reestablishment of black male pride and she instinctively reacted against a black nationalism which rejected Marxism as ''a white man's thing'' and which reduced her to a supportive role in the black man's struggle for identity.

Her first experience of jail followed her involvement in a radical student protest against American action in Vietnam. It was a minor skirmish, and the district attorney was forced by university officials to issue an apology. Nevertheless, the incident served to establish her credentials.

But she needed to find an organization through which she could work. Not yet ready to join the Communist Party, she became a member of the Black Panther Party, a local group distinct from the party formed by Huey Newton and Bobby Seale. The coincidence of the name caused violent friction, and, having been physically threatened, she purchased a gun which later became the basis of the murder charge leveled against her. The immediate solution to the problem was to merge the local party with SNCC. The first joint venture of the new group was a mass meeting to call for the release of Huey Newton, then the most widely known black prisoner. And when Rap Brown was subsequently arrested, they also organized a campaign on his behalf. Though the organization was strengthened by the anger released as a consequence of Martin Luther King's assassination in April 1968, internal disputes quickly led to its collapse. And in July 1968, Angela Davis joined the Communist Party USA and later visted Cuba. On her return, she found that her teaching job at UCLA was at risk and she became engaged on several fronts: struggling to finish her Ph.D., to maintain her job, and to continue her political activities, as the official assault on the Black Panther Party reached a climax and she became involved in the campaign to release George Jackson and the other Soledad brothers.

Then, on August 7, 1970, in an attempt to secure the release of his brother, seventeen-year-old Jonathan Jackson produced a gun in the middle of a trial presided over by Judge Harold Haley and, with the help of the accused prisoners, forced the judge, the district attorney, and several jurors into a waiting van. The San Quentin guards opened fire, killing Jonathan, the judge, and two of the prisoners. The gun which Jonathan had used turned out to be the one Angela Davis had purchased during the feud between the two Panther parties. It was registered in her name. Accordingly, in the eyes of the police, she became an accomplice to kidnapping and murder and, when she became a fugitive, she was promoted to the FBI's ten most-wanted list—a testimony to J. Edgar Hoover's paranoia rather than to any evidence connecting her to the crime. Eventually captured in New York, she, in turn, became a focus for worldwide protest groups.

Her eventual acquittal, together with that of the Soledad brothers (too late for George Jackson), seemed to stand as a vindication of everything she had fought for and, hence, of the identity which her autobiography was concerned with dramatizing—an identity projected only as an emblem of the community to which she lay claim. It is, she herself half implied in a letter which was read at her trial, perhaps a regrettable view of the self, but one demanded by the exigencies of a situation which makes the "individual escape . . .an evasion of the real problem."[41] As she said, "We have been forbidden to reach out for the truth about survival—that it is a collective enterprise and must be offensive, rather than defensive—for us, the principle of survival dictates the annihilation of all that compels us to order our lives around that principle."[42] And just as she could say that "the more the movement for my freedon increased in numbers, strength, and confidence, the more imperative it became for everyone to see it not as something exceptional but as a small part of a great fight against injustice,"[43] so this is the sense in which a thirty-year-old woman justified to herself the writing of an autobiography. It was offered as a narrative of a double release: the individual from prison and the group from spiritual enslavement. Her attack on Ron Karenga and LeRoi Jones as cultural nationalists who demand the total submission of the black female as rectification for the "century-long wrongs she has done the Black Male" derived from the same impulse. Liberation could only begin with a mind and imagination freed of the will to dominate others or to subordinate itself to the demands of power. However, once liberated, the self owed its primary allegiance elsewhere. Religion and the Party made similar demands and presented similar programs. The love expressed in the letters to George Jackson, and ignorantly paraded before the court by a prosecutor desperately trying to establish a motive for an invented crime, was indeed a motivating power, but in a sense to which the attorney remained blind. The surrender of the self and a concern for the other is of course a demand made by both religious and secular ideologies—the very rigor of that demand providing part of its attraction.

In contemplating Angela Davis, Huey Newton, and George Jackson, James Baldwin remarked in *If They Come in the Morning* that "what has happened, it seems to me, and to put it far too simply, is that a whole new generation of people have assessed and absorbed their history, and, in that tremendous action, have freed themselves of it, and will never be victims again. . . .I am trying to suggest that you—for example—do not appear to be your father's daughter in the same way that I am my father's son," because "at bottom, my father's expectations and mine were the same, the expectations of his generation and mine were the same . . .But when Cassius Clay became Muhammad Ali and refused to put on that uniform . . .a very different impact was made on the people and a very different kind of instruction had begun."[44]

Their's was indeed a new generation which had been robbed of its youth in a way which had hardly been true before. The fact of race was not simply (simply?) learned in the first meaningless insult delivered by a child of a different complexion, equally baffled by the code he was learning and, at first, unconsciously perpetuating. For the generation born during or just after the war—the generation which wrote these autobiographies—the daily drama of the civil rights movement denied even this brief grace of innocence. Race was front-page news; commitment was not a matter of choice. The sharp divisions were no longer slowly and terrifyingly defined by the developing sensibility; they were at the center of political life and the focus of media attention. This was the moral issue of the day, and the need to articulate black suffering became a moral compulsion.

There is, for the most part, little concern for method in these works. The situation in which they were written determines the form (though Angela Davis is careful to bracket her account of her early life with the more pressing and political realities of the present; past and present being subsumed in the same warping constraints). The pressure of the material leaves little room for imaginative shaping. Indeed, a central theme of these books is the suppression of imaginative as well as physical freedom.

And these are autobiographies written under a paradoxical need to suppress the self which is at the heart of the enterprise. Engaged in a process of definition which is avowedly political, they take as their point of departure the relative insignificance of individual experience. Indeed, the promotion of the self becomes a politically suspect act. So, childhood is seen only in its relation to events which demonstrate prejudice, only insofar as it can account for the education of the mind in the oppressive details of American racism. The ego is defined by external forces, and its resources are in turn external. Meaning is derived either from the fact of resistance or from embracing one's role in a historic drama. The self disintegrates; it is surrendered to process. It is the first and necessary victim of the revolution. Hence, these books tend to focus less on the individual who suffers than on the mechanism of that suffering. The subject of these autobiographies, in some ineluctable way, is America.

Their weakness was equally a product of the moment. They presumed too much. Looking for evidence in the present, they were likely to find it invalidated by time; but, then, their objective was immediate. Hence, their world tends to be Manichean, consisting of the irredeemably corrupt (the capitalists and their agents) and the pure and heroic army of the dispossessed, led usually by the Cubans, the Chinese, and the Vietnamese, or embodied in the liberating power of black consciousness. It was not of course a moral battlefield of their choosing, and they wrote against a political background and in a context in which social and moral problems seemed conveniently to resolve themselves in simple terms. The fact was that a decade later the Vietnamese were fighting skirmishes with the Chinese and the Cambodians, while the Muslim faith showed, from time to time, that it was as capable of producing fanatics as any other religion and, anyway, eventually abandoned its separatist stance. Black nationalists, meanwhile, were forced to acknowledge the complexities of

African politics and the moral ambiguities consequent upon their assault on fellow blacks as "bourgeois," "assimilationist," "Negroes," and "Toms." Some have retained their original convictions, making the necessary subtle adjustments, others have changed abruptly, abandoning the positions which they adopted with such vigor and total commitment in the late 1960s and early 1970s. Others did not survive that period and, hence, are frozen forever in the integrity of their stance.

But none, I think, except possibly H. Rap Brown, was a simple pragmatist, seizing the most convenient ideological weapons. They were forced to react quickly, to shape their lives into something more than a pattern of individual revolt. They felt, more acutely perhaps than had previous generations, that it was as a group that they were under attack and that it was as a group that they would have to revolt. Public visibility was no longer to be a way of evading commitment; it was to be a useful tool. And so they pulled the pieces of private experience together and related these to the shaping formulas which they read about in the books which offered them crash courses in the ideology of black revolt or class revolution. Here they found the theoretical structure which could make sense of the random violence and consistent deprivation which they had experienced as individuals.

Nor is this intended as a patronizing dismissal of the creeds which they embraced. It is simply an observation that the special force of many of these black autobiographies lies in the excited discovery of a way of relating individual experience to a public situation, a discovery which has all the force and perhaps something of the vulnerability of conversion. Perhaps, as Philip Larkin observed of those who marched off to World War I, "Never such innocence again,"[45] though we are dealing here not with ignorance but with an unexamined hope emerging from their own imagery. The prison experience was presented as an analogue of black oppression. The campaigns to free Huey Newton, the Soledad brothers, and Angela Davis were in essence campaigns to free black America. This, in a sense, is the purpose behind these autobiographies. And yet, when they were indeed released, the image collapsed. For the release of those individuals did not lead to the release of black America, though admittedly it did mark a far from minor achievement in demonstrating that such victories were possible, that the institutions of society and hence society itself were vulnerable to assault. Yet the problems remained, and, when the hysteria which provoked these particular public forms of persecution had passed, few fundamental changes had come about. For the inequity of sentencing still continued, as the experience of the Wilmington Ten attested in the late 1970s.

But it is that form of innocence and the energy which it released which distinguishes these autobiographies from a work like *Black Boy*, which concentrated on a pathology of the black American. And, finally, what matters is not the advocacy of a particular strategy—though Angela Davis would of course disagree—but the fact of resistance. Just as Camus fought in the war to save the *idea* of man, so, too, did these writers fight in their war for an idea of man which transcended the more limited analysis which they applied.

Their ardor to live, their passion to win, and their conviction that the other was knowable and hence redeemable, indeed their very enthusiasm, were all at odds with a fashionable nihilism, though it was shared for a while by those who found in the antiwar movement a focus for their commitment. The difference, however, was clear. America withdrew from Vietnam. For the black man and woman there was no withdrawal. Their contact with history was not fickle or even willed. Nor was their objective the same. Most of those who eventually attacked the Vietnam War did so in the name of the status quo; it was, at its most successful, a conservative rebellion. Not so for the black revolutionary who was committed to demythologizing, which, as Sartre has observed, [46] is also a revolutionary act.

There is an extraordinary lack of self-doubt in these books. Following the moment of conversion, there is little or no uncertainty about the self which emerges or its relationship to the world. Indeed, the opposition of the public world creates an unquestioned identity, with a manifest solidity. It is true that autobiography tends to be the story of the undefeated, but the struggle of these individuals is so much with a world external to the self that the self emerges through a struggle with that externality. For most of them, that battle begins early, and the dialectical struggles within the sensibility of the individual, the painful process of handling human relationships, emerging sexuality, religious faith, and the problems of career are simply absent. The dialectic operates between an assured self and a society which, though apparently implacable, is vulnerable to assault by the individual whose sensibility has been reduced to the fact of resistance. There is a great deal missing from these books—an area of private life which is at best sketched because the authors value only that experience which is instructive and utilizable. It is not the uniqueness of the individual's experience which is stressed but its typicality. Only Malcolm X dwells at length on his youth, and then only as the religious convert who is always liable to deploy the dissolute nature of his past in order to demonstrate more effectively the redeemed nature of his present. As John Bunyan had said, *"I can remember my Fears, and Doubts, and sad Months with Comfort,"* because *"they are as the head of Goliath in my Hand."* [47] These are literally inspirational works in the religious sense. The journey to prison is a correlative of that dive down into selfhood which is at the heart of William James's *The Varieties of Religious Experience* and so many other autobiographical texts. It is the pit from which the individual returns having understood the principles whereby the world functions. The autobiography thus becomes the attempt to make that experience intelligible to others. The very existence of these books is a testament. It is evidence of a command of experience which is often contrasted with the largely mute suffering of the previous generation. Their exclusions tend to be exclusions of the frivolous and irrelevant, as judged by a mind for which the present is the commanding reality and the public world the world of real moral seriousness. They are offered as representative destinies. The resurrection of the self which they offer is a political rebirth, a sudden detection of the historical resonance of a private experience which could only be seen as unique through a failure to locate it in its cultural and economic context.

At the heart of these books is a single theme—the growth of an individual from innocence to knowledge and of a race from impotence to power, power not necessarily over the public world but over the self. And this self is projected, not as a romantic image of alienation, but as the basis of community, as a model of authentic hope and social action. The note of naive faith which carries the individual through experience, even in some cases to death, is an expression of his sense of meeting that experience on a wholly new basis. There is the clear feeling that theirs is a generation which can tackle America on its own terms. The tone is that of exuberant, confident adolescence. It celebrates a newly lost innocence, expresses fiercely held convictions, and is vibrant with a commitment which will allow no room for ambiguity, which feels itself to be the fulcrum of history. It was an image enhanced by the dark and powerful forces which they challenged. Just as young white Americans were feeling themselves to be the resurgent conscience of America, these black writers saw themselves as the moral catalyst transforming themselves and the state. The answer, whether contained in the myths and symbols of socialism or in the Muslim faith, lay finally in the courage to confront America with its hypocrisy and the black American with his ability to determine his own fate. In the words of Margaret Walker's "For My People," quoted at the beginning of *Revolutionary Suicide*, "Let a new earth arise. Let another world be born. . . . Let a second generation full of courage issue forth, let a people loving freedom come to growth. . . .Let the martial songs be written, let the dirges disappear. Let a race of men now rise and take control!"[48] These polemical essays and autobiographical works are those martial songs and these writers are that second generation. They begin with the material of a deterministic dirge and end with a celebration of a new world.

Black Drama: The Public Voice

8

One of Addison Gayle, Jr.'s, less helpful remarks is his observation that "the novel is the one genre which attempts in dramatic and narrative form to answer the questions, what are we? and what is it all about?"[1] Even his use of the word "dramatic" does not seem to have alerted him to the literary myopia which his remark implies. In fact, for many people in the 1960s, it was theatre and not the novel which engaged their enthusiasm most directly. It was on the stage that the Black Arts movement was born, with LeRoi Jones's Black Arts Repertory Theatre, and it was drama which provided a model of that direct relationship between artist and community which was the essence of the Second Renaissance. In its collaborative nature, it also stood as an image of black cooperative endeavor, which was not without its relevance to a threatened minority. Indeed, a quite contrary claim had been made as early as 1947 by Edith Isaacs, for whom "when the theatre is at its height it is the art best fitted to interpret men to one another."[2]

The theatre is a public art, the only art conducted in the present tense; not only does it rely for its effect on an immediate rapport between artist and public, but its very "present" nature contains the possibility of that empathy being raised to the level of secular ritual, of epiphany. It was a direction that the American theatre itself took in the 1960s, with the experiments of people like Julian Beck and Richard Schechner. But for the black dramatist, such moments of consonance, the insistence on the permeability of the membrane between performer and public, was not an experiment conducted in the name of transcendental unity, but was itself an assertion of political potential and cultural solidarity. The path from the theatre building to the street, followed by the avant garde theatre of the 1960s, was pursued equally by some sections of the black theatre but for rather different reasons. Beck might assert that life and art were synonymous, meaning by that that art is simply the framing of experience, a means of drawing attention to the dramatic potential of lives which were themselves self-dramatizing mechanisms; the black writer went to the street because that was where his audience lay, that was where he could find those whose consciousness he wished to assault with the truth of their existence and their cultural and political potential, rather than with Artaud's strenuous truths about human experience. The theatre has always exerted a powerful attraction over those for whom the stage and the platform seem generically connected (see, for example, the case of John Dos Passos), but for the black American there was a special potency in a communal art which seemed especially familiar to those used to the church service, the dance hall, and the sometimes desperate communality of the street. The audience was at hand. There may be no established tradition of novel reading, which was, anyway, largely a private experience; but there was a tradition of the public event in one guise or another. And poetry in performance and drama built on that tradition established themselves as the dominant forms of the Second Renaissance. The number of theatre groups expanded dramatically, with black arts theatres being established in cities across the country, the Free Southern Theatre taking plays to those who had never been exposed to drama before, and major subsidized companies being established in New York. This was not a solemn theatre, but it was also not a repetition of the black revues and musicals of the 1920s, though Broadway continued to capitalize on black vitality. For the most part, it was a theatre which engaged the daily reality of the black experience of America (Ed Bullins), proposed revolutionary models (LeRoi Jones), or enacted rituals based on black life (Barbara Ann Teer).

Yet the theatre is cooperative in another respect as well. In its conventional form it is a commercial enterprise whose success depends upon the approbation of the marketplace. It is scarcely surprising, therefore, that black drama should seldom have penetrated into the supposed showcase of the American theatre. It is not for nothing that Broadway is called the Great White Way. But Broadway itself has been in a continual state of decline in recent years so that, paradoxically, the new black theatre, with its roots in the black community, has had a purchase on a shared experience not always available to the American writer whose subject all too often was the failure of communal values. The black writer faced a community homogenized by a common experience in a way that was simply no longer true of white society. But it was not all black writers who wished to address an audience solely defined by its racial composition. It was not all black writers who wished to endorse cultural and moral values which aligned themselves quite so conveniently along racial lines. But, then, the problem of the audience for black writing has been a crucial and persistent issue and one which, the vociferous pronouncements of some black dramatists notwithstanding, was not to be resolved quite as simply as it appeared.

Writing in 1928, James Weldon Johnson identified the problem confronting the Negro playwright as the problem of the double audience. ''The moment a Negro writer picks up his pen and sits down to his typewriter,'' he insisted, ''he is immediately called upon to solve, consciously or unconsciously, this problem of the double audience. To whom shall he address himself, to his own black group or to white America? Many a Negro writer has fallen down as it were, between these two stools.''³ One year earlier, Alain Locke had indicated a possible solution to this dilemma when he published an anthology of *Plays of Negro Life*, in which he called for a national Negro theatre ''where the black playwright and the black actor will interpret the soul of their people in a way to win the attention and admiration of the world.''⁴ But, ironically, even at its very beginning, the black theatre movement was compromised, for although Alain Locke was black, the better-known playwrights in his collection were white.

For James Weldon Johnson, the production of Ridgely Torrence's *Three Plays for a Negro Theatre* in April 1917 paradoxically marked the beginnings of Negro theatre. For although Torrence was white, the plays offered the Negro his first real opportunity in serious drama. Negroes were themselves allowed into the New York audience, then still something of a novelty, and the plays went some distance beyond the usual stereotypes, the central character of *Granny Maumee* having been blinded by fire when her son had been burned to death for a crime he had not committed. The declaration of war on the day following their opening, however, cut short a promising run, while the ironies involved in the white authorship of Negro plays was less striking than the fact that the subject should be tackled at all. The success of O'Neill's work, especially, opened up the subject of the Negro in a way which, despite the ambiguities of work which stressed the supposed primitive aspect of Negro identity, was crucial to the emergence of black writers.

The first serious play by a black writer to appear on Broadway was Willis Richardson's *The Chipwoman's Fortune* (1923), which opened originally at the Lafayette Theatre in Harlem before moving downtown. It was a slight work, a one-act morality play whose characters lack credibility and whose moral is as disturbingly simplistic as the action is punctilious in its threadbare morality. Silas Green, a store porter, is laid off from work because of his failure to maintain payments on a Victrola. He needs fifty dollars to prevent the machine from being reclaimed and to win his job back. The money is rapidly forthcoming when Aunt Nancy, an old woman who survives by collecting wood and coal and who has nursed Silas's wife through a serious illness, confesses that she has saved money for her son who has been in prison. As luck would have it, and with an alarming promptness, he duly arrives and immediately hands over half of the savings—more than enough to save the day. Racial humiliation is hinted at and provides a moral context for the play, but the work lacks any real artistry. It is hard to imagine now why it should have been thought worthwhile to venture such a slight work on Broadway, while the gap between this play and those of O'Neill indicates clearly enough why the theatre did not play a leading role during the First Renaissance. There were attempts to create black theatre, but these early efforts were uneven, as, it must be added, was much white theatre at a time when O'Neill was one of the few writers to show any real awareness of the revolution which had overtaken European drama in the previous few decades.

It is true, however, that the creation of the Federal Theatre in the late 1930s gave a brief boost both to the black and the white theatre in America. The black units did indeed play an active role, though not without considerable difficulty, some groups finding themselves permanently in rehearsal and almost never in performance. But, the achievement of such "black" productions as *Macbeth* and *The Swing Mikado* aside, the black theatre did achieve one considerable success with Hall Johnson's *Run Little Chillun*. This was originally produced on Broadway in 1933, when it ran for three months. Revived by the Federal Theatre, it received numerous productions across the country.

Run Little Chillun is essentially a folk play. The plot is concerned with a struggle for the soul of Jim Jones, son of the Reverend Jones, pastor of Hope Baptist Church. On the one hand are his loving wife and the hypocritical representatives of respectability, who are secretly delighted at his lapse from grace; on the other is the sensuous Sulami, a passionate young woman drawn equally to the paganism of a new mystical cult and the pleasures of the body. This cult, rooted in an African past, offers sensual freedom, where the Baptist Church offers only salvation through suffering. Caught in the middle, Jim, like Emperor Jones, is trapped between two cultures, each fallible but each making a genuine claim on his sensibility. The play ends with a flash of lightning. Sulami falls to the ground. As the stage direction indicates, it remains unclear as to which has triumphed—paganism or the church.

The play did tackle something of the same territory as did O'Neill, and its intelligent use of music, along with a satirical treatment of the black church, and a melodramatic stagecraft, perhaps account for its success. But, like *Emperor Jones*, its view of the Negro as a primitive spirit, the victim of sexuality and superstition, reinforced a stereotype which the black writer has always struggled to escape.

Langston Hughes's *Mulatto* (1935) still dealt in stereotypes, but this melodrama of southern race relations was written with the kind of force and directness which provided something of the momentum behind Wright's *Native Son* five years later. It took as its theme a popular motif of the 1920s—the plight of the mulatto—but projected through this, not only the special dilemma of the individual who shares black and white parents, but thereby the central problem of the American Negro, for whom the double vision is an ineluctable aspect of existence. The choice for both lay in acquiescence or in a dangerous challenge to the system. In a sense, it was a curious play to find Hughes writing in the mid-1930s, at a time when his poetry was stressing the new black identity as worker and ally of the white working class. Certainly the class potential implicit in the play is not stressed. It becomes, rather, a kind of companion piece to Wright's *Uncle Tom's Children*, published in 1938—a warning of the birth of a new generation for whom dignity lies in challenging white dominance, claiming full recognition as a legitimate child of America. The run of *Mulatto* on Broadway was not challenged for another twenty-four years, when Lorraine Hansberry's *A Raisin in the Sun* established a new record for the number of performances of a Broadway play by a Negro author. But the intervening period was not entirely barren, nor were black playwrights unwilling to assert a militant role for the black American.

Theodore Ward's *Our Lan'* was not produced until 1946, appearing first off Broadway and then subsequently on Broadway. Set in 1865, it is concerned with the efforts of freed slaves to establish their right to land on an island plantation off the coast of Georgia. Promised forty acres and a mule by General Sherman, they are eventually deprived of it when President Johnson vetoes the bill which would have confirmed their right to the appropriated land.

The play moves steadily towards an apocalyptic ending. Beneath the conventionalities of a love interest is an attempt to reclaim history, and the leader becomes an image of resistance, of a determined independence, as is made apparent in the tone of Ward's stage direction which indicates that ''he is an expression or symbol if you will, of the best traits of his people. There is a sure sense of dignity about him and his very physical strength bespeaks something of the relentlessness and courage which characterised the bulk of the vilified black men of the period—a people conditioned by the terrors of ruthless oppression who communicated their spirit from generation to generation.''[5] The hero's stubborn commitment to principles of natural justice is contrasted with the moral equivocations of postbellum America and with the temporizing of Negro freedmen who see their own position and their acquisition of power and material benefits as threatened. Of course the play is offered not only as a commentary on the past and the betrayals of late nineteenth-century America but also as a model of relationships in the present. The same bitter ironies were, after all, observable in Theodore Ward's America. It was a debate about the response which the Negro should offer to assaults on his dignity and on his rights.

In *Our Lan'*, the choice is between acquiescence, the acceptance of a relationship with whites dependent on economic subservience, and the assertion of an independence and a personal pride which would be maintained even in the face of violence. So the play ends with a battle between the ex-slaves and the army, which is supposedly acting on behalf of the liberal Freedmans' Bureau but which is actually working on behalf of the economic interest of the Old South. The play ends with many dead on both sides, as the whites prepare to annihilate the survivors with cannon fire. In the original production, the sound of that final explosion closes the play; in the Broadway version, the play ends before the cannon fire, the resultant silence being charged with kinetic energy and expressing perhaps a more accurate sense of an apocalyptic possibility.

Joshua, who as a slave had planned revolt, takes his stand, fully aware that he must lose, but conscious himself of his role as symbol, "Ain't nobody ever got nothin' worthwhile for nothin'. Some of ouah leaders don't understand tha. They's turnin' one Convention after ernother into de graveyard of all ouah hopes. It's got to be up t' us. We ain't many. 'N it's hard t' stand your ground when yuh know deep down in your heart de best yuh can do is serve as er lesson. Remember John Brown. Him 'n his lil handful stood up for ouah freedom 'n they set de whole country on fiah!"[6] Having rejected both accommodation and a bid for political power which, given the realities of American politics, will leave them powerless, he opts for an insistence on natural justice, even though this means a destructive confrontation. Since the play was actually written in 1941, this was a powerful proposal to make at a time when America was itself faced with a similar dilemma over war in Europe.

The relationship between Jericho and a beautiful black girl, Delphine, is admittedly a carefully calculated sentimentality, but Ward adroitly relates a folk dimension to political analysis in a way which makes some of the more graceless moments of dialect dialogue defer to a transcending mythology of resistance and an ironic perception of American values. The unalloyed heroism of Ward's central character lacks the element of self-advertisement displayed by many black rebels of the 1960s. Necessarily his act of rebellion is itself pragmatic as he simply responds to evidence of white political and moral equivocation. In a way, his values are those of American society, freedom implying the inheritance of liberal values; but more importantly, he proposes a model of black community which would be taken up in another form in the 1960s. The difference, of course, is that he lacks any ideological basis for his action. However, he does recognize the value of the ex-slaves creating their own community, and his emphasis on ownership of land as a key to cultural identity was a familiar tenet of Marxist faith and one again reflected later by the Black Muslims.

Theodore Ward was concerned with creating a usable history, with molding images commensurate with an unfolding consciousness of racial autonomy, as were the black writers of the 1960s. The relative lack of response for the play may in part have arisen from the fact that at the hands of writers like Torrence, O'Neill, Paul Green, and DuBois, Hayward the Negro seemed to have become trapped in a stereotype of folksy, dialect-based plays which emphasized the persistence of superstition and the fragility of the black psyche, and that Ward's play appeared to be written in the same vein.

Take a Giant Step (1953), Louis Peterson's sensitive and subtle study of a young black boy's simultaneous initiation into sexual and racial realities, has been equally undervalued. Sharing something of the tone of Salinger's *The Catcher in the Rye*, it is a compassionate account of an adolescent struggling, in a self-destructive way, to deal with an emerging sexuality which he finds as baffling as he does at first the gradual withdrawal of his white friends. The all-male world of his youth, in which race and religion mean nothing to the gang of boys who stage a raid on the local delicatessen, breaks down with puberty. The nexus between race and sex obtrudes into the childhood world of camaraderie. At the school dance he finds himself isolated, as his is a Negro family in a predominantly white area. Increasingly lonely, he deals with his new situation by challenging his teacher's racist remarks and is suspended from school when he is found smoking. He deliberately cuts himself off from his classmates, themselves hyphenated Americans, preempting what he rightly presumes will be their rejection of himself. He makes a half-hearted and largely bewildered visit to a prostitute's room and takes a beer in a bar, in a romantic attempt to crash his way through to an adulthood which he hopes will insulate him from the painful truths of adolescent life. Eventually, he is eased through this mental and emotional barrier with the compassionate understanding of a young black widow—an act of grace which verges on the stereotype but which is saved from the somewhat solemn mood of Anderson's *Tea and Sympathy*. The death of his grandmother, a witty old woman who forges an alliance with her grandson, robs him of a remaining friend.

Take a Giant Step hardly dramatizes the plight of a typical black boy. His disillusionment and desertion are delayed by his unusual circumstances—a middle-class black boy in a white community. He is betrayed as much by his own naive failure to realize the implications of his situation as by the friends whose rejection of him is less a consequence of personal prejudice than of a desire to make themselves socially inconspicuous. Social norms begin to exert an authority which they are unwilling to challenge. Lacking the imagination to understand his situation, they collaborate in his exclusion.

His parents have similarly failed him. Their presence in a middle-class white area is a badge of their achievement, as are the material goods which they have substituted for real affection. To Peterson, the real problem of integration lay less in the direct challenge dramatized by Lorraine Hansberry than in the human costs involved in aspiring to the values of an amoral society. And, in this respect, I find his work more subtle and, in some respects, more honest than Hansberry's. In *Take a Giant Step*, the move from a black slum opens up possibilities for Spence. Like his brother, he has his eye on college. He has an element of self-consciousness which shapes the form of his rebellion. But it leaves him vulnerable in a way, and at an age which would not apply to the black child raised in the heart of the ghetto. The protection of his middle-class background is also a curse which leaves him no method of dealing with his problem except the familiar evasions of middle-class white youth. It is precisely because he is alone, because he is the only black child in the neighborhood, that he can get no support, while his parents, anxious to get him back into school, are unlikely to support him in a clash with those white forces through whom they hope he will gain a freedom from racial prejudice. But the cost is too high. Distraught at his grandmother's death and overcome with a justifiable self-pity, he says the only thing he can say, seeing that it is the essence of the lessons offered equally by his parents and by society. "God damn it—I hate being black . . .I hate it. I hate it. I hate the hell out of it."[7] The play ends with his mother's assertion of her love for him as Spence obediently practices the piano. Having told his friends that he no longer wishes to meet them, he faces a future still bewildering and potentially destructive. "I'm trying to learn. I'm trying as hard as I know how."[8]

The potential for sentimentality in such a play is considerable. It is Peterson's achievement that he allows that impulse such little room to operate. It is perhaps inevitable that the special circumstances of the play would make it seem less significant than a work like *A Raisin in the Sun*, which is set in a black ghetto more typical of the environment facing most blacks in the 1950s; yet, in some ways, it is better constructed, less contrived, and considerably more subtle in its treatment of prejudice and in its recognition of the corrosive power of a society which operates less through implacable fiats and overt challenges than through a soul-destroying contempt for human values, an exclusion of the alien through a spiritual, rather than a physical, banishment. Spence's sense of humor, his ironic view of himself and his surroundings, itself becomes a resource, as is the imperfect love of his parents. There is no hint that political action can transform his dilemma or that an alteration in economic circumstance will provide an easy passage to a redeeming sense of self. His battle is a lonely one, his commitment is to finding his own way of adjusting to the realities which have so suddenly left him abandoned.

Lorraine Hansberry's *A Raisin in the Sun* was a crucial document. Just as the 1950s had begun with the award of a Pulitzer Prize to Gwendolyn Brooks, so it ended with the award of the New York Drama Critics Circle Award to Lorraine Hansberry. Like Wright's *Native Son*, her play was set in the South Side of Chicago and begins with the urgent ringing of an alarm bell, an alarm intended both for black and white America. Like Wright's Bigger Thomas, with dreams of a better life, dreams of escape from the demeaning round of poverty, the emasculating fact of racial and economic subservience, the protagonist is a chauffeur. But where Bigger's dreams are frustrated, Walter Younger's become redefined and realizable.

In many ways the play symbolized the spirit and strategy of the civil rights movement. The Younger family has moved from the South to their present home in the South Side. Their aspirations are blunted by exposure to the bleak realities of the ghetto, but they are now revived by the imminent arrival of a check for ten thousand dollars, the product of a life-insurance policy. Under the impact of this deus ex machina, their hopes are rekindled. It is a mechanism which one might have expected to be treated with some irony, like the similar device in Odets's *Awake and Sing* to which Hansberry's play bears more than a passing resemblance. Instead, it becomes simply an enabling device whose moral and social implications remain largely uninspected. And this is symp-tomatic of an approach which successfully dramatizes moral issues but which too often fails to press beyond the public poses to an underlying reality.

Walter Younger sees the money as making it possible for him to revive his damaged pride by buying a liquor store, unquestioningly accepting the legiti-macy of the American dream, much as Miller's Willy Loman had done. If the business of America is business, then the obvious way to achieve acceptance as an American is through a Franklinesque self-reliance and enterprise. His daughter, Beneatha, regards the cash as making possible the medical career which she trusts will provide a means of escape from a world in which she feels so out of place. Her mother, however, is committed to buying a new house in order to rescue the family from its deepening alienation and its imminent disintegration.

When Walter feels his manhood threatened by her disposition of the money, she entrusts a large part of it to him. Inevitably—and that very inevitability raises interesting and unanswered questions about Hansberry's social and metaphysical assumptions—he squanders the money, entrusting it to a black friend who duly absconds with it. The loss provokes a crisis. The house alone remains as a bolt-hole from their present difficulties. But even this is threat-ened when Walter, in an effort to restore his authority and in an attempt to retrieve some of the lost money, offers to accept a bribe offered by the representative of a white residents' association and agrees to sell their new house, which turns out to be in a white area (this being the only place in which his mother could secure a reasonably priced property). However, when the man arrives, Walter is stung into resistance by the contempt with which his wife and mother treat him. The play ends with his new commitment to challenge the white world.

The difficulty is that the decision to take on the overt hostility of the white world is a product of that same desire for self-respect which had earlier made Walter long for a liquor store. Lorraine Hansberry does not successfully distinguish between the two dreams, nor can one have much confidence in the family's ability to sustain the inevitable tensions consequent upon the move since we have seen how easily these characters capitulate in the face of difficulties. The logic of the action implies the emergence of a new pride and family unity; the logic of the characters implies the collapse of both under the pressure of time and social hostility. Moreover, the fact of the inheritance, without which such a potentially redeeming action is impossible, is made contingent on an event wholly external to the characters and to the community which they exemplify. Though initially the move is seen by the mother as itself potentially transforming, by the end the meaning of their lives has become ineluctably and dangerously linked to the fact of white opposition. The pre-judice of the whites creates the need for a resisting self. It is an inescapably ambiguous source of identity and an even more ironic creator of family unity.

Either way, these ambiguities lie outside the play, as they do outside the sensibilities of the characters. Indeed, the move itself hardly constitutes a fundamental change in their circumstances; what it does is to render visible and overt the determining power of white society, which is usually concealed and implicit.

It was of course a basic strategy of the civil rights movement to break down housing segregation since this was a key to desegregation in education and eventually in employment. But, in this play, the escape to the middle-class white area is itself seen as liberating. There is another unexamined paradox, however. For the other value which Hansberry identifies is the emergence and shaping of a black identity which derives from an acknowledgement of cultural independence. Beneatha brings an African student to the house, and though the author implicitly criticizes Beneatha's unthinking adoption of African modes of dress, she does endorse the untested values which he proposes and exemplifies. And the relationship between this identity—racially based, internalized, spontaneous—and the one to be distilled out of the clash with white society is unclear.

Walter Younger is established as a black Willy Loman, self-deceiving and self-destructive. Even his challenge to the white world is delivered at the instigation of his mother and daughter, so that, in a sense, the play is less concerned with social and racial issues, though these create the determinants within which he moves, than with the interplay between the social and the psychological. But therein lies a problem, for insofar as Walter's weakness is psychological, the social critique is diluted; insofar as it is socially derived, he becomes simply evidence of socal determinism. Either way the risk is that he will become merely evidence of racial pathology. The ebb and flow of his confidence thus derives, not from a moral view of the world nor yet from personal commitments, but shifts in the private or public subsoil. Moreover, insofar as it is never convincingly established that Walter's character is a product of his racial circumstances, his failure and his less believable renewed confidence cannot really be seen as an indictment of American racism. His poverty and the destruction of his aspirations arguably derives from a failure of moral nerve, not from the opposition of the white world. If he believes in the icons of American society, then so did Willy Loman and for much the same reasons. In a world apparently lacking in transcendence, he values only those things which society itself seems to value.

Indeed, it is perhaps best to read this play not so much as an assault on American racism as an attack on its substitution of material for spiritual values, of which the reduction of individuals to racial stereotypes is merely the most striking example. Both Willy and Walter deceive themselves and others; both yearn for the restoration of human values, though neither can see that his illusions are themselves the chief obstacle to the realization of such a need. They fail because they can see no way of relating the self either to the social world or to those whose offer of love cannot be acknowledged because it seems to demand a material sanction in wealth, achievement, or status. The psychosis at the heart of their lives neutralizes the social critique, for, although their sense of alienation may be socially derived and the precise configuration of their dreams defined by national myths, there is no evidence that a modification of that society would have destroyed that alienation. Would Willy or Walter have succeeded under any social system? They are not without their sense of loss; both of them reach for something which they can only define in material form but which is in essence a missing sense of transcendence in their lives. Both men value the cash value of life-insurance policies because these seem to offer a way of buying into the dreams which they inherit and which they take for reality; but both are equally deceived. At least they seem to be. The irony of *A Raisin in the Sun*, however, is that this money does buy a dream; it does turn out to be the key which Walter took it to be. And though this is not quite in the simplistic way he had imagined, the author still has a moral problem to confront, for she seems, through a plot contrivance, inevitably to endorse the very materialism against which she is in revolt, apparently believing that the inheritance is simply a dramatic device which will be perceived as such and forgotten. Any Marxist would have told her otherwise.

The climax towards which the play moves, then, implies moral and social progress. The individuals are rescued from despair and self-hatred. They are shown in the process of making a new commitment. What is unclear is the nature and extent of their redemption and the object of their commitment. Walter's rejection of the proffered bribe may restore his pride (though even this is doubtful since he had to be bullied into it and is, anyway, susceptible to the quixotic gesture), but nothing else has changed. For Lorraine Hansberry, however, his gesture is mythic; it is an act of courage which links him with tragic heroes from literature and life. In an article in *The Village Voice*, she claimed that ''he becomes, in spite of those who are too intrigued with despair and hatred of man to see it, King Oedipus refusing to tear out his eyes, but attacking the Oracle instead. He is that last Jewish patriot manning his rifle in the burning ghetto at Warsaw; he is that young girl who swam into sharks to save a friend a few weeks ago; he is Anne Frank, still believing in people; he is the nine small heroes of Little Rock; he is Michelangelo creating David, and Beethoven bursting forth with the Ninth Symphony. He is all those things because he has finally reached out in his tiny moment and caught that sweet essence which is human dignity, and it shines like the old star-touched dream that is in his eyes.''[9] The truth is that this is how Walter Younger would wish to see himself; it may even be a state to which he briefly aspires when he enacts his version of an African dance, but the fragility of his character has been too faithfully recorded, his attraction for the grand gesture (pressing desperately needed money into his son's hand, gambling everything on a black friend) too accurately demonstrated. We have no reason to believe in his transformation beyond the fact that his latest bid for attention and dignity comes at the climax of the play and thus implies a conversion which has yet to be established in terms of character.

In reality, nothing has changed. Beneatha cannot now become a doctor, if she ever could. Walter is still only a chauffeur, if his inadequate record has not by now precipitated his dismissal. All he has to look forward to is the increased expense caused by life in the suburbs and the presence of another mouth to feed. The mother, whose stubbornness had forced the move, is an old woman. Hence, the implications of moral and social progress are unsubstantiated, the hope illusory, the logic of individual and hence cultural realization contradicted by the fact of character as by a social reality which the author merely projects just beyond the perception and experience of her characters. The materials for an independent black pride are identified: the stubborn endurance and practicality of the mother and the new pride in origins of Beneatha. But neither is without irony; the mother's authority undermining her son's masculinity and Beneatha embracing an inadequately perceived and romanticized version of Africa. Far from the dream now bearing a chance of realization, it has apparently simply changed its form. Indeed, the confusions in the play were in part a reflection of similar confusions in the civil rights movement, for the problem is that assimilation into a white world is potentially destructive of precisely that confident black identity which is a prerequisite for such a venture.

In a sense, this is implicitly recognized by Lorraine Hansberry's second play, *The Sign in Sidney Brustein's Window* (1964), since here the single black individual confronts an alienation which has scarcely been dispelled by integration and which is identified as deriving from a more fundamental dissonance between reality and appearance, hope and actuality, than that proposed by race. For Harold Cruse, indeed, her desertion of black characters and of an art directed single-mindedly to the probing of black identity was a matter for indictment, if not constituting the reason for its failure. Her concern in this play is with asserting the need for a compassion which is constantly threatened by a self-obsession which she sees as lying at the heart of political corruption, the failure of personal relationships, and the collapse of integrity in art.

Sidney Brustein is a white liberal who has tired of causes but who can always be rallied behind any slogan sufficiently close to his own dreams of innocence and moral concern. Idealism becomes a form of evasion, while his tolerance is constantly in danger of concealing a fundamental lack of passionate commitment. Life becomes a glorious game in which nothing is finally too serious, and this year's cause can always be traded in on next year's. His wife Iris is bemused by his shifting allegiances and struggles to play the various roles in which he casts her. But to Lorraine Hansberry, such innocence can be deadly, and the willful refusal to engage the complexity and, indeed, the cruelties and deprivations of life is a fundamental denial of moral responsibility. For Sidney, a conscience is a badge, a sign to hang in his window. As a consequence, he fails to realize that his efforts have secured the election of a corrupt politician and that his own marriage is crumbling under the impact of his dedication to unreality. Yet, Lorraine Hansberry was equally repelled by those who denied all responsibility, who allowed themselves to be shocked into belief in an absurdist world in which no values could operate and in which art was merely an expression of entropy. And she equally rejected those who settled for the role of detached observer, those who protected themselves by simulating a neutral stance. Iris is one such; her family name, Parodus, pointedly being the Greek word for chorus.

When put to the test, each character in the play fails. Gloria Parodus, a neurotic call girl, sees the chance for some happiness in a relationship with the play's only Negro character, Alton Scales. But when he discovers her past, he drops her with a cruelty akin to that shown by Mitch towards Blanche DuBois in *A Streetcar Named Desire*. None of the play's characters helps Gloria in her extremity of suffering, and eventually she commits suicide, an indictment of all those who can so easily deploy their excuses for what is a failure of humanity. But it is that simple act of humanity which, for the playwright, constitutes the single immutable value to oppose to an absurdist universe and a corrupt social system alike. Inhumanity, she suggests, is not born of particular systems, nor is it an extrusion of metaphysical truths; it is a product of self-interest and of a willful refusal to see the world for what it is and human needs for what they are. Racism is simply one example of such a failure. For her, the responsibility of the individual and of the artist is to describe reality, but also to direct attention to ways in which that reality can be changed or perceived. As Gloria remarks, ''I was taught to believe that—creativity and great intelligence ought to make one expansive and understanding. That if ordinary people, among whom I have the sense at least to count myself, could not expect understanding from artists . . .then where indeed might we look for it at all—in this quite dreadful world.''[10] This, of course, might account for the hollow optimism of *A Raisin in the Sun*, and despite her assurance, in an article in *Mademoiselle*, that she was not calling for clichés of affirmation, all three of her major works tend to end on such notes, subtle ambiguities being swallowed up in a necessary drive through despair or self-doubt to a new social vision.

And the point towards which she ruthlessly drives her characters is the point of commitment: Walter Younger seeks to rescue his pride through an act of social commitment; Sidney Brustein, having discovered that he has been deceived by the supposedly reform politician, says that ''you have forced me to take a position. Finally—the one thing I never wanted to do. Just not being for you is not enough. . . .I have been forced to learn that I have to be *against* you'';[11] in *Les Blancs*, the black intellectual, torn between personal and intellectual ties which link him to Europe and the demands of a revolutionary situation in Africa, opts for revolt. Always, it seems, the social act is seen as redeeming; an external drive is presented as solving an internal dilemma. Yet, behind the social act is a sentimentality which she works very hard to convert into active principle.

Like Baldwin, in *The Sign in Sidney Brustein's Window* she presents love as a value which can neutralize social alienation—a value whose sentimentality is purged by a necessary suffering. The agency through which this love will operate is more problematic, and we are back in the same circular logic. If love becomes an active moral principle, then the agencies of its operation may become possible; but love cannot be generated by social mechanisms already penetrated by the corrosive influence of self-interest. So that love can only derive from a suffering consequent upon its failure.

It was a popular stance, a flight from the political and social into the metaphysics of relation, the morality of the sensibility, equally visible in the work of Edward Albee (*The Zoo Story* and *Who's Afraid of Virginia Woolf?*), in the attenuated liberalism of Arthur Miller (*After the Fall*) and, later, in the casual sentimentalities of performance drama and the neoromantic vogue for the authenticity of the body. To be true, the civil rights movement itself derived its impetus from a similar piety, resting its case on the liberal principles of the Constitution and the injunctions of the New Testament, which proposed precisely that model of human brotherhood and mutual moral responsibility which provided their sanction as well as their paradigm. The contempt of Harold Cruse and others derived from a conviction that such language had been historically negated, that it lacked both a credible political and cultural correlative. Thus, the thrust of *A Raisin in the Sun* became an unsubstantiated piety and *The Sign in Sidney Brustein's Window* became an assertion of the need for abstract commitment which fails to acknowledge the special circumstances of black deprivation or the cultural and communal resources available to the black American.

The play may attack absurdist reductivism and the idea that art should be self-serving or ironic, but, to Cruse, it fails to offer anything more than a generalized gesture which takes as its premise precisely that universality denied by the prejudice which it is invoked to neutralize. For Hansberry, however, the point of the play is that commitment is a serious matter which requires the rejection of slogans which imply the perception of issues only in their most immediate and obvious form. It would, perhaps, be fanciful to see this as a critique of her own early play, but she was clearly intent on dramatizing her conviction that the transformations which she sought to foster lay in a courageous determination both to live with human contradictions while insisting on the responsibility to renew love, and to struggle for the persistence of values which are not adequately described by or contained within an assault on the superficial evidences of alienation. The irony is that, arguably, *A Raisin in the Sun* was guilty of just such a failure, while *The Sign in Sidney Brustein's*

Window shows a treatment of character which is itself lacking in that acknowledgement of ambiguity and complexity which she suggests to be implicit in the notion of love.

She insists that the individual's responsibility is to look beyond the surface, to penetrate the anguish of private and public life and she offers Sidney and Iris's failure to do this as an indictment of their human failure; the failure of David, himself a playwright, similarly stands as her rejection of an art which sees no purpose beyond an elaboration of absurdity. Yet her own portraits are similarly simplified; David being a parody of the absurdist dramatist and Gloria, a clichéd call girl. Even the sole Negro character exists only as the embodiment of a stereotypical attitude. In the context of the moral world which she proposes, it is potentially a fatal flaw.

Lorraine Hansberry's second play was the last produced during her lifetime. In common with Baldwin's *Blues for Mr. Charlie*, its run was prolonged with the aid of donations by the familiar liberal well-wishers, black and white. But, when she died of leukemia at the age of thirty-four, the play was closed. She left behind her several works, in particular, *Les Blancs*, which was her response to Genet's *The Blacks* and which expresses her conviction, a conviction hinted at in the figure of Asagai in her first play, that the fate of the black American and that of the African were in some way indissolubly linked. Her uncle, William Hansberry, had himself been a scholar of African antiquities and, as a young woman, she had taken a seminar under W. E. B. Du Bois. She was an active supporter of Jomo Kenyatta and, as an associate editor of *Freedom*, she was exposed to the question of African liberation. Indeed, two weeks before the opening of her first play she said that " . . .more than anything else, the compelling obligation of the Negro writer, as a writer and citizen of life, is participation in the intellectual affairs of all men, everywhere. The foremost enemy of the Negro intelligentsia of the past has been and in a large sense remains—isolation . . . . And I for one, as a black woman in the United States in the mid-Twentieth Century, feel that I am more typical of the present temperament of my people than not, when I say that I cannot allow the devious purposes of white supremacy to lead me to any conclusion other than what may be the most robust and important one of our time: that the ultimate destiny and aspirations of the African peoples and twenty million American Negroes are inextricably and magnificently bound up together forever."[12]

Lorraine Hansberry is nothing if not a moralist. All her major plays are about the need for commitment, a commitment violently resisted because of everything it implies about the need to sacrifice private dreams, but a necessary engagement with the need to sustain a moral image of the world at a time when society seems governed by nothing more than self-interest and greed. Like a great deal of black literature, her work projects a belief in the purifying and transcendent nature of moral concern, which had largely disappeared in white American writing, to flare up in a particularly innocent way in the public, but not for the most part the literary, world of the 1960s. If her work demonstrates an awareness of the painful ambiguities implied by that commitment to a degree which was alien to the political and cultural assurances of the Black Arts movement, which itself was born in the year of her death, this did not diminish her belief in the necessity for change and the compulsory involvement of those whose responsibility could not be casually shrugged off in the name of objectivity or art.

As a preface to *Les Blancs*, she quotes Frederick Douglass's observation that ''if there is no struggle there is no progress. . . .This struggle may be a moral one, or it may be a physical one, and it may be both moral and physical, but it must be a struggle. . . .Find out just what any people will quietly submit to and you have found out the exact measure of injustice and wrong which will be imposed upon them, and these will continue till they are resisted with either words or blows, or with both.''[13] It could equally have been the epigraph to any of her plays.

In *Black Theatre* magazine, issue number five, there appeared an editorial comment, presumably by Ed Bullins, or at least issued with his authority, which stated that ''the editors of *Black Theatre* magazine do not think that any Black people should see *The Blacks*'' because ''Jean Genet is a white, self-confessed homosexual with dead, white Western ideas—faggoty ideas about Black Art, Revolution, and people. His empty masochistic activities and platitudes on behalf of the Black Panthers should not con Black people. Genet, in his writings, has admitted to seeing himself as a so-called 'nigger.' Black people cannot allow white perversion to enter their communities and consciousness, even if it rides on the back of a Panther. Beware of whites who plead the Black cause to their brothers and fathers who oppress us; beware of Athol Fugard of South Africa and Jean Genet, a French pervert; disguised white missionaries representing Western cultural imperialism. Black people, in this stage of the struggle, have no use for self-elected 'niggers.' ''[14] The tone of moral absolutism typified the Black Arts movement, but Lorraine Hansberry felt an equal revulsion, regarding Genet's play as ''a conversation between white men about themselves.''[15] And though the play that was to become *Les Blancs* already existed in note form, it was the American production of *The Blacks* in 1961 which proved the final catalyst.

Her objection to *The Blacks* was very different from that voiced by *Black Theatre*, for she saw its chief fault as lying in its perpetuation of a myth of racial difference; its evasion of a fact which increasingly alarmed her—namely, that failure of moral commitment and simple humanity which could be traced to its root in human nature. Like Arthur Miller, she felt obliged to deal with a collapse of ethical concern which could not be conveniently dismissed as social, national, or racial in origin. As she explained, ''The problem in the world is the oppression of man by *man*; it is this which threatens existence. And it is this which Genet evades with an abstraction: an elaborate legend utilized to affirm, indeed, entrench, the quite *different* nature of pain, lust, cruelty, ambition presumed to exist in blacks. . . .In *The Blacks* the oppressed remain *unique*. The Blacks remain exotic in 'The Blacks.' And we are spared therefore the ultimate anguish—of *man's* oppression of man.''[16] The kind of moral commitment which she envisages is not to be easily satisfied by rituals of violence which absolve guilt by reducing the individual to convenient racial ciphers. What she demands is an engagement with human complexity, even with the ambiguity implicit in a revolution conducted in the name of an imperfectly perceived humanity. She recognizes the need for action, but rejects a revolt which can only sustain itself by denying the very principles in whose name it is conducted. Like Wright and Ellison before her, she is concerned with the need to renounce a metaphoric role. For she believes, with Tshembe in her play, that ''racism is a device which of itself explains nothing. It is simply a means. An invention to justify the rule of some men over others.''[17] And though the individual is forced to revolt in the name of that imposed identity, he must, she feels, always recognize a distinction between such social fictions and the humanity which they were invented to deny.

Les Blancs is set in Africa, in a country struggling towards independence. The familiar ritual of a desperate rearguard action by whites, bemused by the sudden violence of people on whose willing subservience they had counted for their own self-image, is played out in and around a mission compound and hospital. A white American journalist, emotionally committed but with the painful and necessary, if ambiguous, detachment of the writer, witnesses the anguished battle as whites harden themselves into a defensive unity and a black intellectual sets aside the Western traditions and personal ambitions to which he has laid claim to become a grudging rebel, destroying in order to create. Outside of the tactical simplicities of the military and of the black rebels, the tone is one of moral confusion—a mixture of guilt and reluctant confession.

Tshembe, trained in the West and married to a white woman, returns to his country to see his dying father. Though in favor of the independence movement, he feels himself uninvolved. His attention has shifted to his private life. Like Bigger Thomas, he has discovered a private meaning in existence. His brother, Abioseh, has also found meaning outside of the struggle, having joined the church. But the momentum of revolt cannot be so easily resisted. Beneath the subservient exterior of the mission's native servant is a rebel leader who tries to win Tshembe back to his responsibilities.

The missionaries are dedicated people, but, as the play progresses and as terrorists press their attacks closer to home, they begin to temporize, and eventually it is apparent that the paternalism of their leader, the Reverend Neilson, a Schweitzer-like figure whom we never see and who is eventually killed, had been an expression of his spriritual collaboration with the colonial powers, who now begin a ruthless attempt to stamp out revolt.

In the middle is the pathetic figure of Eric, a young man who is a product of an illicit affair between the white military commander and the wife of the tribe's black leader. The melodramatic action of the play concerns Abioseh's betrayal of the black leader—a Christian duty as he sees it—and the transformation of Tshembe into the black rebel whose first act must be the ritual killing of his traitor brother. But the revolt necessarily involves the murder of Madame Neilson, a symbolic and willing martyr to the new cause. Though blind, she sees clearly enough the necessity for her own death and recognizes that the martyrdom which she now embraces is more meaningful than any she could have suffered in the name of an abstraction. Inevitably a member of the rebel band, and the one who destroys the mission with a hand grenade, is Eric, who, having freely chosen the identity of guerilla, is no longer a pathetic drunk. The play ends with Tshembe placing the dead white woman's body beside that of his brother and emitting an anguished cry of grief which is an expression of his lament at the necessities which he has been forced to acknowledge.

The debate is a familiar one. The need for revolt is clear enough. The old system is, by turns, patronizing and repressive. It imposes its own image of native inferiority. But, for the intellectual, for the heir to Western liberal tradition, the act of revolt implies a moral absolutism, a surrender of a valued detachment, and an involvement in history which carries with it a disturbing responsibility and guilt. It was an issue which the British dramatist Christopher Hampton would take up a few years later in his play, *Savages*, about the Brazilian treatment of the Indians. The problem for Tshembe is the same as that which confronts the dramatist herself. His desperate cry, "I HAVE RENOUNCED ALL SPEARS!!!"[18] equally applies to the dramatist for whom art necessarily involves a degree of detachment, a retreat from the barricades. As Tshembe remarks, "There are men in this world...who see too much to take sides."[19] The African rebel leader, Peter, offers a cautionary tale by way of response, providing, perhaps, a rationale for much of the revolutionary black drama of the 1970s. He recounts the story of an animal whose ability to grant equal justice to both sides of an argument leads directly to its own destruction. The moral is obvious and is one taken seriously by playwrights distrustful of liberal equivocation in politics and a studious commitment to moral balance in art.

The play provoked violently contradictory responses. A polemical document, it was challenged for what was felt to be its justification of the slaughter of whites and for the stereotypes which it parodied as a way of justifying a failure to engage a human reality which would resist such casual manipulation. Alternatively, it was seen as a sensitive attempt to engage a central moral issue of the age and, more sentimentally, as an opportunity to record the passing of a black writer whose significance had perhaps not been sufficiently acknowledged when she was alive. There was some justice in the attacks. The action is predictable throughout, the characters tracing a familiar path. Too often, internal conflicts are allowed to bubble to the surface in language rather than in action. Tshembe is thus forced to rehearse the alternative possibilities available to him, as Madame Neilson is obliged to spell out the extent of and reason for her support of the black rebellion which has killed her husband. The final gesture of the play is a sentimentality not wholly redeemed by its neat encapsulation of Tshembe's ambivalence. It seems hard to see why he should have been chosen as leader when his heart is so palpably not in it. Though he may have been lured on by his revolutionary muse—cast, perhaps mistakenly, in the person of a fantasy woman—he has clearly not steeled himself to the task which faces him. Like so many other black rebel leaders in the drama and fiction of the 1960s, he is riven by self-doubt.

Les Blancs was not produced until 1970, by which time it no longer had quite the relevance it might have had a decade before. But, then, Lorraine Hansberry's real significance for the development of black theatre lay in her first play, which placed the situation of the black American squarely before the American people at a crucial moment and which, more importantly, acted as a reminder of the dramatic potential of black life.

But the times were changing, and Lorraine Hansberry's debate over idealism and commitment, focused as it was in her first play on the middle-class aspirations of a black family and in her second on a Jewish intellectual in Greenwich Village, seemed remote from the drama then being played out in the streets of America. People were dying, not because they were abused call girls whose hopes had disintegrated, but because they were black, or had espoused the cause of the blacks, and were encountering the far from subtle assaults of institutionalized racism. Lorraine Hansberry's focus was too distant to convey the sharpness of a conflict which was now waged in terms of physical confrontation rather than philosophical debate. The optimism of a play like Loften Mitchell's *A Land Beyond the River*, with its confident faith in the power of legislation, had likewise deferred to a different spirit. And this may account for the relative success of James Baldwin's *Blues for Mr. Charlie* (1964), as it most certainly did for the emergence of a black revolutionary theatre in the mid-1960s.

Baldwin's engagement with the theatre has not been entirely a happy one. *The Amen Corner* was originally written in 1952 and, despite a production at Howard University, it did not reach Broadway until 1965, a year after *Blues for Mr. Charlie*. This latter play had been inspired by the 1955 murder of Emmet Till and was finished under the shadow of the death of Medgar Evers. It takes as its setting the contemporary South of the civil rights marches and the debates over the legitimacy and effectiveness of nonviolence as a strategy. As Baldwin himself remarks, "The play . . .takes place in Plaguetown, USA, now. The plague is race, the plague is our concept of Christianity; and this raging plague has the power to destroy every human relationship."[20] But once again, Baldwin was aiming at a double audience. The play was, after all, called *Blues for Mr. Charlie*, not *Blues for the Black Man*, an ambivalence that largely escaped critical attention, and his introduction to the published text showed a familiar pronominal equivocation. For, when he asserts of the play's southern white murderer that "we, the American people, have created him, he is our servant; it is we who have put the cattle-prodder in his hands, and we who are responsible for the crimes that he commits. It is we who have locked him in the prism of his colour,"[21] it was not likely to be only blacks who would wish to dissociate themselves from this view. More importantly, however, this ambivalence permeates a play which, like so much of his work, rushes simultaneously to assert the absoluteness of white perfidy and the present possibility of redemption, the necessity for violence and the equal need for the continuance of love. As ever, Old and New Testaments neutralize each other, leaving the audience committed to a hope whose substance he has effectively already destroyed. It is, he insists, "one man's attempt to bear witness to the reality and the power of light" in a "terrible darkness,"[22] but his own melodramatic conscience is too Calvinist to grant any real force to a hope which relies on anything as fragile as the human spirit.

The play was produced by the Actors Studio in a mood of mutual suspicion and recrimination. The original version was five hours long, and Baldwin resisted cuts, quoting O'Neill's *Strange Interlude* by way of justification. But its faults have less to do with its length, or even with his private fear that he would be unable to draw a valid portrait of the white murderer, than with its confused moral viewpoint, its unearned affirmation, and a style which lurches awkwardly from naturalism to impressionism.

The action concerns the murder of Richard Henry by a white storekeeper, Lyle Britten. Richard has returned from the North embittered and truculent, the very fact of his return implying a self-destructive drive which is confirmed by his northern experiments with drugs. Meanwhile, his father, the Reverend Meridian Henry, leads a nonviolent civil rights group, and the play effectively opens and closes with a protest march. From the first of these marches they return bearing the literal and psychic bruises which seem an inevitable consequence of life in the South and of the passive nature of their protest. For Richard, whose mother had probably been murdered by southern whites, such a passive approach is humiliating and pointless, and his father's failure to avenge his mother's death is the root cause of his own bitterness. He carries a gun. But slowly he is weaned away from what Baldwin sees as his self-destructive urge by a dawning love for a black girl, Juanita. Before anything can come of this, however, he is involved in a confrontation with Lyle Britten, who charges him with insulting his wife. Both men are trapped in a myth. Neither can back down without damaging his self-image and without breaching what they imagine to be immutable rules of behavior. Richard is shot dead, having previously surrendered his gun to his father. And though Parnell, a white liberal, salves his conscience by forcing a trial, when the moment comes to challenge white hypocrisy he is unable to do so. Lyle is freed. The play ends with the marchers once again assembling, with Meridian still equivocating, and with Parnell asking to join the blacks in their protest.

It could easily have been transformed into a play about hypocrisy; about Meridian's continuing failure to face the reality of his situation, about Parnell's irremediable detachment from the real and from the justice which he thinks he serves. But the irony is that the movement of the play is quite otherwise. Baldwin's public commitment to the cause, his determination to bear witness to the light, leads him hopelessly to compromise the logic of the play's development, just as his parallel need to assault the white liberal forces him to deny Parnell the integrity which is a necessary component of the hope for the future which he believes himself to be endorsing.

Parnell's attraction for justice turns out to be not at all an abstract virtue. It was born, as all such commitments seem to be born in Baldwin's work, out of a sexual relationship. As a young man, he had fallen in love with a black girl and, in the self-revelatory monologues with which Baldwin punctuates the trial scene, he admits to himself that "all your life you've been made sick, stunned, dizzy, oh, Lord! driven half mad by blackness. Blackness in front of your eyes. Boys and girls, men and women—you've bowed down in front of them all!...Black boys and girls! I've wanted my hands full of them, wanted to drown them, laughing and dancing and making love—making love—wow—and be transformed, formed, liberated out of this gray-white envelope."[23] In the same way, his attempt at the end of the play to join the marchers is compromised by his sexual designs on Juanita. As ever, Baldwin confuses Eros and Agape, but here the confusion is potentially destructive of the very hope to which it was originally intended that such commitments should bear witness.

Richard likewise poses a problem. Baldwin deliberately makes him unsympathetic in an attempt to avoid the stereotype of black heroism and purity confronting white evil. His point was that such arrogance and posturing deserved censure but hardly merited death. But there is a confusion here, too. For the bitter young man who returns from the North is nearly deflected from his anger by a dawning love for Juanita. "I been in pain and darkness all my life. All my life. And this is the first time in my life I've ever felt—maybe it isn't like that. Maybe there's more to it than that."[24] For Baldwin, this is a real alternative, and, yet, it is because of this new commitment that Richard becomes vulnerable, while the relationship itself seems to offer little more than a means of expunging his anger and narcotizing his spirit. He himself recognizes that it is something of an evasion.

We are left, then, with a central ambiguity. Did he die because his new commitment to love led him to surrender the gun which might have saved his life, or did he die because he persisted in his determination to challenge the white world? And did his relationship with Juanita ever constitute a desirable alternative, given the realities of the South as Baldwin presents them? The play is certainly a dance of death in which neither of the main characters can escape his history or break out of the images which both take to be an adequate and complete account of the real. Baldwin's failure is that his own compulsions prevent his giving any substance to the alternatives which his own conflicting convictions lead him to establish. The stereotype has as potent an influence on the playwright as it does on his characters.

Hence, Juanita, who offers Richard the grace of love and who is regarded by the white community as the epitome of black promiscuity, does indeed turn out to be remarkably catholic in her dispensing of sexual grace. By the same token, the liberal is by definition an equivocator. Meanwhile, the minister, who speaks ominously of the Bible and the gun, is frozen in an impotent passivity which Baldwin both admires and rejects. It is a play in which the writer himself tries to have things both ways—to insist on the logic and justice of violence and, simultaneously, to assert the necessity for love. It is a play which splits in two as sharply as does the stage set during the trial scene when black and white town confront one another.

Part of Baldwin's failure in the play lies in his moral equivocation, part lies in his failure of dramatic imagination, and part, in his weakness for the rhetorical flourish at the expense of character. Richard dominates the play because, unlike the nonviolent protestors, he challenges the white world directly, hurling his anger in its face until it is forced to respond. And yet, the logic of the play insists that it is these marchers, these minor figures who exist in the shadow of his life and his death, who hold the real clue to social transformation. But since their leader, the Reverend Meridian Henry, has passively accepted the murder of both his wife and son, it is as hard to grant any real substance to such an implied emphasis as it is to grant any integrity to the white liberal whose honest commitment is equally necessary to the play's final image.

Too often, Baldwin relies on exposition rather than action. In order to penetrate the inner lives of his characters, he freezes the action and permits them lengthy monologues in which they explain rather than present their confusions and convictions. Or, more disastrously, he grafts onto their dialogue a rhetoric which has less to do with their characters than with his own inflated language, a linguistic sentimentality which is the mark of so much of his work. Wishing to raise the private relationship to the level of social and moral exemplar, he creates a hyperbolic language whose resonances, he seems to believe, will do the trick. Sometimes the effect is hopelessly and embarassingly bathetic—as when Juanita remarks, "When Richard came, he —*hit*— me in some place where I'd never been touched before." Although she hastily adds, "I don't mean just physically," the unfortunate appropriateness of the remark cannot but destroy the ponderous banalities which follow, as she confesses that "he took all my attention—the deepest attention, maybe, that one person can give another."[25] To this, Pete, who had formerly been considering marriage with Juanita, unbelievably replies, "there's a lot of love in you, Juanita. If you'll let me help you, we can give it to the world. You can't give it to the world until you can find a person who can help you—love the world.''[26] It's a brave actor who survives speeches like that.

It seems likely that Baldwin's painful relationship with the Actors Studio inhibited the kind of editing which could have given the play the kind of consistency which it lacks and which could have pruned some of the more painful examples of inflated rhetoric. But relations were not good, and the play was produced complete with its structural weaknesses and its confusions of character and action. What it retained was a melodramatic power, generated in part by its subject matter and in part by the moral significance of a play which attempted to tackle not only the cruder conflict of racial antagonism but also the self-destructive urge created by continued injustice.

The play opened on April 23, 1964 at the ANTA theatre. It received mixed notices, and, one month later, closing notices were posted. Baldwin, who by then was scarcely on speaking terms with the producing company, accused them of incompetence and bad management. There then began a campaign to rescue the production, with well-wishers paying for advertisements in the national press and offering donations of cash. These came primarily from those very white liberals whose commitment Baldwin denies in the play. In the end, and with this assistance, the play ran for another three months. But, by then, Baldwin had retreated to Europe.

Amen Corner, written more than a decade earlier, reached Broadway in the following year. It derived from much the same experience which produced his first novel, *Go Tell It On The Mountain*, and is set in a Harlem church. It takes as its subject the downfall of Sister Margaret, the pastor of the church, as the result of a petty campaign by jealous church members. But, at base, it is concerned with the struggle for meaning which, paradoxically, leads the individual to renounce that very humanity which is his chief consolation. The principal hope for meaning lies in the person of the pastor's son, whose new grasp on life, on sexuality, and on the pleasures of the physical world is offered as a key to meaning in a world which offers little in the way of social or metaphysical purpose.

It was a slight piece, but sensitively realized and impressive in the counter-point which he created between the hymns of the saints and the compulsions of a physical life. It was not, however, a play which was likely to appeal either to a liberal white audience or to a black community which was beginning to respond to a theatre which deployed more obvious and direct forms of black rebellion. Indeed, the difference in mood bewteen Baldwin's two plays, separated in time by more than a decade, was itself evidence of the changes which now began to accelerate.

Baldwin's dramatic efforts to save his own play, together with the tenuous existence of Lorraine Hansberry's second play, showed that Broadway was no longer prepared to support plays whose chief claim to attention lay in their moral concern. Meanwhile, the black theatre was itself beginning to turn in other directions, and the next decade was dominated by the creation of new black theatres, both in New York and elsewhere, which became the real basis for a quite astonishing explosion of playwriting talent. Writing about Negro playwrights in 1961, Darwin Turner suggested that "after a struggle of many years they could now regard themselves as artists, writing about the Negro race only because that is the group with which they are most familiar."[27] It was a hopeful thought and well within the tradition of American pluralism. The confidence which inspired his declaration, however, did not survive the decade. The good-natured wit of Ossie Davis's *Purlie Victorious* and Douglas Turner Ward's *Day of Absence*, and the cheery optimism of Lorraine Hansberry's *A Raisin in the Sun*, could make little of Watts, the racial murders of 1967, or the assassinations of 1968. They were the products of the integrationist years; the cultural evidence of a social strategy which increasing numbers of blacks were preparing to abandon. The sheer scale of operations in Vietnam, combined with the slow decay of America's cities and the imaginative poverty of political and popular response, were breeding a situation in which escalating militancy appeared more attractive and productive than civil disobedience and an ethnic solidarity seemed a genuine resource. Thoreau's ideas were proving singularly inappropriate to a situation in which Sunday-school children were blown to pieces and civil rights marchers were gunned down in front of the police.

The Negro family in Lorraine Hansberry's first play, anxious to integrate into a hostile white community, and the cunning blacks in Douglas Turner Ward's *Day of Absence*, eager to prove their utility to a southern community, were now replaced by the black rebel of LeRoi Jones's *The Slave*. He, in turn, was then displaced by less sophisticated tokens of black achievement—by the black revolutionary, speaking the language of the streets and acting out agitprop scenes and image-building fantasies. Martin Luther King's assassination provided an appropriate and highly visible symbol of changing attitudes. His death showed what really happened to a dream deferred. In a very real sense, the 1960s did witness the passing of a whole generation. It saw the death of Langston Hughes, Richard Wright, Lorraine Hansberry, and, perhaps most significantly, W. E. B. Du Bois.

The explosion of talent resulted, on the one hand, in Douglas Turner Ward's call for a permanent Negro repertory company and, on the other, in LeRoi Jones's establishment of the Black Arts Repertory Theatre in Harlem. The two ventures were quite distinct from one another and emerged from profoundly different visions of the function of art. Nevertheless, they were both breaking with the kind of stance represented by Ossie Davis, who, in an article in the *New York Times* in August 1964, insisted that the theatre "cannot escape the law of supply and demand: who lives to please must please in order to live. . . .Let us artists, set before Man not only the magnitude of the tasks before him, but also the magnificence of the resources that lie deep within himself to accomplish these tasks . . . all the preaching, and teaching, and screeching has not yet liberated man from his petulant preoccupation with his own smallness . . .'' Just one year after the Alabama Sunday-school bombings this seemed singularly inappropriate to many black writers, as did the curious juxtapositions of his further comment on the power of the theatre to inspire sympathy and see in specific individuals merely reflections of some ''universal'' man. ''Once I feel the truth,'' he insisted, ''the internal is-ness of, say, a Negro, a Jew, a Gentile, a Catholic, a Communist, a homosexual or a Nazi, I can no longer pretend that he is a stranger, or a foreigner, or an outcast. What is more, I will be so pleasured in my new knowledge that I would not want to so pretend. I will myself have become, at one and the same time, all of these things.''[28] Having but recently emerged both culturally and socially from an imposed obscurity, blacks were not overly anxious to become ''invisible'' in the service of some vague vision of universal man while trusting in the ''magnificence of the resources'' which had been difficult to detect during years of prejudice and discrimination.

In terms of the theatre, therefore, the second half of the 1960s saw determined efforts to establish some kind of ethnic drama. Douglas Turner Ward stated baldly in August 1966, ''If any hope, outside of chance individual fortune, exists for Negro playwrights as a group—or, for that matter, Negro actors and other theatre craftsmen—the most immediate, pressing, practical, absolutely minimally essential first step is the development of a permanent Negro repertory company.'' For Ward, this was a matter of practicalities and had little or nothing to do with social strategy. Indeed, he insisted that ''this is not a plea for either a segregated theater, or a separatist one,'' for while the Negro Ensemble Company, as it was later called, was to concentrate primarily on ''themes of Negro life,'' it was also to be ''resilient enough to incorporate the best of world drama'' and was to allow whites to participate ''if they found inspiration in the purpose.''[29] For many, this brought back visions of interracial MacBeths and Swing Mikados, and, while the company has thus far avoided this approach, it has found itself in a series of paradoxical positions. To begin with, it was financed by money from the Ford Foundation. Secondly, its first production, *Song of the Lusitanian Bogey*, was by a white European playwright, Peter Weiss, and, thirdly, its audience was initially 70 percent white—a fact which is scarcely surprising given its location on the Lower East Side. It's location, according to Ward, was, however, a matter of deliberate choice. ''In the first place, we designed a project which was not a community theatre project. People interested in community theatre would have to locate in the midst of that community—in Harlem or Bedford-Stuyvesant. Our project was designed for the entire metropolitan area. Therefore, we wanted a central location that would be easy to reach from all the outlying Black communities. . . . It was not designed as a cultural arm of a community.''[30] The audience was thus to be substantially black, and, while it has managed to move away from its ambiguous beginning, actually reversing the percentage of black to white in the audience, it has been less successful in other areas. Its workshop and training programs, in some ways the most important aspect of its work, suffered from an undue emphasis on major productions. This, in turn, was necessitated by the Ford Foundation's eagerness for the company to become self-supporting. As a consequence, it has not always been ready to embrace those writers whose work is most exciting dialectically or dramaturgically. Thus, reportedly, both Ed Bullins's *In the New England Winter* and Charles Gordone's Pulitzer Prize-winning *No Place to Be Somebody* were rejected by the NEC, which chose, instead, to rely on the less caustic work of Alice Childress, Ted Shine, Ray McIver, and Lonne Elder. In a review of an evening of one-act plays staged by the NEC at the St. Mark's Playhouse, Robert Pasolli remarked that "as for the writing, it was...entertaining: conventional character drama in the case of Alice Childress's 'String,' and conventional situation comedy in the case of Ted Shine's 'Contribution,' and conventional exotica-tropica in the case of Derek Wolcott's 'Malcochon.' Blacks, you see, can do as well as whites."[31] The NEC, in other words, was in danger of repeating the mistakes of the past, appealing to a predominantly middle-class intellectual audience by catering to its artistic and social conservatism. One of the NEC's early successes was such a product.

Lonne Elder's two-act play, *Ceremonies in Dark Old Men*, is set in a barbershop on 126th Street, between Seventh and Lennox avenues in Harlem. Russell B. Parker, congenitally allergic to work, is persuaded by his sons to open an illegal liquor establishment. Blue Haven, chief operator and con-man, convinces the family that they should sell corn whiskey and "guarantees" their immunity from arrest. He is the self-styled prime minister of the Harlem De-Colonization Association—a group which does not believe in "picketing, demonstrating, rioting, and all that stuff."[32] He is more concerned with liberating the merchandise from white-owned stores in the neighborhood: "We're different...We're non-violent"[33] (a line dangerously close to one in *Purlie Victorious*).

With his new-found wealth, Russell Parker is able to declare his independence from a daughter who had begun to get a little oversensitive to his studious inactivity and buy himself the company of a young girl. The play ends as he staggers into his home, unaware that one of his sons has been killed while stealing from the nearby stores. The irony is finely controlled, but the situation is a little too reminiscent of O'Casey's *Juno and the Paycock*.

The play has its effective moments. Parker's final speech is carefully modulated and even poignant: "You and Blue with your ideas of overcoming the evil of white men—to an old man like me, it was nothing more than an ounce of time to end my dragging about this shop—it sent me sailing out into those streets to live a time—and I did live myself a time. I did it amongst a bunch of murderers, all kinds of 'em—where at times it gets so bad, til it seems that the only thing that's left for you is to go out there and kill somebody before they kill you.''[34] But finally, Elder is trying too consciously to repeat the effects of *A Raisin in the Sun* and *Purlie Victorious*. The play is unadventurous in form and content.

Elder's response to such criticism was to assert that critics found his work conventional ''because I took the time, the care, put a lot of energy into it to make it workable, from moment to moment, from scene to scene.''[35] A more plausible explanation, however, is offered by the fact that he was a great admirer of Lorraine Hansberry and her work and had even appeared in the Broadway production of *A Raisin in the Sun*. Moreover, although *Ceremonies* was first performed in 1969, Elder had actually started work on it in 1963, before the Black Arts Repertory Theatre and before the violence of the mid- and late 1960s. And, anyway, he rejected the premise which lay behind Jones's work and the assertions of writers like Harold Cruse who, in *The Crisis of the Negro Intellectual*, had declared that the Negro playwright could only survive and operate in an ethnic theatre. Elder's response to this was to insist that ''it's crude, it's ludicrous, it's unreal and it's unbelievable. I'm sick and tired of people telling other people what they can do and what they cannot do.''[36] Yet, he looked forward to a time when the NEC would no longer need white foundation money and would draw exclusively on black playwrights appealing to black audiences: ''You no longer try to appease a theatre-going audience which is basically white. If you write for the theatre you've got to be writing for a white audience. I'm writing for an audience which at this time doesn't really exist. Thanks to the Negro Ensemble and the black theatre movement in America this audience is being cultivated.''[37] The chief accomplishment of the NEC thus far is indeed its attempts to create such an audience. Ten years after its foundation, it continued to offer a limited season, attracting 77-percent-capacity houses but still relying, for three-quarters of its income, on unearned income, though this is a plight which it shares with many other companies.

The Free Southern Theatre holds the middle ground between the NEC and the Black Arts movement. It is an attempt to build a different kind of theatre. It was founded in September 1963 with the motto, ''Theatre for people who have no theatre.'' Based in New Orleans, it toured the southern states in an attempt to bring theatre to black communities otherwise denied access to drama. Entry was free, and performances were frequently given in the open air and at times convenient to local audiences. Despite the assertion of John O'Neal, one of the theatre's founders, that the ''black artist suffers from the white audience because he must speak from a divided consciousness to a mentality that refuses to acknowledge the most essential part of that consciousness,''[38] the FST, unlike the NEC, was not born from a desire to provide work for black writers and artists, but rather from a wish to serve the black community. Both O'Neal and his cofounder, Gilbert Moses, had gone south to work in the civil rights movement. They were primarily concerned with living "a life of useful engagement"; creating a theatre which could serve the black community rather than with forging an audience for frustrated black artists. The audience was to be created for social rather than artistic reasons: "In the creation of a relevant theatre the development of an active and critical rather than a passive audience is the most important task. It is not enough that a particular theatre group be composed of Black people or even that it be physically located where Black people live, if the theatre is not addressed to the needs of Black people and grounded in their experience. 'Exposure' is not only a patronizing concept—it does not develop an audience."[39]

In some senses, the group has promised far more than it has achieved. Ideologically, it has been uncertain as to its precise role. The initially racially mixed company became almost entirely black dominated—a parallel to the similar shift in the civil rights movement itself in the late 1960s. As O'Neal admits, "That question—the relationship between what we were doing and our peers in the 'movement' were doing—consumed the largest part of the philosophical struggle."[40] At the same time, its initial choice of plays inspired considerable criticism from those who doubted that works by white dramatists could really be "addressed to the needs of Black people."[41] Certainly the first plays which the FST produced were by Duberman, O'Casey, Beckett, Ionesco, and Brecht, a choice which, with the exception of Duberman, might seem somewhat strange in view of O'Neal's further comment that the theatre is anyway "largely foreign to the cultural experience and heritage of the Black audience." But, writing in 1968, he admitted that the plays he would really like to perform, plays which grew directly out of the experience of those watching, had yet to be written. Most plays by blacks were still directed largely at white audiences. To rectify this situation, a community workshop program was established in New Orleans, but lack of finance prevented the extension of this project.

In December 1966, the FST received a grant of $62,500 from the Rockefeller Foundation, thus placing itself in the same position, potentially, as the NEC. But, as LeRoi Jones demonstrated with the Black Arts Repertory Theatre in Harlem, acceptance of white money is scarcely of necessity emasculating. The range of plays produced by the FST gradually broadened. And, as indicated earlier, the emphasis slowly switched away from didacticism and towards a concern with theatrical ideas. It also became a more avowedly regional theatre.

By far the most important movement of the 1960s, however, was the attempt to create black theatre—a development which placed drama at the heart of the Black Arts movement. There have been many attempts to establish racially homogenous groups. Montgomery Gregory, director of the Howard Players in the early 1920s, announced that "our ideal is a national Negro Theatre where the Negro playwright, musician, actor, dancer, and artist in concert shall fashion a drama that will merit the respect and admiration of America. Such an institution must come from the Negro himself, as he alone can truly express the soul of his people.''[42] Despite proliferating groups such as the Negro People's Theatre, the Harlem Suitcase Theatre, the Rose McClendon Players, and the Negro Playwrights' Company, however, there was little success in this direction. Only the Negro units of the Federal Theatre project in the 1930s and the American Negro Theatre in the 1940s came close to realizing the dreams of Gregory and Locke. But, paradoxically, the most successful productions staged by the New York Negro unit were Orson Welles's production of *Macbeth* and a swing version of *The Mikado*. Thanks to a cheap ticket policy (twenty-five cents a seat or free to those carrying a Department of Welfare card), these productions were well supported, but while they played an important role in giving work and experience to many Negro writers and performers, they did little to create the kind of audience necessary to sustain a permanent Negro repertory. The Negro units were finally closed down with the rest of the Federal Theatre, following allegations of left-wing activity.

The American Negro Theatre, founded in 1939, staged its first performance in 1940. Its eventual failure in the second half of the decade has been largely ascribed to the success of its best-known production, *Anna Lucasta*, a play by Philip Yordan adapted for Negro production. This transferred to Broadway, taking with it some of the personnel from the ANT and thus weakening the permanent company.

In terms of the 1960s, black theatre became less a question of establishing specific repertory groups, though Ed Bullins's New Lafayette Theatre was one such, than of creating a drama responsive to the needs and interests of black people and performed in the black communities which it serves. And at the heart of this enterprise, creating the institutions which could facilitate it and elaborating the images, the myths, and the forms of this new theatre, was, most crucially, a single man—LeRoi Jones. It was as a modernist poet, drawing on European and American models, that LeRoi Jones first came to prominence; it was as the colleague of white writers that he first established a reputation, founding *Yugen* Magazine and Totem Press in 1958 and coediting *The Floating Bear* magazine with Diane DiPrima in 1961.

But a changing social world, nationally and internationally, exerted the same moral pressure on Jones that it did on James Baldwin who had been living in Paris while the first events of the civil rights movement were being enacted in America. The change which eventually came over LeRoi Jones was a profound one, one which affected his private, public, and artistic life and made him the most important black writer of the 1960s—a shift, moreover, symbolized by a change of name. He abandoned his "slave name" for an appellation which indicated his new stance—Imamu (leader) Amiri (warrior) Baraka (blessing). In fact, from the beginning, his work had grown out of his own sense of cultural identity but where that had been simply the circumstance of his art, in the late 1960s it became the basis of an artistic and political philosophy. In many ways Baraka has contained within himself the conflict within the black community: avant-garde artist and committed spokesman, putative Black Muslim and secular politician, black nationalist and Marxist ideologue. And the gap between these opposing compulsions—like the space between American promise and fulfillment, revolutionary rhetoric and reality —is always liable to be filled with violence sublimated in artistic form. And it was partly as a writer whose powerful plays were luminous with violent images and articulate anger that he became the leading black playwright of the last decade and a half.

Baraka's arguments with himself have, in essence, been the arguments which split the black community. The irony is that now, as a Marxist-Leninist, he has spent the last few years struggling to escape from a myth of his own construction, that of black political and cultural separation, as in the late 1960s he had had to exorcise his earlier career as experimental writer and proponent of a modernist aesthetic. The alliance which he now seeks between black and white members of the ''advanced'' working class constitutes a synthesis of the terms of the dialectic which he had identified in the 1960s as constituting mutually exclusive symbolic systems and socially unassimilable propositions. If he was never the true poet of violence which he was taken to be, he was a writer for whom social action and imaginative fiat were symbiotically related. And though he retains that conviction, the components which form his imaginative universe today differ fundamentally from the Manichean elements which constituted his moral battleground a few years ago.

Although his early poetry lays claim to the modernist tradition, there was from the beginning a social compulsion in his work, a drive through the word to the fact. And his admiration for the Beats was, in part at least, an admiration for people who located a specific environment which became not merely the reason for the literal and stylistic quest, but also, in some ways, its subject. It was very much a literature of witness, even though the external world was finally only a mirror of the self, which, in the case of Kerouac at least, became its neoromantic center. They were also interested in the socially and metaphysically disinherited, the outcast. The cityscape pictured by John Rechy, Hubert Selby, Jr., or Jack Kerouac was likely to be that of the ghetto, the vacant lot, the neglected underside of reality and of the American psyche. The homosexual, the addict, the Negro are projected in their works as resisters of American reality, part victims but also part heroic survivors of a civilization in decline, possessors of secret knowledge. And these were the writers whom Jones admired and published in his anthology of new writing in America, *The Moderns*, and who constituted his literary confreres in the late 1950s and early 1960s.

But the public situation was changing. Africa now stood as a model of revolution rather than as a romantic image of primal innocence as it had in the 1920s. In 1960, well over a dozen African nations secured independence. The Cuban revolt brought revolution close to home. When Patrice Lumumba was murdered in 1962, Jones was among those who went to the United Nations to protest. His work, too, was changing. In 1963, he published *Blues People: Negro Music in White America*, and, in 1964, his powerful one-act play, *Dutchman*, was produced at the Cherry Lane Theatre with the assistance of Edward Albee's Playwrights Unit. It was not his first play. *A Good Girl Is Hard to Find* had been produced in Montclair, New Jersey, in 1958, and early in 1964 *The 8th Ditch* (an excerpt from his forthcoming novel, *The System of Dante's Hell*) and *The Baptism* made brief appearances. But it was *Dutchman*, a powerful fable of American race relations, which established his reputation as a dramatist and which turned his career in a new direction.

The play is set in a subway car, in what Jones calls the "flying underbelly of the city." It takes as its subject the mythic encounter of white woman and black man. Lula, a beautiful young woman, seeks out and then in turn seduces and provokes Clay, a middle-class black who has long since sublimated his anger and bitterness in his literary concerns and in his aspirations to success. She skillfully taunts him with his acquiescence in his own spiritual emasculation, probing to see whether mask and reality are synonymous, whether he retains any dignity and identity apart from his bourgeois performance. And the weapon she uses is her sexuality, the totem of a society which has made the white woman mark the limit of black freedom. She is Eve tempting Clay to a self-knowledge which will ultimately be damning. Like Jerry in Edward Albee's *The Zoo Story*, she deliberately goads him into action; but her intention is not redemptive. She is intent on exposing the real power she suspects is still concealed behind the façade of accommodation. And, at last, she succeeds in provoking the violence which she both fears and desires. Clay strikes her and dominates the stage through the sheer strength of his anger. He steps outside his public role and meets her for a moment as a man, challenging both this individual woman and the culture of which she is an expression. But it is an ambiguous anger, itself partly the creation of the whites at whom it is directed. And, as an intellectual, he himself is struck by the ironies involved. As a consequence, he retreats from his own spontaneous action. He falls back on language, resisting the urge to power, trying to break out of the myth which contains them both. But the myth is stronger than he suspects. Lula, having confirmed the persistence of a black identity, but discovered also Clay's unwillingness to express and inhabit that identity, is able to destroy him. She sticks a knife in his chest and, with the help of the other passengers who have remained mute throughout, throws him out of the train. His middle-class appearance offers no more protection than does a rage which lacks the power to sustain itself. As the play ends, Lula prepares to repeat the ritual with another young Negro who now enters the compartment. She is as trapped in the myth as he is and as the Flying Dutchman, implied in the title, had been in his.

Like the mysterious agents of Eliot's *The Cocktail Party* or Albee's *Tiny Alice*, Lula is fated to perform a familiar ritual. She is both temptress and avenger, provoking the response which she must then punish. Indeed, this oscillation between attraction and repulsion, this diminuendo and crescendo, provides the rhythm of a play which creates a racial counterpoint of stunning power. The subject of the play is, as Lula confesses, Clay's manhood. Everything about his appearance and language suggests that he has surrendered to white society, aping its values, aspiring to its middle-class anonymity. But beneath the surface is a residual menace, a submerged identity, suppressed in the interests of ambition and a peaceful life. It is that identity which is the source of white fears; that independence of mind and being which potentially threatens white equanimity. It is an identity charged with a physical potential which may realize itself in terms of sexuality or violence, the two being inevitably connected. It is a source of anarchic power which threatens the ordered inertia of society and which must therefore be purged. As Lula says, "You mix it up. . . .Change change change. Till, shit, I don't know you . . .you change. . . .And things work on you till you hate them."[43] As a putative white man, he is wholly knowable, so that Lula can accurately provide him with details about his life and aspirations; as a black man in disguise, he is an enigma and as such, a threat. It is a threat thoroughly sublimated, however. For Clay is a writer. His anger is deflected into language, his bitterness is displaced into an aesthetic code, and his anarchic potential subsumed in poetic structures. As with Jones himself, his art is potentially an act of denial as well as an act of affirmation.

In order to destroy him, Lula has to break through his protective mask. As Jerry did with Peter in *The Zoo Story*, she tries first with language, goading him with insults, taunting him as an "escaped nigger" who is full of white man's words. When this fails, she tries to induce Clay to join her in a dance, a grotesque parody of the sexual contact which would give her the excuse to precipitate violence. Yet, she is herself torn by ambiguous and contradictory feelings. While programmed to destroy him, she is aware that the response which she is endeavoring to provoke is also potentially liberating. "Clay. Clay, you got to break out. Don't sit there dying the way they want you to die. Get up."[44] On the other hand, this response, too, would be determined by whites, and here is the familiar paradox of revolt. While its coherences seem to be liberating, revolt, by definition, is defined by the force which it opposes—a force which, even in succumbing to the violence which it provokes, imposes its own pattern on the rebel.

At last stirred into action, Clay clubs a white drunk to the ground and beats Lula into silence. But even then he rejects the power which seemingly follows from the act. "I could rip that paper out of his hand and just as easily rip out his throat. It takes no great effort. For what? To kill you soft idiots? . . .You telling me what I ought to do. Well, don't. Don't tell me anything."[45] He asserts his right to remain a mystery, to conceal his identity behind disguises impenetrable to those who take appearance for reality and who try to create a clarity of outline by molding black identity into a form in which it can be dealt with. But black life is essentially a code, a sublimation of a more logical revolt. Black music, black literature, he suggests, are revolt transposed into art—an observation which could clearly apply equally to *Dutchman* itself. Art is neurosis; but sanity would result in murder, as murder would constitute sanity. So that if the rationalism which leads Lula to wish to penetrate the black disguise were to spread to the black man, the result would be a murderous sanity. And so, he suggests, "Let them alone. Let them sing curses at you in code and see your filth as a simple lack of style. Don't make the mistake, through some irresponsible surge of Christian charity, of talking too much about the advantages of Western rationalism or the great intellectual legacy of the white man, or maybe they'll begin to listen. And then, maybe one day, you'll find they actually do understand exactly what you are talking about, all these fantasy people. . . .And on that day . . .when you really believe you can accept them into your fold, as half-white trusties late of the subject peoples . . .they'll murder you, and have very rational explanations. Very much like your own."[46]

The admission precipitates his death. But this is less a result of his confirmation of a violent potential than a consequence of the fact that as a writer he turns away from that violence, saying, "But who needs it? I'd rather be a fool. Insane. Safe with my words, and no deaths, and clean, hard thoughts, urging me to new conquests."[47] The body is thrown off the train by the anonymous white subway travelers whose indifference is itself a necessary part of the ritual as it is of social life. Another young Negro enters the carriage, and the process begins again.

Dutchman remains one of the best plays ever written by a black author and one of the most impressive works of recent American theatre. Like *The Zoo Story*, it is a potent parable of alienation. If Jones's control of language is reminiscent of Albee's, as is his sense of musical structure, in the person of Clay he has created a far more complex character than Albee's Peter, whose stereotypical role is the one serious flaw in what is otherwise the most impressive first play ever written by an American dramatist. *Dutchman* is a reflexive work. At its heart is a consideration of the artistic process, a debate over the legitimacy of sublimating social anguish into aesthetic form. It addresses itself to a central problem of the black artist who is alive to the evasion which may be implied in the act of writing. It is a debate which Jones has continued throughout his career without ever finding a wholly satisfactory answer.

In part, of course, the play can be read as Jones's confession or critique of his own safe refuge in words, of his own attempts to sublimate racial tensions in art. If this is so it was even more true of a subsequent play, *The Slave*, which is intensely autobiographical and in which he accuses himself and others of remaining slaves to a liberalism which can no longer be validated by reality. *Dutchman* was awarded an Obie by *The Village Voice*.

Later the same year, two of his plays were performed at St. Marks Playhouse, *The Toilet* and *The Slave*. The former is a one-act play in which racial violence breaks out in a school lavatory. Yet, beneath the apocalyptic clash is a curiously contradictory belief in the efficacy of love—a Baldwin-like sentimentality expressed in a sexual grace which transcends social realities. The ending, which he explains to have been "tacked on," is strangely out of key with the main thrust of the play. But it does appear to validate his own continuing commitment to the interracial ethos of his Greenwich Village existence. So, black and white come together in the concluding moment of the play in an epiphany, suggesting thereby that dispossession and exclusion are not exclusively racial experiences.

The Slave, however, pursues racial tensions to their logical conclusion. It takes place at the moment of a black revolt in America. The revolutionary leader, Walker Vessels, formerly married to a middle-class white woman, now visits her and her husband, a white liberal professor, as his troops move in on the city. Himself a writer, he had abandoned the word for the act. But his own presence in his ex-wife's apartment shows that he has not escaped his past, he is still a slave to old ideas and associations. His denunciation of the white liberal is thus largely an exorcism of his own former self. But it is also an assertion that it is precisely liberal equivocation that has transformed the slave into the rebel. Despite his own reservations, however, the logic of his position and of the history in which they are all trapped leads to his shooting the white professor. The play ends as shells hit the building, his former wife is crushed underneath a fallen beam, and the screams of his two children are heard.

For all the violence of the action, the most striking aspect of the play lies in the reservations which it expresses about the act of revolt. He is aware of, and in part still feels, liberal ambiguities about violence and about a social transformation which depends on simple inversion. Lacking any ideological structure for his work, he is left with presenting revolt as generating its own values. In some ways, therefore, it is a work, like Lowell's *The Old Glory*, dedicated to presenting the paradox of revolution. Change is necessary, but the violence of revolt closes the moral gap between oppressed and oppressor.

The play begins with a prologue in which the rebel leader, Walker, appears dressed as a field slave. His language is strangely at odds with his appearance. It is the language of a detached observer, an intellectual able to see even the ambiguities and contradictions of his own stance, aware, too, that art is by definition deceptive, that artistic form may itself operate as a mechanism which denies the thing it wishes to express by deflecting social concern into aesthetics, by implying the existence of an order which the work is designed to deny. Hence, the prologue becomes a paradigm of the doubt which invades the work itself; it offers a critique of the process of invention which lies at the heart of the play and which is seen as being dangerously akin to the process of social manipulation, the way in which each individual invents the world in which he lives and thus becomes responsible for its configuration. As Walker observes, "Whatever the core of our lives. Whatever the deceit. We live where we are, and seek nothing but ourselves. We are liars, and we are murderers. We invent death for others. . . .Stone possible lovers with heavy worlds we think are ideas.''[48] The problem, he suggests, is less ignorance than a "stupid longing not to know,'' which becomes a central strategy for survival to which no one is immune. Thus, he seems to imply what the following two acts elaborate, that the central theme of the play is less the direct racial conflict which provides the action than the human danger involved in becoming slaves to ideas, to myths, and to presumptions which seem too self-evident to challenge. As Walker observes in the prologue, "It is a deadly filth that passes as whatever thing we feel is too righteous to question, too deeply felt to deny,'' for, finally, you should "figure, still, that you might not be right. Figure, still, that you might be lying . . .to save yourself. Or myself's image.'' Hence, it becomes neces- sary to accept that ideas "need judging,'' that "just because they're beautiful and brilliant . . .just because they're *right* . . .doesn't mean a thing. The very rightness stinks a lotta times.''[49] And despite its own deceptions, art provides a possible metalanguage, a way of literally dramatizing truths otherwise too easily evaded. For one thing, the theatre has the power simultaneously to present appearance and essence, to reveal deception even as it is practiced. And so, with a metadramatic gesture ("metadrama,'' as I use the term, being concerned with foregrounding technique, with drawing attention to the fictive status of the work and implying a postmodern doubt about its coherences, since these are as usurped by manipulative ironies as are those of the public world on which they are presumed to comment) he announces, "A poem? Lastly that to distort my position? To divert you . . .in your hour of need . . .Discovering racially the funds of the universe. Discovering the last image of the thing.''[50]

And that play is, of course, apocalyptic. But the worlds which collide are not so easily delineated by racial distinctions despite the nature of the battle which is being conducted on the streets outside the apartment. For all three characters are the slaves not only of their ideas but also of their history, their myths, and even of their language. As Walker, now a rebel leader who has paradoxically taken time off from leading his troops to justify himself before his white ex-wife and to visit and possibly remove his own children, remarks, "I did come into the world pointed in the right direction. Oh, shit, I learned so many words for what I've wanted to say. They all came down on me at once. But almost none of them are mine.''[51] In moving from advocacy of a restored liberal idealism to the deployment of literal revolt, he is still contained within that alien language, still held by a past which can apparently only be shattered by an assault on all the things which he values. He is conscious of being a primary victim of the anarchy which he has unleashed and which he had hoped would prove cathartic. He is all too aware that he will only be changing "the complexion of tyranny'' and that he has "killed for all times any creative impulse''[52] he might have had. He knows that though the revolt is conducted in the name of humanity, human values will themselves have to be sacrificed to the exigencies of that revolt. It is his very awareness of these paradoxes which has brought him to his ex-wife's apartment and which leads to his near collapse there. He recognizes the truth of his wife's assertion that he wished to ''reshape the world after the image''[53] he has of it. Indeed, his later remark that ''I've never aligned myself with anything or anyone I hadn't thought up first''[54] is itself a description of the potentially dangerous subjectivism which seems the only possible alternative to enslavement by the public world. The choice does indeed seem to be that between victim and hangman.

But, in the circumstances of oppression, the act seems to have a justification of itself. Certainly to a writer like Walker it seems to have a validity which his own craft does not. As he explains, ''The aesthete came long after the things that really formed me. It was the easiest weight to shed. And I couldn't be merely a journalist . . . a social critic. No social protest . . . right is in the act.''[55] For LeRoi Jones, who earlier in his career had rejected those writers with social pretensions, the ironies multiply, and buried within the play is not merely a debate about the nature of art, but an ironic presentation of a central debate about the function of art. The action, however, proves purely destructive. Walker kills his wife and her white husband and then leaves the stage in the guise of the old man of the prologue. Having precipitated chaos, he is no less a slave than he had been before the revolt which was designed to be an act of liberation. It is a central irony which went virtually unremarked by critics who tended to take Walker as a model for the black rebel. The play's theatrical subtleties, its debate over form and language, its concern with the paradoxical nature of action and the dominating power of imaginative structures, public and private fictions, were swiftly swallowed up in the political events of the day. Jones's own subsequent career likewise discouraged a consideration of these elements in a work which was increasingly seen as a prelude to his later revolutionary plays. Ironically, such an imaginative restructuring of the play's meaning was itself primary evidence for the assertion which lies at the very center of its concerns.

On the verge of a profound change in his personal life and in the racial situation in America, Jones is all too aware that ideas need judging, that revolutionary symbols fail to deal adequately with the complexity of private or public action. But the play deploys a level of subtlety and ambiguity which he rapidly dispensed with as his own analysis of American society and the racial situation led him to a more stringent and unambiguous stance.

The ironies of the play are magnified when one realizes that shortly afterwards Jones left his white Jewish wife and his two daughters and moved his activities to Harlem where he became the focus for the Black Arts movement of the late 1960s. *The Slave*, therefore, stands as a personal act of exorcism, and the works which followed advocated a clear cultural and political nationalism of a kind which left no space for self-doubt.

When Jones's plays were performed downtown, they were regarded as powerful rituals, articulate dramatic parables of disaffection; transferred to Harlem, they assumed a political dimension which led to the discontinuance of a grant from the Office of Economic Opportunity. But in its brief life, the Black Arts Repertory Theatre established a pattern for similar theatres which sprang up in a number of American cities in the course of the next few years. It marked the birth of the whole Black Arts movement in America. The plays which he now produced were presaged by the 1965 production at St. Marks Playhouse of *Experimental Death Unit 1*, which took as its subject the ritual killing of two white homosexuals and a black prostitute by a disciplined army of black militants. The revolution was under way. As he has said, ''In works like *Dutchman* . . .the line is defensive but still positive, in the sense of what Clay says to Lula about not wanting to be suffocated under the whole American white oppression. But at the same time he gets killed. He is still a victim in that sense. The same way with Vessels—the slave of the title of the play. So, then, looking at that, I said, 'Well, that still is a kind of capitulationist line, because I should not be trying to write from the perspective of the victim, except insofar as the victim is getting ready to turn the tables.' ''[56]

A Black Mass is a dramatization of the Black Muslim creation myth in which mad black scientists create the white man in a Faustian experiment which goes disastrously wrong. The white beast destroys them all, and the audience is warned that the beast is still at large, devouring the world. *Madheart* parodies the black obsession with white values and features the ritual destruction of a white devil lady. *Great Goodness of Life* takes as its central character Court Royal, a black traitor who shoots his own revolutionary son in order to ingratiate himself with the white power structure. These are, then, agitprop sketches, brief consciousness-raising exercises, cultural rituals aimed directly at a black audience. Indeed, in *Madheart*, the audience is explicitly invited to think about themselves and about their lives as they leave the play.

The plays displayed simple images and an inflated rhetoric, but, as Roland Barthes has said, in revolutionary times truth ''demands the very forms of theatrical amplification.''[57] For Jones, this was a revolutionary period, and such a theatrical amplification was an attempt to raise fact to the status of myth. Subtleties of character and ambiguities of motive had no place when seen in the context of injustice.

When the Black Arts Repertory Theatre closed down, Jones moved his activities to New Jersey, founding Spirit House in Newark in 1966. In the course of the next few years, he elaborated his ideas on black nationalism, advocated the wearing of African dress and the learning of African languages. He adopted the name Imamu Amiri Baraka. During the Newark riot, he was arrested and charged with carrying a concealed weapon, a charge eventually dismissed, though he still carries the scar on his forehead from a blow with a police weapon. Increasingly, he concerned himself with the political situation, working for the election of a black mayor and organizing black political groups. As the secretary-general of the National Black Political Assembly, he became one of the only unifying voices in an otherwise hopelessly schismatic black movement.

Yet, from the beginning, he had been suspicious of those who became "fluent in the jargon of power" and he became increasingly doubtful of a logic which was leading him into reform politics and a cultural nationalism which offered no clear analysis of the nature and direction of political power beyond the advocacy of an alternative life-style and a rejection of the worst excesses of American capitalism.

The most successful play to emerge out of this period showed a similar distrust of white language. *Slave Ship*, produced in 1967, was an attempt to charge black language with mythic significance; it built a ritual out of enslavement and cultural destruction, out of the screams of suffering and a Yoruba language which was slowly and symbolically broken down by the language of the slave master. *Slave Ship* was a pageant, a celebration of black fortitude, and a reminder of black suffering. Written just before the Newark "riot," it was, in Jones's words, "a hot note of rage to be expanded, so that the bitterness becomes an environment in which we can all learn to be ourselves, now."[58] Its intention was to make suffering the cause of present action. But the rebellion implied in this and other plays has more to do with style than with substance. He urged blacks to break free of American decadence, but offered no model of an alternative system. And there was an inescapable romanticism about this vision, as there had been a sentimentality of violence in some of his short plays.

He himself came to feel that his work was ideologically inadequate, as he moved steadily towards a Marxist-Leninist stance. By the mid-1970s he felt that in simply creating black alternatives to a supposed white sterility he was only strengthening the hands of the real enemy, just as in fighting to support the election of black candidates he had simply been trying to reform a system which should be destroyed. The weakness of *Slave Ship*, he felt, was its failure to analyze the capitalist nature of slavery. By 1975 he had come to the conclusion that "the only solution to our problems . . .is socialist revolution."[59] In a reversal of his previous work, he now saw racial separation as a deliberate strategy of the ruling class. *The Motion of History* and its associated work, *S-1*, is an expression of this growth in revolutionary consciousness.

The Motion of History, as its title implies, is an attempt to identify the forces which manipulate and determine the direction of human lives. Beginning with scenes from black slave revolts, he sets out to show that racial hostility derives, not from inborn prejudice, but from the political need of the aristocracy and then the bourgeoisie to divide and rule. In a sequence of thirty scenes, which press gradually towards the present, he laments the failure of white workers and black leaders to perceive the real nature of their oppression. But the play ends with these historical lessons finally learned, with the realization, in other words, that capitalism constitutes the real enemy and that in order to fight it a new, nonrevisionist Communist party of the USA has to be formed. It is, perhaps, not surprising, therefore, that the final lines should be so strikingly reminiscent of 1930s proletarian drama: ''FORWARD TO THE PARTY! FORWARD TO THE PARTY! LONG LIVE SOCIALIST REVOLUTION!.''[60]

Baraka has said that *S-1* can be seen as an addendum to *The Motion of History*. It is set in 1976 and concerns the establishment of a fascist state in America. The main instrument of this state is S-1, a bill actually debated by the Senate Judiciary Committee in that year but in Baraka's play enacted by Congress and declared constitutional by the Supreme Court, which effectively negates the first, fourth, fifth, sixth, eighth, and ninth amendments to the Constitution. It is a bill which outlaws the Communist Party, restricts freedom of speech and assembly, and introduces arbitrary powers of arrest and detention. It is, Baraka implies, a logical extension of ''the most recent government moves . . .the ideas being pushed in the superstructure, particularly movies and television'' and a likely product of ''the crisis that monopoly capitalism and imperialism is in.''[61] As a conventional war breaks out between the super-powers, so black and white Americans come together, shouting, ''defeat S-1! Forward the party!. . .Build a revolutionary Marxist-Leninist Communist Party based on Marxism-Leninism-Mao Tse-tung Thought!''[62]

Asked, in 1977, what his view of the whole Black Arts movement of the 1960s was, he replied, ''There are still progressive black artists who relate what they are doing to the Black Liberation Movement, and to revolution, which is the positive aspect of that. I think the negative aspect has actually been co-opted by the bourgeoisie—I mean the part of black art that just rested with skin identification, so that the very people who first opposed us are given the grants and the money to open the Black Arts Theatres, all around the country, the Negro Ensemble Company, the New Lafayette Company. And now you have exploitation flicks talking about black arts, and there are several people on television who were in plays of mine in the 1960s, who considered them-selves revolutionary black artists but who became involved simply with the skin aspect of it. What is black art? It's about black people, they thought. But the point is, it's supposed to be about revolution.''[63] It is a view, of course, which necessarily makes him blind to the accomplishments of a work like Ntozake Shange's ''Choreopoem'' *For Coloured Girls Who Have Considered Suicide When the Rainbow Is Enuf*, which had its first performance in 1974 and reached Broadway two years later. But, then, he has replaced the rigors of one ideological stance by those of another which leaves little space for lyricism.

In his own eyes, of course, the development from *Dutchman* to *S-1* repre-sents ''a leap from partial truth to a more wholesided reality,'' from ''the feeling and rage against oppression to the beginnings of actual scientific analysis of this oppression and its true sources.''[64] To others, it might appear that he had simply moved from one ideology to another, pressing experience to its extreme edges, to the point at which meaning seems to render itself up only in moral absolutes of chilling determinism. There is indeed a clear line of development visible in his work. Whether or not it is a move in the direction of truth, however, is more debatable. Dramatically, he has abandoned rituals as ''bourgeois nationalism'' and forsworn the subtleties of his own early work as simply inadequate to confront what he takes to be the unsubtle conflicts of capital and labor. His plays are, he admits, ''vehicles for a simple message,''[65] and their weakness is perhaps apparent in that description.

His work is now, I suspect, overarticulate. It operates wholly on the surface. All hidden powers are exposed, and the result is both an oversimplified view of political process and a dissipation of dramatic power. No longer interested in the energy generated by the collision of conscious and subconscious or in the potent rhythms of submerged passions, he resolves all tensions into the battle for economic hegemony; all violence becomes literal and political. Character is crushed as effectively by the playwright as it is by the reactionary forces against which he pitches his work. And the risk, clearly, is that in identifying those historical forces which account for the drive towards Marxist-Leninism, he fails to dramatize those human forces which must finally validate it. History remains an implacable force, once on the side of the capitalist, now on the side of the worker, but with a momentum quite separate from the parabola described by the victim of those forces. It is an irony which Walker Vessels, the black revolutionary, would have seen clearly enough, even while pressing forward his commitment.

But Baraka is not unaware of the problems involved in creating ideological drama. His artistic credo is taken from Mao Tse-tung's *Yenan Forum on Art and Literature*: ''What we demand is the unity of politics and art, the unity of content and form, the unity of revolutionary political content and the highest possible perfection of artistic form; . . .we oppose both works of art with a wrong political viewpoint and the tendency towards the 'poster and slogan style' which is correct in political viewpoint but lacking in artistic power.''[66] As he has indicated in a recent interview, this still eludes him. But he obviously believes that what he has lost—the imaginative brilliance of *Dutchman*, the subtle analysis of *The Slave*, the controlled rhythms and potent rituals of *Slaveship*—is adequately compensated for by the historical significance of his new career. At the moment it is difficult to endorse that view. The question is whether he can yet find a form and a language adequate to his self-imposed task or whether the logic of his present position may not drive him beyond theatre altogether.

Clearly, the pressure for ideological commitment in Baraka is strong, whether it be the shaping myths of black nationalism or those of Marxist-Leninism. But he is a writer of genuine integrity for whom art must always be seen as a public act. His struggle to find a structure capable of expressing the needs of the individual and those of society, his search for a form of transcendence which lies neither in aestheticism nor in a convenient surrender of historical truth, has in essence been that of all black writers in the last two decades. It should not be unduly surprising that in the midst of the anarchic enthusiasms of that period ideology should have been seen as offering such a persuasive sense of order, locating, as it does, irrational prejudice and social deprivation in a coherent mythological or "rational" context. Nor should it be surprising that drama—a public art, a shaping mechanism—should itself have been seen as a primary agent in this process.

Baraka was important, not only in his own right, but also as a profound influence on other black writers. He was a shaping influence on the black revolutionary plays of the 1960s, which, Larry Neal has suggested, were the cultural equivalent of the black power concept. This theatre was concerned primarily with defining and even creating black pride. Its strategy was twofold: to indict the whites as the sources of all evil and corruption; and to denounce those in the black community who, by their desire to share the values and standards of the dominant society, become traitors to the new vision of black dignity and solidarity. As the playwright William Mackey explained, the new black theatre was "a spit at the black middle class for turning their backs on the black masses still in bondage."[67] But Jones was also the inspiration of a writer whose work revealed a much greater range than that of most "revolutionary" playwrights and who was a moving spirit behind the founding of another black theatre institution—the New Lafayette Theatre.

In *Street Sounds: Dialogues with Black Experience* (1970), Ed Bullins presents a collage of monologues by those whose lives, taken together, offer an impressionistic account of black experience, a literary pointilism gradually building up a picture of the black community. And one such figure is the Black Critic, whose censure of the black dramatist's concern with the more brutal and demeaning aspects of ghetto life is Bullins's parody of the criticism directed at his own earlier works. These plays, in distinction from those produced in the early 1970s, are not so much concerned with forging images of revolt as with declaring a hegemony over black experience and a commitment to the real world of private passions locked within a public world characterized by economic and social constrictions.

The Black Critic insists, much as had those of the First Renaissance, that "you're irresponsible! You're not fulfilling any of the needs of the people that I can see. Look at what you're doing to yourself and the negative image of the race you create. We've had it hard enough. We don't need to be showing them that side of us. It's a disgrace, that's what it is. I wasn't raised that way. Nobody I knew was. We were refined, man. And here you are, at this late date, creating profanity, filth and obscenity and displaying it to the masses, the black people you so hypocritically harp about forever into the future, as art and culture.''[68] Bullins's own rejection of such an assault is indicated, as it frequently is in his work, by the critic's self-conscious retreat into jargon, by his eagerness to ally himself, on the one hand, with the values and language of aesthetic criticism (''The work lacks range and its author fails to demonstrate a measurable degree of responsibility to the depiction of the unlettered masses,''[69]) and, on the other, to the new conventionalities of black language and national consciousness (''Sure is a heavy game. I wanna thank you. Just doin' mah thang. Salaam, ahke? Kill the night blackness and groove.''[70]).

It is more remarkable that such a character should be presented in a collection of plays in which Bullins's own introduction insists that ''Black Art is to express what is best in us and for us Black People.''[71] But the best may, of course, have little to do with good taste as perceived by others or with political utility of the kind which reduces the relationship between art and the public world to the slogan that ''Art and Politics Should Be Identical.'' Bullins's response to this is ''be serious.''[72] And, from the very beginning, his work showed a strong satiric component, a suspicion of cant and of a demogoguery which was ultimately self-serving and remote from the actual concerns of the black community which the black artist must address. Hence, his early play, *Dialect Determinist* (1965), was a vicious parody of Marxist ideologues who hide behind the mask of an African identity.

At the same time, the plays which Bullins wrote in the second half of the 1960s did project precisely that sense of a brutalized world to which his own Black Critic had taken such objection. Love devolves into a violent sexuality in which communion becomes simple possession, a struggle for mental and physical dominance. Money is a dominating reality, and alcohol and drugs, like sexuality, the only relief. The tone of the plays is one of desperation and frustration. Individuals are locked together by need, trapped by their own material and biological necessities. Women are dominated by men and men, by their environment. Race is only one, and perhaps not even the dominant, reality.

In *It Has No Choice*, a black man and a white woman are hopelessly enslaved within their own histories. Even their language becomes a source of potential pain and misunderstanding. They enact a ritual of love and hatred, sealed by an act of violence which is as potent and meaningful a moment of contact as is the sexual unity which is, anyway, undercut by political, cultural, and racial presumptions. A less subtle version of the same conviction is observable in *A Minor Scene* (1966), which, like the former play, was a product of Black Arts-West Repertory Theatre in San Francisco. In this brief play, a young black man, with the symbolic name of Peter Black, accosts the equally symbolically named Miss Ann. With a stream of invective, sexual abuse, and implied threats, he succeeds in gaining her acquiescence—a parody of white liberal masochism which is little more than a joke about white guilt and the violence which is a latent aspect of sexual relationships.

But, more typical are works like *Clara's Ole Man* (1965), *Goin' a Buffalo*, (1966), and the sequence of plays *In the Wine Time* (1967), *In the New England Winter* (1967), and *The Corner* (1968), works which, in their reductive view of human nature and their sense of the black ghetto as lacking in any redeeming sense of community or moral values capable of transcending a concern with the self or the brutal dialectics of survival, would seem to merit the kind of reproaches aimed at such works by the Black Critic.

In *Clara's Ole Man*, set in the mid-1950s, Jack, a twenty-year-old black man going through college prep on the GI bill, is beaten insensible when he fails to understand the relationship between young Clara and her presumably lesbian companion Big Girl. The stage is peopled with grotesques: with Miss Famie, an elderly alcoholic; with Baby Girl, a mentally retarded teenage girl who mouths the obscenities taught her by her domineering sister; and with a gang of young street fighters who obligingly break the young man's body when requested to do so by Big Girl. The play's ironic subtitle, *A Play of Lost Innocence*, applies equally to all the characters. It is a James Purdy world of partial beings, obsessive figures, desperate souls. And, although Jack's pretentious language is mocked and the street gang is in flight from the police, there is no sense in which race is made the focus of the play or in which the distortions of the psyche are traced to racial origins.

The play is set in a slum kitchen in South Philadelphia, but the image which dominates the play is a nonspecific sense of human desolation, frustrated hopes, and the evanescent nature of available consolations. Baby Girl is too evident a symbol of human potential for the play to generate any confidence in the individual or in the possibility of communal actions and values.

Much the same could be said of *The Corner*, which is concerned with events which predate those of *In the Wine Time* and *In the New England Winter*. Set in the early 1950s, it concerns a group of young blacks, one of whom is a twenty-four-year-old alcoholic with a mental age of sixteen. It, too, turns on a brutal view of human relations. Feelings are scarcely articulated by individuals for whom money, wine, and sex are the dominant realities. Cliff Dawson, a young black man, abandons his girl to get married, but before doing so, has intercourse with her in the back of a car and then invites his companions to take their turn. It is a casual cruelty for which the play offers no real alternative. Cliff's decision to marry another girl is prompted by her pregnancy and by a general sense of insufficiency in his life. As he says, "What's like me, huh? To be a bum? To drink wine and fuck bitches in junky cars? To stand half the night on some street corner that any fucken cop can come up and claim?" But this sense of hollowness is imperfectly perceived, and marriage clearly offers no real means of neutralizing his discontent, as is shown clearly enough in the other plays of the sequence.

However, *In the Wine Time*, first produced in 1968, does begin with a lyrical prologue about the birth of a relationship between Ray, Lou's nephew, and a mysterious young woman whom he meets on the street and who stands as an idealized image of an alternative world beyond that forged by the love, the hate, and the ever-present alcohol which he shares with Cliff and Lou, his uncle and aunt, and which are slowly stifling him even as he presses towards manhood. As the young woman explains, she will be ''out in the world, little boy, out in the world. Remember, when you're ready, all you have to do is leave this place and come to me, I'll be waiting. All you'll need to do is search!''[73] But these plays repeatedly stress the impossibility of breaking away, the inevitable loss of innocence, the destruction of lyricism, and the collapse of hopes which are simply transposed into the immediate relief of sex, alcohol, drugs, religion, and a violent action which gives the illusion of accomplishment.

The play is once again set in the 1950s, in the small side street of a large northern industrial city. In a series of houses, one is occupied by whites. But they all share the limited world of daily frustration and fanciful hopes. Ray wants to escape the neighborhood and the limitations of his life by joining the navy. But we have Cliff's example to show that this offers no real alternative, for he had been in the navy, and, though he now chooses to sentimentalize that experience, it had failed to offer him the meaning which he sought. Meanwhile, the casual violence, the constant threat of chaos, is outlined in the scenes set in the Avenue.

The baby which Lou carries simply threatens new levels of deprivation and a further hostage to fate. Cliff's illusion of studying stands in sharp contrast to the reality of his life. His sense of this breeds a rage which is barely controlled, ''There's a big rich world out there'' he observes, ''I'm going to get me part of that world or stare your God in the eye and scream *why*. I am not a beast . . .or animal to be used for the plows of the world. But if I am then I'll act like one, I'll be one and turn this fucken world of dreams and lies and fairy tales into a jungle or a desert.''[74] These are, indeed, the two poles between which the characters move. Their loud manners don't allow them to fit easily into the street in which they live, but they try to keep a distance between themselves and the simple brutalities of the Avenues. The only moments of transcendence are those in which they indulge their fantasies—Ray, for his girl; Cliff, for the free life of the sailor—lyric invocations which can find no correlative in action. Ray's dreams are smashed by a spasm of violence, itself an articulation of a world reduced to elementals. Cliff protects his nephew by killing the man who threatens and taunts him.

For the polite inhabitants of the Avenue, for those whose ears are attuned only to gospel songs or the narcotic drone of the radio commercial, it is evidence of anarchy best shut out. For those on the street, it is simply confirmation of the closed world of desire and death—a world which is not explained as a consequence of race, but as the product of a life without transcending ideals which can be transformed into action. In a sense, the ideal girl, the myth woman pursued by Ray, is close kin to Daisy Buchanan—a way to restore a primal innocence, to charge the ordinary processes of life with meaning, to redeem and justify a life spent in a world whose reality is corrupting and whose principles have become lost in the simple process of survival. And the ironies are the same as those in Fitzgerald's novel, as the myths turn into ironic commentaries, as they desert the individual and leave him to his fate. The play ends with Cliff being taken away by the police and the community immediately slipping back into its narcosis.

In the New England Winter picks the story up after Cliff's release. He no longer harbors any illusions about college; these have been displaced onto his half-brother Steve, with whom he is in covert competition. The prologue details an armed robbery easily effected and successful. The rest of the play suggests that this is simply an idealized form of the crime which they are preparing to commit and which they rehearse with ever less conviction. The gang is an unlikely alliance. Cliff and his half-brother are joined by two untrustworthy companions. Cliff continues to drink because "it's good for fighting off my distorted sense of reality."[75] Again, the play slips into an occasional lyricism, a fantasy world reinforced by changes in lighting and by music. It is this world of fantasy which provides the motivation for the crime. The money is not valued in itself; it simply buys access to their dreams. In Steve's case, it is to facilitate the move to New England and his dream woman, who plays the same function as Ray's fantasy girl in the earlier play. She is an image of the future, of possibility. But for Cliff, there is no such ideal. Lou has left him while he was serving his sentence. As he says, "The future is with us right now, brother. We drown in our future each breath we take; . . .phoney promises leak into our brains and turn them to shit."[76]

The rhythm of the play, indeed, is provided by an alternative pulse of lyricism and brutal reality. Steve's girlfriend has dreams of the baby which they will have: "And we'll take our baby sleddin' in the snow and skatin' across the ice. We'll take our baby swimmin' in the California Pacific. He'll be with us in the mountains and camp with us in the desert. The world is ours." But, at the same time, she is frightened of the future when "they might come for him . . .come to steal him away. Steal his blackness . . .steal his spirit and soul."[77] Such lyricism, however, is taken for madness, more especially since it is so out of tune with a context in which softness is taken for stupidity and hope is seen as a failure of perception. So, too, feelings are regarded as creating a dangerous vulnerability. As Steve says, "I don't have feelings, emotions, sympathy, tenderness, compassion . . .It slows you up."[78] But this disavowal of feeling is somewhat contradictory and unreal. In fact, he is totally vulnerable, and when Liz is genuinely driven mad by the pressure of events, his world collapses, "Madness madness madness. . . .God, I can't take this. . . .I can't live this out. It can't be *this* way."[79]

Once against the play is not *about* race. Race provides its context; the social pressures of the ghetto stand as a concrete example of the anarchic thrust of existence. But Steve's desire for order, for a platonic ideal, for a version of the real capable of sustaining a sense of purpose, is a familiar enough theme of modern drama. His insistence that "this isn't it . . .there must be order . . .perfection . . .there must be form . . .there must be reason and absolutes. . . .There can't be only madness and reaching out and never touching the sides. . . .There *has* to be something for me besides this emptiness . . .this living death. . . .this white coldness"[80] lies equally at the heart of Miller's liberal laments and the absurd's ironic comments. That the play ends with a conventional reversal in which it is revealed that Steve had been Lou's lover, a revelation which Steve tries to stifle by murdering the man who intends to tell his half-brother, is both surprising and regrettable. The fact that Cliff had known the truth all the time merely reduces the more fundamental ambiguities of the play to a somewhat trite irony.

Though race is not the point of these plays, it is clearly its circumstance. His characters are outcasts, pressed back into a desperately small physical and emotional space. They eke out their existence in the interstices of a social world which they do not command and which hardly features as a conscious element of their daily existence. Political impotence demands a stress on sexual potency; social insignificance creates a determination to establish a local reputation for violence or sexual dominance. Anger is deflected from its logical target until it becomes reflexive, self-destructive. Dominance denied on a public level must be continually exerted on a private one—even a dominance over death, an assertion of contempt for human life which is a defensive response to the negative value placed on their own. This, he recognizes in his early plays, is not an experience exclusive to blacks. But he increasingly came to feel that for the black American it was the norm. Black ghetto life was a losing rearguard action against an absurdity which was socially, rather than metaphysically, derived. There is, indeed, a shift in emphasis in his work which seems to have come about in 1970. *The Duplex*, produced in May of that year, was a transitional work (though a brief *Black Commercial #2*, produced in San Francisco in 1967, had already suggested that there was a need to deflect art into a specifically political utility and the destructive violence of the ghetto into a rejuvenating sense of community.)

The Duplex, originally produced by the New Lafayette Theatre in 1970 and later given what Bullins felt to be an unsatisfactory production at Lincoln Center, is subtitled *A Black Love Fable in Four Movements* and contains the same Steve Benson who had featured in his earlier play. Together with *In the Wine Time, In the New England Winter*, and *Goin' a Buffalo*, it constitutes part of a planned twenty-part series called The Twentieth-Century Cycle.

Once again, Bullins offers a closed world of sadomasochistic sex and violence orchestrated into arias or the overlapping monologues which pass for conversation. For the women, dreams are focused on past or future lovers; for the men, on their pride in their success with women, their luck at cards, or their success in repaying insults. But now Bullins has the central character point the racial moral at the heart of the play when he asserts:

Nobody knows me . . .what's in my mind and guts . . .they'll never understand the thoughts that flash through my head and scorch the back of my eyes . . .these eyes that see the flames of the hell that we all live in . . .live our black lives in here . . .getting ready to become something we ain't now or will never be . . .really. Some names like what? Colored insurance man, postal clerk, negro journalist, teacher, lawyer, afro-american dentist, actor, horn blower, whiskey pourer . . .clown? Don't marry anything black . . . .Because she's nobody . .a little black female nothing with babies she don't even know how they come so fast . . .and she shouldn't be in my together program anyway 'cause I'm due for greater things. Yeah . . .greater things . . .ha ha. . . .Well I'm not, you know . . .not due, that is . . .not due for anything more than I'm due for now . . .and that is only to be a nigger . . .or be black . . .nothing short of those two absolutes. To work in this white man's land . . .or build one of my own . . .to give a last ditch try to save my balls. . . .And to make some children so that they can climb up over my bloated sweating carcass once it falls . . .falls in the service of them. . . .That we call progress . . .ha ha ha . . .don't get too close to her because she's not going anywhere. . . .But where in the hell are we going, brother? Where? Into the machine maze of IBM. . . .Into the confines of teaching the slavemaster's offspring . . .into the insanity of thinking we can teach them their own language . . .my poor brother, language is more than words . . .it is deeds and gestures . . .and silence . . .what history can we teach those who hide from history . . .those who believe their lies and fears create history . . .can we teach them their own sterility of soul that we slaves learned better than they that call it their civilization?[81]

It is a powerful aria, a sermon indicting the white world which created the context for black life, the black world which acquiesces in its own destruction, and the self which seeks to make a separate peace with absurdity by compounding it. The weakness lies not in the language nor even simply in its incongruity but in its inconsistency with respect to the character who voices this highly self-conscious sentiment. Steve's imaginative world is presented as limited, his emotional life oscillating between an exploitative arrogance and a disabling sentimentality. Like many of Bullins's protagonists, he is studying under the GI bill, but there is little evidence of intellectual self-possession or of a consistent view of the future which he here perceives as vacuous and destructive. On the one occasion when he reads to Velma, his landlady-lover, Bullins has him read from *In the Wine Time* a piece of solipsism which is potentially destructive, since not only is Steve's brother a character in that play but it implies a level of perception and sensitivity in Steve and a degree of fictive awareness by the writer which is simply not sustained by the play.

Once again the action turns on sexual jealousies, and an imminent violence charges events with a deceptive significance. The momentary glimpses of potential harmony and of a future not hedged around by irony are shattered by the familiar rhythm of sex, drink, and violence. And nowhere in the play does

Bullins identify an alternative to the destructive visions which Steve describes so eloquently, unless it is in the desperate, unthinking opiate of sexual relationships, which at best parody that sense of communal values and purposive action which now became the central justification and function of his drama. The inconclusive ending, true enough to the frustration and the closed world of emotions which consume themselves with no spiritual or social residue, was alien to the mood of the late 1960s and to Bullins's own increasing commitments. His early plays, from *How Do You Do* onwards, had admittedly had a satiric edge, but these had mostly given way to a naturalistic account of the warping effects of ghetto life, lightened only by moments of lyric potential, passages of pure fantasy which necessarily collapsed under the weight of a hermetic mental and physical environment. Now he took a more determinedly revolutionary stance.

In 1967, he began talking to Robert Macbeth about the possibility of building a black theatre ensemble company. This led to the creation of the New Lafayette Theatre, of which he became resident dramatist. Immediately prior to this he had been working with Eldridge Cleaver, Marvin X, Amiri Baraka, and Sonia Sanchez in Black House, San Francisco. This had been an alliance of political and artistic members which eventually broke up over the role to be ascribed to white radicals. Cleaver had called for a coalition, but Bullins and the other writers favored the development of a black art wholly separate from white influence. At the same time, he confessed that his own early works had been "swept away in the Black revolutionary emotionalism and resulting fratricide of the '60s."[82] Now he came to feel that "the conditions must be created for sweeping social and cultural change. It is the black artist's creative duty to plant, nurture and spread the seeds of change."[83] The future of black theatre he felt would lie "in its evolution into a profound instrument for altering the slave mentality of Black Americans."[84] And, employing the very rhetoric which had blunted appreciation of his own earlier plays, he suggested that "in an evil, white world of shifting values and reality, for the Black man there must be a sanctuary for re-creation of the Black spirit and African identity. In racist, madmen America, the Black theatre has carved out this part of the future for itself."[85] But even now, he endeavored to keep a certain distance between himself and those political activists whose reduction of complex realities to radical simplification was even more menacing for the artist than it was for the ordinary individual. Hence, he asserted, "If all around us are losing their heads . . .it may be provident for the black artist to attempt to hold onto his, which is a conservative impulse, true, but radical in terms of heretical viewpoints. Political theorists of the Black Arts," he suggested, "are confused and disappointing. . . .'The dogs may bark but the caravan passes on.' "[86]

In *A Black Quartet* (1969), a group of four plays by black writers, he contributed *The Gentleman Caller*, which was a parody of white condescension and a call for cultural awareness. A black maid is transformed into a revolutionary, much as Jones's fieldslave had been transformed into a rebel in *The Slave*. The play's humor—he plays elaborate games with racial stereotypes as he had in his first play, *How Do You Do*—finally gives way to the invocations to black pride which, for a time, were the sine qua non of black writing. "It is time for Black people to come together. It is time for Black people to rise from their knees and come together in unity, brotherhood and Black spirituality to form a nation that will rise from our enslaved mass and meet the oppressor. DEATH TO THE ENEMIES OF THE BLACK PEOPLE! All praise is due to the Blackman."[87] But, given the ironic detachment of a play like *Street Sounds* and the anguished debate of *Death List*, it seems clear that this slogan is not to be taken literally and that the revolution is to be in the consciousness of black America. By the same token, *A Short Play for a Small Theatre*, in which the white members of the audience are shot in the face by the single black actor, is offered as a provocative image of black emancipation rather than as a literal program for action. It is not performed much, any more than is *The Play of the Play*, in which the audience is locked inside a theatre so that "anything can be laid on the people that you wish through light, images, sound, movement and colour;"[88] an ironic image of the kind of revolutionary art which Bullins's own works transcends. In *Death List* (1970), a black man lists those prominent Negroes whom he considers to be the enemies of black people around the world, slowly loading a high-powered rifle as he does so. But, as a black woman points out, not only does this presume an arrogant right to define and police the nature of blackness, but it also involves a demeaning and ultimately self-destructive violence. Such rituals of black purity must eventually proscribe everyone, including the black woman and eventually the black man himself. It is a point repeated in his screenplay *Night of the Beast*, which blends realism and fantasy in an account of a revolution in Harlem. But here, the impulse to press the idea of a revolution in consciousness to the point of literal revolt leaves the play ambiguously balanced.

Bullins's evaluation of himself as "almost without peer in America—black, white or imported," his suggestion that his projected cycle of plays was of "surpassing greatness in its scope"[89] might imply a detachment from reality of amazing proportions. But in all his work, no less than in this statement, there is a fundamental irony working against the implacable absolutes of the period in which he wrote. His suggestion that he claims supremacy for his own work "because there is practically no one in America but myself who would dare"[90] hints at the humor which is equally an identifying feature of his art. Certainly, despite the revolutionary images generated by works like *Night of the Beasts*, he was one of the few black writers of the 1960s who kept a cautious distance from a black drama which defined itself solely in political terms. As he said in his introduction to the 1974 collection *The New Lafayette Theatre Presents*, "In the recent past, preoccupation in addressing mainly social and political issues may have been Black literature's major flaw.''[91] He welcomed the fact that such compulsions had now ''changed from a social-protest oriented form to one of a dialectical nature among Black people.''[92] And, in this respect, his work has proved a model for a black theatre which is not only a vital part of the black community's debate with itself, but also, paradoxically, an essential element in a revivified American theatre.

Today, black theatre is a fact of American cultural life, from the avowed ethnicity of Barbara Ann Teer's National Black Theatre founded in 1968, or Fred Hudson's Frederick Douglass Creative Arts Center (an outgrowth of the Watts Writers Workshop) established in 1971, to the multiethnic New Federal Theatre founded by Woodie King, Jr., in 1970. And if the ever-present Joe Papp is showing an increasing interest in black creativity, this is no longer seen as quite the threat it might have been only a few years ago. The main thrust of black arts may have passed, the shrill voice of protest may have become muted, and the more strident political imperatives may have been modified, but the impact of that movement has been considerable, not only on the black community, but also on the society with which that community has been in such long and ambiguous struggle.

The Black Poet as Cultural Sign   9

It has become common among critics to lament the beginnings of black poetry in America as evidencing an unfortunate but unavoidable submissiveness. Sterling Brown, in his pioneering study, says of Phillis Wheatley (1753-1784) that ''the real griefs she experienced herself or could have witnessed are missing'' and that this is ''cause for regret.''[1] But the truth is that it is a mistake to see in her work only a series of self-denying, derivative pieties. For, from the very beginning of the history of black poetry in America, there is an implied engagement with the special circumstances of its creation—a concealed assertion of identity projected against a public imagery which is otherwise almost wholly reductive. To be a poet at all was a public gesture, but buried within the poetry are implied claims and attitudes designedly at odds with the values of those who read it.

The constraints offered by the heroic couplet—a closed structure which offers a subtle blend of fixed form and imaginative transcendence—was an appropriate metric for Phillis Wheatley to employ. And in celebrating her ''release'' from pagan Africa and her spiritual liberation in slave-owning America, she could scarcely be unaware of the resonating ironies. As Henry Louis Gates, Jr., has shown, in a fascinating thesis on *The History and Theory of Afro-American Literary Criticism, 1778-1831*, the mere fact of black literary accomplishment was inevitably subsumed in a more general argument about the validity of slavery and the nature of the Negro. Black poetry from the beginning was a code, a public gesture whose implications transcended the sentiment expressed. The struggle to find imaginative freedom within a fixed and determined form was an obvious, if submerged, image of the situation of those for whom the rhythms of life were fixed by the rise and fall of the sun, by the imposed and artificial metronome of sowing and harvesting. While her celebration of man's submission to God implies a parallel submission to man, her work constitutes a claim, not only for personal attention, but also for a full acknowledgement of her humanity. In the context of an active debate about the nature of the Negro and his origins, a debate which even contemplated an animal origin, her appeals to God to guide her ''soul'' and raise her ''mind'' to ''seraphic strain,'' her use of the word ''race'' to mean the human race, and her insistence that ''the noble frame of man'' and the rest of nature were ''all lovely copies of the Maker's plan''[2] amounted to more than a simple piety; it was an assertion of a truth still strongly resisted by many and used by them to justify a process of enslavement. And how would Sterling Brown account for the none-too-subtle ironies so evident in the middle stanza of her poem to the Right Honourable William Earl of Dartmouth:

> Should you, my lord, while you puruse my song,
> Wonder from whence my love of *Freedom* sprung,
> Whence flow these wishes for the common good,
> By feeling hearts alone best understood,
> I, young in life, by seeming cruel fate
> Was snatch'd from *Afric's* fancy'd happy seat:
> What pangs excruciating must molest,
> What sorrows labour in my parents' breast?
> Steel'd was the soul and by no misery mov'd
> That from a father seiz'd his babe belov'd.
> Such, such my case. And can I then but pray
> Others may never feel tyrannic sway?[3]

Given the nature of this stanza, one wonders how James Weldon Johnson could say that "one looks in vain for some outburst or even complaint against the bondage of her people, for some agonising cry about her native land."[4] Indeed, he calls this very stanza "unimpassioned." Given the general level of poetry at the time, Thomas Jefferson's comment that "religion has produced a Phillis Wheatley, but it could not produce a poet; her poems are beneath contempt"[5] seems a curiously revealing outburst of a particularly self-justifying kind.

By the same token, it is difficult to read wholly without irony the following lines by Jupiter Hammon (ca. 1739-1800) from "An Evening Thought: Salvation by Christ With Penetential Cries":

> Salvation now comes from the Lord,
>   He being thy captive slave
>
> Dear Jesus, let the Nations cry,
>   And all the People say,
>
> Salvation comes from Christ on high
>   Haste on Tribunal Day.[6]

On one level, it expressed a conventional wish for the truth and solace of Judgement Day; on the other hand, it is a recognition that since the only available source of salvation lies in Christ, the sooner that day comes, the sooner will come release for the captive slave. Likewise, his poem "A Dialogue Intitled the Kind Master and the Dutiful Servant as follows" contains the following ambiguous stanza:

> Dear Master, now I'll follow thee,
>   And trust upon the Lord;
> The only safety that I see,
>   Is Jesus' holy word.[7]

The point of the poem seems to reside in the irony whereby the parts of the dialogue operate on wholly different levels; the master preaching submission and the servant acknowledging the desperate plight which makes that religion the sole source of release. Other poets were more direct. George Moses Horton (1797–1883) lamented his plight in verses designed to secure his manumission. The fact that they failed to do so merely compounded the painful reality of his situation.

Literature was not always a reliable avenue of escape, though it proved so for Phillis Wheatley. But it was clearly perceived as an important weapon by the abolitionists. It was one thing to enslave the dumb, the inarticulate, the insensitive—those, in short, who could scarcely lay claim to the liberal principles of the Great Experiment since, not being men in the eyes of their enslavers, they could scarcely qualify for the promised equality. When these same slaves succeeded in articulating their plight, in revealing an imaginative and intellectual capacity beyond that required by mere literacy, a whole line of moral argument disintegrated, and the poem became a potent instrument for liberation. And clearly the closer the form and language approximated to that of dominant white modes, the more forceful was the argument. So these were to be no stuttering, incoherent attempts at verse; their fluency was in large degree their point, as was their derivative nature. William Lloyd Garrison, in his introduction to *The Narrative Life of Frederick Douglass* (1845), chose especially to emphasize the author's "fluency of language." Also, since they were now directed at the conscience of America, they were addressed in a clear vocative mood.

> Say, Righteous Sire, shall Afric ever mourn
> Her weeping children from her bosom torn?
> Chained, sold, scattered far in Christian lands;
> Scourged, beaten, murdered, too, by Christian hands![8]

Nor were these poems particularly supplicatory. James M. Whitfield began his poem "America" with the words:

> America, it is to thee,
> Thou boasted land of liberty,—
> It is to thee I raise my song,
> Thou land of blood, and crime, and wrong.[9]

If fluency was a necessary tactic for abolitionist poetry, after emancipation there was a premium on dialect verse—a market to which Dunbar responded but in which he became eventually trapped. Dying at the age of thirty-three, he never succeeded in forging a personal poetic style which satisfied him or which he could confidently expect to be published. The use of dialect was a device which had some authenticity but which, as James Weldon Johnson suggested, quickly became formularized, the basis of a potentially demeaning stereotype. The son of a slave, Dunbar negotiated a psychic territory of his own, but it was one in which compromise became as necessary in literature as it was in life. Ironically, the wheel had come full circle by 1976, and now it was a black critic who regretted Dunbar's private resistance to his own dialect poetry. Onwuchekwa Jemie has said that "it is mainly on looking back from the vantage point of our own era that one might be inclined to blame Dunbar for not seeing the transformational possibilities of plantation dialect, and for so stubbornly preferring his poems in standard English."[10] William Dean Howells's ambivalence with regard to Dunbar was equally instructive. Like the abolitionists, he still saw Dunbar's achievement as vindicating the civilized state of the Negro and hence working to diminish and eventually eradicate prejudice by asserting an "essential unity of the human race, which does not think or feel black in one and white in another, but humanly in all." Yet, he also valued what he called "a precious difference of temperament between the races," which he saw as exemplified in the dialect poetry. And here, in embryo, is the idea of a black cultural experience distinct from that of white America. For all his praise of Dunbar, however, his notion of black artistic endeavor is not untinged with paternalism, for he regrets that in an earlier essay he had failed to point out that Pushkin, as well as Dumas, had been black, excusing himself with the remark that "these were both mulattoes, who might have been supposed to derive their qualities from white blood vastly more artistic than ours."[11]

The First Renaissance did not end compromise; neither was it uniform. Some poetry of the 1920s was still offered as part of a continuing appeal for justice (James Weldon Johnson's "O Southland, dear Southland!"), some was defiant challenge (Claude McKay's "If We Must Die"), and some was entirely detached from the race problem (Countee Cullen's "Timid Lover"). There was no single ideology, but simply a new confidence, a lack of apology, and a positive assertion of cultural values. And poetry was central to this new experience, as was music. It was not, for the most part, innovatory. Countee Cullen's simple metrics were paralleled by Claude McKay's sonnets. A simple imagery of release charged Africa with an iconic force, and an undertow of neoromanticism gives much of the poetry an air of naivety. But at the heart of most of it was an attempt to isolate an imagery adequate to the task of self-definition. If blackness was not the icon it was to become in the Second Renaissance, it was the attempt at imaginative possession of black experience which animated the movement. The South, Harlem, Africa, the clichés of the minstrel, the reality of segregation, and the equal reality of emotional release and musical fulfillment were all inspected for a meaning which could define a self capable of transcending the simple fact of circumstance. And this was a highly self-conscious movement which required the individual poet to stake out his territory. Hence, Claude McKay could say that "frankly, I have never regarded myself as a Negro poet. I have always felt that my gift of song was something bigger than the narrow confined limits of one people and its problems,"[12] and Countee Cullen could confess that though "a number of times I have said I wanted to be a poet and known as such and not as a Negro poet . . .in spite of myself . . .I find that I am activated by a strong sense of race consciousness. This grows upon me as I grow older, and although I struggle against it, it colors my writing."[13] The mere fact of such statements reveals the extent to which it was perceived as an issue. The shaping consciousness of Alain Locke and the continuing pressures of prejudice created a social imperative which charged the public act of the artist with a significance beyond itself. Just as for Phillis Wheatley, its meaning lay partly in the act itself. Even a simple lyric contained a socially derived kinetic energy. Alain Locke was thus not wholly correct in saying that "our poets have now stopped speaking for the Negro— they speak as Negroes. Where formerly they spoke to others and tried to interpret, they now speak to their own and try to express."[14] Certainly a black audience was now perceived, and the vocative case tended to disappear. But the social role was still implicitly acknowledged, perhaps never more clearly than when it was being publicly disavowed. The "democracy of art"[15] was not as self-evident as Paul Kellogg believed.

Despite its heterogeneous nature, the essence of the First Renaissance and what links it with the Second is contained in the description offered in the Chicago *Whip* in January 1920: "The group styling themselves the New Negroes are those who have conceived a new line of thought, a new method of approach and a new ultimatum. The new line of thought is that the intrinsic standard of Beauty and aesthetics does not reside in the white race. . . .The new method of approach is a militant campaign against those who have corrupted public opinion and . . .have contented themselves with a 'back seat and half a loaf.' The ultimatum . . .is that a new racial love, respect and consciousness may be created."[16] It was just such an amalgam which was to typify the late 1960s, which produced a group of writers as young as that which defined the nature of the Harlem Renaissance (Arna Bontemps, Countee Cullen, Langston Hughes, Jean Toomer, and Zora Neale Hurston were in their twenties; Claude McKay and Alain Locke were in their thirties).

If McKay and Cullen resisted too exclusive a racial mode, others self-consciously developed a verse form and an approach which drew on specifically black modes. Hence, James Weldon Johnson, while working as the secretary of the NAACP for the passage of the Dyer Anti-Lynching Bill, published *The Book of Negro Spirituals* in 1925 and two years later produced

God's Trombones, which attempted to capture the rhythms of the black preacher. And, more centrally, Langston Hughes tried to create a poetic form which would express a distinctive metrical structure derived from black music. As he said, "Most of my own poems are racial in theme and treatment, derived from the life I know. In many of them I try to grasp and hold some of the meanings and rhythms of jazz."[17]

Hughes did indeed structure much of his poetry on rhythms derived from both jazz and the blues. In that, of course, he was not unique. Vachel Lindsay, in particular, was there ahead of him and, despite that poet's lapse from grace in his racially suspect poem "The Congo," which makes his an ambiguous name to invoke, his handling of jazz rhythms was at least as subtle and powerful as Hughes's. For Lindsay, the jazz poem constituted only one of a series of experiments with poetic form, but for Hughes it was paradigmatic. It was the assertion of a poetic, a statement not only of the relationship between verse and music, but of the cultural role in which he cast himself. Both men saw poetry as a public and spoken, or "sung," art (Lindsay's other, more private self, only now being plumbed), but Hughes spoke directly to an audience for whom such an art and the rhythms which it expressed were an everyday experience.

Of course, such a poet, whose work is designed to be immediately and readily available, poses a number of problems for the literary critic of a kind which have become all too familiar in the last decade. Indeed, a recent study of Hughes's work, written against the new orthodoxies of the Second Renaissance, expresses the dilemma of that critic who wishes to defend the poet's simplicity of language and line (though hardly of rhythm). Thus, in his study of Hughes, Onwuchekwa Jemie attempts to establish the significance of his poetic by attacking what he sees as a necessarily opposing tradition. He denounces, in particular, the "excessive devotion to formal complexity, which characterises the modernist sensibility" and which he sees as being responsible for Hughes's modest reputation, and rejects what he sees as the "elitist, antidemocratic, modernist schoolmen" who respond only to "masses of esoterica and obscure allusions."[18] But since he wants to say that, though simple, Hughes's poetry does not consist of lyrical banalities, he contrasts his work with that of Countee Cullen whose poetry, Jemie tells us, is "self-centred, death obsessed, weak and effeminate in the worst Keatsian tradition."[19] This method of establishing the significance of the black aesthetic by the denunciation of those poets whose social vision is unacceptable, or by a systematic distortion of an opposing tradition, becomes an unfortunate characteristic of much criticism in the Second Renaissance. One way to establish the importance of black culture, it is presumed, is to dismiss white culture as decadent, effete, pseudosophisticated, elitist, and inhumane. Thus, Jemie's assertion that Hughes's "Madame" is preferable to Eliot's "Prufrock" on the dubious grounds that the former "affords the reader a more profound insight into human realities," while the latter, "despite its sonorous phrases," is "devoid of ultimate insight,"[20] says more for the defensive posture of the critic than it does about either Hughes or Eliot. And so Braithwaite ("effete and vacuous") and Cullen ("whines and complains") are at one end of the spectrum, with Langston Hughes ("producing art whose matter and manner were relentlessly rooted in the black folk experience") at the other. Toomer ("married a white woman . . .and disappeared into the great anonymity of the white race"), McKay ("turned his back on the folk rhythms and dialect of his early work"), and Johnson ("despised blues even more than . . .jazz" and reiterated "the 'universal' – 'white' equation"), because of redeeming qualities, occupy the middle ground. And neither did the next generation win a place in Jemie's abbreviated pantheon of black writers, for Melvin Tolson's work was "a compendium of esoteric learning . . .obsessively pedantic, willfully obscure, allusive to the point of lunacy and frivolity,"[21] while Robert Hayden concentrated on expressing his Baha'i faith—a faith, Jemie informs us, alien to the black community, "and since religion is a controlling element in any culture, one can only infer that his over-all attitude to his Afro-American culture is correspondingly negative."[22] Even Gwendolyn Brooks is "academic and mannered," though she is saved in her later work and "must be counted fortunate to have lived long enough and had the strength and humility to participate as creature and creator in the black transformation of the 1960s and 1970s."[23] At times, Jemie reads more like a theologian than a critic, and there are few who shall enter by the narrow gate which he constructs unless they are fortunate enough to be born after World War II and show the proper regard for blackness as defined by the ruling orthodoxy.

Alain Locke said of black writing and black life in the 1920s that it was "finding a new soul" and "a fresh spiritual and cultural focusing." And it is best to regard the period as process rather than as expressing a clearly definable stance. Jemie was at least correct in stressing the range of attitudes, forms, and intent which went to form the First Renaissance. And if experimentation took radical form only with Hughes and Tolson, it was an unprecedented attempt at cultural definition and one whose significance was reflected in the sales of the special issue of *The Survey*, a journal devoted to social problems, which was eventually expanded and republished in book form as *The New Negro*. *The Survey* sold 30,000 copies in two weeks, and another printing was ordered. Yet, little of the poetry in the collection was specifically aimed at a black audience. Of the nine poets represented, six had spent time at university, and, though they did not for the most part produce a particularly academic poetry, neither did they aim at a specific new urban black reader. It was not, like much of the poetry of the Second Renaissance, designed primarily for public performance. There was no ideological norm to which it conformed, and there were no black critics to police such a norm—except a vague conservative desire to see a "positive" image of the Negro projected, a Negro metaphorically clutching Booker T. Washington's key to middle-class white acceptability—the toothbrush. There was no agreed poetic, no acknowledged social and political objective. And, despite the bitter realities of the 1920s, the prevalence (if relative decline) of lynching, and the ironies of black existence in postwar America, there was no sense of an agreed social imperative behind the artistic act which required the poet to conform to the rigors of a militant orthodoxy in the way that would be true four decades later, though bitter poems of protest were produced. Nonetheless, there was a largely unexpressed conviction that race was itself a generator of specific values as well as a product of historically definable experience. It suggested a history, an attitude, a mood, an approach. At the same time, Jemie's comments notwithstanding, the use of the sonnet form by Claude McKay was in itself a forthright reminder of the humane values which, if upheld in art, were systematically abrogated in life; the tension between the thought and the form potentially constituting part of the force of the poem. The poet was not merely using the form, he was taking possession of it for his own cultural purposes, as is made clear in McKay's "If We Must Die" and in "To the White Fiends." McKay was all too aware that he had been born, in the words of his poem, "Outcast," "Under the white man's menace, out of time."[24] His return to time is marked by an acceptance of his own responsibility for his fate, his acceptance that "segregation is not the Whole sin, / The Negroes need salvation from within."[25] And, despite Jemie's casual dismissal, it is in McKay that we find a claim that became familiar in the Second Renaissance and that became a basic tenet of proponants of the black aesthetic. Hence, in "The Negroes Tragedy," he asserts that "only a thorn-crowned Negro and no white can penetrate into the Negro's ken," adding that "what I write is urged out of my blood. / There is no white man who could write my book."[26] Thus, in a conventional sonnet, he announces a limit to the white writer's and white critic's power to possess imaginatively an experience which defies assimilation. The form is familiar; the assertion of cultural distinctiveness and even opacity contradicts the claims implied in that familiarity. And it was James Weldon Johnson who proposed the intensity of race consciousness, defensive in origin but fiercely assertive in consequence, and which was an implication of the more forthright aspects of black independence, when he suggested that if integration failed as a strategy "there will be only one way of salvation for the race that I can see, and that will be through the making of its isolation into a religion and the cultivation of a hard, keen, relentless hatred for everything white."[27] And literature, as he saw it, was at the heart of this process, with a responsibility to destroy distorted images of black life, for "just as these stereotypes were molded and circulated and perpetuated by literary and artistic processes, they must be broken up and replaced by similar means."[28]

And if there was still a timidity about the poetry of these black writers, a sense of the derivative and the precious, this was a criticism which could be applied more widely. Less than a decade earlier, Ezra Pound had queried whether it was possible to teach the American poet that poetry was not "a pentrametric echo of the sociological dogma printed in last year's magazines?" and asked whether there was one of them "that can write natural speech without copying clichés out of every Eighteenth Century poet still in the public libraries."[29] Still, by the time of the First Renaissance, the fruit of the Chicago Renaissance provided an alternative model, though admittedly the decline of the latter coincided with the rise of the former. And there are echoes to be found, principally, though not exclusively, in the work of Langston Hughes. Indeed, he paid tribute to the influence:

> Carl Sandburg's poems
> Fall on the white pages of his books
> Like blood-clots of song
> From the wounds of humanity.
> I know a lover of life sings
> When Carl Sandburg sings.
> I know a lover of all the living
> Sings then."[30]

It is an influence which can be seen even in his most famous poem, "The Negro Speaks of Rivers."

In terms of the history of twentieth-century American poetry, it must be admitted that the First Renaissance amounted to little more than a footnote to the rebellious spirit and neoromantic energy of the first two decades of the century. The sentimentalities of a remote Africa provided a kind of coda to the midwestern nostaglia of Edgar Lee Masters and Carl Sandburg and the occasionally tricksy rhythmic power of Vachel Lindsay. The 1920s were certainly the end of something, as F. Scott Fitzgerald saw so well; but they were also the beginning of something. And, although the eclecticism of Pound and Eliot and that of surrealism was quite capable of recognizing a liberating image in the Negro and a usable ironic commentary in the seriocomic rhythms of jazz, it was to Europe and to the more confident values of the past that they looked for a modernist aesthetic, rather than to the emergent energy of the black poet. The ironies which undercut the lyricism of black poetry were different from those which created the undertow in Eliot and Pound. The black poets inhabited a wasteland all too real. Since disillusionment was for them not a product of the war nor of the newly discovered emptiness of the material world, their poems, for the most part, displayed either an unfashionable social commitment or a lyricism which seemed merely quaint because it was located in a black mythological African past rather than in a white mythological European past. The

First Renaissance, if it was acknowledged at all, was perceived primarily as a social phenomenon, as the emergence of a new urban art by a formerly suppressed group. What was less clear was that a number of these poets, and in particular James Weldon Johnson and Langston Hughes, were laying claim to a tradition which was nonetheless real for being submerged—a tradition of experience, of specific and identifiable rhythms and forms, and of poetry as potentially a communal and public art. Nor is it adequate to dismiss quite so casually those writers like Claude McKay and Countee Cullen who adhered to conventional verse forms for, as I have suggested, there is another tradition in black writing—that of subverting the familiar, commenting upon the implications of literary form—which is equally supportive of individual and cultural dignity.

The 1930s marked an abrupt end to the First Renaissance and a shift in literary strategy. The old order was aging. In December 1934, Rudolph Fisher and Wallace Thurman died; while James Weldon Johnson published no poetry and died in 1938. As James Young points out in *Black Writers of the Thirties*,[31] black writers produced less than one volume of poetry a year between 1929 and 1942. Claude McKay and Arna Bontemps were supported by the Federal Writers Project, and Langston Hughes turned largely to prose, giving poetry readings as a way of remaining financially solvent and publishing only three pamphlets of poetry throughout the decade. And the exigencies of economic collapse bred an inevitable shift in emphasis as the black man was seen as simply one example of exploitation. Cullen's observation that

> never shall the clan
> Confine my singing to its ways
> Beyond the ways of man.
>
> No racial option narrows grief,
> Pain is no patriot[32]

was increasingly reflected by other poets in a more directly political form.

Yet, he did not wholly ignore the racial situation. In ''The Black Christ,'' he drew a parallel between the sufferings of Christ and those of the Negro (see also Langston Hughes's ''Christ in Alabama''), and together with others he responded bitterly to the Scottsboro case, directing a poem at his fellow American poets (''Scottsboro, Too, Is Worth Its Song,'' 1935):

> Remembering their sharp and pretty
> Tunes for Sacco and Vanzetti,
> I said:
> Here too's a cause divinely spun
> For those whose eyes are on the sun,

Here in epitome
Is all disgrace
And epic wrong,
Like wine to brace
The ministrel heart, and blare it into song

Surely I said,
Now will the poets sing.
      But they have raised no cry.
      I wonder why.[33]

The bathetic ending was not atypical of Cullen's poetry. He was also a little late in his appeal since in 1932 Langston Hughes had produced *Scottsboro Limited*, a pamphlet containing some poems and a verse play. And Scottsboro was, of course, the focus for the Party's attempt to woo the Negro. Falsely accused of rape, nine Negro boys found themselves the victims of a southern justice intent on playing out its myths irrespective of reality. Recognizing the significance of the case, the Party entered into an unedifying struggle with the NAACP for the right to defend the boys who became the focus for a worldwide campaign. It was a shrewd move designed to show the way in which black suffering could be linked to that of the oppressed throughout the world. It is hardly surprising that black writers should have responded to such a move or that the imagery of human unity should prove so appealing.

Langston Hughes's 1936 "Union" expressed the classic conviction of the period:

Not me alone
I know now—
But all the whole oppressed
Poor world
White and black
Must put their hands with mine
To shake the pillars of their temples
Wherein the false gods dwell.[34]

And in 1934 the young Richard Wright submitted his poem "I have Seen Black Hands" to the *New Masses*, which published this work by an unknown black writer less because of its intrinsic value, as Joseph North has remarked, than because they wished to encourage him.

I am black and have seen black hands
Raised in fists of revolt, side by side with the
      white fists of white workers,
And some day—and it is only this which sustains me

Some day there shall be millions and millions of them
On some red day in a burst of fists on a new horizon![35]

But this was not a shift to the mainstream—the mainstream was, anyway, not on the barricades. Nor was it a wholesale rejection of the cultural identity so recently staked out, though it did imply a more fiercely social deployment of that identity and a suspension of that individuality which Hughes had seen as an essential protection against American conformity. It was a period which seemed to invite a class, rather than a racial, analysis, or rather one which tended to regard race as synonymous with class (not without some justification, given the realities of the day). It was a period which consequently regarded too great an insistence on the individual sensibility as politically inopportune and inexcusably bourgeois. It was ironic that no sooner did the black writer aspire to the status of bourgeois artist than this status came to be regarded with contempt. But the racial component of that individuality was not wholly surrendered, and to Hughes this had been the essence of the individualism which he valued. It was a matter of a coincidence of interests. The black and white hands which consititued such a familiar image of interracial cooperation remained black and white, but those terms tended to lose the subtlety which they had had in the previous decade, or, rather, blackness now acquired the same simplified contours which had been ascribed by the First Renaissance to whiteness. It now stood for suffering, poverty, and heroism; it was a badge which of itself established solidarity with the poor white, for what else could black represent in a period of mass unemployment than a deprivation raised by a new sense of cultural identity to an image of resistance. Sometimes, however, the interracial cooperation is offered as such a brief coda to a catalog of white violence enacted on the black body, as in Langston Hughes's verse play *Don't You Want to Be Free* (1938), that the new alliance fails to carry complete conviction, and the writer who had inveighed against a nonracial art in the crucial essay "The Negro Artist and the Racial Mountain" (1926) predominates over the servant of the proletarian cause.

But the play, which utilizes the racially based poems from his earlier collections *The Weary Blues* (1926) and *The Dream Keeper*, nonetheless moves towards a conventional 1930s climax:

> Oh, who wants to come and join hands with me?
> Who wants to make one great unity?
> Who wants to say, no more black or white?
> Then let's get together, folks,
> And fight, fight, fight![36]

Yet, for all his insistence on group solidarity, Hughes did not join the Party. And in his account of his tour of Russia in 1931 and 1932, which is included in the second volume of his autobiography, *I Wonder as I Wander* (1956), he recalls a conversation with Arthur Koestler in which he explains that he had not joined because "the Party . . .was based on strict discipline and the acceptance of directives that I, as a writer, did not wish to accept. I did not believe political directives could be successfully applied to creative writing. They might well apply to the preparation of tracts and pamphlets, yes, but not to poetry or fiction, which to be valid, I felt, had to express as truthfully as possible the *individual* emotions and reactions of the writer, rather than mass directives issued to achieve practical and often temporary political objectives'' (page 122). It was a familiar dilemma, certainly one shared by Richard Wright. The problem was to negotiate a synthesis from this determined individualism, from an insistent racial consciousness, and from the new commitment to class solidarity. (Wright's attempts in this direction were described in Chapter 1.) But the subtlety and, it must be said, the contradictions of his essay ''A Blueprint for Negro Writing'' were not, for the most part, reflected in his poetry, which showed little of the anguished debate between competing ideologies which one finds in his prose.

The 1940s were a different world. Their tone was in some ways set by Robert Hayden, whose first book of poetry appeared in 1940. Despite his authorship of some conventional committed poetry, a product of the previous decade, his new stance of social and aesthetic detachment was a natural reaction against that decade and seemed to mark, in some senses, an extreme perimeter to Negro art in the following decades. He declared that he was ''opposed to the chauvinistic and the doctrinaire,'' that he saw ''no reason why a Negro poet should be limited to 'racial utterance' or to having his writing judged by standards different from those applied to the work of other poets.''[37] And, although he wrote this in 1967 when the claims of an alternative tradition were immediate and real, it was an accurate description of his attitude and of a desire to escape what was increasingly seen as a literary parochialism. Certainly his poems were articulate and skilled, and they revealed an engagement with those developments in American poetry which had gone largely unremarked by the black writer.

At the other extreme, apparently, was Margaret Walker who, in her 1942 volume *For My People*, had called for a second generation to arise, a generation which would write its own martial songs. The reality of black writing in the 1940s and 1950s lay somewhere in the middle. For most black writers, as for most blacks, there was no escaping the fact of color which had been charged with significance by the dominant white society and subsequently by their own experience. At the same time, the mere fact of color was, of course, no guarantee of poetic force. As Gwendolyn Brooks herself said:

> Every Negro poet has ''something to say.'' Simply because he
> is a Negro, he cannot escape having important things to say.
> His mere body for that matter, is an eloquence. His
> quiet walk down the street is a speech to the people.
> Is a rebuke, is a plea, is a school.

> But no real artist is going to be content with offering raw
>   materials. The Negro poet's most urgent duty, at present,
>   is to polish his technique, his way of presenting truths
>   and his beauties, that these may be more insinuating and,
>   therefore, more overwhelming.[38]

For Margaret Butcher, who in 1956 edited the papers of Alain Locke into the book entitled *The Negro in American Culture*, this view symbolized "what must be the objective of Negro poets: to be basically poets, American poets, who at the proper time, and in a proper way can be Negro poets, spokesmen for their innermost experiences."[39] Exactly what she meant by "the proper time" and "in a proper way" is not clear, but the comment is very much in keeping with the spirit of a period in which Allen Tate could hail the publications of Melvin Tolson's "Libretto for the Republic of Liberia" in the July 1951 edition of *Poetry* magazine by remarking that Negroes should "not limit themselves to provincial mediocrity in which one's feelings about one's difficulties become more important than poetry itself."[40]

Such a comment by a white southern writer or, indeed, by anyone else would not have been possible in the mid-1960s, and his suggestion that the above assumption had made "Mr. Tolson not less but more intensely Negro in his apprehension of the world" would have been received as the piece of racial affrontery which perhaps it is. Certainly William Styron's incautious claim to inhabit the black sensibility brought him up against a group of blacks less willing to place aesthetic considerations before social ones, no matter how dubious some of their arguments may in fact have been from an historical and aesthetic point of view.

As late as 1963, Herbert Hill could say that "the greater part of contemporary American Negro writing is characterised by a determination to break through the limits of racial parochialism into the whole range of the modern writer's preoccupations," using "the concepts of 'Negro' and 'race' as universal symbols in a new concern with the problems of individual consciousness."[41] If this was in part an accurate enough observation, his language was dangerously ambiguous, while he failed to address himself to the central question of how race—which in America had been defined precisely as that which is unassimilable within any conception of universality which addresses itself to ideals of common humanity and shared experience—was to be utilized as a symbol of that universality without raising issues destructive of the smooth transcendence of a parochialism never chosen but imposed. And his remark that "self-pity and dreary rage are clearly no longer enough"[42] implied both an inaccurate perception of twentieth-century black writing and a social insensitivity surprising from someone on the executive board of the NAACP.

It remains true, however, that, while in the 1930s the articulation of suffering and the strident announcement of a newly discovered faith were seen as the essence of a modern art, the 1940s and 1950s constituted a reconsideration, a period of consolidation. Robert Hayden and Gwendolyn Brooks were aware of American poetic tradition and experiment to a greater degree than those who had preceded them.

In college, Hayden had admired Countee Cullen and had even written a long poem on Africa in imitation of Cullen's "Heritage." He had read widely in the works of Jean Toomer and Langston Hughes, but also in that of Edna St. Vincent Millay, Hart Crane, and Carl Sandburg. In graduate school, he worked under W. H. Auden. When he did set himself the task of addressing himself to his racial past, it was, perhaps paradoxically, as a result of reading the passage in Stephen Vincent Beneét's poem, "John Brown's Body," in which the author had confessed that he could not sing of "the black spear" and that this would await another poet. Hayden hoped to be that poet and planned a long work dealing with slavery and the Civil War. He hoped to "correct the false impressions of our past, to reveal something of its heroic and human aspects."[43] He wrote "Middle Passage" in the 1940s, but never completed the project. Yet, the fragment which he did complete is a subtle work whose ironies emerge from a shifting persona—a dramatic dialogue with the American past conducted in the voices of the ships' logs, court records, and reminiscences interpolated with brief echoes from the religious pieties with which the slavers, like America itself, had sought to protect themselves from the moral implications of their actions. The names of the ships ("Jesus Estrella," "Espiranza," "Mercy"), the detailed depositions about the persistent lust and murders aboard, and the apparently ineluctable connection between slavery and American wealth and independence create enfolding ironies which provide the tone and purpose of a poem whose strengths lie in his subtle combination of a language which is by turns self-revealing in its hypocricies, as the American voice seeks to justify its past, and lyrical, as it expands that past to mythic dimensions. Hence, the prayer of the pious capitalists

> We pray that Thou wilt grant, O Lord
> safe passage to our vessels bringing
> heathen souls unto Thy chastening.
> Jesus Saviour.[44]

is contrasted with the blood and excrement below the decks, the reality below the surface on ships that

> plough through thrashing glister toward
> fata morgana's lucent melting shore,
> weave toward New World littorals that are
> mirage and myth and actual shore.
>
> Voyage through death,
>   voyage whose chartings are unlove.[45]

The lyricism is ambiguous. It contains the elements of both mythology and demythology at the same time—the language straining to cut itself adrift from the realities which pull it back to human suffering, but also locating that suffering against a wider sense of betrayal which would see this failure of humanity as part of a more general collapse of idealism.

Hayden is not without his commitments, as poems like "Runagate, Runagate," "The Ballad of Nat Turner," and the anti-Vietnam War poem "In the Mourning Time" make clear. But he is also aware of the competing orthodoxies which could deprive him of his personal voice. In "A Ballad of Remembrance," which appeared in his 1966 collection *Selected Poems*, he identified the nature of these orthodoxies:

> Accommodate, muttered the Zulu king,
> toad on a throne of glaucous poison jewels.
> Love, chimed the saints and the angels and the mermaids.
> Hate, shrieked the gun-metal priestess
> from her spiked bellcollar curved like a fleur-de-lis.![46]

But there were other compulsions and aesthetic imperatives which create the tension from which a personal voice can emerge. As he has said in an interview, "I object to strict definitions of what a poet is or should be, because they usually are thought up by people with an axe to grind—by those who care less about poetry than they do about some cause." Like Langston Hughes, he felt menaced by the anonymity of the times, but resisted regimentation as a solution, the idea that "in order to be free, you must submit to tyranny, to ideological slavery."[47] And since his definition of the role of the poet involved the need to "affirm the humane, the universal, the potentially divine in the human creature," it was likely that he would find himself opposed to a tendency, or what he called "almost a conspiracy," to "delimit poets, to restrict them to the political and the socially or racially conscious."[48] So that in 1969, when Hoyt Fuller asked him whether he saw any future at all for the school of black writers then seeking to establish a black aesthetic, his reply was predictable: "It seems to me that a 'black aesthetic' would only be possible in a predominantly black culture. Yet not even black African writers subscribe to such as aesthetic. And isn't the so-called 'black aesthetic' simply protest and racist propaganda in a new guise."[49] The tenor of his reply was a measure of the stridency of the demands then being made, for, as ever, the irony was that any definition of a black aesthetic had to take account of the achievement of a writer like Hayden whose accomplishment as a poet arises from his fusion of his identity as black and as American and whose skill is not unconnected with his ability to bring those traditions together, throwing American history into a sharp relief achieved by the successful dramatization of that clash. The sparks struck by such a collision are not irrelevant to the task of defining the nature of black creativity and its special contribution to literary development.

His own Baha'i faith led him to a belief in the unity of mankind, a unity which would ultimately be achieved by love—a force which, like Baldwin, he is anxious to distinguish from sentimentality. And though he recognizes the existence and power of injustice, violence, and suffering, his work tends to be an affirmation of human potential. He is what he himself has called a "romantic realist." Much of his poetry is written in the present tense, which is an insistence both on the mediating presence of the poet and the immediacy and relevance of the experience itself. It is an implicit claim to relevance which is not without justification.

Gwendolyn Brooks is aware that, in the words of her 1967 poem "The Chicago Picasso," "Art hurts. Art urges voyages."[50] The voyages are partly aesthetic experiments with language and form, attempts to find verbal and symbolic equivalents for experience; and partly they constitute internal journeys, dangerous encounters with the self. The racial element of her poetry was, she asserted, "organic, not imposed," for she saw it as her function to "present Negroes not as curios but as people" while vivifying "the universal fact."[51] She was aware, both in the form of her poetry, whose metrics derived from folk ballad and contemporary experimentalism alike, and in its subjects that she was heir to a double tradition. But she was also aware of the social and experimental prohibitions which deny access to that tradition for many of those whom she took as her subjects.

In her first volume of poetry, *A Street in Bronzeville* (1945), she celebrates that double tradition, but also expresses her sense of the distance between its opposing poles, a distance which is rooted in the nature of daily life. In "The Sundays of Satin-Legs Smith," she describes the simple, uncomplicated life of a man who inhabits the narrow world of proximate experience, unconcerned at the restrictive boundaries defined by remote and largely unfelt forces. His life expressed its meaning on the surface; his apprehensions are those shaped by a past of which he remains largely unaware, for

> Down these same avenues
> Comes no Saint-Saens, no piquant elusive Grieg,
> And not Tchaikovsky's wayward eloquence
> And not the shapely tender drift of Brahms.
> But could he love them? Since a man must bring
> To music what his mother spanked him for
> When he was two: bits of forgotten hate,
> Devotion: whether or not his mattress hurts:
> The little dream his father humored: the thing
> His sister did for money . . .
>
> . . .The pasts of his ancestors lean against
> Him.   Crowd him.   Fog out his identity.[52]

And yet the war had pulled the Negro into that wider world. Sanctions were momentarily relaxed and democracy was invoked as a principle worth defending abroad if not enacting at home. And interspersed with the lyricism and the subtle ironies with which she celebrates black ghetto life and as a corollary of the domestic pain and loss which she identifies in poems like "The Mother" and "De Witt Williams on His Way to Lincoln Cemetary," are ironic poems like "Negro Hero" and "Gay Chaps at the Bar," which address a hypocrisy highlighted, but not created, by the war. This was a period, after all, when the first cracks began to appear in the edifice of segregation, but experience had taught that things could move in either direction. This series of what she called "Soldier Sonnets" was written in an "off rhyme" which is itself an expression of the disjunction between the ideals for which black men fought and the realities which had determined their lives. And so the Negro hero asks himself:

> Still—am I good enough to die for them, is my blood bright
> enough to be spilled,
> Was my constant question—are they clear
> On this?   Or do I intrude even now?

The horror remains that once the war is concluded

> . . .they might prefer the
> Preservation of their law in all its sick dignity and their
> knives
> To the continuation of their creed
> And their lives.[53]

It was her second book, *Annie Allen* (1949), however, which really established her reputation, and in 1950 she became the first Negro ever to win the Pulitzer Prize for poetry. Despite the curious conditions of that prize, there was no sense in which she abandoned the continuing subtext of her work; and, indeed, in "The Womanhood," she debated with herself the function of poetry for a writer drawn to lyric celebration but constantly alive to a social reality which denies such lyricism. Just as a mother assumes a responsibility not felt by those without children, a responsibility which is simultaneously a grace and a burden, so the poet, who speaks as a representative of oppressed people and as the voice of those whose experiences she unavoidably shares, accepts a similar joy and curse. The questions are: which truth should be dramatized, does the reality of pain preclude the possibility of beauty? This is a metaphysical problem experienced as a social reality by that writer who recognizes, not only the "malocclusions, the inconditions of love,"[54] but also the pressing truths of poverty and prejudice. The result is a compromise, an order of priorities, which places the need for social transformation before the need for consonance. It was an indication of the direction her thoughts were taking and a conviction which she felt with increasing force in the following decade. She advises herself to "Fight fight. Then fiddle."

> . . .carry hate
> In front of you and harmony behind.
> Be deaf to music and to beauty blind.
> Win war. Rise bloody, maybe not too late
> For having first to civilize a space
> Wherein to lay your violin with grace.[55]

And the effort to do just that—to civilize a society to the point at which it could conceive of the moral as well as the superficial force of beauty—was the main social project of the 1950s and lay at the heart of her 1960 collection *The Bean Eaters*. The civil rights movement, however, created its own compulsions. But though these were felt to reveal a more socially-conscious poet than the earlier volumes, this view was simply a consequence of a failure to perceive the social thrust of works whose lyricism was offered more as ironic commentary than as absolute value. Indeed, "The Chicago Defender Sends a Man to Little Rock: Fall, 1957" is written less out of a bitter revulsion than a baffled encounter with the paradox of people whose lives respond to the common rhythms of hope and despair but who make room in those lives for an illogical and implacable hatred. Likewise, "The Last Quatrain of the Ballad of Emmet Till" is remarkable more for its restraint than for its intensity, while the verse form itself offers a conscious bathos rather than the crescendo of feeling that the theme would seem to suggest.

But the pressures of the 1960s did exert a continuing strong pull on Gwendolyn Brooks. In an interview conducted in 1969, she was confronted with her earlier remarks, quoted above, that the "Negro poet's most urgent duty, at present, is to polish his technique . . . ," a comment made originally in 1950, and she said, "I still do feel that a poet has a duty to words, and that words can do wonderful things, and it's too bad to just let them lie there without doing anything with and for them. But something different is happening now."[56] Jemie's earlier comments notwithstanding, her change lay less in any radical revision of her own poetic than in her energetic defense of the stance adopted by other writers. She was fully aware that "black poets today . . .are interested in speaking to black people" and felt that "there is also a brief to be put forward for those who are just very much excited about what is going on today and are determined to get that rich life and urgency down on paper."[57] And she was to say that she did not think "we can turn our backs on those people and say airily, 'That is not good poetry' because for one thing the whole concept of what 'good poetry' is is changing today."[58] But at the same time, she sees this as a temporary phenomenon and looks forward to the time when her comments of twenty years before will again become appropriate.

The poems included in her 1968 collection *In the Mecca*, like those in *Riot* (1969), express a changed reality but no less a commitment to a rigorous aesthetic. While quoting approvingly Ron Karenga's observation that "the fact that we are black is our ultimate reality," blackness did not, to her, require simplification of language, symbol, or of moral perception. It meant, as it always had, an engagement with the black experience refracted through a personal sensibility which recognized, but did not embody, the functional simplifications of the purely didactic writer. She was, she insisted, not a polemical poet. Her shift in emphasis was a consequence of a changed social scene. As she confessed, "Many things that I'm seeing now I was absolutely blind to before."[59] And one reality was the possibility of communicating directly to those in the black community whom she had earlier described as severed from cultural concerns. Together with a group of young black poets, she attended an impromptu reading in a Chicago bar. It suggested a new direction, and she confessed that "there *is* something different that I want to do. I want to write poems that will be non-compromising. I don't want to stop a concern with words doing good jobs, which had always been a concern of mine, but I want to write poems that will be meaningful to those people . . .things that will touch them. . . .I want to write poetry—and it won't be Ezra Pound poetry, as you can imagine—that will be exciting to such people. And I don't see why it can't be 'good' poetry."[60] Yet she was still equivocal, insisting in the same interview that "I am not writing poems with the idea that they are to become social forces. I don't feel that I care to direct myself in that way."[61] But by example, she became, in herself, a social force. Hence, the "poet laureate" of Illinois became, in her fifties, the inspiration for a number of young black poets, running her own writers' workshop and sponsoring poetry prizes.

But if her poetry inevitably shows the imprint of the changed self-perception of the black American, it is still true to say that her early work shows an equal understanding of the peculiar pressures which are at work on the black writer. And if her more recent work has revealed a desire to speak more directly to the black audience, she has chosen a dialogue which still balances ironies against certainties and avoids a cabalistic recitation of social evils and too definitive an attribution of vices and virtues. Her concern remains what it has always been—to dramatize the experience of the black community, to articulate her own and that community's changing perceptions of that experience. That she should come to see a connection between the transformations of her poetry and those of society was scarcely surprising, that she does not offer that poetry as an agent of transformation, but rather as a committed commentary, is what distinguishes her from many of those younger poets whom she inspired and

whose other model was likely to be that paradigm of black cultural independence and revolutionary nationalism—LeRoi Jones.

LeRoi Jones did not respond immediately to the stirrings of black political
activism in the 1950s. The poems which appear in his first collection, *Preface
to a Twenty-Volume Suicide Note*, were written between 1957 and 1960 and
bear the impress of influences other than those of a stirring social world or of a
black literary tradition. Indeed, the shaping influences on these early poems
are, as he explained in an interview conducted in 1960, the surrealism of
Lorca, which itself helped to neutralize an earlier influence by Eliot, and the
work of William Carlos Williams, Robert Creeley, and Charles Olson. He saw
the abandonment of Eliot as a necessay break with academicism in poetry. The
tradition he wished to identify with, and the one he saw as restoring American
poetry to the mainstream of modern verse, was that of twentieth-century
modernism, just as he saw the prose writing of Jack Kerouac, Hubert Selby,
Jr., and Edward Dorn as a demotic modernism. From Williams he learned
"mostly how to write in my own language—how to write the way I *speak* . . .to
write just the way it comes to me, in my own speech, utilizing the rhythms of
speech rather than any kind of metrical concept. . . .From Pound, the same
concept that went into the Imagist's [sic] poetry—the idea of the image and
what an image ought to be. I learned, probably, about verse from Pound—how
a poem should be made, what a poem ought to *look* like. . . .And from Williams
how to get it out in my own language."[62] From Olson he derived the connection between line length and breathing. In his magazines, *Yugen*, edited with
his wife, Hettie Cohen, and *The Floating Bear*, edited with Diane DiPrima, he
published mostly the work of the Beats, together with the San Francisco poets
and those who had been at Black Mountain College.

Despite his concern for a modernist engagement with the process of writing,
with writing as subject as well as process, he was equally concerned that the
new poetry and prose should exist as social reality—that it should be both an
expression and an essential part of a social dynamic. At the time this did not
imply a polemical literature, but one which, in its language and in its social
presumptions, was not simply detached, ironic, autonomous. By "social" he
seems to have meant primarily a linguistic and intellectual consonance between art and public activity, rather than a direct response to political change.
Hence, the Beats both articulated and were part of that sense of disaffiliation
which seemed to typify a generation of Americans in the 1950s.

At the same time, it seems curious that Little Rock and the beginning of the
civil rights movement should have had such little effect on his work. And,
indeed, it is one of the minor ironies of the Beats that their dismissal of the
established political and social machine should have extended to those who
sought most actively to alter it. Rebellion was to be metaphysical not actual;

alienation was a spiritual condition not a business of actual deprivation (witness Kerouac's naive distortions of Negro life which he could perceive only in terms of the emotional and sensual release which he himself pursued through the ghetto streets of Denver and on into Mexico).

Jones's was a decidedly urban setting, and the world to which he related was primarily that of the literary avant-garde. Indeed, in the 1960 interview, he suggested that he did not in fact know many Negroes—a sense of detachment from racial origins which he later suggested he had exaggerated. His wife was white, and his immediate milieu was that of Greenwich Village. The political world was tangential. And yet, insofar as he defined the poetic landscape, in Olson's sense, as what the poet sees from where he is standing, there was a level on which his racial background was bound to inform his work. And, three years later, Olson's phrase had indeed become the basis for an avowedly political stance. In a violent denunciation of James Baldwin in *Kulchur* magazine, he insisted that "it is deadly simple. A writer must have a point of view, or he cannot be a good writer. He must be standing somewhere in the world, or else he is not one of us, and his commentary is of little value."[63] The bitterness of the assault was, at least in part, an indictment of his own former sense of uninvolvment; his accusation that Baldwin had wished to live free of the fact of racial struggle was an expression of his own sense of guilt at having done precisely the same thing. In 1960, however, his sense of racial identity was more general. Hence, he accepted that it was an unavoidable influence and that it gave him access to a special experience denied to others. But that provided only an unvoiced tone and context for his work in contrast to the poetry of Langston Hughes for whom it was subject. The fact of his racial identity was something he "would deal with . . .when it has to do directly with a poem and not as a kind of broad generalization that doesn't have much to do with a lot of young writers today who are Negroes."[64] Indeed, he implied that the inferior quality of much black writing had been a consequence of its sociological bias. Only one poem in his first collection directly addressed the question of his racial identity. In "Notes for a Speech," he expressed his sense of remoteness both from emergent Africa and from his fellow Negroes in America, to whom he is related by color and by his sense of alienation but from whom he is divided by circumstance and vocation.

> African blues
> does not know me.   Their steps, in sands
> of their own
> land.   A country
> in black and white, newspapers
> blown down pavements
> of the world.   Does
> not feel
> What I am . . .

```
    . . .they conduct
    their deaths apart
    from my own.   Those
    heads, I call
    my "people."⁶⁵
```

Yet the pressure of his black experience comes through. It is there in "The Screamers," an early story in which his ironic observation of a dance hall threatens to devolve into a legitimization of racial battle. The story appeared, however, in a collection of prose pieces which he edited under the title *The Moderns*; he was the only black author among fourteen.

The transformation of LeRoi Jones into Amiri Baraka, a black committed poet and political activist, was gradual, but traces of his development are there to be seen. When President Kennedy was assassinated, he wrote a poem which was literally pasted into the winter edition of *Kulchur* magazine, of which he was music editor. While this acknowledged a belief in the integrity of Kennedy and the reality of the hopes inspired by his presidency which he would later have disavowed, there is a strong sense in the poem of an historical caesura which provides something of a rationale for his own determined separatist mentality in later years. For the future which he sees is hopelessly compromised:

> From now on we will sit in nightclubs with jewish millionaires
> listening to the maudlin political verse of a money narcissist.
>
> And this will be the payback for our desires.
> For history, like the ringing coin
>
> that will not bend
> when we bite it.⁶⁶

The collection of poems published the following year, *The Dead Lecturer*, expressed the same growing concern with his cultural identity. In "Green Lantern's Solo," he asked

> . . .What man removed from his meat's source, can
>   continue
> to believe totally in himself?⁶⁷

Though most of them show a continuation of the concerns and forms to be found in his first volume, now he dedicates one poem to Robert Williams, with whom he had traveled to Cuba and who had been forced to flee the country. In this he protests the

>   . . .deadly idiot
>   of compromise
>   who shrieks compassion, and bids me love my neighbor. Even
>   beyond the meaning
>   Of such acts as would give all my father's dead ash to fertilize
>   their bilious
>   land.[68]

and asserts that

>   I am deaf and blind and lost and will not again sing your quiet
>   verse.   I have lost
>   even the act of poetry.[69]

Indeed, one poem, ''Black Dada Nihilismus,'' anticipates the commited black poetry which followed the publication of this volume. But, amidst the apocalyptic imagery of black murder and rape, there is a last plea, an equivalent of the hesitation implied in his powerful play of black revolt, *The Slave*, which also appeared in 1964. For the final stanza prays:

>   May a lost god damballah, rest or save us
>   against the murders we intend
>   against his lost white children
>   black dada nihilismus[70]

When the change came, when he left his wife and white friends and fellow writers and moved from the Village to Harlem, discovering, as he felt, the full meaning and potential of his blackness and shaping it into a lesson for others, the revulsion which he felt for his own past was so sharp that it was expressed in a corruscating language designed to burn out his past equivocations and exorcise what now seemed to him his defection from responsibility. In ''For Tom Postell, dead black poet,'' he confessed:

>   You told me, you told me
>   a thousand years ago. And the white man thing
>   you screamed on me, all true . . .
>
>   . . .You
>   screamed and slobbered on me, to hear you. And I
>   didn't. Shacked up with a fat jew girl. Talking about
>   Shakespeare. I didn't hear
>   you brother . . .
>
>   . . .I laughed among the beasts
>   and meateaters. I strode with them, played with them,
>   thought myself
>   one with them, the jews were talking through
>   my mouth.[71]

Just as in *The Slave* where, symbolically, he kills his white wife and his two children (the persistence of their screams at the end suggesting that even symbolically this is a necessity which he cannot realize), so, here, he reviles his own treachery in a language so absolute as to lay any remaining ghosts of a personal or cultural affection at odds with the responsibility laid upon him by history and the daily catalog of brutalities. Nor was it enough simply to identify a new direction for his art. It became obligatory to attack the tradition within which he had worked—''the poetry of straightup Christian White America.''[72] And, while recognizing that writers like Richard Wilbur and Allen Ginsberg were not simply agents for and expressions of the establishment, he felt that they were still unavoidably ''meaning-horns for the inch of filth they represent.'' His assertion that he did ''not mean this derogatorily'' hardly carries conviction, as he tenders another metaphor with even more dubious implications. They are, he suggests, ''tied end to end a string of rats, all the way down the line.''[73] And yet the poetry remains true insofar as it, like the work of Burroughs and Beckett, constitutes an apocalyptic vision, a confession that white culture and civilization is intellectual, is cut off from feeling and spirit and from a revivifying energy, is exhausted and on the point of collapse. He felt the best glimpsed the need for an art deriving from intuition and passion, but were encysted in a culture which denied it. Only the black, removed now from the demeaning and destructive context of an alien tradition (Jones himself had been the only black poet in an anthology of postwar American poetry), was in touch with a sense of a transcendent spirit, an animating rhythm deriving from the circumstances of his life and from a tradition waiting to be reclaimed by those who had liberated themselves from the demeaning self-images and constricting cultural presumptions of a dominant white America.

LeRoi Jones was not the only pioneer of a Black Arts movement, but he did become its moving spirit and chief exemplar. The Black Arts Repertory Theatre in Harlem flourished only for a brief time and was essentially a small-scale venture. But, partly because of the high-level reaction which it provoked, it acquired a symbolic significance. It attracted Ed Bullins, who later founded Black Arts West in San Francisco, while he himself moved back to New Jersey where he had been born and established Spirit House in Newark. For Jones, the Black Arts Repertory Theatre was an expression of his growing conviction that ethics and aesthetics are inseparable; and, though both *Dutchman* and *The Slave* offer oblique and even ambiguous responses to a public role which he still feels contradictory of the artistic impulse, there was no doubting the drive towards a new commitment. He was all too aware that articulateness can constitute an evasion—can, indeed, ally the victim with his oppressor—and that the tradition of writing to which he responded drew on the energy released by irony, ambiguity, and a suspicion of the unqualified act. So that it was perhaps less the plays that his theatre produced which generated a growing absolutism than it was the fact of its existence—a black theatre producing plays for blacks.

But in 1965, he also produced the first of his revolutionary plays, *Experimental Death Unit #1*, and, in the following year, he outlined his ideas on revolutionary theatre in a way which made clear enough the direction his art would take, in a language whose excesses were a conscious element in a strategy involving the simultaneous creation of new black myths and the demythologizing of white language, values, and symbols. The revolutionary theatre was to force changes, it was to ''EXPOSE! Show up the insides of these humans, look into black skulls. White men,'' he announced, ''will cower before this theatre because it hates them. . . .It must Accuse and Attack because it is a theatre of Victims.'' It must ''show the missionaries and wiggly Liberals dying under blasts of concrete. . . .It is a political theatre, a weapon to help in the slaughter of these dim-witted fatbellied white guys who somehow believe that the rest of the world is here for them to slobber on. . . .And what we show must cause the blood to rush, so that pre-revolutionary temperaments will be bathed in this blood, and it will cause their deepest soul to move.''[74]

It was an essay still not wholly drained of his earlier commitments. He still expressed the Beats' suspicion of technology, their commitment to restoring the spirit and the sensibility to a central position; he still conveyed a surrealist's conviction about the centrality of the imagination as a primary transforming mechanism, ''a profound vector from the soul.''[75] Yet it was clearly the announcement of a new aesthetic, and he was all too aware that the response to the mythic heroes and villains which he created, to the assault on the black and white psyche which he initiated, though seeking its justification in social experience, would indeed be based on aesthetic grounds—a response which he necessarily holds to be not only irrelevant but hostile. It was an accurate prediction and indicates clearly enough his awareness of the aesthetic implications of an art in which the form was to be dictated by social and cultural necessities other than those which constrained the art of the white American writer, and whose heroes would no longer be the free spirit confronting American nature or the urban wastelands of the psyche, but ''Crazy Horse, Denmark Vesey, Patrice Lumumba, and not history, not memory, not sad sentimental groping for a worth in our despair.'' These, he added, ''will be new men, new heroes, and their enemies most of you who are reading this.''[76]

His emphasis on victims was not intended to suggest that he was intent on creating a simple literary pathology. On the contrary, the sole purpose and justification of the art which he proposed was to alert the black individual to the reality of his situation in order to provoke a response, to stimulate an assertion of cultural independence. Yet, buried in his language was an ambiguity which he himself came to recognize a decade later. For, in calling for ''actual explosions and actual brutality,''[77] he was in danger of destroying the distinction between metaphor and reality without proposing an ideological framework in which that problem could be resolved and language could discover a correlative in action. In a curious sense, the judge who later read one of his poems into the court record as evidence against him was applying a literal interpretation which Jones himself could not wholly deny. This, indeed, was a chief deficiency of the Black Arts movement which, for the most part, failed to address itself to the fundamental economic and political realities which were the cause of cultural alienation. It was an art which contented itself with tackling the symptoms rather than the disease, with projecting images of a revolt and of a cultural autonomy which could never be wholly convincing when located against the implacable realities within which they were deployed. To an extent, they even relied on the agencies of that system to propagate their views, the majority of black drama and poetry anthologies being issued through white publishers for whom black cultural invective represented a good return on the dollar.

But such ironies were unavoidable and should not diminish the significance of the Black Arts movement which dominated the remainder of the decade. It is possible, after all, for a body to harbor the agents of its own destruction or transformation, and the alteration of black consciousness was a necessary prelude to revolt. This was a conviction which Jones shared with Malcolm X, and his poem marking the assassination of that leader stressed the need for spiritual transformation, making Malcolm the first of a new line of heroes:

> For all of him, and all of yourself, look up,
> black man, quit stuttering and shuffling, look up,
> black man, quit whining and stooping, for all of him.
> For Great Malcolm a prince of the earth, let nothing in us rest
> until we avenge ourselves for his death.[78]

Inevitably, his commitment to a new socially directed art created its own compulsions. In particular, if he were to address himself directly to the black masses, he, like Gwendolyn Brooks, realized that it was necesary to

> say it straight to be
> understood straight, put it flat and real
> in the street . . .
> say what you mean, dig
> it out and put it down, and be strong
> about it.[79]

It was not an injunction which he was always to follow, but he was clear that poetry was to become both an expression of the "live words of the hip world live flesh and/coursing blood" and a weapon, "poems that kill/Assassin poems, Poems that shoot/guns."[80] At this stage he saw no room for a lyricism which might emerge from that live world. In a revolutionary situation, the softer impulses had to be denied, a truth of revolutionary art which Brecht had likewise noted and which Jones insisted upon:

> Let there be no love poems written
> until love can exist freely and
> cleanly . . .[81]

Yet, at some future time, another kind of literature could become possible, and, in ''Three Modes of History & Culture,'' he confessed that he thought

> . . .about a time when I will be relaxed.
> When flames and non-specific passion wear themselves
> away. And my eyes and hands and mind can turn
> and soften, and my songs will be softer
> and lightly weight the air.[82]

And, indeed, the simple repetition of evils, the vilification of whites, the deliberate destruction of language, and the decreative acts of abdication and revulsion were not infinitely repeatable. It was clearly not enough to create a poetry wholly out of denial. In a way, the unpoetic poetry of abuse was a confession of the power of the objects of that abuse. His assertion that ''poems are and have been and will be written about hating white people, or knocking them off''[83] has an air of hysterical defensiveness, and, indeed, it was not a necessity which delayed him for long.

The more important task was the need to identify an opposing tradition, to assert that black life was not mere pathology, that it constituted a resource of values which opposed the antihuman reductiveness ascribed to the white world. So that if he called 1969 the ''year of reconstruction,'' he identified 1970 as the year of separation. In both his political and poetic life he set out to establish the unity of black experience, to expunge the accommodationist impulse, and to identify the basis of a black national spirit and identity. And the consequence was a restored lyricism which reasserted itself through an emphasis on an African past (a common origin generating a persistent, if vestigial, sense of community and a rhythmic consonance) and a shared perception of the present. Most obviously with *It's Nation Time* and *In Our Terribleness* (1970), his poems became hypnotic mantras, cabalistic chants, tribal incantations, magical formulae, public ceremonies. As he explained in *In Our Terribleness*, ''The rhythm of beings is the reason for being.''[84]

Both of these poems were recorded against a background of African and jazz music, the unity of the music and the harmonious relationship of words and music itself standing as an image of a powerful black identity restored to its original wholeness. It was an image which derived from his political conviction that the separate black nation which the Black Muslims called for already existed in the inner areas of America's major cities. As he explained in the symbolically black-edged pages of *In Our Terribleness*,

Man woman child in a house is a nation. More than them
we become large cities that shd have, domes, spires, spirals
pyramids . . .
. . .The cities the cities our dominion[85]

And the man and the woman become the first citizens of this nation. Hence, love, rejected as counterrevolutionary in 1966, now becomes the unifying force of the black community:

Love I hear you from way cross the
sea . . .in East Africa . . .Arabia.
Reconstructing the grace of our
long past . . .[86]

The result is a studied romanticism, a curious echo from the First Renaissance. This is a sentimentality, however, now carefully calculated for its social effect—an effect achieved on record by the blending of words and music and (in the case of *In Our Terribleness*) in book form by the interweaving of verse of photographs from the black ghetto. So, the poet becomes "a black priest interpreting the past and future" of his people. And rhythm becomes grace, a pulse uniting a black African past with a black American present. Thus, the poem "All in the Street" devolves at times into a verbal jazz beat, held and repeated until it resembles a liturgical chant, a deliberately hypnotic strobe of language designed to approximate, if not induce, an emotional trance in which the self dissolves into a mystical unity, a magical state in which time collapses and black cultural unity becomes a present reality. And so the poet-priest chants out:

The energy the energy the energy the rays
of God roared thru us all . . .
I am in an ecstacy a swoon in
actual touch with everything

These future rulers
are black
I see and hear them
now
I am in touch
with them. They speak and
beckon to me
Listen they speak thru
my mouth

Come on—
Come on—
Come on—
Come on—
Come on—
Come on—[87]

It is a romanticism familiar in its location of meaning in the sensibility, in the feelings; in its conviction that knowledge derives from the heart.

> If knowledge were
> anything
> It could not
> (be) but
> matter
> The vibration
> The heart's pulse
> In the instant
> all is transformed
> Great cities erected
> in a waste land
>
> Say only what you know
> Clearly & freely & swiftly, as it comes
> Springing from
> the heart![88]

The principles which he embraced were those identified by Maulana (Ron) Karenga, founder of the organization US: unity, self-determination, collective responsibility, collective economics, purpose, creativity, and faith. The criteria for a culture, likewise: mythology, history, social organization, political organization, economic organization, creative motive, and ethos. The principles of the future were discovered in the past, "The past and the future. The circle complete." The conceit is a familiar one, as is his sense of the oneness of life, of poetry as vatic rite, and of the individual as an expression of an oversoul, a community of the spirit. And its derivation was hardly as distinct from white tradition as he would have wished. The echoes of Whitman and Emerson, of the symbolists, and even the surrealists, are clear, though the idea of poetry as black spells, as imprecations to facilitate cultural reconstruction, redirects the energies of transcendentalism and the emotional correspondences of the senses into a racial religion of redemption. The true poem was to be the black life, and the poet simply a celebrant, identifying mythic origins, projecting a community of souls, and producing hymns to a god whose kingdom was within.

The consequence was a lyrical poetry whose flowing lines reflected the rhythms of African music and of Coltrane; the inflections of street talk and the arabesques of the conscious poet. But, paradoxically, this was offered as a utilitarian lyricism. Where usually the poetry of rebellion and of cultural reconstruction is liable to take a strident, self-announcing, staccato form in which the retreat from lyricism is offered as one of the necessary sacrifices demanded of the revolutionary artist—a position which he had adopted earlier and a mannerism in which too many black poets became trapped—he now saw the celebration of beauty and the generation of poetic harmonies as a necessary expression of a rekindled black awareness.

This, too, has its banalities, and repeated invocations of black beauty, the pride of a masculine warrior heritage, and a feminine resource of grace and love themselves threaten to devolve into stereotype. A culture may indeed be created by accumulation and a myth by repetition, but, in his poetry, as in his prose pieces, he began to show signs of an exhausted imaginative range. The real cause lay, perhaps, in a gradual reexamination of his political and cultural stance. The unreality of an attempt to restructure the black community within an existing politically and culturally dominant white society slowly became apparent. Black political leaders whose election he helped to secure found themselves operating in a world immune to the symbols of emergent black nationalism. Increasingly, he came to suspect that a nationalist analysis was simply not adequate to precipitate change at a level which could affect the conditions of black life. And Marx and Lenin, earlier rejected as "dirty Lenin" and "terrible Marx," increasingly seemed to offer the kind of approach which could make sense of a world situation in which color was no longer to be regarded as the primary principle. Ironically, in a speech delivered at Rockland Palace in 1969, he had said that "nationalism is a beginning step,"[89] a phrase reminiscent of that used by Richard Wright more than thirty years earlier. At the time, Baraka saw nationalism as a step towards the development of the self, on the one hand, and the elaboration of a mystical community of the spirit, on the other. By the mid-1970s, he had come closer to Wright's meaning, though without the equivocations which even then had undercut Wright's public commitment to Marxism. And this implied, once again, the acceptance of a dipthongized culture (Baraka's term), at least insofar as it became necessary to accept that the drive to separate had appropriated to race a suffering and, subsequently, a grace and hegemony of virtue which was more properly seen as the common lot of the dispossessed. Blackness remained an identifiable quality, but the willful sundering of the black community from the white, on a moral as well as a cultural level, was, he came to feel, an error.

Owen Dodson, black novelist and poet, has said that "the black writer has no obligation to 'blackness.' "[90] It was not a popular position to adopt. To him, the vogue for a racially distinct literature was an excuse for poor writing, and, in an interview, he produced an impromptu parody of a Nikki Giovanni poem. It is certainly true that much of the poetry produced by the Second Renaissance lent itself all too easily to parody, the black aesthetic implying a social, rather than a literary, criterion which was liable to praise the poet for the orthodoxy of his views and the authenticity of his racial stance rather than for the manner in which those virtues and that authenticity was expressed. If white poetry could somewhat cavalierly and inaccurately be characterized by such writers as ''art for art's sake,'' then an overconcern for form, language, irony, and ambiguity implied cultural defection. Language was to be direct, to express and speak to the black masses. Thus, the resonances of that language had to be contained within the immediate experience, or located in a cultural context from which the American experience and the echoes of a literary past had to be ruthlessly excluded.

Don Lee's early poetry, although immensely popular, is weak in precisely this way, expressing a new orthodoxy, but failing to find a form adequate to the task. Thus, like Baraka, he rejects his former self, meditating

> About my blackness and my early escape
> period, trying to be white.[91]

and contemplating the implicit treachery of the black bourgeoisie, but does so in a poem, ''Understanding But Not Forgetting,'' which fails to locate the source of the poetic which he works to pitch against this presumed decadence. He identifies his uneducated grandmother as the source of pure wisdom because, untainted by the corrupting influence of a suspect literacy,

> Behind all those ain'ts, us'ens and we's lies
> a mind with wisdom that most philosophers would
> envy[92]

but fails, at first, to engage the implications of this observation for his own poetry. Too often, as in ''The New Integrationist,'' ''The Cure All,'' or ''Contradiction in Essence,'' he is content to settle for a simple aphorism extruded into poetic form only by an unconventional typography. But a rationale for a deliberate contempt for poetic form was of course built into the black aesthetic and is most consciously evident in the deliberately ironic contradictions of ''Two Poems.'' And here it becomes clear that the studied antipoetic nature of much of Don Lee's poetry, especially the early work, is itself a statement:

> i ain't seen no poems stop a .38,
> i ain't seen no stanzas brake a honkie's head,
> i ain't seen no metaphors stop a tank,
> i ain't seen no words kill
> & if the word was mightier than the sword
> pushkin wouldn't be fertilizing russian soil/
> & until my similes can protect me from a night stick
> i guess i'll keep my razor
> & buy me some more bullets.[93]

It does little good to refer to such works as ''hate poems,'' as Arthur Davis has done; coming from a poet, such a poem is clearly not even intended to be taken seriously. It is simply a recognition of the pressures which mold the black poem.

Certainly this was a point astutely seized upon by Gwendolyn Brooks who, in an introduction to Lee's 1969 collection *Black Words That Say: Don't Cry, Scream*, observed that ''he knows that the black man today must ride full face into the whirlwind—with small regard for 'correctness,' with limited concern for the possiblities of 'error.' He knows that there are briefs even for the Big Mistake. The Big Mistake is at least a violent change—and in the center of a violent Change are the seeds of creation. Don Lee knows that nothing human is elegant. He is not interested in modes of writing that aspire to elegance. . . .He speaks to blacks hungry for what they themselves refer to as '*real* poetry.' These blacks find themselves and the stuff of their existence in his healthy, lithe, lusty reaches of free verse. The last thing that these people crave is elegance. It is very hard to enchant, with elegant song, the ears of a fellow whose stomach is growling. He can't hear you. The more interesting noise is too loud.''[94]

It is a statement which exposes the reason for both the strength and the weakness of much black poetry, which forebears a transcendent function in the name of immediacy and relevance, which regards a concern for form as too clear a remnant of the modernist poetic against which it is in a necessary revolt. As Lee himself insisted in ''Black Poetics/for the many to come,'' ''The most significant factor about the poems/poetry you will be reading is the *idea*. . . .Black poetry in its purest form is diametrically opposed to white poetry. . . .Black poetry in form/sound/word/usage/intonation/rhythm/repetition/ direction/definition & beauty is opposed to that which is now (& yesterday) considered poetry.''[95] In imposing an artificial homogeneity on white poetry, such statements were themselves akin to the black poetry which they described. But, while he accurately identifies some important characteristics of black poetry, his concept of inherently and absolutely contradictory cultures was a necessary fiction invoked to lay the groundwork for an art still trying to create a space between itself and the traditions which it wished to deny.

Unlike Baraka, he began his life as a black poet. He did not need to tackle within his own sensibility a commitment to an alternative poetic tradition, but he did feel it necessary to denounce those Negro poets to whom that tradition continued to exercise an attraction. In ''History of the Poet as a Whore,'' he wrote of the writer who was

> yeats in brown tone
> ultrablack with a whi-te tan,
> had a dangerous notion that
> he/she
> wd be famous yesterday.

a paper prostitute
with ink stained contraceptions.
still,
acute fear of colored pregnancy
forces poet to be poet
& not "negro poet"[96]

But, as his poem to Gwendolyn Brooks suggests, he was not unaware that a simple insistence on blackness carried its own dangers, and he also wished to establish a distinction between a militant black art and one which transmutes suffering into melodics; "we ain't blue," he insisted, "we are black."[97] Yet, for all his insistence on the necessary political nature of black poetry, like Baraka he progressed to lyrical works like "A Poem Looking for a Reader," believing with Baraka that lyricism can have a political content.

In terms of influence, Lee has recognized Robert Hayden for his style and craftsmanship, Sterling Brown for his control of idiom, Hughes for his use of musical metrics, and Baraka for the correctness of his political thrust. But his own development, like that of many other black poets of the late 1960s, showed an increasing concern for incorporating jazz rhythms. In a volume of criticism, *Dynamite Voices: Black Poets of the 1960s*, he recognized that "the language of the new writers seemed to move in the direction of actual music. The poets were actually defining and legitimizing their own communicative medium."[98] It was a development which invariably meant that increasingly his poetry was written for performance, the text lapsing into exultant screams and jazz scats. Despite the phenomenal sales of his books, books which originally he had sold personally on the streets of Chicago (250,000 copies were sold in the first few years), it is in performance that his poetry finds its real purpose, and perhaps nowhere is this more apparent than in "Move Un-noticed to be Noticed, A Nationhood Poem" from his collection *We Walk the Way of the New World*:

when u goin be something real, Clean?
like yr/own, yeah, when u goin be yr/ownself?

the deadliving
are the worldmakers,
the image breakers,
the rule takers: blackman can u stop a hurricane, mississippi
          couldn't.
blackman if u can't stop what mississippi couldn't, *be it. be it*.
blackman be the wind, be the win, the win, the win, win, win:

          wooooooooooowe boom boom wooooooooooowe bah
          wooooooooooowe boom boom wooooooooooowe bah
if u can't stop a hurricane, be one.
          wooooooooooowe boom boom wooooooooooowe bah
          wooooooooooowe boom boom wooooooooooowe bah

be the baddest hurricane that ever came, a black hurricane.
         woooooooooowe boom boom woooooooooowe bah
         woooooooooowe boom boom woooooooooowe bah[99]

The same emphasis on performance applies equally to Sonia Sanchez and, to a lesser extent, Nikki Giovanni. Sonia Sanchez, like many of the other black poets of the 1960s, is a college graduate (the list of those attending university would also include Amiri Baraka, Hart Bibbs, Edwin Brooks, F. J. Bryant, James A. Emanuel, Julia Fields, Bob Fletcher, Nikki Giovanni, Charles Gordon, David Henderson, Calvin Hernton, Alicia Johnson, Julius Lester, Audre Lorde, Larry Neal, Michael Nicholas, N. H. Pritchard, Dudley Randall, Ishmael Reed, Conrad Kent Rivers, Carolyn Rodgers, Herbert Simmons, A. B. Spellman, Darwin Turner, Ron Welburn, Marvin X), but the distinguishing characteristic of her work is a language which catches the nuance of the spoken word, the rhythms of the street, and of a music which is partly jazz and partly a lyricism which underlies ordinary conversation. It is not surprising that she should turn to drama because much of her poetry is written in dialogue form or has a conversational tone which makes it particularly effective on stage. She plays complicated games with linguistic registers; cultural games which express precisely that gap between the black and white sensibility, or between the experience of the poor and of those who try to accommodate that experience to alien theories of action which generate the ironies of black life. And Sonia Sanchez is an ironic poet, her sense of irony saving her from the worst excesses of black poetry during the 1960s and creating a subtle commentary on her own failings and those of the world through which she moves. In "221-1424 (San/francisco/suicide/number)," she offers a dialogue which is one side of a conversation between a black person planning suicide and the social worker at the other end, unseen but fully realized:

                 what's that
u say? When did I first
feel that honkies?
                 Yeh, honkies
yeh. I'll spell it for u. HONKIES . . .
were tryen to kill me?
                 well, man, it ain't
exactly my discovery
                 but it's been happenin
for bout 400 yrs.
                 what's that
can i au-then-ti-cate that
                 how you
spell that man? Oh yeh?
now what that mean? Oh yeh?

well that ain't one of my words.
but mannnn.
                        don't u read the fucken papers?
don't u live?
                        what's that? u say it's
all improven for us negroes.
                        what kind
of fool are u? . . .
    . . .   what's that u say?
i do.
                        feel like go/en out and
do/en in a couple of honkies.
yeh, honkies. hey, u still there?
yeh. well i'm gonna split
hey. u know what?
                        u don't sound so gooood.
yehhhh if i wuz u
                        i'd hang it up mannnNN.
                                bye now![100]

For Sanchez the aberrant spelling and the typographical layout are function-al, and these and the ironic humor are far more subtle and persuasive agents of cultural reconstruction than the direct assaults of Baraka's middle period, Don Lee's early poems, or the work of Nikki Giovanni. And while creating a poetry which is designed to serve the purpose of instilling pride, she is also aware that language alone is not capable of transforming, that it carries its own risk. In "blk/rhetoric," she asks

who's gonna make all
that beautiful blk/rhetoric
mean something
                        Like
i mean
            who's gonna take
the words
            blk/is/beautiful
and make more of it
than blk/capitalism.[101]

And again, in "To Fanon, culture meant only one thing—an environment shaped to help us & our children grow, shaped by ourselves in action against the system that enslaves us,"

the cracker is not to be played with.
he is the
enslaver/
       master.   we the slaves
the evilllll he does is not new
cannot be resolved
         thru rhetoric/
         hate/
           poems/[102]

Indeed, with a homeopathic logic, in ''TCB'' she dedicates a whole poem to the familiar litany of racial abuse so that she can fulfill her supposed responsibility and move on to more constructive issues. Most of her poetry, indeed, is a poetic equivalent of political attempts at the reconstruction and consolidation of the black community. Her poems and the performances in which they are presented are attempts to rebuild pride and respect; they are secular sermons displaying a revolutionary puritanism. Hence, she attacks the self-directed violence of the ghetto, denounces the use of drugs and drink, and insists that black men and women should honor and respect one another. Like Don Lee, she rejects the blues as a passive assimilation and acceptance of suffering:

am I blue?
      sweet/baby/blue/
              billie
no. i'm blk/
    & ready[103]

And, like Baraka, she takes as her model Coltrane (see ''a/coltrane/poem''). And though the liberation of the black individual is to be won initially through a rejection of white models of thought and a consolidation of the black personality, there is in Sanchez a recognition of more fundamental problems raised both by the existence of prejudice and the brutal struggles of ghetto life—problems not neutralized by language, by utilitarian symbols, or even by the ennobling fact of revolt. ''Small Comment,'' admittedly ironic in intent, at least recognizes the persistence of metaphysical questions, even if its tone implies that this is finally an evasion. And so she recognizes the argument that

the name of the beast is
man or to be more specific
the nature of man is his
bestial nature or to
bring it to its elemental terms

> the nature of nature is
> the bestial survival of the
> fittest the strongest the richest . . .
> . . . .
>   but to really
> be with it we will say that man
> is a natural beast . . .[104]

The deflating comment, ''you dig?'' which ends the poem is the assertion that in the context of a community intent on rebuilding its morale, metaphysics constitute a retreat from commitment. But, at the same time, for Sonia Sanchez, commitment can extend to love poetry and to an examination of the sensibility; nor does she demand that the individual enroll in a corporate identity in order to build a racial selfhood.

The same combination of private and public poetry is observable in the work of Nikki Giovanni, but the personal poem defers quickly to the public rite, and it is not hard to see why Owen Dodson felt it easy to parody her bursts of poetic militancy. ''The True Import of Present Dialogue, Black vs Negro'' is the kind of work that Sanchez disposed of so effectively in ''TCB'':

> Nigger
> Can you kill
> Can you kill
> Can a nigger kill
> Can a nigger kill a honkie
> Can a nigger kill the Man
> Can you kill nigger
> Huh? nigger can you
> kill
> Do you know how to draw blood
> Can you poison
> Can you stab-a-Jew[105]

For Nikki Giovanni, black poetry is an instrument of change. It is a polemical medium which translates a political imperative into persuasive form. Its strength lies in its response to the moment as well as its vision of the future. Hence, her injunction contained in the ''Poem for Black Boys''

> DO NOT SIT IN DO NOT FOLLOW KING
> GO DIRECTLY TO THE STREETS
> This is a game you can win[106]

is only intensified by the assassination of Martin Luther King, Jr., which is seen as evidence of a continuing war and which leaves the individual only with the question,

What can I, a poor Black woman, do to destroy america?
This is a question, with appropriate variations, being asked
in every Black heart. There is one answer—I can kill. There
is one compromise—I can protect those who kill. There is
one cop-out—I can encourage others to kill. There are no
other ways.[107]

The collapse of poetic structure parallels the collapse of everything but the prosaic need for violence. It is not a collapse which produces compelling poetry, nor is it one which takes account of the ironies which surround a continued commitment to life as a writer. She, herself, becomes guilty of a cop-out, celebrating slaughter without examining its function or its ideological meaning. Her work offers a new litany which is essentially recessive:

Blessed be machine guns in Black hands
All power to grenades that destroy our oppressor
Peace Peace, Black Peace at all costs . . .
Blessed is he who kills[108]

And yet, in "The Great Pax Whitie," she is capable of a poetic containment of her bitterness, of a solemn lament for failed values and the death of principle, whose insistent rhythms, highlighted by the recording on which the poem is recited to a background of gospel singers, do raise the fact of death to a mythic level. But, for the most part, her work is a catalog of betrayal and death, which she meets with a deification of brutality, to be justified as the boomerang of history coming back to strike those who set that history in motion. The occasional love poem merely accentuates the forces which crush equally the self and the lyric potential of poetry. But, judged on its own terms, it is doubtful that the observation that "the worst junkie or black businessman is more humane/than the best honkie"[109] has anything of value to offer either as poetry or as consciousness-raising invocation. The elaboration of stereotypes serves neither the poetic nor even, finally, the revolutionary spirit, but, as she suggests in "For Saundra," perhaps "these are not poetic/times/at all."[110]

The new black writing was not without its contradictions. Just as Bertolt Brecht had sat in East Berlin denouncing the antihuman reductivism of capitalist society while clinging carefully to his Austrian passport, so these black writers still retained their American "passport," in the form of an American identity which provided something of the material and cultural context of their revolt. It was an inadvertent nationality, but one which conveyed certain privileges which were claimed and whose ironies were not acknowledged. Thus, not only were many of these writers graduates of American universities, but they continued to teach in them. Despite the appearance of a number of black publishers, many continued to reach their black public and denounce the agents of white culture precisely through those agents and to denounce capitalism on a ten-percent royalty. And this was not simply an unavoidable irony; it, and the whole complex interplay of an American and a black cultural identity, was a relationship which demanded an examination beyond caricature and casual dismissal. Du Bois's double consciousness could not be negated simply by ignoring it and by denying the force of the language in which separation was simultaneously proposed and contradicted.

There was a further ambiguity, however, and that, a familiar one. In the 1920s, the Austrian writer Hugo von Hofmannsthal had remarked that "our time is unredeemed; and do you know what it wants to be redeemed from? . . . The individual. . . .Our age groans too heavily under the weight of this child of the sixteenth century that the nineteenth century fed to monstrous size. . . .We are anonymous forces. Potentialities of the soul. Individuality is an arabesque we have discarded. . . .I should go so far as to assert that all the ominous events we have been witnessing in the last twelve years are nothing but a very awkward and longwinded way of burying the concept of the European individual in the grave it has dug for itself."[111] Certainly the 1930s vindicated this assumption, but the decade also revealed a moral implication of such a stance. For morality was likely to be interpreted solely in terms of social pragmatics, which could vindicate equally the Moscow show trials and the Nazi holocaust. If the individual was himself no longer a value, morality was replaced by history with its own relentless logic. What, after all, was a single soul in the context of a thousand-year reich or a continuing revolution which projected the reappearance of the individual only in some distant future when the state had obligingly withered away?

The black poet, similarly committed to a version of history as a convulsive surge towards eventual liberation, offers the same hostages to time. Again the word "individual" becomes synonymous with traitor, and morality becomes the simple identification of a model whose force derives less from moral needs than from historical necessity. The consequence is not only the constant threat of a literature which is tested for its adherence to agreed formulae (much as 1930s literature had been inspected for its orthodoxy), one necessarily simple in contour because of its drive towards social utility, it is the danger of a writing whose moral force is blunted both by that simplified vision and by the existence of a formula which acts as a barrier between the writer and an ethical sensitivity which dissipates on encounter with the abstract, or which substitutes preferred modes of behavior for the socially nonutilitarian.

The black poet Alvin Aubert has seen the Western stress on individualism as evidence of a social fragmentation—a fear of community. Yet, that same Western culture has proved itself equally capable of generating atavistic images of community which have been forged into potent weapons for projecting the individual into a world in which obedience is offered as the only substitute for a nonteleological existence. This is not to imply that all images of community are equally recessive, but that the moral implications of a strenuously policed prescriptive version of that sense of homogeneity require inspection. And the threat is not simply abstract. Hence, Amiri Baraka and Nikki Giovanni can write poems which any European would regard as shamelessly anti-Semitic and retreat from the ethical implications of that act by asserting a symbolic role for the Jew as the image of the exploiter in the new mythological canon of black art. The ironies of this in a poetry dedicated to smashing the familiar icons, the necessary symbols of white cultural and political supremacy, should have been manifest, but they were swallowed up in a larger irony—namely, the fact that release from one image was to be secured by the creation of others. And the point is not even whether some Jewish entrepreneurs, at times as readily identifiable by their names and even appearance as blacks, were guilty of exploitation; it is that in the act of declaring independence from the images and methods of the white world such writers should have slavishly perpetuated both those images and that methodology in their own work. Announcing their freedom, they did so in a way which made plain the extent to which they remained trapped within a mode of thought which could define cultural value only in opposition to a demeaned image of the other. This was, after all, precisely the method of the racist, and though I do not accuse these writers of being racist, they are, it seems to me, vulnerable to the accusation that they have failed to examine the implications of their stance, failed to perceive a possible flaw in the black aesthetic. A reductive image was to be replaced not by an engagement with complexity and the acknowledgement of ambiguity—this was seen as dysfunctional, being too reminiscent of a liberal view of the self and a familiar American literary tradition—but by the elaboration of symbols which could be embraced with pride. The reductivism lay in the *process* of conforming rather than in the constituent elements of the model; in the idea that the substitution of symbols was an adequate response to an all too tangible world. And the black poet was also in danger of liberating the black individual from a demeaning metaphor of the self only to pitch him into a universe which was likely to become absurd if that individual chose to press experience beyond the parameters traced out by the new truths of black pride, heroism, and beauty. If experience failed to locate a social correlative for these images, the danger was that black art would detach the individual and the community from a realistic appraisal of the actual strengths and vulnerabilities of a system which expresses itself through corrosive economic and political realities.

The criticism which has attempted to deal with this poetry has also, at times, been disappointingly formulaic. In *Understanding Black Poetry*, Stephen Henderson charts a critical convention which purports to embrace the unique quality of black art. Starting with the flatly erroneous view that "literature . . .is the verbal organization of experience into beautiful forms,"[112] he asserts that "black poetry in the United States has been widely misunderstood, misinterpreted . . .especially by white critics" but also "by many black academics whose literary judgements are self-consciously 'objective' and whose cultural values, while avowedly 'American,' are essentially European."[113] The distinction between European and American cultural values remains unexamined, as do the identities of the critics, but the essence of his argument is the strangely tautologous one that black poetry "is somehow structurally black . . .identifiably Black, in terms of structure, theme, or other characteristics." It is written by "an identifiably Black person whose ideological stance vis-à-vis the history and the aspirations of his people since slavery is adjudged by them to be correct."[114] And, although he accepts the problems raised by such a definition and indeed identifies some of them, he himself then proceeds to work within it, choosing to analyze black poetry by theme, structure, and "saturation," by which, again tautologously, he means "the communication of Blackness and fidelity to the observed or intuited truth of the Black Experience in the United States."[115] Having assumed what he wants to prove, he can with safety suggest that "the ethnic roots of Black poetry . . .are ultimately understood only by Black people themselves."[116] However, since he later feels able to say that though Don Lee's use of the word "neoteric" is "not 'Black,' the casual virtuoso way that he drops it on us—like 'Deal with that'— *is an elegant Black linguistic gesture*, a typical gesture,"[117] it is hard to take some of his claims for privileged insight entirely seriously. His suggestion that "there is this tradition of beautiful talk with us" is the sheerest self-serving critical cant, disturbing not simply because of its invention of a false and unsupported distinction, but because it detracts from some of his more sensible observations about musical structure, codified language, and verbal rhythms.

My point is not that there are no identifiable qualities in black poetry, but that the critic who closes his mind to the cultural context within which the black poet operates—a context which includes the tradition of American poetry as well as the realities of black cultural life, assertions by black poets to the contrary notwithstanding—is likely to have a difficult time establishing the nature of his definition. This is a fact which Dudley Randall acknowledged in an interview[118] in which he remarks on the considerable influence of white poetry on even those black poets most concerned with distinguishing themselves from that tradition. Indeed, he points out the degree to which Baraka's poetry bears the imprint of European and American poetry; this, in turn, becoming a model for young black writers.

Black poetry is a great deal more varied and inventive than its own claims for polemical status would suggest and a great deal more eclectic than any racially based criticism would seem to imply. Even Don Lee has insisted that "what the black critic must bring to us is an extensive knowledge of world literature, along with a specialized awareness of his own literature."[119] It is hard, for example, to see how Henderson would deal with the surrealist poems of Ted Joans (as opposed to his simplistic aphorisms) or the ironic and inventive assaults of Ishmael Reed, whose poems embrace the language of the black aesthetic in order to reject its authority over him. To statements such as that made by Alvin Aubert, that "the Black poet has an obligation to always affirm Blackness in his writing. He should never forget that he is Black and that he has an obligation to Black People—to uplift their spirit . . .to encourage them to liberate themselves,"[120] Reed's response would be to imply that the poet determines the nature of his obligations, which may be as well served by oblique and subversive humor as by a solemn commitment to the parading of black values and virtues. Indeed, in "catechism of d neoamerican hoodoo church," Reed identifies as the enemy of poetry those who attempt to prescribe its content:

> a little red wagon for d black bureaucrat
> who in d winter of 1967 when i refused to
> deform d works of ellison & wright—his betters—
> to accommodate a viewpoint this clerk thot irresistible,
> did not hire me for d teaching job
> which he invitd me to take
> in de first place.
>
> this is for u insect w/ no antennae, goofy
> papers piling on yr desk—for u & others. where
> do u fugitives frm d file cabinet of death get
> off in yr attempt to control d artist? . . .
> . . . .
>
> our pens are free
> do not move by decree. accept no memos
> frm jackbooted demogs who wd exile our minds.
> dare tell d artist his role. issue demands on
> cultural revolution . . .[121]

He rejects those who tell him

> this is how yr ears shd feel
> this is what u shd eat
> this is who u shd sleep w/
> this is how you shd talk
> this is how u shd write . . .[122]
> . . . .
>
> these are d new gods we made for u . . .

And yet his poems are as much a vital part of black creativity as the most polemical Nikki Giovanni poem. Indeed, he makes essentially the same defense of an assault on language and grammar as do writers like Don Lee

> & by d way did u hear abt grammar?
> cut to ribbons in a photo finish by
> stevie wonder . . .[123]

while his work represents an equally conscious attack on American cultural tradition, the difference being that he accomplished his objective by guerilla warfare, using a parodic Negro dialect simultaneously to mock both the white tradition and the white image of the Negro:

> its not my fault dat yr tradition
> was knocked off wop style & left in
> d alley . . .
>
> ·
>
> ought to do something abt yr security or
>   mend yr fences partner
> dont look at me if all dese niggers
> are ripping it up like deadwood dick;
> doing art d way its never been done.[124]

Like Dudley Randall, he does not believe that the poet should be "programmatic." As Randall, himself the publisher of many of the new black writers, remarked, "He may be programmatic in his outside life, but, in poetry, you *cannot* lay down a blueprint or a program for revolution. . . . Being a preacher's son, I've heard too many sermons."[125]

But preaching was what the late 1960s and early 1970s were about as far as most black poetry was concerned, and, in some ways, it makes no sense to ask what the decade produced in terms of lasting literary value. Black poets did not see their work as a series of artifacts, an anthology of monuments. They were less concerned with establishing a corpus of black literature than with engaging in a dialogue with the black community. It was not for nothing that they tended to reiterate the appropriateness of music, not merely as the basis for poetic rhythm, but as an image of black art. The poems which they wrote constituted a kind of phatic communion, whose meaning lay in their performance and in the success with which they engaged their audience. And, though there was a certain absurdity in Carolyn Rodgers's refusal to "write well" because this meant to conform to alien standards, and in her refusal to use "white" language, more especially the word "poem" (an absurdity manifest in the fact that virtually every word she used was "white" in some sense), there was an appropriateness in the word which she chose to substitute—a word, however, no less white than the one she rejected. She proposed the word ''song'' and saw the poet as a ''singer''; and that is indeed what the black poet aimed to be in many senses.

And once the ritualistic assaults on whitey and the Jews were out of the way, as they were in a very short time, the prevailing tone became one of celebration. A black poem was an epiphany, and if the prosaic nature of print and the passage of time detracted from its impact, as in some cases it did, then this mattered less than that it should have resonated in the minds of black people at the moment when their identities and, for some, their lives were menaced. The confident identity deployed today in black art and life is a tribute to these poets whose occasional deficiencies of an aesthetic and, more alarmingly, of a moral kind were eventually less important than their value as celebrants of a new-born cultural identity. They may have been disturbingly prescriptive in the images which they offered and unduly contemptuous of those whose sufferings were as great as theirs but whose response they found hard to understand, but their energy and their confidence, their commitment to the notion of art as a liberating force, placed them at the heart of the cultural reawakening which was the Second Black Renaissance.

Afterword

The debate about the nature and extent of black literary achievement continues. Though muted somewhat in recent years, there is still an active disagreement over the role of the black writer and the rights, responsibilities, and limitations of the critic. In the 1960s and early 1970s, there were those who wished to dictate, not only the content and tone of black art, but also the audience which could legitimately respond to it. But a work of art finds many audiences. It derives its life from a series of interactions. This is clearly not the book which would have been written by a black American. It is not offered as such. In a sense, therefore, there will be those who see it as a challenge to black critical hegemony. I recognize the force of the argument, as I do the cogency of Gramsci's theories of cultural control. But I continue to insist on the legitimacy, if not the innocence, of this enterprise, finding it, at least in part, in that very liberal undertow which I have tried to demonstrate in the tide of black writing and partly, I admit, in my own refusal to be denied access to a body of work which I respect.

It is true that my experience is not that of the black American, but I have the assurance of writers as various as Richard Wright, Ralph Ellison, James Baldwin, Lorraine Hansberry, John A. Williams, Ishmael Reed, Amiri Baraka, Eldridge Cleaver, Bobby Seale, and George Jackson, among many others, that the fluctuation between anguished self-appraisal and a confident assertion of values, between personal anomie and a sense of shared experience, is one which is of immediate and pressing relevance beyond the boundaries of America and outside the perimeters of racial identity. Clearly, not all black art works on such assumptions. Neither can culture be reduced to some undifferentiated international sea. That is not my point. What I am insisting on is that literary works are created and re-created by their readers or their audience. They are multifaceted, and we diminish them by denying them this quality. They are, indeed, in this case, primarily an expression of black cultural life. But they also inhabit a wider world. The black experience is, perhaps ineluctably, bound up with the American experience, as that is intimately related to a European experience. Of course, black culture is more than that, precisely how much more being the subject of much debate by black critics in recent years.

That the African experience is remote does not mean that it is irrelevant or that its impact is slight.

What I have tried to do in this book, however, is to see the black writer primarily in his American context, to take him (or her) at his (or her) word, and to chart the changing perception of self and community at the heart of works which were consciously offered as part of the process of private and public definition.

The Second Renaissance was and is a remarkable phenomenon. It was a literary movement which was coterminous and inextricably bound up with one of the most impressive social and political movements of twentieth-century America. This book simply tries to attest to this fact and to indicate what seems to me, from a European perspective, to be the nature and extent of the achievement of writers who knew themselves to be in the eye of the storm.

Notes

INTRODUCTION

1. Richard Wright, *Black Power* (London: Dobson, 1968), p. 118.
2. Ibid., p. 12.
3. Quoted in David Ray and Robert Farnsworth, *Richard Wright: Impression and Perspectives* (Ann Arbor: University of Michigan Press, 1973), p. 11.
4. Gunnar Myrdal, *An American Dilemma* (New York: Harper, 1944), p. 7.
5. Lionel Trilling, *The Liberal Imagination* (New York: Doubleday, 1953), p. viii.
6. Ibid., p. xii.

CHAPTER 1

1. Jean-Paul Sartre, *Anti-Semite and Jew*, trans. G. J. Becker (New York: Schocken, 1965), pp. 66-67.
2. Alain Locke, *The New Negro* (New York: Atheneum, 1968), p. 15.
3. Amritjit Singh, *The Novels of the Harlem Renaissance: Twelve Black Writers, 1923-1933* (University Park, Pa.: Pennsylvania State University Press, 1976), p. 32.
4. Dorothy Blair, *African Literature in French: A History of Creative Writing in French from West and Equatorial Africa* (Cambridge: Cambridge University Press, 1976), p. 146.
5. John H. Bracey, August Meier, Elliott Rudwick, eds., *Black Nationalism in America* (Indianapolis: Bobbs-Merrill, 1970), p. 410.
6. Ibid., pp. 421, 422, 427.
7. Locke, *The New Negro*, p. 48.
8. Ibid., p. 356.
9. Nathan Huggins, *Harlem Renaissance* (New York: Oxford University Press, 1971), p. 202.
10. Locke, *The New Negro*, p. 48.
11. Ibid., p. xvi.
12. Ibid., p. 11.
13. Ralph Ellison, *Invisible Man* (New York: Random House, 1952), p. 130.
14. Irving Howe, *The Decline of the New* (London: Gollanz, 1971), p. 95.
15. Stuart Rochester, *American Liberal Disillusionment* (University Park, Pa.: Pennsylvania State University Press, 1977), p. 91.
16. James O. Young, *Black Writers of the Thirties* (Baton Rouge, La.: Louisiana State University Press, 1973), p. 4.
17. Michel Fabre, *The Unfinished Quest of Richard Wright*, trans. Isabel Barzun (New York: William Morrow, 1973), p. 582.
18. Raymond Wolters, *Negroes and the Great Depression: The Problem of Economic Recovery* (Westport, Ct.: Greenwood Press, 1970), p. xiii.
19. Richard Wright, "Blueprint for Negro Literature," *Amistad* 2 (New York: Vintage Books, 1971), p. 7.

20. Ibid.
21. Ibid., p. 9.
22. Ibid., p. 10.
23. Ibid., p. 11.
24. Ibid., p. 16.
25. Dan T. Carter, *Scottsboro: A Tragedy of the Modern South* (Oxford: Oxford University Press, 1969), p. 332.
26. W. E. B. Du Bois, *The Seventh Son: The Thought and Writings of W. E. B. Du Bois*, vol II, ed. Julius Lester (New York: Vintage Books, 1971), p. 173.
27. Ibid., pp. 320-21.
28. Ibid., p. 313.
29. James Baldwin, *Notes of a Native Son* (London: Corgi, 1965), p. 137.
30. James Baldwin, Emile Capouya, Lorraine Hansberry, Nat Hentoff, Langston Hughes, Alfred Kazin, "The Negro in American Culture," in *The Black American Writer*, vol. 1, ed. C. W. E. Bigsby (New York: Penguin, 1969), p. 81.
31. David Ray and Robert Farnsworth, *Richard Wright: Impressions and Perspectives* (Ann Arbor: University of Michigan Press, 1973), p. 124.
32. Ibid., p. 137.
33. Ibid., pp. 137-38.
34. Ibid., p. 46.
35. James Joyce, *The Portrait of the Artist as a Young Man* (London: Jonathan Cape, 1930), pp. 231, 281.
36. Richard Wright, *Twelve Million Black Voices* (London: Drummond, 1947), p. 30.
37. Horace R. Cayton and St. Clair Drake, *Black Metropolis* (London: Jonathan Cape, 1946), p. xxxii.
38. Irving Goffman, *The Presentation of the Self in Everyday Life* (Harmondsworth, Eng.: Penguin, 1954), p. 45.
39. William V. Spanos, *A Casebook on Existentialism* (New York: Thomas A. Crowell, 1966), p. 148.
40. Frantz Fanon, *The Wretched of the Earth*, trans. Constance Farrington (Harmondsworth, Eng.: Penguin, 1968), p. 74.
41. Tony Tanner, *The City of Words* (London: Jonathan Cape, 1971), p. 16.
42. Roland Barthes, *Writing Degree Zero*, trans. Annette Lavers and Colin Smith (London: Jonathan Cape, 1967), p. 92.
43. Richard Wright, *Black Boy* (London: Readers Union, 1947), pp. 274-75.
44. Richard Wright, *American Hunger* (New York: Harper & Row, 1977), p. 146.
45. Locke, *The New Negro*, p. 47.
46. Sartre, *Anti-Semite and Jew*, p. 134.
47. Ibid., p. 135.
48. Ibid., pp. 55-57.
49. Ibid., p. 137.
50. Eldridge Cleaver, *Post-Prison Writings and Speeches* (London: Jonathan Cape, 1969), pp. 57-72.
51. Sartre, *Anti-Semite and Jew*, p. 136.
52. Fabre, *The Unfinished Quest*, p. 274.
53. LeRoi Jones, "Brief Reflections on Two Hot Shots," *Kulchur* 3, no. 12 (Winter, 1963): 3.
54. LeRoi Jones, *Dutchman and the Slave* (New York: William Morrow, 1964), p. 75.
55. Addison Gayle, Jr., *The Way of the New World* (New York: Doubleday, 1975), p. xii.
56. Tanner, *The City of Words*, p. 16.
57. Wright, *Black Boy*, p. 214.
58. Daniel Bell, *The End of Ideology: On the Exhaustion of Political Ideas in the Fifties* (New York: Collier, 1962), p. 404.

59. Barthes, *Writing Degree Zero*, p. 27.

60. Ibid., p. 28.

61. Ibid., p. 22.

62. Ibid., p. 20.

63. Herbert Hill, *Anger, and Beyond: the Negro Writer in the United States* (New York: Harper & Row, 1966), p. 19.

64. Mercer Cook and Stephen E. Henderson, *The Militant Black Writer in Africa and the United States* (Madison, Wisc.: University of Wisconsin Press, 1969), p. 68.

65. LeRoi Jones, *Home* (New York: William Morrow, 1966), p. 61.

66. Ibid., p. 76.

67. Ibid., p. 85.

68. Ibid., p. 86.

69. Ibid., p. 112.

70. Ibid., p. 114.

71. Ibid., p. 115.

72. Jones, ''Brief Reflections on Two Hot Shots,'' p. 2.

73. Jones, *Home*, p. 121.

74. Ibid., p. 168.

75. Ibid., p. 212.

76. Ibid., p. 211.

77. Ibid., p. 246.

78. Stokely Carmichael, *Black Power: The Politics of Liberation in America* (London: Jonathan Cape, 1968) p. 45.

79. Stephen E. Henderson, ''Survival Motion: A Study of the Black Writer and the Black Revolution in America,'' in *The Militant Black Writer*, by Mercer Cook and Stephen E. Henderson, p. 79.

80. Arna Bontemps, ''Artist in an Age of Black Revolution,'' *Arts in Society* 5, no. 2 (Summer-Fall, 1968): 220.

81. Ibid., p. 230.

82. Ibid., p. 229.

83. John Oliver Killens, ''The Black Writer and Revolution,'' *Arts in Society* 5, no. 3 (Fall-Winter, 1968): 398.

84. LeRoi Jones and Larry Neal, eds., *Black Fire* (New York: William Morrow, 1968), p. xvi.

85. Ed Bullins, ''Open Letter,'' *Black Theatre* (February 1971), n.p.

86. Dudley Randall, ''Black Publisher, Black Writer: An Answer,'' *Black World* 24, no. 5 (March 1975): 32-37.

87. Addison Gayle, Jr., ''The Black Aesthetic,'' *Black World* 24, no. 2 (December 1974): 34.

88. Addison Gayle, Jr., *The Black Aesthetic* (New York: Doubleday, 1972), p. xxii.

89. Ibid.

90. Ibid., p. 7.

91. Ibid., p. 46.

92. Jones and Neal, *Black Fire*, p. 656.

93. Gayle, *The Black Aesthetic*, p. 31.

94. Armstead L. Robinson, Craig C. Foster, and Donald H. Ogilvie, eds., *Black Studies at the University* (New Haven, Ct.: Yale University Press, 1969), p. 47.

CHAPTER 2

1. Richard Wright, *Black Boy* (London, 1947), p. 223.

2. Richard Wright, *American Hunger* (New York, 1977), p. 85.

3. Ibid., p. 5.

4. Ibid., pp. 134-35.

5. Ibid., p. 135.
6. Ibid.
7. Richard Wright, "The Man Who Lived Underground," in *Cross Section*, ed. Edwin Seaver (New York: L. B. Fischer, 1944), p. 85.
8. Ibid., p. 79.
9. Ibid., p. 86.
10. Ibid., p. 87.
11. Ibid., p. 82.
12. Ibid., pp. 89-90.
13. Ibid., p. 102.
14. Ibid., p. 65.
15. Wright, *American Hunger*, p. 69.
16. Albert Camus, "The Human Crisis," in *Civil Liberties and the Arts: Selections from Twice a Year*, ed. William Wasserstrom (Syracuse: Syracuse University Press, 1964), p. 246.
17. Ibid., pp. 243-44.
18. Ibid., pp. 244-45.
19. Ibid., p. 256.
20. Ibid., p. 250.
21. Ibid., p. 249.
22. Ibid.
23. Ibid., p. 252.
24. Ibid., p. 251.
25. Ibid., p. 254.
26. Ibid., p. 253.
27. Alfred Kazin, *On Native Grounds* (New York: Overseas Editions, 1942), p. 386.
28. Ibid., p. 387.
29. Georg Lukacs, *The Meaning of Contemporary Realism*, trans. John and Necke Mander (London: Merlin, 1962), p. 19.
30. Wright, *American Hunger*, p. 63.
31. Ralph Ellison, *Invisible Man*, (New York, 1952), p. 439.
32. Richard Wright, *Native Son* (New York: Harper & Row, 1966), p. 67.
33. Ibid.
34. Ibid., p. 141.
35. Ibid.
36. Ibid., p. 225.
37. Ibid.
38. Ibid., p. 232.
39. Ibid., p. 256.
40. Richard Wright, *Uncle Tom's Children* (New York: New American Library, 1963), p. 192.
41. Wright, *Native Son*, p. 222.
42. Houston Baker, *Richard Wright* (Englewood Cliffs, N.J.: Prentice-Hall, 1972), p. 80.
43. Ibid., p. 58.
44. Wright, *Native Son*, p. 113.
45. Ibid., p. 164.
46. Ibid., p. 257.
47. Richard Poirier, *A World Elsewhere* (London: Chatto, 1967), p. 37.
48. Wright, *Native Son*, p. 365.
49. Wright, *Black Boy*, pp. 282-83.
50. Ibid., p. 283.
51. Wright, *American Hunger*, p. 7.
52. Wright, *Native Son*, p. 22.
53. Ibid., p. 366.

54. Ibid., p. 367.
55. Wright, *American Hunger*, p. 133.
56. Wright, *Native Son*, p. 48.
57. Ibid., pp. 67-68.
58. Gayle, *The Way of the New World*, p. 209.
59. Ibid.
60. Ibid., p. 202.
61. Ibid., p. 204.
62. Ibid., p. 205.
63. Ibid., p. 206.
64. Ibid., p. 207.
65. Ibid.
66. Ibid., pp. 207-208.
67. Ibid., p. 208.
68. Fabre, *The Unfinished Quest*, p. 193.
69. Richard Wright, *The Colour Curtain* (London: Dobson, 1956), p. 179.
70. Fabre, *The Unfinished Quest*, p. 273.
71. Ibid.
72. Richard Wright, *The Outsider* (New York: Harper, 1953), p. 78.
73. Ibid., p. 79.
74. Ibid., p. 82.
75. Ibid.
76. Ibid., p. 83.
77. Ibid., p. 119.
78. Ibid., p. 131.
79. Ibid., p. 386.
80. Ibid., p. 175.
81. Ibid., p. 275.
82. Ibid., p. 276.
83. Ibid., p. 212.
84. Ibid., p. 225.
85. LeRoi Jones, *Dutchman and The Slave* (New York: William Morrow, 1964), p. 73.
86. Wright, *The Outsider*, p. 332.
87. Ibid., p. 347.
88. Ibid.
89. Ibid., p. 330.
90. Ibid., p. 391.
91. Ibid., p. 404.
92. Ibid.
93. Arthur Miller, *After the Fall* (London: Secker and Warburg, 1965), p. 58.
94. Wright, *The Outsider*, pp. 303-304.
95. Ibid., p. 299.
96. Ibid., p. 173.
97. Richard Wright, *The Long Dream* (London: Panther, 1963), p. 105.
98. Ibid., p. 218.
99. Ibid., p. 219.
100. Ibid., p. 92.
101. Ibid., p. 198.
102. Ibid., p. 210.
103. Ibid., p. 214.
104. Ibid., p. 230.
105. Ibid., p. 204.

106. Ibid., p. 314.
107. Ibid., p. 204.
108. Ibid., p. 315.
109. Ibid., p. 94.
110. Ibid., p. 218.
111. Fabre, *The Unfinished Quest*, p. 80.
112. Ralph Ellison, *Shadow and Act* (London: Secker and Warburg, 1967), p. 261.
113. Fabre, *The Unfinished Quest*, p. 354.
114. Richard Wright, *White Man, Listen!* (New York: Doubleday, 1957), pp. 71-72.
115. Ibid., p. 105.
116. Ibid., p. 120.
117. Richard Wright, "Blueprint for Negro Literature," *Amistad* 2 (New York, 1971), p. 9.
118. Wright, *White Man, Listen!*, pp. xvi-xvii.

CHAPTER 3

1. Ralph Ellison, "On Becoming a Writer," *Commentary* 38, no. 4 (October 1964): 59.
2. Ibid.
3. Ralph Ellison, "Mister Toussan," *New Masses*, 41 (November 4, 1941): 19.
4. Ellison, "On Becoming a Writer," p. 57.
5. Clifford Mason, "Ralph Ellison and the Underground Man," *Black World* 20, no. 2 (December 1970): 25.
6. Ernest Kaiser, "A Critical Look at Ellison's Fiction," *Black World* 20, no. 2 (December 1970): 57.
7. Ralph Ellison, "Flying Home," in *Cross Section*, ed. Edwin Seaver (London: L. B. Fischer, 1944), p. 471.
8. Ibid., p. 483.
9. Ibid., p. 471.
10. Ibid., p. 483.
11. Ibid., p. 472.
12. Ibid.
13. Ibid., p. 477.
14. Ibid., p. 484.
15. Ibid., p. 485.
16. Ralph Ellison, *Invisible Man*, (New York, 1952), p. 333.
17. Ibid., p. 5.
18. Ibid., p. 6.
19. Ibid., p. 7.
20. Ibid.
21. Ibid., p. 86.
22. Ibid., p. 87.
23. Ibid., p. 88.
24. Ibid.
25. Ibid.
26. Ibid., p. 72.
27. Ibid., p. 111.
28. Ralph Ellison, "Society, Morality and the Novel," *The Living Novel: A Symposium*, ed. Granville Hicks (New York: Macmillan, 1957), p. 59.
29. Ralph Ellison, "Under the Bar," in *Soon, One Morning: New Writing by American Negroes, 1940-1962*, ed. Herbert Hill (New York: Knopf, 1963), p. 244.
30. Ellison, *Invisible Man*, p. 118.
31. Ibid., p. 143.

32. Ibid., p. 119.
33. Ibid., p. 118.
34. Ibid., p. 180.
35. Ibid., p. 183.
36. Ibid., pp. 184-85.
37. Ibid., p. 181.
38. Ibid., p. 197.
39. Wright, "Blueprint for Negro Literature," p. 10.
40. Ellison, *Invisible Man*, p. 268.
41. Ibid., p. 285.
42. Ibid., p. 286.
43. Ibid., p. 288.
44. Ibid.
45. Ibid., p. 332.
46. Ibid., p. 334.
47. Ralph Ellison, *Shadow and Act* (New York, 1972), p. 102.
48. Ibid., p. 383.
49. Ibid., p. 418.
50. in Hicks *The Living Novel: A Symposium*, p. 67.
51. Ellison, *Invisible Man*, p. 435.
52. Ellison, *Shadow and Act*, p. xxiii.
53. Ibid., p. xix.
54. Ellison, *Invisible Man*, p. 3.
55. Ellison, "Society, Morality and the Novel," p. 20.
56. Ibid., p. 21.
57. Ellison, *Shadow and Act*, p. 179.
58. Quoted in Wright, *White Man, Listen!*, p. 99.
59. Ellison, *Shadow and Act*, p. 104.
60. Ibid., p. 117.
61. Addison Gayle, Jr., *The Way of the New World* (New York, 1975), p. 257.
62. Ellison, *Shadow and Act*, p. 147.
63. Ibid., pp. 189-90.
64. Jean-Paul Sartre, "We Write for Our Own Times," in William V. Spanos, *A Casebook on Existentialism* (New York, 1964), p. 149.
65. Ibid., p. 147.
66. Ellison, *Shadow and Act*, p. 38.
67. Paul Tillich, "The Courage to Be," in *A Casebook on Existentialism*, p. 329.

CHAPTER 4

1. James Baldwin and Margaret Mead, *A Rap on Race* (London: Corgi, 1972), pp. 245-46.
2. Quoted in Frederick Hoffman, *The Mortal No* (Princeton, N.J.: Princeton University Press, 1964), p. 332.
3. James Baldwin, *Notes of a Native Son* (London: Corgi, 1965), p. 3.
4. Stokely Carmichael, *Black Power: The Politics of Liberation in America* (London: Jonathan Cape, 1968), p. 36.
5. Baldwin, *Notes of a Native Son*, p. 141.
6. Ibid., p. 19.
7. Baldwin and Mead, *A Rap on Race*, p. 58.
8. Ibid., p. 180.
9. James Baldwin, *Nobody Knows My Name* (London: Corgi, 1965), p. 98.
10. Ibid., p. 17.

11. Baldwin, *Notes of a Native Son*, p. 5.
12. James Baldwin, *Going to Meet the Man* (New York: Dell, 1966), p. 76.
13. Ibid., p. 127.
14. Ibid., p. 129.
15. Baldwin, *Nobody Knows My Name*, p. 11.
16. Ibid., p. 87.
17. Ibid., p. 169.
18. Ibid.
19. Baldwin, *Notes of a Native Son*, p. 15.
20. Ibid., p. 17.
21. Ibid., p. 11.
22. Ibid., p. 102.
23. Ibid., p. 104.
24. Ibid., p. 35.
25. Ibid., p. 148.
26. James Baldwin, *Go Tell It on the Mountain* (London: Corgi, 1954), p. 136.
27. Ibid., p. 222.
28. Ibid., p. 226.
29. Ibid., p. 230.
30. Ibid., p. 90.
31. Ibid., p. 74.
32. Fern Maria Eckman, *The Furious Passage of James Baldwin* (London: Michael Joseph, 1968), p. 137.
33. Baldwin, *Nobody Knows My Name*, p. 128.
34. Eckman, *The Furious Passage*, p. 32.
35. James Baldwin, *Giovanni's Room* (London: Corgi, 1964), p. 68.
36. Alfred Kazin, *Bright Book of Life*, (Boston: Little Brown, 1973), p. 222.
37. Baldwin, *Giovanni's Room*, p. 20.
38. Ibid., p. 30.
39. Baldwin, *Nobody Knows My Name*, p. 105.
40. Eckman, *The Furious Passage*, p. 147.
41. Ibid., p. 179.
42. Ibid., p. 181.
43. James Baldwin, *Another Country* (New York: Dell, 1970), p. 351.
44. Ibid., p. 296.
45. Ibid., p. 341.
46. Ibid., p. 181.
47. Ibid., p. 168.
48. Ibid., p. 180.
49. Ibid., p. 215.
50. James Baldwin, with James Mossman and Colin MacInnes, "Race, Hate, Sex, and Colour," *Encounter* 25, no. 1 (July 1965): 56.
51. James Baldwin, *The Fire Next Time* (Harmondsworth, Eng.: Penguin, 1964), p. 81.
52. Ibid., p. 43.
53. Ibid., p. 68.
54. Ibid., p. 72.
55. Ibid., p. 76.
56. James Baldwin, Nathan Glazer, Sidney Hook, Gunnar Myrdal, "Liberalism and the Negro," *Commentary* (March 1964), p. 38.
57. Ibid., p. 41.
58. Eckman, *The Furious Passage*, p. 242.

59. James Baldwin, *Tell Me How Long the Train's Been Gone* (London: Michael Joseph, 1968), p. 42.
60. Ibid., p. 89.
61. Ibid., p. 99.
62. Ibid., p. 365.
63. Ibid., pp. 316-17.
64. James Baldwin, *No Name in the Street* (London: Michael Joseph, 1972), p. 117.
65. Eldridge Cleaver, *Soul on Ice* (London: Jonathan Cape, 1969), p. 99.
66. Baldwin, *No Name in the Street*, p. 87.
67. Ibid., p. 119.
68. Ibid., p. 29.
69. Ibid., p. 141.
70. Ibid., p. 163.
71. Ibid., p. 166.
72. Ibid., p. 39.
73. James Baldwin, *If Beale Street Could Talk* (London: Michael Joseph, 1974), p. 226.
74. James Baldwin, interview with the author, London June 24, 1974.
75. Baldwin, *If Beale Street Could Talk*, p. 146.
76. Baldwin, interview.
77. Ibid.
78. Baldwin, Mossman, and MacInnes, ''Race, Hate, Sex, and Colour,'' p. 56.
79. Baldwin, interview.
80. Baldwin and Mead, *A Rap on Race*, p. 214.
81. Ibid., p. 186.
82. Ibid., pp. 186-87.
83. Sartre, *Anti-Semite and Jew*, p. 16.
84. Baldwin and Mead, *A Rap on Race*, pp. 192-93.
85. Ibid., p. 202.
86. Ibid., p. 250.

CHAPTER 5

1. Saul Bellow, *Mr. Sammler's Planet* (London: Weidenfeld and Nicolson, 1970), pp. 277-78.
2. Saul Bellow, ''Some Notes on Recent American Fiction,'' *Encounter* 21, no. 5 (1963): 29.
3. Quoted in Harold Kaplan, *Democratic Humanism* (Chicago: University of Chicago Press, 1972), p. viii.
4. Walt Whitman, *Walt Whitman Complete Poetry and Selected Prose and Letters* (London: Nonesuch, 1938), p. 3.
5. Walt Whitman, *Democratic Vistas and Other Papers* (London: Scott, 1888), p. 26.
6. Arthur Miller, *The Theatre Essays of Arthur Miller*, ed. Robert A. Martin (New York: Penguin, 1978), p. 5.
7. Ibid., p. 14.
8. Saul Bellow, *Herzog* (London: Weidenfeld and Nicolson, 1965), pp. 74-75.
9. Miller, *The Theatre Essays*, p. 261.
10. Bellow, ''Some Notes on Recent American Fiction,'' p. 26.
11. Saul Bellow, *Dangling Man* (Harmondsworth, Eng.: Penguin, 1963), p. 75.
12. Saul Bellow, *To Jerusalem and Back*, (London, 1976), p. 95.
13. Bellow, ''Some Notes on Recent American Fiction,'' p. 29.
14. Saul Bellow, *The Adventures of Augie March* (Hamondsworth, Eng.: Penguin, 1966), p. 173.
15. Saul Bellow, *Henderson the Rain King* (London: Weidenfeld and Nicolson, 1958), p. 49.

16. Saul Bellow, "An Interview with Myself," *The New Review* 2, no. 18 (1975): 55.
17. Bellow, *Mr. Sammler's Planet*, p. 33.
18. Ibid., p. 181.
19. Ibid., p. 304.
20. Ibid., p. 305.
21. Ibid., p. 236.
22. Ibid., p. 234.
23. Thomas Pynchon, *Gravity's Rainbow* (London: Jonathan Cape, 1973) p. 758.
24. Bellow, *Mr. Sammler's Planet*, p. 54.
25. Ibid., p. 182.
26. Saul Bellow, *Humboldt's Gift* (London: Secker, 1975), p. 431.
27. Bellow, *Mr. Sammler's Planet*, p. 261.
28. Ibid.
29. Ibid., p. 313.
30. Eldridge Cleaver, *Soul on Ice* (London, 1969), pp. 94-95.
31. Jean-Paul Sartre, *Situations*, trans. Benita Eisler (London: Hamilton, 1965), p. 98.
32. Ralph Ellison, *Interviews with Black Writers*, pp. 67, 70.
33. John O'Brien, ed., *Interviews with Black Writers*, (New York: Liveright, 1973), p. 237.
34. Leon Trotsky, *Literature and Revolution* (Ann Arbor: University of Michigan Press, 1960), p. 226.
35. Alain Locke, *The New Negro*, (New York, 1968), p. 47.
36. Langston Hughes, *Not Without Laughter* (London: Collier, 1969), p. 262.
37. Herbert Marcuse, *Negations*, trans. Jeremy J. Shapiro (Harmondsworth, Eng.: Penguin, 1972), p. 240.
38. Ishmael Reed, *Interviews with Black Writers*, p. 179.
39. Ibid.
40. Ishmael Reed, *Yellow Back Radio Broke Down* (New York: Bantam, 1972), p. 18.
41. Ibid., p. 40.
42. Sigmund Freud, *The Future of an Illusion*, trans. W. D. Robson-Scott (London: Hogarth Press, 1928), p. 8.
43. Jean-Paul Sartre, *St. Genet*, trans. B. Frechtman (New York, 1963), p. 55.
44. James Baldwin, interview with the author, London, June 24, 1974.
45. Erika Monk, "Up from Politics: An Interview with Ed Bullins," *Performance* 1, no. 2 (April 1972): 56.
46. John O'Neal, "Performing in the South," *Performance* I, ii (April 1972), p. 45-46.
47. Carl Justav Jung, *Modern Man in Search of a Soul*, trans. W. S. Dell and C. F. Baynes (London: Routledge, 1966), pp. 227-28.
48. John A. Williams, *Mothersill and the Foxes* (New York: Doubleday, 1975), p. 238.
49. Alice Walker, *Meridian* (New York: Pocket Books, 1976), p. 219.

CHAPTER 6

1. John A. Williams, *This Is My Country, Too* (New York: Signet, 1966), p. 153.
2. Ibid., p. 156.
3. James Baldwin, *The Guardian*, December 12, 1970, p. 9.
4. Richard Wright, *White Man, Listen!* (New York: Doubleday, 1957), pp. 108-09.
5. John A. Williams, *Sons of Darkness, Sons of Light* (London: Eyre and Spottiswoode, 1970), p. 194.
6. John A. Williams, *The Man Who Cried I Am* (London: Eyre and Spottiswoode, 1968), p. 370.
7. John O. Killens, *Youngblood* (London: The Bodley Head, 1956), p. 137.
8. Ibid., p. 560.
9. John O. Killens, *'Sippi* (New York: Trident Press, 1967), p. 295.

10. John O. Killens, *And Then We Heard the Thunder* (New York: Knopf, 1968), p. 132.
11. Ibid., p. 174.
12. Ibid., p. 482.
13. Ibid.
14. Ibid., p. 483.
15. Ibid., p. 485.
16. John O. Killens, *Slaves* (New York: Pyramid Books, 1969), p. 142.
17. William Melvin Kelley, *A Different Drummer* (New York: Doubleday, 1969), p. 151.
18. John A. Williams, *Night Song* (London: Collins, 1962), p. 110.
19. John A. Williams, *Journey Out of Anger* (London: Eyre and Spottiswoode, 1965), p. 18.
20. Williams, *Night Song*, p. 84.
21. Williams, *The Man Who Cried I Am*, p. 50.
22. Ibid., p. 68.
23. Ibid., p. 188.
24. Ibid., p. 370.
25. Williams, *Sons of Darkness, Sons of Light*, p. 6.
26. Ibid., p. 181.
27. Ibid., p. 258.
28. John A. Williams, ed., *Beyond the Angry Black* (New York: Mentor, 1971), p. xvii.
29. John O'Brien, ed., *Interviews with Black Writers* (New York, 1973). p. 229.
30. Alice Walker, *Meridian* (New York: Pocket Books, 1976), p. 201.
31. Ibid., p. 213.
32. Toni Morrison, *The Song of Solomon* (New York: Knopf, 1977), p. 222.
33. O'Brien, *Interviews with Black Writers*, p. 194.

CHAPTER 7

1. Alfred Kazin, *On Native Grounds*, (New York: Overseas Editions, 1942), p. 490.
2. Ibid., p. 491.
3. Ibid.
4. Frantz Fanon, *The Wretched of the Earth*, trans. Constance Farrington (Harmondsworth, Eng.: Penguin, 1968), p. 11.
5. Angela Davis, *Angela Davis: An Autobiography* (New York: Random House, 1974), p. x.
6. Thomas Cooley, *Educated Lives: The Rise of Modern Autobiography in America* (Columbus: Ohio State University Press, 1976), p. 12.
7. Huey Newton, *Revolutionary Suicide* (London: Wildwood House, 1974), p. 11.
8. Cooley, *Educated Lives*, p. 5.
9. Malcolm X, *The Autobiography of Malcolm X* (New York: Grove Press, 1966), p. 150.
10. Ibid., p. 90.
11. Ibid., p. 27.
12. Ibid., p. 91.
13. Ibid., p. 185.
14. Ibid., p. 273.
15. Bobby Seale, *Seize the Time* (London: Hutchinson, 1970), p. 251.
16. Ibid., p. 262.
17. Newton, *Revolutionary Suicide*, p. 5.
18. Malcolm X, *Autobiography*, p. 366.
19. Eldridge Cleaver, *Soul on Ice* (London: Jonathan Cape, 1969), p. 59.
20. Ibid., p. 83.
21. Ibid., p. 192.
22. Richard Gilman, "White Standards and Negro Writing," in *The Black American Writer*, vol. I. (New York, 1971), ed. C. W. E. Bigsby, p. 36.
23. Ibid., p. 37.

24. Newton, *Revolutionary Suicide*, p. 7.
25. Gilman, ''White Standards and Negro Writing,'' p. 37.
26. Bobby Seale, *Seize the Time*, p. 262.
27. Newton, *Revolutionary Suicide*, p. 99.
28. Ibid., p. 304.
29. Ibid., p. 163.
30. George Jackson, *Soledad Brother: The Prison Letters of George Jackson* (London: Jonathan Cape, 1971), p. 18.
31. Ibid., p. 27.
32. Ibid., p. 83.
33. Ibid., p. 86.
34. Ibid., pp. 210-11.
35. Ibid., p. 214.
36. Ibid., p. 194.
37. Ibid., p. 85.
38. Ibid., p. 105.
39. Ibid., p. 94.
40. Ibid., p. 126.
41. Angela Davis, *An Autobiography*, p. 372.
42. Ibid.
43. Ibid., p. 382.
44. Angela Davis, ed., *If They Come in the Morning* (London: Orbach, 1971), p. 20.
45. Paul Fussel, *The Great War and Modern Memory* (New York: Oxford University Press, 1975), p. 18.
46. Jean-Paul Sartre, *Politics and Literature*, trans. J. A. Underwood and J. Calder (London, 1973), p. 31.
47. Quoted in John N. Morris, *Versions of the Self* (Baton Rouge, La.: Louisiana State University Press, 1966), p. 91.
48. Newton, *Revolutionary Suicide*, p. 3.

CHAPTER 8

1. Addison Gayle, Jr., *The Way of the New World* (New York, 1975), p. xi.
2. Edith Isaacs, *The Negro in the American Theatre* (New York: Theatre Arts, 1947) p. 16.
3. Quoted in Adam David Miller, ''It's a Long Way to St. Louis,'' *The Drama Review* 12 (Summer 1968), p. 147.
4. Quoted in William Couch, Jr., *New Black Playwrights* (Baton Rouge, La.: Louisiana State University Press, 1968), p. xii.
5. Theodore Ward, *Our Lan'*, in *Black Drama in America: An Anthology*, ed. Darwin Turner (Greenwich, Ct.: Fawcett, 1971), p. 130.
6. Ibid., p. 195.
7. Louis Peterson, *Take a Giant Step*, in *Black Drama in America*, p. 359.
8. Ibid., p. 374.
9. Lorraine Hansberry, *Les Blancs: The Collected Last Plays of Lorraine Hansberry* (New York: Vintage, 1973), p. 13.
10. Lorraine Hansberry, *The Sign in Sidney Brustein's Window* (New York: Random House, 1965), p. 64.
11. Ibid., p. 141.
12. Ibid., pp. 40-41.
13. Ibid., p. 49.
14. Ed Bullins, ''Comment,'' *Black Theatre* no. 5 (1971), p. 3.
15. Hansberry, *Les Blancs*, p. 42.

16. Ibid.
17. Ibid., p. 121.
18. Ibid., p. 106.
19. Ibid., p. 125.
20. James Baldwin, *Blues for Mr. Charlie* (London: Michael Joseph, 1965), p. 10.
21. Ibid.
22. Ibid., p. 11.
23. Ibid., p. 110.
24. Ibid., p. 93.
25. Ibid., p. 42.
26. Ibid.
27. Darwin Turner, "The Negro Dramatist's Image of the Universe, 1920-1960," in *Black Voices*, ed. Abraham Chapman (New York, 1968), p. 690.
28. Ossie Davis, "Plays of Insight Are Needed to Make Stage Vital in Our Lives," *New York Times*, August 23, 1964, Section II, p. 1.
29. Douglas Turner Ward, "American Theatre: For Whites Only?" *New York Times*, August 14, 1966, Section II, pp. D1, D3.
30. Negro Ensemble Company program.
31. Robert Pasolli, "Theatre: An Evening of One Acts," *The Village Voice*, April 10, 1969, p. 47.
32. Lonne Elder, *Ceremonies in Dark Old Men*, in William Couch, Jr., *New Black Playwrights*, p. 104.
33. Ibid.
34. Ibid., p. 153.
35. Lonne Elder, "An Interview," in *The Black American Writer*, vol. II, ed. C. W. E. Bigsby (New York, 1969), p. 220.
36. Ibid., p. 223.
37. Ibid., p. 222.
38. John O'Neal, "Motion in the Ocean," *The Drama Review* 12 (Summer 1968), p. 72.
39. Ibid., p. 77.
40. Ibid., p. 72.
41. Ibid., p. 77.
42. Quoted in Doris E. Abramson, *Negro Playwrights in the American Theatre* (New York: Columbia University Press, 1969), p. 25.
43. LeRoi Jones, *Dutchman and The Slave* (New York, 1964), pp. 28-29.
44. Ibid., p. 31.
45. Ibid., pp. 3-4.
46. Ibid., p. 36.
47. Ibid., p. 35.
48. Ibid., p. 43.
49. Ibid., p. 44.
50. Ibid., p. 45.
51. Ibid., p. 53.
52. Ibid., p. 66.
53. Ibid., p. 67.
54. Ibid., p. 71.
55. Ibid., p. 75.
56. Amiri Baraka, "The Theatre and the Coming Revolution," *Theatre Quarterly* 8, p. 31.
57. Roland Barthes, *Writing Degree Zero* (London, 1967), p. 27.
58. Amiri Baraka, *The Motion of History and Other Plays* (New York: William Morrow, 1978), p. 11.
59. Ibid., p. 13.

60. Ibid., p. 122.
61. Ibid., p. 209.
62. Ibid., p. 206.
63. Baraka, ''The Theatre and the Coming Revolution,'' p. 34.
64. Baraka, *The Motion of History*, p. 16.
65. Ibid., p. 13.
66. Ibid., p. 14.
67. Quoted in Couch, *New Black Playwrights*, p. xxii.
68. Ed Bullins, *The Theme Is Blackness: The Corner and Other Plays* (New York: William Morrow, 1973), p. 168.
69. Ibid.
70. Ibid., p. 169.
71. Ibid., p. 15.
72. Ibid.
73. Ed Bullins, *The Electronic Nigger and Other Plays* (London: Faber, 1970), p. 105.
74. Ibid., pp. 138-39.
75. Ed Bullins, *New Plays for the Black Theatre* (New York: Bantam, 1969), p. 137.
76. Ibid., p. 160.
77. Ibid., p. 150.
78. Ibid., pp. 161-62.
79. Ibid., p. 167.
80. Ibid.
81. Ed Bullins, *The Duplex* (New York: William Morrow, 1970), pp. 120-22.
82. Bullins, *The Theme Is Blackness*, p. 11.
83. Ibid.
84. Ibid., p. 14.
85. Ibid.
86. Ibid.
87. Ed Bullins, *A Black Quartet* (New York: Mentor, 1970), p. 136.
88. Bullins, *The Theme Is Blackness*, p. 83.
89. Ibid., p. 12.
90. Ibid.
91. Ed Bullins, ed., *The New Lafayette Presents* (New York: Anchor, 1974), p. 4.
92. Ibid.

CHAPTER 9

1. Sterling Brown, *Negro Poetry and Drama and the Negro in American Fiction* (New York: Atheneum, 1969), p. 6 [reprint of 1937 edition].
2. Phillis Wheatley, ''Thoughts on the Work of Providence,'' in *Early Black American Poets*, William H. Robinson (Dubuque, Iowa: William C. Brown, 1969), pp. 101-105.
3. Dudley Randall, *The Black Poets* (New York: Bantam, 1971), p. 38.
4. James Weldon Johnson, *The Book of American Negro Poetry*, p. 28.
5. Ibid., p. 25.
6. Benjamin Brawley, ed., *Early Negro American Writers* (New York: Dover, 1970), p. 24.
7. Ibid., p. 27.
8. Ibid., pp. 157-58.
9. Ibid., p. 228.
10. Onwuchekwa Jemie, *Langston Hughes* (New York: Columbia University Press, 1976), p. 150.
11. Paul Laurence Dunbar, *The Complete Poems* (New York: Dodd, Mead and Company, 1913), p. viii.

12. Nathan Huggins, *Harlem Renaissance* (New York: Oxford University Press, 1971), p. 219.
13. Jemie, *Langston Hughes*, p. 7.
14. Alain Locke, *The New Negro* (New York: Atheneum, 1968), p. 48.
15. Paul Kellogg, ''The Negro Pioneers,'' in *The New Negro*, p. 276.
16. Quoted in ''Introduction,'' in *The New Negro*, pp. v-vi.
17. Jemie, *Langston Hughes*, p. 11.
18. Ibid., p. 195.
19. Ibid., p. 158.
20. Ibid., p. 193.
21. Ibid., p. 162.
22. Ibid., p. 166.
23. Ibid., p. 171.
24. Claude McKay, *Selected Poems* (New York: Harcourt Brace, 1953), p. 41.
25. Ibid., p. 51.
26. Ibid., p. 50.
27. James Young, *Black Writers of the Thirties* (Baton Rouge, La.: Louisiana State University Press, 1973), p. 30.
28. Ibid., p. 156.
29. Bernard Duffey, *The Chicago Renaissance in American Letters*, (Westport, Ct.: Greenwood, 1972), p. 185.
30. Langston Hughes, *The Big Sea* (New York: Harcourt Brace, 1940), p. 29.
31. Young, *Black Writers of the Thirties*, p. 166.
32. Ibid., p. 169.
33. In *Modern and Contemporary Afro-American Poetry*, ed. Bernard W. Bell (Boston: Allyn and Bacon, 1972), p. 52.
34. Donald Dickinson, *A Bio-Bibliography of Langston Hughes 1902-1967* (Hamden: Archon Books, 1972), p. 66.
35. Joseph North, ed., *New Masses: An Anthology of the Rebel Thirties* (New York: International Publishers, 1969), p. 51.
36. Langston Hughes, *Don't You Want to Be Free?*, One Act Play Magazine, October, 1938, p. 392.
37. Abraham Chapman, *Black Voices* (New York: Mentor, 1968), pp. 438-39.
38. Margaret Butcher, *The Negro in American Culture* (New York: Mentor, 1956), p. 113.
39. Ibid., p. 114.
40. Ibid., p. 111.
41. Herbert Hill, *Soon, One Morning* (New York, 1963), p. 3.
42. Ibid., p. 4.
43. John O'Brien, ed., *Interviews with Black Writers* (New York, 1973), p. 118.
44. Dudley Randall, *The Black Poets*, pp. 123-24.
45. Ibid., p. 126.
46. Ibid., p. 132.
47. O'Brien, *Interviews With Black Writers*, p. 115.
48. Ibid.
49. Addison Gayle, Jr., *The Black Aesthetic* (New York, 1972), p. 380.
50. Randall, p. 169.
51. Chapman, *Black Voices*, pp. 460-61.
52. Gwendolyn Brooks, *Selected Poems* (New York: Harper & Row, 1963), p. 16.
53. Ibid., pp. 20-21.
54. Ibid., p. 52.
55. Ibid., p. 54.
56. ''An Interview with Gwendolyn Brooks,'' *Contemporary Literature* II, no. 1 (Winter 1970): 6.

57. Ibid., p. 3.
58. Ibid., p. 6.
59. Ibid.
60. Ibid.
61. Ibid., p. 7.
62. David Ossman, ed., *The Sullen Art* (New York: Corinth Books, 1963), p. 80.
63. LeRoi Jones, *Kulchur* III, xii, p. 3.
64. Ossman, *The Sullen Art*, p. 81.
65. LeRoi Jones, *A Twenty-Volume Suicide Note* (New York: Totem Corinth, 1961), p. 47.
66. Jones, *Kulchur*, p. 68.
67. LeRoi Jones, *The Dead Lecturer* (New York: Grove Press, 1964), pp. 68-69.
68. Ibid., p. 46.
69. Ibid., p. 47.
70. Ibid., p. 64.
71. Paul Breman, ed., *You Better Believe It* (Harmondsworth, Eng.: Penguin, 1973), p. 333.
72. LeRoi Jones, *Raise, Race, Rays, Raze* (New York: Random House, 1971), p. 18.
73. Ibid., p. 20.
74. LeRoi Jones, *Home* (New York, 1966), pp. 210-13.
75. Ibid., p. 213.
76. Ibid., p. 215.
77. Ibid., p. 214.
78. Dudley Randall, ed., *Black Poetry* (Detroit, 1969), p. 32.
79. Quoted in Kimberley Benston, *Baraka: The Renegade and the Mask* (New Haven, Ct.: Yale University Press, 1976), p. 123.
80. Randall, *Black Poetry*, p. 33.
81. Ibid., p. 34.
82. Benston, *Baraka*, p. 130.
83. Jones, *Raise, Race, Rays, Raze*, pp. 120-21.
84. LeRoi Jones, *In Our Terribleness* (Indianapolis: Bobbs-Merrill, 1970), n.p.
85. Ibid., n.p.
86. Ibid., n.p.
87. Ibid., n.p.
88. Jones, *Raise, Race, Rays, Raze*, p. 50.
89. Ibid., p. 98.
90. O'Brien, *Interviews with Black Writers*, p. 56.
91. Don Lee, *Think Black!* (Detroit: Broadside Press, 1970), p. 13.
92. Ibid., p. 12.
93. Don Lee, *Black Pride* (Detroit: Broadside Press, 1968), p. 13.
94. Don Lee, *Black Words That Say: Don't Cry, Scream* (Detroit: Broadside Press, 1969), p. 9.
95. Ibid., p. 15.
96. Ibid., p. 40.
97. Ibid., p. 28.
98. Abraham Chapman, *New Black Voices* (New York: Mentor, 1972), p. 43.
99. Bernard W. Bell, ed., *Modern and Contemporary Afro-American Poetry*, p. 168.
100. Sonia Sanchez, *We A BaddDDD People* (Chicago: Broadside Press, 1970), pp. 12-13.
101. Ibid., p. 15.
102. Ibid., p. 50.
103. Ibid., p. 54.
104. Clarence Major, *The New Black Poetry* (New York: International Publishers, 1969), p. 114.
105. Nikki Giovanni, *Black Feeling, Black Talk, Black Judgement* (New York: William Morrow, 1968), p. 19.

106. Ibid., p. 50.
107. Ibid., p. 54.
108. Ibid., p. 57.
109. Ibid., p. 84.
110. Ibid., p. 89.
111. Lionel Abel, *Metatheatre* (New York: Hill and Wang, 1963), p. 89.
112. Stephen Henderson, *Understanding Black Poetry* (New York: William Morrow, 1973), p. 4.
113. Ibid., p. 3.
114. Ibid., p. 6.
115. Ibid., p. 10.
116. Ibid., pp. 7-8.
117. Ibid., p. 33.
118. Dudley Randall, "A Conversation with Dudley Randall," *Black World* 21, no. 2 (December 1971): 30.
119. Don Lee, "Voices of the Seventies: Black Critics," *Black World* 19, no. 11 (September 1970): 28.
120. Charles H. Rowell, "The Black Poet in the Afternoon," *Black World* 22, no. 10 (August 1973): 48.
121. Ishmael Reed, *catechism of d neoamerican hoodoo church* (London, 1970), p. 18.
122. Ibid., p. 26.
123. Ibid., p. 14.
124. Ibid., p. 11.
125. Ibid., p. 34.

Index